The
Political
Novels
of Joseph Conrad

The Political Novels of Joseph Conrad

A CRITICAL STUDY

by Eloise Knapp Hay

THE UNIVERSITY OF CHICAGO PRESS

CHICAGO AND LONDON

Quotations from the book, *Joseph Conrad:
Life and Letters*, by G. Jean-Aubry, copyright
1926, 1927 by Doubleday & Company, Inc., used
by permission of the publisher

THE UNIVERSITY OF CHICAGO PRESS, CHICAGO 60637

The University of Chicago Press, Ltd., London

*International Standard Book Number: 0–226–32041–3
Library of Congress Catalog Card Number: 63–13066*

To Stephen

Preface

After living intensively for ten years with this book in my mind, I find it odd to recall that my interest began with a simple question: "What is it about *Lord Jim* that no one has adequately explained?" Having been brought up to discipline vague questions into concrete terms, I began at once to examine the implications of the seaman's code (which Jim tragically breaks) and of Jim's remark "that he could never go home now" (p. 79). I was not the first who turned with my queries to the non-English aspects of Conrad's own experience. Nor was I the first to fasten very quickly on the political imperative as the peculiar force behind both Jim's romantic sense of mission and Marlow's (as well as Jim's own) classical sense of a fixed standard of conduct. If I was first in anything, it was in the naïveté of my belief that I could scrupulously trace the origins and permutations of this political imperative in Conrad's fiction, without fully knowing the histories and literatures of Poland, France, England, and Russia.

I now see that to do absolute justice to the subject, I should have learned at least the Polish language and read meticulously through many more volumes than I did of Polish history from the beginnings of the Jagellonian dynasty to the present. I should have read all the Polish studies of the Korzeniowski and the Bobrowski families. I should have read not a select few but all the several hundred works on Conrad written in Polish by his fellow countrymen.

What deterred me from this course, quite apart from the brevity of life, was the long appeal of art—that is to say, my impatience with studies that would take me too far from my real subject and interest, Conrad's English novels. The only attempt I dared to make, therefore, was to isolate for a spell the political novels of Conrad and, while concentrating on how his art itself addresses us, to describe as concisely as possible the main historical, political, and personal influences suggested by Conrad's motifs and accents in the novels.

The result leaves room for further speculation, documentation, and (I hope) correction. These will be facilitated by the forthcoming volume of Conrad's Polish documents and correspondence, edited and translated into English by Zdzisław Najder (London, Oxford University Press), which unfortunately has not been available to me. Conrad's first great biographer, G. Jean-Aubry, in his *Life and Letters*, made use of many of the important materials in Najder's collection before sending them to Poland between the two world wars. Although the result of the Second World War caused these papers to be ignored or inaccessible for a decade to many Conrad enthusiasts, there has been in the post-Stalin era an extraordinary rebirth of Polish interest in Conrad. This revival has produced numerous assessments and reassessments of the political Conrad, as well as of Conrad the novelist. With the help of Polish friends and translators, I have tried to catch the various strains of the new Polish criticism—both inside and outside Poland—and to weigh it for evidence of Conrad's own Polish stresses.

Jocelyn Baines's excitingly comprehensive *Joseph Conrad: a Critical Biography* appeared in England after the major part of my study was written. This is my only excuse if I have not sufficiently retraced my steps by its light, or if I have failed to give his book the enormous credit it deserves. Similar words might be said of Leo Gurko's *Joseph Conrad: Giant in Exile*; and of Róża Jablkowska's *Joseph Conrad, 1857–1924*, which has re-examined the Conrad papers in Warsaw and Cracow and includes an up-to-date bibliography of Polish studies not listed in our indexes.

In the end, *Lord Jim* both abides our question and magnificently exceeds the caviler's grasp. One is left with the luxury of reading Conrad—and the other luxury of writing about the enlarged view of the human spectacle his novels open.

Acknowledgments

Without a blush, I am willing to admit that the completion of this study has been due to the wit and energy of the most generous of gadflies, Albert J. Guerard. His counsel and encouragement remained constant over ten years of time, conveyed often as readily by letters to me in India as by word of mouth in his own offices at Harvard University. The example he set as craftsman and scholar was no small part of the incentive he supplied. If his image appears less exalted than one would expect in the following pages, it may be partly because of another, most unusual sort of encouragement he provided: the nerve to speak my own mind forcefully at whatever points we disagreed in evaluating Conrad's thought and writing. The delights of argument with a mind so deeply engaged as Albert Guerard's kept the pages coming.

Second only to Guerard in helpfulness was Wiktor Weintraub, whose profound knowledge of the Polish and Russian languages became a prop without which I could not have proceeded. I heard of him first not at Harvard, where I should have begun looking, but in London, where the Polish colony of Conrad enthusiasts held his name in reverence. It was in London, too, that I found other lifelines to my subject: in the Polish physician and critic Wit Tarnawski, in the stimulating English critics Douglas Hewitt and Jocelyn Baines, the novelist Jerzy Pietrkiewicz, and the editor of *Wiadomości*, Mieczysław Grydzewski, all of whom were most friendly and helpful. Joseph Conrad's son John, the architect, entertained me most cordially at his house in Canterbury and greatly enriched my understanding of his father's character. In Paris, Maria Kasterska gave me long hours and invaluable insights. Finally, while naming the writers who helped the book take shape, I owe gratitude to Maria Kuncewiczowa and Thomas C. Moser for criticism, suggestions, and courtesies; and to Howard Mumford Jones, without whom the book would still be in manuscript form.

It is impossible to thank all the dedicated and astute librarians who helped me to find my way in the manuscript collections on which the book has relied so heavily. John D. Gordan, well known for his own book on Conrad, opened the secrets of the Berg Collection at the New York Public Library. Carolyn Jakeman was tireless in attendance on my needs at Houghton Library, Harvard, as was William H. McCarthy, of the Rosenbach Foundation in Philadelphia. Bellary Kesavan, director of the National Library in Calcutta, sent me a fine, complete edition of Conrad's works by train to the Indian village where my husband and I were living in 1955, and I was able to use the excellent facilities of Mr. Kesavan's library on many different occasions thereafter. At the University of Chicago Library, Helen M. Smith, Christine Reb, and Joseph Gregg solved numberless difficulties for me with incredible patience. The entire staffs of the manuscript collections at Dartmouth and Yale spent days of intensive activity in the service of this project.

George C. Walter, versatile and generous curator of the Polish Museum of America in Chicago, kept me supplied with up-to-date Polish publications on Conrad. I should not have known how to read them, of course, without the help of friends and neighbors who know Polish: Ilona Karmel Zucher, Isabella Wellisz, Mrs. Walter Drzewieniecki, and Mitchell Winthrop.

For permission to quote from Conrad's manuscript letters and works, I am indebted to the British Museum, the Dartmouth College Library, the Henry W. and Albert A. Berg Collection of The New York Public Library, the Harvard University Library, Yale University Library, and to the Philip H. and A. S. W. Rosenbach Foundation. The right to quote from these manuscripts and from Conrad's published works has kindly been granted by the Trustees of the Joseph Conrad Estate, Doubleday and Co., Inc., and Messrs J. M. Dent.

A grant from the University of Illinois Research Board made possible a last, thorough review of my materials and the verification of my manuscript. The index was prepared by Theodora P. Bobrinskoy.

Contents

Illustrations

Introduction

Like Keats's "chameleon Poet," Gustave Flaubert sharply registered the social colors of his period in *Madame Bovary* and *L'Éducation sentimentale*. It was Flaubert who passed on to Joseph Conrad and all other succeeding novelists a clear prohibition against personal coloring in matters of politics, nationality, and religion. The artist, he said, "*should have neither religion, country, nor even any social conviction.*" [1]

As if consciously obedient to the master, Conrad had neutralized himself in all three of these points by the time his writing life began in 1889, when he was thirty-one. Born a Roman Catholic, he had long given up practicing the faith to which his devout parents had pledged him. Born into the hotly nationalistic Polish gentry, he had established his legal and affective allegiance to the British Crown in 1886. As to social conviction, by the time he was thirty he seems to have fully prepared the noncommittal response he offered in one form or another to partisans of every ideology (for example, to the British socialist Edward Garnett): "My misfortune is that I can't swallow any formula and thus am wearing the aspect of enemy to all mankind." [2]

We have the word of Conrad's collaborator Ford Madox Ford that these apparently evasive attitudes were not, however, to be

[1] Letter of April 26–27, 1853, in *The Selected Letters of Gustave Flaubert*, translated and edited by Francis Steegmuller (New York: Farrar, Straus and Young, 1953), p. 151. The italics are mine.
[2] Letter of Sept. 24, 1919, in *Letters from Joseph Conrad, 1895–1924* (Indianapolis: Bobbs-Merrill Co., Inc., 1928), p. 265.

1

interpreted as negations of personal involvement on Conrad's part. Quite to the contrary, according to Ford: ". . . above all things else . . . Conrad was a politician. . . . He was, that is to say a student of politics, without prescription, without dogma, and, as a Papist, with a profound disbelief in the perfectibility of human institutions."[3]

For a man to be thus intensely and personally engaged with politics, and from a religiously oriented point of view, but without commitment to any particular doctrine or policy, is difficult for us to understand. For at least half a century after his first novel, *Almayer's Folly*, appeared in 1895, Conrad's readers failed to find any political interest in the novels and stories that came out year after year. Even Ford's challenging assertion, made just after Conrad's death in 1924, called forth neither agreement nor denial. It was only in 1941, when novelists in the United States, France, and Russia had long been employing fiction for revolutionary social themes, that an English critic, M. C. Bradbrook, commented on the importance of the political voice in Conrad's works. "Whatever else in Conrad has dated," she wrote, "his politics are contemporary."[4]

The stamp of Conrad's politics that Miss Bradbrook called "contemporary" has a complex character. To be politically contemporary, presumably, is to prove one's thought and art relevant to the political experience of one's age. The artist may approve of the tendencies and conflicts of his period, or he may disapprove of them, but if he is to go on being "contemporary" in the years after his death, his evaluations must mirror the deepest political experiences of his time. His rendering, furthermore, must so represent the present state of politics as to register faithfully how it developed from its past and how it is likely to affect the future.

Miss Bradbrook clearly accepts Conrad's evaluation of this complex experience. She therefore implies that for Conrad to have been "contemporary" was also to have been "right." It may soon enough be apparent where I stand on the question of Conrad's political judgments, but we should allow at once that an artist's

---

[3] *Joseph Conrad: A Personal Remembrance* (London: Duckworth, 1924), p. 58.
[4] *Joseph Conrad: Poland's English Genius* (New York: Macmillan Co., 1941), p. 8.

importance as a reflector of his age is not necessarily determined by the objectivity of his vision or by his ability to render justice to the partisans of every cause. If such were the case, the social conscious- ness of a Plutarch, Dante, Shakespeare, or a Dostoevsky would be pronounced insignificant. Conrad's political vision is still con- temporary because he experienced more of the political tensions and realities of his period and could interpret them more clearly than any other novelist of the last hundred years. This claim is what will stand or collapse as an answer to those of his readers (many of whom live in Communist or "neutralist" nations) who hold that his political vision was sadly out of date even in his own time.

The fact remains that for the last twenty years critics have referred increasingly to "the political novels" of Conrad as though he had a political message to convey, or at least as if he found in politics a background against which his characters and plots could best come to life. Most readers today will say that only the latter case (if either) could fit a writer who concentrates as closely as Conrad does on the isolation of individual men—often self-exiled— from their native communities. On the other hand, what most brings Conrad to our notice is that he does not, like Trollope, James, Orwell, or Pasternak, treat politics as an external milieu or force impinging on the private life of individuals who could live more happily without it. If we have any reason to consider the political novel today as a genre, we have reason to see in Conrad the unique example of a "pure artist" who could not think of men at all without thinking of the individual's immediate reliance upon, and obligations to, a politically defined community.

The exact nature of that reliance and those obligations was for Conrad a subject for broad investigation. His novels pursue the subject far beyond the issues of loyalty and defection that have been associated with his fiction so insistently since Gustav Morf wrote of the guilt complex he believed to have haunted Conrad as a result of his "deserting" Poland.[5] No one has yet freed Conrad's most interesting characters from the suspicion that they embody

---

[5] *The Polish Heritage of Joseph Conrad* (London: Sampson Low, Marston [1930]).

the tormenting self-accusations of a political deserter. Only V. S. Pritchett offered Morf any argument on this important subject. "The Poles suggested," Pritchett noted, "that Conrad felt the guilt of the émigré, a guilt all the sharper because he was the son of a man who had been a national martyr. Conrad did not evade the criticism and answered it very sensibly." Pritchett then added, "I do not think that Conrad had any feeling of personal betrayal." Unfortunately, even Pritchett has recently shifted his weight to windward, the direction of those finding a "guilt complex" somewhere in the theme of every novel Conrad wrote.[6]

Any analysis begun from a special point of view, whether political or psychological or whatever, runs the risk of emphasizing aspects of an artist's work which are minor or even irrelevant. With the now venerable New Critics, one would like to read every Conrad novel away from all magnetic fields that might pull pieces of the work apart from the whole. One would like to avoid the distracting pull of Conrad's biography and personal psychology. But we have reached a point where we must use his life critically to help us decide what is *not* conveyed in his fiction, as well as what may sensibly be admitted to be there.

The recent biography by Jocelyn Baines offers new material in support of a different emphasis than the desertion motif stressed by Morf. Did Conrad desert his fatherland, or was he persuaded that, in his peculiar circumstances, a life leading away from Poland was the only means of survival? One begins to see in Baines's pages that there were reasons why Conrad's family came to approve of his desire to go to sea and thus join a service that could be found only outside Poland. There was the matter of his blinding teen-age infatuations, first with a neighbor's daughter and then with an older cousin. Worse, there was his chronic illness and depression, his habit, as his uncle called it, of "yielding unnecessarily to impressions, feelings and thoughts inappropriate" to his age.[7] Although his guardian uncle, Tadeusz Bobrowski, sympathized deeply with

---

[6] "The Exile," in the *New Statesman* (London), Aug. 24, 1957, p. 229. In "The Moralist of Exile," in the *New Statesman* of Jan. 30, 1960, p. 157, Pritchett seems to have come round to Gustav Morf's view.

[7] *Joseph Conrad* (London: Weidenfeld & Nicolson, 1959), p. 27.

this orphaned, only child of martyred parents, he continually stressed the inappropriateness of Conrad's character to life in Poland at the time. While urging practical application to ordinary studies, Bobrowski argued even more forcefully for the choice of a profession that would build "strength of character and endurance," a man's ability to "work by himself and direct himself."[8]

Dictated both by childhood reading and by unconscious desires to seek what he had lost or never found, Conrad's first important decision in life was to leave Poland for life at sea. The ultimate consequences of this choice, made when he was only fifteen, could not be foreseen, but it turned out to be a political decision, taken with due regard to what his family expected of him at every point. If he later in life felt the constant, haunting presence of the family and nation left behind, he recognized the specter at every turn as part of his unavoidable fate, the secret sharer of his destiny. In view of the fact that the nearest and dearest members of that past had died in agony before he was twelve, it is not surprising that he visualized the whole past and the defeated nation they loved as removed forever from life. Their ghosts, like Hamlet's father, spoke to him equivocally of political realities dead or dying. Immobilized for thirty years by all that concerned them, he attended to their memories when he wrote.

In the last years of his life, Conrad assumed that the reason his English readers loved his sea stories and belittled his other works was that, as he said, the "public mind fastens on externals, on mere facts, such for instance as ships and voyages, without paying attention to any deeper significance they may have." The way one should generalize upon "authors and their material," he suggested to the critic Richard Curle, is to observe "how they transform it from particular to general, and appeal to universal emotions by the temperamental handling of personal experience."[9] This lead may be pursued to particular advantage in reading the political novels of Joseph Conrad.

---

[8] Quoted in Baines, *op. cit.*, p. 26.
[9] Letter to Curle, July 17, 1923, in G. Jean-Aubry, *Joseph Conrad: Life and Letters*, II (New York: Doubleday, Page, 1927), 320–21.

"It requires a certain greatness of soul to interpret patriotism worthily—or else a sincerity of feeling denied to the
vulgar refinement of modern thought which cannot understand the august simplicity of a sentiment proceeding
from the very nature of things and men."

"Prince Roman"

"I am not indifferent to what interests You. Only my interest is elsewhere, my thought follows another course, my
heart longs for something else, my soul suffers from another kind of impotence. Do You understand? You who
devote Your enthusiasm and Your talents to the cause of
humanity, You will understand undoubtedly that I must
—I have a need to—preserve my thought intact as a last
homage of fidelity to a cause that is lost. This is all that I
can do. I have thrown my life to all the winds of the sky,
but I have preserved my thought. It is a small thing—it is
everything—it is nothing—it is life itself."

Translated from the French in Conrad's letter to
R. B. Cunninghame Graham, February 8, 1899.

CHAPTER
ONE

"The Artist
of the Whole Matter"

The extent of Conrad's importance as a political novelist was first noticed in 1949, when George Orwell called him "one of the few true novelists that England possesses," representing "a sort of grown-upness and political understanding which would have been almost impossible to a native English writer at the time." Orwell classed Conrad with T. S. Eliot, Henry James, Joyce, and Yeats as foreigners "who in the present century civilized English literature and brought it back into contact with Europe, from which it had been almost severed for a hundred years."[1] G. D. H. Cole, who gave

---

[1] In "Conrad's Place and Rank in English Letters," Wiadomości (London), April 10, 1949. Actually, Orwell's words seem almost a paraphrase of Ford Madox Ford's remark before Conrad's death: "Nevertheless, the works of Mr. Conrad that the present writer most tremendously remembers are Heart of Darkness, Nostromo, Under Western Eyes—that finest novel in the English language—and The Secret Agent, that immense failure of comprehension! Each of these is a political parable, and so, you might add, is An Outpost of Progress; and so, for the matter of that, is, with its atmosphere of Arab and Malay intrigue beneath the shadow of Dutch suzerainty, Mr. Conrad's first book, Almayer's Folly" (Thus to Revisit [New York: E. P. Dutton & Co., 1921], pp. 90–91). A few pages further on (p. 101), Ford adds: "Mr. Conrad, coming from Poland—even as Henry James coming from New England—has once more put Anglo-Saxondom into contact with the main stream of human art."

his opinion in the same collection of critiques on Conrad in which Orwell's appeared, singled out *The Secret Agent* and *Under Western Eyes* as having passed almost unnoticed among Conrad's works, although deserving of the highest regard.

If Orwell was right in suggesting that Conrad's political understanding enlarged and "civilized" the English point of view, it was possible only because as a Pole Conrad symbolized a cause with which most Englishmen had instinctive sympathy, while at the same time he represented a people whose political outlook was in many ways utterly alien. The Poland known to the English throughout the greater part of the nineteenth century, according to E. H. Carr,

> represented both the essence of nationalism and the essence of democracy. The oppressors of Poland were the three traditional opponents, since the Congress of Vienna, of democracy and nationalism: Austria, Russia, and Prussia. France and Great Britain, who ruled over no subject races in Europe, were free to indulge the liberal sentiments which they professed by sympathizing with the subject Poles. . . . In the hands of the nineteenth century democrats the cause of Poland became a symbol of international righteousness.[2]

Conversely, the England admired by Polish patriots in the nineteenth century was a land that symbolized political hope, even for men who professed hopeless indifference. In the year before Conrad was naturalized as a British citizen (1886), he wrote from Singapore to his Polish friend Spiridion Kliszczewski, living in Cardiff, that the newspapers announcing the defeat of England's Liberal government (with its policy of friendship toward Russia) had given him reason for "expecting great things":

> I saw with pleasure the evidence of improved relations with Germany, the only power with whom an anti-Russian alliance would be useful, and even possible, for Great Britain . . . Events are casting shadows, more or less distorted, shadows deep enough to suggest the lurid light of battlefields somewhere in the near future, but all those portents of great and decisive doings leave me in a state of

---

[2] *Michael Bakunin* (London: Macmillan Co., 1937), p. 139.

despairing indifference: for whatever may be the changes in the fortunes of living nations, for the dead there is no hope . . .[3]

The deceased nation had yet her scattered heirs, with their allegiance to mankind, if nothing else. In the same letter Conrad added,

I agree with you that in a free and hospitable land even the most persecuted of our race may find relative peace and a certain amount of happiness, materially at least; consequently, I understood and readily accepted your reference to "Home." When speaking, writing or thinking in English, the word home always means for me the hospitable shores of Great Britain.

There was a side to Polish politics, however, which the English mind (the American mind as well), priding itself on liberalism and evolutionary progress, chose not to recognize and shrank away from whenever agitation for Polish freedom became too strong in Parliamentary circles. This was the side of his own mind which Conrad muted in his fiction through the English accents of his narrators—Marlow, the professor of languages, and the seaman who recalls the voyage of the "Narcissus." It was the part of Conrad's mind that the English called morbid[4] because it preferred resistance and death to compromise in the face of overwhelming adversity. It was the side that defended fanaticism as the source of some of the noblest human passions as well as the most degrading. It was the side that yearned after "a fixed standard of conduct" that could be recognized universally, and thought that doubt in such a standard was of man's creation.

But to seek out the "political Conrad" is by no means to suggest that Conrad, the novelist, wrote as a Polish partisan, or any other kind of partisan. Even the months he spent smuggling arms from Marseilles to Spain in the service of the Carlists—a period for which we have little documentation beside Conrad's own glamor-

[3] Letter to Kliszczewski, Oct. 13, 1885, in G. Jean-Aubry, *Joseph Conrad: Life and Letters*, I (New York: Doubleday, Page, 1927), 80–81.
[4] See Author's Note in *Lord Jim*, further discussed in chap. ii. All references to Conrad's works are to the Collected Edition (London: J. M. Dent, 1946–55), unless otherwise specified.

ous but self-deprecating accounts, fictional and autobiographical—even these months seem to savor more of the fantasy from which books are made than of calculated political activity. The only case to be made is that accidents of national origin and family background compelled him from earliest childhood to see in life a political dimension that strongly affected his perspective of all human affairs.

Many of Conrad's least political works convey to us the psychopolitical image of men bent on sailing to utopia but turned back by disaster, futility, or both. In *The Nigger of the "Narcissus,"* the ship is a "little world" that

> went on its curved and unswerving path carrying a discontented and aspiring population. They found comfort of a gloomy kind in an interminable and conscientious analysis of their unappreciated worth; and inspired by Donkin's hopeful doctrines they dreamed enthusiastically of the time when every lonely ship would travel over a serene sea, manned by a wealthy and well-fed crew of satisfied skippers.[5]

And in "Youth" the aging Marlow recalls how once, in fantasy, he had been able to transcend the pattern of existence which the voyage of the "Judea" symbolized, one of those voyages that seem "an illustration of life," where you

> fight, work, sweat, nearly kill yourself, sometimes do kill yourself, trying to accomplish something—and you can't. Not from any fault of yours. You simply can do nothing, neither great nor little—not a thing in the world—not even marry an old maid, or get a wretched 600-ton cargo of coal to its port of destination.[6]

England had no recent experience of this kind of "voyage" when Conrad made his home there. She knew only the peace of the *pax Britannica*, a peace rooted in her policy of delicately balancing one hostile power against another, of avoiding challenges to any power on a hard basis of right and wrong. Even today, wherever one finds a Polish colony, one will hear the peculiar Polish defense of British freedom mixed with resentment of Britain's methods of maintain-

[5] *The Nigger of the "Narcissus,"* p. 103.
[6] *Youth*, p. 4.

ing it—methods which persistently refused official recognition of Polish right against Russian might.[7]

If Conrad had a maturing effect on English letters, it was in part because he called attention to the sheer horror in certain political realities that were being overlooked by comfortable, law-abiding English citizens and politicians. A sense of impending disaster, probably founded in childhood memories, seems to have been as ingrained in Conrad's temperament, as it was in that of Lord Jim, who had no such childhood experience. (Hence, perhaps, Conrad's inability to understand why Jim's sensitivities baffled many English readers.) Conrad's early life, as seen through his uncle's letters particularly, makes us wonder to what extent his chronic drift toward reverie may have caused his fear of emergency situations—his fear that he would go blind like Captain Whalley, for instance[8]—and to what extent the tendency to dream was itself caused by early experiences of disaster.

At any rate, Conrad seems to have distrusted in himself the "morbid excess" that Coleridge named in Hamlet: the loss of "*equilibrium* between the real and the imaginary worlds," as a result of which "the images of his fancy are far more vivid than his actual perceptions."[9] A line might be traced from Hamlet through Conrad to Lord Jim, suggesting the intimate alliance between political necessity and imaginative flight in men with a keen sense of responsibility to their social commitments.

While trying to relate Conrad's political thinking to the politics of his time, one keeps meeting a curious riddle: Why is a Polish émigré like an English Tory? Those who think first of Conrad's

---

[7] For an interesting study of the episode when Lord Palmerstone inconclusively attempted to send aid to the Polish insurrectionists of Apollo Korzeniowski's fatal rebellion, see W. E. Mosse, "England and the Polish Insurrection of 1863," *English Historical Review* (January, 1956), pp. 28–55.

[8] ". . . the story of the captain who went blind in 'The End of the Tether' had its source, according to Captain Craig, in Conrad's fears for his own eyes aboard the 'Vidar.' " G. Jean-Aubry, *La Vie de Conrad*, translated by Helen Sebba as *The Sea Dreamer* (New York: Doubleday & Co., Inc., 1957), p. 239.

[9] Samuel Taylor Coleridge, "Hamlet," *The Complete Works*, IV, ed. W. G. I. Shedd (New York: Harper & Bros., 1884), 145.

nostalgia for lost legitimacies in the courts of Europe (specifically in Spain and France) brand him a Conservative, failing to note that the main attraction of these royalist causes was not that they were legitimate but that they were (like the Polish cause) lost. No one of the English parties favored the ideals of government in Conrad's mind. As his son John reports,[10] he was never known to vote in an English election in the thirty-eight years of his British citizenship. He was born, and remained, "a man without a country." The nation that existed only in his mind was wonderful indeed, for it was governed without having a government. The abolished constitution of the old Polish Republic remained for him, as it had for his father, both vague and correct, a marvelous paradox of freedom and control as eternally mirrored in "the Polish temperament":

> Nothing is more foreign than what in the literary world is called Slavonism to the Polish temperament with its tradition of self-government, its chivalrous view of moral restraints and an exaggerated respect for individual rights: not to mention the important fact that the whole Polish mentality, Western in complexion, had received its training from Italy and France and, historically, had always remained, even in religious matters, in sympathy with the most liberal currents of European thought.[11]

To suggest that Conrad's political philosophy was based upon a never-never land and not conceived for practical purposes might be to discourage some readers from further inquiry into the political aspects of his fiction. Because it was detached perforce, however, from the patriotism that Samuel Johnson called "the last refuge of a scoundrel," Conrad's mind had the advantage of greater freedom in criticizing the actual and imagining the unattained. What he lost through the impossibility of direct action he may have gained in the heightened reality he found in his reading and the imaginative power with which he imbued his limited political experience. "No one has known—for intellectual use—the things you know," Henry James wrote him in 1906; ". . . you have, as the artist of the whole matter, an authority that no one has approached."[12]

---

[10] Interview with John Conrad, Canterbury (England), June 17, 1956.

[11] *A Personal Record*, pp. vi–vii.

[12] Letter to Conrad, Nov. 1, 1906, in *Selected Letters of Henry James*, ed. Leon Edel (New York: Farrar, Straus and Cudahy, 1955), p. 157.

Conrad's stature as a novelist is apparent to us, however little we may be aware of it, by the immense range of his perceptions and interests. He neither neglects nor belittles anything of importance on the human stage. He outdistances novelists like Ford Madox Ford, Virginia Woolf, and E. M. Forster, who sometimes wrote on the same themes he chose and were often more adroit technicians and more appealing storytellers, by his continued application to the whole human story and his resulting humility as a writer within it. His ambition as a writer was appalling if one thinks of it: ". . . literary creation being only one of the legitimate forms of human activity has no value but on the condition of not excluding the *fullest recognition to all the more distinct forms of action.*"[13]

Politics, surely the most distinct and comprehensive form of human action, has for Conrad a broader applicability than for many English-writing novelists of the last century. And yet we find politics treated in a purer form in *Nostromo, The Secret Agent,* and *Under Western Eyes* than in many novels which are now coming to be classed as political. Conrad's characters and incidents, with rare exceptions, recurrently open a double perspective into their private and public significance. For this reason, even such novels as *The Nigger of the "Narcissus," Lord Jim,* and *The Secret Sharer* bear the impress of the politically engaged Conrad. Nearly all his principal characters fall into situations where their personal action or thought is challenged by public forces with which they are incompatible and with which they must be reconciled. Justice, which for Plato and Aristotle was the aim of all political controversy, is the objective toward which his characters tend. And they end, like Lord Jim and Razumov, by giving up the struggle for their private causes and standing for judgment before the common conscience of their readers, which their trials have helped to enlighten.

If we consider two of the most readable books written in recent years on the subject of the political novel, we discover that no category has been made to accommodate Conrad. Morris Speare's *The Political Novel, Its Development in England and America*[14]

---

[13] "Books," *Notes on Life and Letters,* p. 7. The italics are mine.
[14] Morris Edmund Speare, *The Political Novel: Its Development in England and America* (New York: Oxford University Press, 1924).

limits itself almost entirely to novels that center on Parliament or Congress. Irving Howe's provocative *Politics and the Novel*[15] skilfully evades any definition of politics at all, but the introductory essay is crucial. Howe points out that, in the nineteenth century, the political novel developed when the novelist's attention was forced away from "the luxury of being able to take society for granted" and "had necessarily to shift from the gradations within society to the fate of society itself." At this point, "the *idea* of society, as distinct from the mere unquestioned workings of society, has penetrated the consciousness of the characters in all of its profoundly problematic aspects . . ."[16]

I do not think it would be an annoying quibble to ask a question that Howe omits to consider. Can we discuss the general subject of politics—"the idea of society"—in the novel without establishing at least a tentative definition of what we mean by politics, or even what we mean by society? Perhaps prudently, Howe prefers to let his readers infer the meanings of these words (which may be many) from his discussion of the individual novelists. Yet through his essays one grows increasingly aware that the critic's definitions inevitably refract the light he throws upon his subjects. Howe's own genuine political concern appears to reflect the opinion most common to American political novelists—Hawthorne, James, Faulkner, Robert Penn Warren, and others who are such good bait for his hook—that politics, regardless of its origins, is a soul-sullying or at best a tragic business. This point of attack may serve our reading of American novelists, but it will not do for Conrad, whose idealism, though ultimately not much hardier than the Americans', leads him again and again to sympathetic consideration of the positive bases of government in human nature.

Howe finally looks on politics, in negative terms chiefly, "as both temptation and impediment," and he singles out the main characteristic of the political novel as a turn towards "apolitical temptation." Thus he rates Conrad below Dostoevsky as a political novelist by reading in the messages of *Nostromo* and *Under Western Eyes*

[15] Irving Howe, *Politics and the Novel* (New York: Horizon Press, 1957).
[16] *Ibid.*, p. 19.

an ultimate retreat from political engagement to "the resources of private affection and gentleness."[17]

The alternation Howe examines between the political novelist's imaginative engagement in a historic cause and subsequent retreat to a pastoral celebration of private life (which may have been sacrificed in the political struggle) need not always be a veering between opposites. For Conrad particularly, every individual life contains the elements of commitment and withdrawal that characterize the political dilemma. Indeed, his much-discussed preoccupation with human isolation is both cause and result of his strong sense of man's necessary involvement in social effort.

Man cannot retire. Conrad does not dream poetically, as did Boris Pasternak, of a society in which retirement is possible. Politics is implicit in the ego. Man is a political animal for Conrad as much as for Plato and Aristotle, whose writings he knew directly or indirectly through his Catholic background or his school reading.[18] "There must be a union of those who cannot exist without each other," Aristotle reasoned, and the necessary association of families must finally lead to establishment of "a single complete community, large enough to be nearly or quite self-sufficing." At this point, said Aristotle, the state comes into existence, "originating in the bare needs of life, and continuing in existence for the sake of a good life."[19]

This fundamental definition of politics is implicit in Conrad's writing but comes through his novels carrying the terrible burdens

---

[17] *Ibid.*, p. 23.

[18] "While I was a boy in a great public school [in Austrian Cracow] we were steeped in classicism to the lips, and, though our historical studies were naturally tinted with Germanism, I know that all we boys, the six hundred of us, resisted that influence with all our might, while accepting the results of German research and thoroughness." Letter from Conrad to George T. Keating, Dec. 14, 1922, in *Life and Letters*, II, 289.

[19] Aristotle, *Politica*, translated by Benjamin Jowett, in *Introduction to Aristotle*, ed. Richard McKeon (New York: Random House, 1947), pp. 554–55.
Aristotle's argument epitomizes the more diffuse argument of Plato. But for Plato, unlike Aristotle, politics is less interesting as a study in itself than as an activity to be defined in seeking the nature of the ideal state, or of justice, which Plato finds only in a strict division of labor. See *The Republic of Plato*, translated by F. M. Cornford (Oxford: Oxford University Press, 1941), pp. 52–57.

modern history has placed upon it. "The good life" (the main theme of the pastoral convention, incidentally) for which the state exists is a tragic fugitive in *Under Western Eyes*, symbolized specifically in a recurring image of winged youth. In *Nostromo* it is achieved at awful cost and built from faulty materials on the edge of a precipice.

Conrad makes difficulties for his readers—often unconsciously, sometimes deliberately, in such complex works as *Heart of Darkness* and *Nostromo*—by concentrating on the self-deceptions that lead virtuous men astray in their pursuit of the good life, which must be a life of public as well as private good. Whether these deceptions are inherent in human nature or result from the pride of Western civilization, whether they are part of the plan of creation or only the effect of unscrupulosity in man's thinking—these speculations crowd in upon the reader, throwing a dense foliage across the path of the story. The author finally seems to waver uncertainly between two possibilities and to conclude by leaving them in the form of a paradox that would doubtless have grated upon the mind of the rationalist Aristotle. The possibility that man is fundamentally good, potentially able to achieve the social harmony he mentally projects, stands against the possibility that man is basically corrupt and his utopian schemes "fairy tales" that create political miseries for the unimaginative, who wish only to be left alone. Conrad's subtlety in contemplating these alternatives may be inferred from the wildly different conclusions critics reach on some of his works— *Lord Jim*, for example. This novel is typical of Conrad's best work, tending as it does toward an insoluble paradox of human perfectibility within imperfection. Each star, each butterfly, each blade of grass, "the mighty Kosmos in perfect equilibrium produces— this," says the German Stein in *Lord Jim*. By contrast, he adds, "Man is amazing, but he is not a masterpiece."[20] But perfection, the reader may conclude on the final page, is a dream of men like Jim, not of butterflies. For Stein, the pursuit of illusion is the mark of the romantic, and the romantic is the most fully realized man. There is something of Aristotle's philosophy of perfectly realizable

---

[20] *Lord Jim*, p. 208.

potentialities in Stein's reverie, but there is nothing in Aristotle of Stein's quasi-Christian praise of human suffering as the means of self-realization.

As we shall see, from earliest childhood Conrad had good reason for dramatizing an opposition between "romanticism" and "realism," politically as well as personally. Furthermore, the shift he made from eastern to western Europe during his maturing years gave him a view of European politics from an objective vantage point superior to that of Gulliver or the Chinese "Citizen of the World." For Conrad was at once more deeply involved in the fate of the cosmopolitan community and less deeply involved than Swift or Goldsmith in the specific national grievances that date their writings for later readers.

This advantage for Conrad, one must add, is the source of another difficulty for his readers. We are never sure of the exact position of the mind reflecting behind the composition—whether it is, as it were, with the English reader or against him; whether it presents its case for our mutual sympathy and understanding or for our edification and improvement.

At a critical moment in Conrad's writing life, when he had dropped *The Rescue* to write *Heart of Darkness* and *Lord Jim*, his friend R. B. Cunninghame Graham invited him to a pacifist meeting in London in the spring of 1899 (about the same time as the Hague Peace Conference of that year). Conrad's answer provides us with our most concise text on his political point of view. It is especially interesting because it seems to follow a train of thought that Conrad was pursuing in his fiction, and its tone is unequivocal, registering a stern corrective to the British point of view from the profound experience of a foreigner. The voice throughout the letter is the voice of a travel-weary European realist, grimly set upon disenchanting his idealistic British friend. "I am simply in the seventh heaven to find you like the 'H. of D.' so far," he begins, referring to the first installment of *Heart of Darkness* that had appeared in the February, 1899, issue of *Blackwood's Magazine*.

> You bless me indeed. Mind you don't curse me by and bye for the very same thing. There are two more instalments in which the idea is so wrapped up in secondary notions that you, even you!—may

miss it. And also you must remember that I don't start with an abstract notion. I start with definite images and as their rendering is true some little effect is produced. So far the note struck chimes in with your convictions,—*mais après*. There is an *après*. But I think that if you look a little into the episodes, you will find in them the right intention, though I fear nothing that is practically effective.[21]

At once Conrad has fixed the lines of the argument. Definite images, truly rendered—this is the only effective artistic technique. Cunninghame Graham will agree to this, but there is more in *Heart of Darkness* than art. Conrad goes on to say that in politics, too, if the terms of argument are indefinite and untrue to life, all effect is lost. Practical effectiveness is the thing to try for. He fears that his efforts in this direction in *Heart of Darkness* are futile.

From the start of the letter Conrad lapses into French to warn his correspondent of a non-British emphasis. French is, among other things, the traditional language of mediation between England and the continent.

Cunninghame Graham is going to talk at the peace conference, and Conrad writes,

> If you want me to come I want still more to hear you. But I am not a peace man, not a democrat (I don't know what the word means really) . . . I can't be an accomplice after or before the fact to any sort of fraternity that includes the westerness [?] whom I so dislike.

The word "westerness," thus transcribed by Jean-Aubry with a question mark, is in the manuscript at Yale obviously "westerners" (*zapadniki*), a term in the political vocabulary of Russia which at that time referred to an assortment of Russians who sympathized with western European traditions. Peter Chaadaev and Paul Milukov were among their best known apologists. The word had this specific application, though Conrad might have used it also for the Americans, second only to the Russians in his contempt at that period, for reasons that will appear. He goes on to say,

> I cannot admit the idea of fraternity, not so much because I believe it impracticable, but because its propaganda (the only thing really

---

[21] Letter to Cunninghame Graham, Feb. 8, 1899, *Life and Letters*, I, 268–70.

tangible about it) tends to weaken the national sentiment, the preservation of which is my concern.

International brotherhood, Conrad stresses, is not a valid political aim.[22] Even if it could be, its profession at this moment is a dangerous red herring that will be used by malicious forces to fool and finally trample the credulous within free nations. The "illusion" of international fraternity "imposes by its size alone":

> There is already as much fraternity as there can be,—and that's very little and that very little is no good. What does fraternity mean? Abnegation,—self-sacrifice means something. Fraternity means nothing unless the Cain-Abel business. That's your true fraternity. Assez.

There is more to this fragile cynicism than at first meets the eye. Conrad is in effect hardly less sanguine politically than was Aristotle, for whom the basis of politics was not in brotherhood (an abstraction) but in a pragmatic "union of those who cannot exist without each other." Aristotle (again following Plato), while appealing to the far-reaching principle that the whole (in this case society) must have priority over the part, nonetheless set a limitation upon the size of societies, determining them not by the whole race of men but by integrations formed for efficiency: communities "large enough to be nearly or quite self-sufficing."[23] For Conrad, especially the Conrad of *Heart of Darkness*, efficiency is an inadequate criterion for the determination of size in a national state. With good reason, too, since one time-honored justification presented by Russia for her annexations of Polish territory was, and has continued to be, on the basis of a politically efficient union of lands and peoples. In the letter to Cunninghame Graham Conrad speaks for the first time to a British subject out of the depths of his

---

[22] Some six years later, in 1905, Conrad writes that the beginnings of European fraternity were squelched by the Franco-Prussian War: "The idea of a Europe united in the solidarity of her dynasties, which for a moment seemed to dawn on the horizon of the Vienna Congress through the subsiding dust of Napoleonic alarums and excursions, has been extinguished by the larger glamour of less restraining ideals. Instead of the doctrines of solidarity it was the doctrine of nationalities much more favorable to spoliations that came to the front, and since its greatest triumphs at Sadowa and Sedan there is no Europe." *Notes on Life and Letters*, p. 103.

[23] Aristotle, *op. cit.*, p. 555.

Polish political background. He has risen to defend not Poland but nationalism—"national sentiment, the preservation of which is my concern."

The national state, suffering persecution in the name of internationalism and brotherhood among other things, is an established fact. Conrad makes no effort to defend it except on the strength of its concrete existence. *"Il faut un principe défini,"* he writes in the French half of the letter in which his positive ideology is expressed.

> Si l'idée nationale apporte la souffrance et son service donne la mort, ça vaut toujours mieux que de servir les ombres d'une éloquence qui est morte, justement parce qu'elle n'a pas de corps.

Although this is the extent of his apology for the nation state, more can be inferred from what is really the crux of the whole letter and, significantly, the turning point at which Conrad lapses completely into French, a language of clear definitions. The crucial term *"l'égoïsme"* which he poses against the English "fraternity" is made to suggest not only the care for self that sets man against his brother, but also the care for the nation, which has set him, Conrad, against "international fraternity." His childhood exposure to German (antiromantic) historiography may well have led to an interest in the historical works of Hegel and Nietzsche and fortified a Polish romantic tendency toward identification of the nation with the self.[24] For Hegel, and for Nietzsche after him, the nation represented the highest expression of human destiny in man's progress toward self-realization and perfect freedom. The clashes of nation against nation, far from tending toward an international synthesis as in Marx, would produce (according to Hegel and Nietzsche) an ever increasing refinement of national spirit and a breed of supermen to defend it. Conrad was deprecating in his references to these German historians,[25] but their tracks are evident in his political

---

[24] See above, n. 18.

[25] "The Germanic Tribes had told the whole world in all possible tones carrying conviction, the gently persuasive, the coldly logical; in tones Hegelian, Nietzschean, war-like, pious, cynical, inspired, what they were going to do to the inferior races of the earth, so full of sin and unworthiness." "The Crime of Partition" in *Notes on Life and Letters*, pp. 124–25.

I don't even mention two neighbouring streets. Two ribs of the same street. There is already as much fraternity as there can be – and that's very little – and that very little is no good. What does fraternity mean. Abnegation – self sacrifice means something. Fraternity means nothing unless the Cain – Abel business. That's your true fraternity. Assez.

L'homme est un animal méchant. Sa méchanceté doit être organisée. Le crime de l'existence organisée. La société est essentiellement criminelle – ou elle n'existerait pas. C'est l'égoïsme qui sauve tout – absolument tout – tout ce que nous abhorrons tout ce que nous aimons. Et tout se tient. Voilà pourquoi je respecte les extrêmes anarchistes. – "Je souhaite l'extermination générale" – Très bien. C'est juste et ce qui est plus c'est clair. Au fait des compromis

Conrad wrote this letter to R. B. Cunninghame Graham (manuscript, Yale University Library) on February 8, 1899. The socialist Cunninghame Graham, with his aristocratic (part Spanish-Catholic, part Scot) background, provoked in Conrad's letters some of the novelist's most fundamental political comments.

fiction. The evidence in the letter to Cunninghame Graham is to be inferred only from the circumstance of his pairing egoism and nationalism against fraternity and internationalism. Typically, Conrad restyles whatever he may derive from political idealists into personal convictions edged with a wry realism. In the letter to Cunninghame Graham, his train of thought on egoism and nationalism leads him to consider the nature of man in its aspect of eternal perversity rather than its godlike potentialities. Human society has its origins, its present, and its future in the conflicts of human egoism, out of which comes everything that we hate, but also everything that we love:

> L'homme est un animal méchant. Sa méchanceté doit être organisée. La société est essentiellement criminelle,—ou elle n'existerait pas. C'est l'égoïsme qui sauve tout,—absolument tout,—tout ce que nous abhorrons, tout ce que nous aimons. Et tout se tient. Voilà pourquoi je respecte les extrêmes anarchistes.—'Je souhaite l'extermination générale.' Très bien. C'est juste et ce qui est plus, c'est clair. On fait des compromis avec des paroles. Ça n'en finit plus. C'est comme une forêt où personne ne connaît la route.

Between the lines we may read the experience of a man (and a people) whose past knowledge of anarchy and present knowledge of oppression have revealed not only the need for organized society but the need to dissolve it when it has been turned against him. Suppression, since 1772 (the first partition of Poland), has discovered to him his formerly unexploited powers for rebellion.

But the urge back to anarchy sits uneasily upon a people who pride themselves upon a flair for political justice and stability (pride all the stronger because the old Polish Republic is beyond the test of practical politics). Their political cynicism, except as it is directed toward oppression, is consciously nurtured as a measure of self-defense and a refuge:

> C'est un égoïsme rationnel et féroce que j'exerce envers moi-même. Je me repose là-dedans. Puis la pensée revient. La vie recommence, les regrets, les souvenirs et un désespoir plus sombre que la nuit.

The political animal for Conrad has a dual nature, empowered with titanic good and titanic evil, as a result of which he is at war both with himself and with his fellow men. To the British Cunninghame Graham, Conrad writes as Thomas Hobbes wrote to the whole English nation, trying to waken it from a dream of utopias to the daylight of a Machiavellian *Realpolitik* that the continent had been digesting for over a century. Hobbes, too, probed into the egoism that is the motive force toward both criminal behavior and social good. But Hobbes, like many of his contemporaries, was bent on convincing his readers of something in which Conrad had no faith—the possibility of an empirical demonstration for all truth. Utilitarian democracy, the "enlightened self-interest" of Hobbes, Bentham, and Mill, as of the American Transcendentalists, is surely the "lovely phantom" of democracy which Conrad derides for his friend's benefit. Leashing its hope to a dream of material wealth like the English hero of *Nostromo*, this phantom has opened the way for a form of government that will force, rather than allow, men to have what they need. Over a decade earlier Conrad had written to Spiridion Kliszczewski that "England was the only barrier to the pressure of infernal doctrines born in continental back-slums." But as a result of an untimely extension of the suffrage, socialism was inevitable, he said, and "must inevitably end in Caesarism." "These things must be. It is a fatality."[26]

Finally, the egoism that asserts the inalienable truth of national existence for Conrad is no more like the egoism of Hobbes than it is like the egoism of Nietzsche. His resort to French is meaningful in another way here, I believe. Some seven years earlier he wrote in French to his relative Marguerite Poradowska of the same faculty for self-sacrifice that, in the letter to Cunninghame Graham, he holds to "mean something," having its source in egoism rather than brotherhood. To Madame Poradowska, a Frenchwoman married to a Pole, he traces "that mysterious urge toward abnegation and suffering which guides womanly feeling" back to its source in charity. "For Charity is eternal and universal Love, the divine virtue, the sole manifestation of the Almighty which may in some manner justify the act of creation.

---

[26] Letter to Kliszczewski, Dec. 19, 1885, *Life and Letters*, I, 84.

"Hence the longing for self-sacrifice, for returning good for evil . . ."[27] Words written to a woman, to a devout Roman Catholic, but the only words he gives anywhere for the origins of the urge toward heroism. And he adds, even to her, the essence of his message to Cunninghame Graham:

> Unfortunately . . . in my opinion abnegation carried to an extreme . . . is not only profoundly immoral but dangerous, in that it sharpens the appetite for evil in the malevolent and develops (perhaps unconsciously) that latent human tendency towards hypocrisy in the . . . let us say, benevolent.

The British socialist and the French Catholic bring out in Conrad two sides of the same thought. Sympathetic with both correspondents, he yet corrects what he takes to be Cunninghame Graham's utopian conception of human nature and the foundations of society, and the Catholic woman's uncritical trust in benevolence.

But the English-speaking reader often mistakenly identifies Conrad's political dualism with arch-conservatism for want of understanding its Polish frame of reference, particularly in the letter to Cunninghame Graham. The difficult passage is the crucial *"l'homme est un animal méchant. Sa méchanceté doit être organisée. Le crime est une condition necéssaire de l'existence organisée. La société est essentiellement criminelle,—ou elle n'existerait pas."* To British and American readers, with their history of relative political security and slowly evolving democratic institutions, Conrad appears to stand "on the lunatic fringe of conservatism." Such is the opinion of one American reader, who then concludes: "The respect for tradition, for law, for convention, [was] a product of his belief that society arose not as a manifestation of similar qualities in individuals, and hence to be subordinate to them, but that it was imposed as a necessary restraint upon man's innate depravity."[28] The trouble with this is that *méchanceté*

---

[27] *Letters of Joseph Conrad to Marguerite Poradowska, 1890–1920*, translated and edited by John A. Gee and Paul J. Sturm (New Haven: Yale University Press, 1940), p. 42.

[28] Henry Steele Commager, Jr., "The Problem of Evil in *Heart of Darkness*," Bowdoin Prize Essay, Harvard University, 1952, p. 7.

is not—as Jocelyn Baines, too, translates it in the concluding pages of his recent biography—"depravity" (a single quality—evil unqualified) but something better rendered as "perversity" (which is dual, implying a norm of goodness and a straying from it). This is, in fact, the common quality in all men of which organized society is the full manifestation. Society is thus formed not as an imposition upon evil human nature, but arises out of the expression of that nature, good and bad. Just as each man must organize his own perversity in order to live with himself, he and his fellows must organize one another's perversity so that they can all live together. Conrad lays a heavier onus upon organized society (*essentiellement criminelle*) than upon man (*méchant*). Man is lovable in his perversity, but organized society is a necessary evil. A strong satiric theme in *The Secret Agent* follows logically from this: The lawkeepers have the same criminal instincts as the lawbreakers, otherwise the whole legal apparatus would collapse (*n'existerait pas*). It takes two to make an argument, a thief to catch a thief.

Conrad's political thought is less like arch-conservatism than it is like the lunatic fringe of Polish liberalism,[29] characteristically jealous of the privilege of anarchy but conscientiously hopeful of preserving each man's rights against his neighbor.

Both the German submissiveness (idealistic as it may be) and the Russian lawlessness (fed on the corruption of all the virtues) are utterly foreign to the Polish nation, whose qualities and defects are

---

[29] Poles have long prided themselves on the early democratization of their political institutions, developed between the fourteenth and eighteenth centuries, before the abolition of the Polish Republic. Among their advances during this period were the grants of personal inviolability by the king to the nobility in 1428, the institution of a parliamentary system (the Polish Diet) and constitutional monarchy in 1505, the invention of the veto power (*Liberum Veto*, 1652), and the extension of political rights to nearly 12 per cent of the whole population. By contrast, "the Liberal France of Louis-Philippe did not grant such rights to 1 per cent of her citizens. . . . In Great Britain, before the reform of 1832, less than 2 per cent of the inhabitants had the right to vote." The myth concerning Polish conservatism, many Poles believe, was created and popularized by German historians who labeled the Polish Republic an Aristocratic Oligarchy, without taking into account that the Polish aristocracy made up a small portion of the voting nobility. See *Poland, An authorized version of Petite Encyclopédie Polonaise*, ed. Erasmus Piltz (London, 1909), pp. 28–29 n. and pp. 389–416.

altogether of another kind, tending to a certain exaggeration of individualism and, perhaps, to an extreme belief in the Governing
Power of Free Assent: the one invariably vital principle in the internal government of the Old Republic.[30]

"*C'est l'égoïsme qui sauve tout . . . tout ce que nous abhorrons,
tout ce que nous aimons.*" An apt summary of Poland's experience
with the *Liberum Veto*, which from 1652 (when it was first applied
—it had been introduced earlier) till its abolition in 1791 gave each
deputy of the Diet the right to defeat any resolution before the
legislature by his single opposition. Out of this wild experiment in
utopian democracy came not only the freedom Poland loved but the
disunion that finally destroyed her. She was, nevertheless, heading
toward a form of government that would reflect as fully as possible
the demands of human nature.

The kind of order required by man should be congruent with his
nature rather than contradictory to it. This is the essence of Conrad's message to Cunninghame Graham. Socialism, robbing men of
natural incentives to self-government and inner moral restraint,
leads on to "Caesarism." "Democracy," on the other hand, has
corrupt connotations for Conrad because it is tainted with the
abstractions that incited the French Revolution or the lawlessness
of American bossism in the West, and in eastern Europe it is a
mounting battle cry for revolutionary forces quickened by hatred for
much that is good as well as much that is corrupt in Western civilization. Conrad distinguishes sharply between Cunninghame Graham's democratic instincts (in the letter: "*vous êtes essentiellement
un frondeur. . . . C'est les nobles qui ont fait la Fronde, du reste.*")
and "that humanitarianism that seems to be merely a matter of
crazy nerves or a morbid conscience."[31] In his novels, Charles Gould
represents the former, Peter Ivanovitch and Donkin the latter.

In an unpublished portion of the manuscript of *Under Western
Eyes*, which must be examined separately, Conrad hinted strongly
at a tragic stalemate that could occur in world politics if Europe

---

[30] "The Crime of Partition," *Notes on Life and Letters*, p. 132.
[31] *A Personal Record*, p. vii.

were to be caught between the two camps of Russian autocratic socialism and American commercial individualism.

Conrad wrote to Cunninghame Graham in the spring of 1899 from the standpoint of a Pole recalling with mingled pride and regret the long history of Polish liberal institutions which had sickened and finally died because Poland had plucked the fruit of democracy before it was ripe. He is in the peculiar position of a man (three generations removed from practical politics) whose inherited memory of it is yet so vivid that he feels justified in admonishing the inexperienced. His advice, furthermore, is not simply against the democracy in which Poland failed, but a subtle compound of faith and despair. It is the inexperience of his adopted English countrymen that calls forth his prophetic insights into modern politics.

"I kept my eye on his shabby plodding with a sort of notion
that it was a punishment for the heroics of his fancy—an
expiation for his craving after more glamour than he could
carry."

Lord Jim

"English critics—for indeed I am an English writer—
speaking about me always add that there is something incomprehensible, impalpable, ungraspable in me. You
[Poles] alone can grasp this ungraspable element, compre-
hend the incomprehensible. *This is my Polishness*. The Polishness which I took to my works through Mickiewicz and
Słowacki. My father read *Pan Tadeusz* aloud to me, and
made me read out loud. Not merely once or twice. I
preferred *Konrad Wallenrod, Grażyna*. Later I preferred
Słowacki. Do you know why Słowacki? *Il est l'âme de
toute la Pologne, lui.*"

Letter written in 1914 from Conrad to Maryan Dąbrow-
ski, quoted in English by Ludwik Krzyżanowski,
Centennial Essays

CHAPTER TWO

Conrad's Polish Background: The Political Imperative

As he says in the opening of A Personal Record, it was with nervous and fitful resolve that Conrad turned back to his early life in Poland, under "the oppressive shadow of the great Russian Empire —the shadow lowering with the darkness of a new-born national hatred fostered by the Moscow school of journalists against the Poles . . ."[1] Something of this Polish past, he said however, must be left for his two sons. For that

> which in their grown-up years may appear to the world about them as the most enigmatic side of their natures and perhaps must re-main for ever obscure even to themselves, will be their unconscious response to the still voice of that inexorable past from which [my] work of fiction and their personalities are remotely derived.[2]

For many years the enigmatic elements in Conrad's fiction have preoccupied critics and biographers, but few have attempted to trace the relationship between the novels and "that inexorable past" from which they were "remotely derived." The works of Gustav

---

[1] A Personal Record, p. 24.
[2] Ibid., pp. 24–25.

Morf, Joseph Ujejski, G. Jean-Aubry, and Jocelyn Baines[3] have come as close to the undertaking as any works available to speakers of only Western languages. British and American writers—until just recently—have understandably shown themselves too wise or too diffident to study a relationship between the novels and a background that has been inaccessible either by reason of the language barrier, the Iron Curtain, or both. Ujejski and Jean-Aubry, who had the necessary Polish materials at their command, were (nevertheless) to a greater or less degree put off balance by them, so that, as V. S. Pritchett says of Jean-Aubry, they each give the impression of one "who simply runs beside" Conrad.[4] Even the full and careful documentation of Jocelyn Baines's critical biography has this quality. One reads these books for the pleasure of finding new light shed upon the man, but with a growing sense of uneasiness. The brightest light that shines on the novelist comes out of his fiction, and the critical biographer sometimes dims that light by the materials with which he surrounds it.

Conrad's creative genius is evident to us largely through its submissive attentiveness to the clash, on the plain of his life, of great forces—both personal and public. What R. L. Mégroz called Conrad's "triumphant passive resistance to life"[5] was his way of dealing with contradictory influences, pitched against each other in his Polish childhood and still struggling for mastery in his English exile. "My point of view, whether on land or sea, is English," he wrote Kazimierz Waliszewski in 1903, "but you must not conclude from that that I have become an Englishman. By no means. The *homo duplex* has, in my case, more than one meaning."[6]

---

[3] Gustav Morf, *The Polish Heritage of Joseph Conrad* (London: Sampson Low, Marston, 1930); Joseph Ujejski, *Joseph Conrad*, translated from Polish to French by Pierre Duméril (Paris: Éditions Edgar Malfère, 1939); G. Jean-Aubry, *La Vie de Conrad* (Paris: Gallimard, 1947), translated by Helen Sebba as *The Sea Dreamer* (New York: Doubleday & Co., Inc., 1957); Jocelyn Baines, *Joseph Conrad* (London: Weidenfeld & Nicolson, 1959).

[4] "The Exile," p. 229.

[5] *Joseph Conrad's Mind and Method* (London: Faber & Faber, 1931), *passim*.

[6] Jean-Aubry, *The Sea Dreamer*, p. 240.

The idea of the divided man as applied to Conrad had been a popular theme with both sides of his Polish family since his childhood. "As far as his heart goes," Apollo Korzeniowski, his father, wrote to the critic Kaszewski when Conrad was seven, "he has his mother's qualities; but his head—poor chap—he got from me."[7] Conrad's maternal uncle, Tadeusz Bobrowski, disputed this point and for years, by letter and word of mouth, drilled Conrad into the belief that what he had inherited from the Bobrowski line was even-tempered rationality; whereas the Korzeniowski influence was all from the "heart": absurd fantasies, erotic passion, moodiness, and poor judgment, particularly in every affair touching economics and politics.

As Jean-Aubry pointed out, the letters Bobrowski wrote to Conrad from his eleventh year (when he was orphaned) till well into his thirties blame the Korzeniowski strain for all Conrad's indiscreet acts and opinions. The Bobrowski line is credited whenever he conducts himself prudently. "You remind me much more of the Korzeniowskis than of my dear sister," Bobrowski wrote in 1876, when Conrad had lost his trunk and belongings in France.[8] Four years later, charging him with instability in the pursuit of his profession, Bobrowski writes, "You would not be a 'Nałęcz' [Korzeniowski], my dear boy, if you did not change your plans."[9] A few weeks later, when the twenty-two-year-old Conrad has decided to persevere in the British Merchant Service, Bobrowski rejoices:

> I see with pleasure that the "Nałęcz" in you has been modified by the influence of the "Bobruszczuki" [little beavers], as your incomparable mother used to call her own family before she flew away to the nest of the "Nałęcz." This time I rejoice over the influence of my family, not, however, without recognizing in the "Nałęcz" a spirit of initiative and enterprise superior to that which runs in our veins. From the blend of these two famous races should emerge a

---

[7] *Ibid.*, p. 36.
[8] *Life and Letters*, I, 39.
[9] *Ibid.*, I, 56.

character so steadfast and so energetic that the whole world will be astonished at it.[10]

It is interesting to speculate how deeply affected Conrad may have been by this long insistence on his divided personality. Most probably, as his uncle surely suspected, it provided a profound and far-reaching expedient: a means of objectifying and simplifying the abnormal conflicts that Conrad had always to contend with in himself. Without such an expedient, he might have surrendered to the psychic paralysis which both uncle and nephew recognized as Conrad's most threatening affliction. This affliction, clearly, was the despot Conrad attempted to "desert" in leaving Poland for a physically rigorous life at sea.

What is most curious is that the Bobrowski-Korzeniowski dualism was a fiction lacking any foundation whatsoever in fact. In a recently published essay on the Bobrowski family, Aleksander Janta has revealed startling evidence that the "fatal inheritance" ascribed to the Korzeniowskis by Bobrowski descended (if it descended at all) from a member of Bobrowski's own family—Seweryn Pilchowski, Tadeusz Bobrowski's maternal uncle, whose very existence was a carefully guarded secret in the family.[11]

Seweryn Pilchowski, one of the most extravagant of the Polish political exiles grouped around Adam Mickiewicz in Paris in the 1840's, had quickly degenerated there from a typically romantic young patriot, adventurer, and lover, into a manic dreamer, a popinjay, a squanderer of funds (entrusted to him for the Polish cause), and a cad. None of Conrad's biographers thus far has ferreted out this fantastic figure. Janta presents evidence to show that Pilchowski's own mother may have hidden the flagrant truth of his Parisian life from the rest of the family. If the truth were unknown to his nephews, however, why would Tadeusz Bobrowski's *Memoirs*—so

---

[10] *Ibid.*, I, 59–60. Baines has newly translated this letter reading "Bobroszczaki" and "excellent races" (also two more minor points) as closer to the original. See his *Joseph Conrad*, p. 66.

[11] Aleksander Janta, *Losy i ludzie* (New York: Polski Instytut Naukowy w Ameryce, 1961), pp. 340–51. This chapter ("*Skąd 'fatalne dziedzictwo' Conrada?*") was translated for me by Mitchell Winthrop.

baldly critical of all other members of the family—omit even the name of the scandalous uncle? After reading the extraordinary case Janta presents, one is inclined to believe that the known facts of Pilchowski's life were so appalling that Bobrowski (like Marlow in Conrad's *Heart of Darkness*) carefully suppressed the truth, feeling that more was to be feared than gained from its example.

The existence of such a personality as Seweryn Pilchowski, distilling the quintessence of all that was worst in the Polish character, seemed to Bobrowski to hover over the family like an evil angel. How to protect the excessively vulnerable Conrad from it became his main concern. By embodying the evil in Conrad's father—an otherwise honorable man—Bobrowski could make it serve his pedagogic purposes. But if this is what actually occurred, the "fatal influence" (as in the possessed swine of the Gospels), to Bobrowski's horror, suddenly turned up in Conrad with seemingly renewed potency. Jean-Aubry and Baines have described the obscure events of 1878, when Conrad as a young seaman in Marseilles took part in a plot to re-establish the Carlists in Spain, squandered his money, ran up crippling debts, engaged in a mysterious love affair, and finally tried to shoot himself through the heart. If one were to assemble the words Bobrowski used to describe Conrad in letters during this time, they would form an exact portrait, not of Conrad's father but of Seweryn Pilchowski: manically inspired by absurd schemes, egotistical, improvident, politically unsound, and irresponsibly amorous.

A further thought is suggested by Janta's discovery. If Conrad, who is as silent as the rest of the family concerning the existence of his great-uncle, had glimpsed the skeleton in the family closet (as seems highly possible) before his adventures in Marseilles, we can imagine his state of mind on discovering that he was re-enacting a family "fatality." Most of Janta's sources of information concerning Pilchowski are from the Mickiewicz correspondence preserved in Paris, which may have come to Conrad's attention, if only by hearsay, during his trips to Paris in the 1870's.[12] Was Pilchowski's dis-

---

[12] *Life and Letters*, I, p. 39 n. Jean-Aubry here mentions that Bobrowski's letter of October 9, 1876, "draws Conrad's attention to the Librairie du Luxembourg at 16 rue

grace to be his own fulfilment of his martyred parents' hopes? Such recognition, added to his other sensations in 1878, might well have driven him to attempt to kill himself.

Impatient as one may be with the whole idea of hereditary influences, one cannot deny the relevance in Conrad's life and fiction of the very different personal influences of his father and uncle.

The head taken by Apollo Korzeniowski to be his chief characteristic expressed itself in social criticism through the medium of verse. Never judged to be a poet of the highest rank, he is known in Poland today as author of a few plays and translations from Shakespeare, de Vigny, and Hugo—but chiefly as a national martyr, and as the father of Joseph Conrad. Readers of Conrad find it significant that Korzeniowski's poems and plays are marked by an inflated romanticism, edged with mordant humor. "The darkest tares of the human spirit—imposture, deceit, hypocrisy, treason—are his chosen adversaries. . . . His raillery wounds to the bone, his irony kills." So read *The History of Polish Literature* in 1877.[13]

In a long essay on Korzeniowski,[14] Czesław Miłosz points out that Conrad's father came in the "second wave" of Polish romantic poets who repeated and amplified the mystic political faith that Adam Mickiewicz (1798–1855) had fabricated out of the vision of the mystic Andrzej Towiański (1799–1878). It was "the prophet" Towiański who fed the wild fantasies of Bobrowski's Uncle Seweryn. According to Towiański's new-made political myth, which Mickiewicz offered an audience of Polish exiles in Paris during the 1840's, Poland is the national incarnation of Christ, destined to become the messiah among the nations of Europe. The

---

de Tournon, Paris, where Władysław Mickiewicz, son of the great Polish poet, was at that time." It would seem from Janta's article that Mickiewicz's son might have been full of anecdotes about Seweryn Pilchowski's activities in Paris, a circumstance that must not have occurred to Bobrowski.

[13] Czesław Miłosz, "Apollo Nałęcz Korzeniowski," *Kultura* (Paris; February, 1956), p. 63. Mrs. Walter Dzewieniecki translated this article from the Polish for me. Other critical studies of Conrad's father are by Stefan Buszczyński (*Mało znany poeta.* Cracow, 1870) and Roman Taborski (*Apollo Korzeniowski; ostatni dramatopisarz romantyczny.* Wrocław, 1957).

[14] Miłosz, *op. cit.*, p. 64.

martyred people of Poland, as part of a mystical body, are destined to rise "on the third day." The first day had been the first capture of Warsaw in 1794; the second day, the second capture of Warsaw in 1831.[15] Mickiewicz did not live to see the third day, but many Poles looked forward to its realization in the 1863 uprising, which was the great political event for which Korzeniowski dreamed and wrote and planned.

Korzeniowski was already a disciple of Mickiewicz before Conrad's birth, when his poems subtitled *Ubi crux, ibi poesia* appeared in 1856.[16] Later, during his exile in Russia, he elaborated the messianic myth in a memoir called *Poland and Russia*, which he managed to smuggle abroad.[17] Russia's vilification and crucifixion of the Polish people symbolized for him the fate in store for all European civilization at the hands of the Russian Empire. A major tenet of Korzeniowski's faith was that Poland's suffering could enlighten and save Europe, if the free nations would profit from the experience of those already absorbed and join forces in the great spiritual conflict.[18]

Miłosz particularly remarks upon Korzeniowski's self-dramatization of the double role he played in the period before his exile in 1861:

> The greater part of his life he had to pass in the Ukraine, where he carried on the functions of administrative steward [in the service of others]. This respectable façade served as a screen for his literary occupations. He remains one of the last rural writers who wielded his pen in seclusion, leading a tenuous life and playing a double role. The theme of a mask which one wears in society, while one apparently goes along with conventional opinions, recurs in nearly all his plays.[19]

---

[15] Wiktor Weintraub, *The Poetry of Adam Mickiewicz* (The Hague: Mouton, 1954), p. 196.

[16] Miłosz, *op. cit.*, p. 63.

[17] *Ibid.*, p. 76.

[18] Conrad's two essays on Poland in *Notes on Life and Letters* echo his father's main points even while repeatedly stressing the importance of a "practical" approach to Poland's political destiny.

[19] Miłosz, *op. cit.*, p. 62. In this connection, George Brandes' comment on Polish dramatic literature at the turn of this century is revealing: "The only place where it is

The exact look of the political rebel beneath Korzeniowski's mask was best revealed, according to Miłosz, in the *Memoirs* of Tadeusz Bobrowski (which slandered so many noble families in Poland that most of the copies were bought and destroyed). Miłosz considers Bobrowski's judgment of Korzeniowski quite trustworthy. According to the *Memoirs*, although Korzeniowski

> considered himself a sincere democrat (and others considered him as a "fanatic" and "red"), he had in him, as I often tried to persuade him, a hundred more times the aristocratic instinct than I had myself—I who never passed for a democrat.
>
> I never managed to understand his political and social views, beyond his rather vague leaning in favor of the old Polish Republic [Rzeczpospolita]. . . . On the peasant question, for example, he hesitated before the emancipation of the serfs. In one sense he sympathized with me (my thought at this time was already precise in 1854); but he showed reticence, affirmed that only those who possessed the land had a right to make a decision on what concerned its redistribution. I am not surprised.[20]

A favorite theme of Conrad's father was the irresponsibility of the Polish aristocracy (a special segment of the broadly based Polish "nobility"), the luxury-loving class that fell into the snares set for it in the eighteenth century by Russian strategists. On this one subject Tadeusz Bobrowski and Apollo Korzeniowski saw eye to eye. They had no use for a class (nominally superior to their own lower nobility) which had won its honors, mostly from the partitioning powers, not because of heroism or public service (as had their own) but because of its material support of the crown before the Partition of 1795. Yet through one of history's ironies, Korzeniowski's criticism of the Polish aristocracy made it hard to distinguish his political intrigues from the activities of Russian socialists and revolution-

---

allowed to speak the Polish language publicly is on the stage. As yet it is not forbidden to give Polish theatrical representations, and this circumstance has given to the theatre a preponderance in Polish intellectual life, which is intelligible, but unfortunate, and so much the more harmful and unnatural as the dramatic literature of the country is rather poor. . . . If many of the best literary men have devoted themselves to theatrical criticism, it is because in the guise of examination and analysis of the ideas put forward in the plays, they can say and suggest much which it would be impossible to advance without this opportunity or veil" (*Poland: A Study of the Land, People and Literature* [New York: Macmillan Co., 1904], pp. 14–15).
[20] Miłosz, p. 69.

aries, whose major effort was—like Korzeniowski's—to destroy the power of the Tsar. Knowing how easily anti-tsarist intrigue could be turned to Russian purposes, many Poles like the antirevolutionary Bobrowski accused Korzeniowski of recklessness.

Bobrowski thought that emancipation of the serfs should be the supreme objective in the years before 1861, according to Miłosz. Korzeniowski insisted that nothing should take precedence over the mobilization of the people for action against the oppressor. "It wasn't that Korzeniowski scorned the people," writes Miłosz, "but he sought in it essentially a capacity for national élan."[21] Miłosz also points out that people from the lower orders of society hardly ever make an appearance in Korzeniowski's plays and poetry. He concentrated on the society of gentlemen, oscillating "between mockery and despair, according to whether he saw in the swinishness around him exceptional meanness or the structure of the universe. In reading his poems we find humanity divided into 'men of feeling' and 'swine'—a romantic division which is at the base of all revolutionary movements created by intellectuals."[22]

In 1855 Korzeniowski plunged into heated activity, trying to synchronize an outbreak of peasants in Poland, Lithuania, and the Ukraine with the arrival of military aid he hoped would come from France and England in time to embarrass Russia crucially, distracted as she was by the Crimean War. The movement failed.

Although even Bobrowski seems to have been uncertain how true the rumors were that Korzeniowski was a "Red," Miłosz hints that the "Party of Daggers" shielded him, and Jean-Aubry confirms that he sympathized with the "Red" party rather than with the "Whites," both of which were formed about this time. The "Reds" were mainly city youths from the petty gentry, the "Whites" chiefly the wealthy landed nobility. The parties seem to have differed only on the extremity of methods needed to achieve the liberation of . Poland in unity with Lithuania and Ruthenia. Jean-Aubry says that Korzeniowski was, in fact, the leader of the "Reds," though he

---

[21] *Ibid.*, p. 70.
[22] *Ibid.*, p. 63.

must have had the confidence of both parties, since he founded the Central Committee, made up of representatives of both parties, which prepared the insurrection of 1863.

Korzeniowski emphatically denied the charge that his political coloring was either communist or socialist. Noting Conrad's protest (in the Preface to *A Personal Record*) that his father was not a revolutionary but a rebel, Ujejski writes:

> In fact, in their views on socialism and communism, the difference between the father and the son was not so great. When, after the publication of Apollo Korzeniowski's play *Komedja* (1856), a critic, "amid tempered eulogies, warned his readers against this work which he accused of being socialist and communist in inspiration," the author, in the preface to his translation of Alfred de Vigny's *Chatterton*, published a year later, hurled back this reproach with passionate indignation. "To backward people," he wrote, "who find their words on the garbage heap of Western theories in order to throw them on each thought that tends to betterment, these words serve as a club to crush all impulses [*élans*] that might interrupt a profound and beloved sleep." But, "no thinking man, if he wishes to be sincere, will believe that Western socialism or communism could flourish among us. . . . Yes, I have defended, I do defend, and I shall continue to defend the cause of the unfortunate, for this cause is remitted by God to the hands of all men who have well disposed hearts. But in defending this cause, I have in sight only its spiritual, moral aspect. Never and nowhere have I sought to prove, and I will not do so in future, that other people's property, torn away from the powerful and distributed among the unfortunate, can be a preventive remedy against social disorders, nor that this property given or restored will not fill with shame the miserable people who receive it."[23]

In 1861 Korzeniowski took up residence in Warsaw, ostensibly to direct a literary journal called *The Fortnightly*, which was about to be founded. The three-year-old Conrad and his mother left their refuge with the Bobrowski's in the Ukraine to join Apollo in Warsaw a few months later. Nothing more of importance has been written concerning Korzeniowski's activities or his exact opinions

---

[23] Ujejski, pp. 71–72. I have translated from the French. Roman Taborski, who places Conrad's father in the ranks of socialist revolutionaries in Poland, has omitted mention of this preface in his recently published biography of Apollo Korzeniowski.

within the "revolutionary government" (*rząd rewolucyjny*) which Miłosz says he had a part in forming.[24] Soon after he had settled in Warsaw, he was arrested by the police and imprisoned in the Citadel. The police, in the course of a persistent inquiry, could find not a single document compromising him, nor did they wrest any useful information from him. All the same, he was kept nine months in the Citadel, where he suffered from rheumatism and scurvy; and there his wife and "Konrad" were allowed to pay him rare visits. In April, 1862, his sentence was finally pronounced: exile to Perm, "in accordance with the desire of the guilty." The governor of Perm, being one of Apollo's old schoolmates at the University of St. Petersburg, might have helped him. But either through coward- ice or a knowledge of Apollo's capacity for political defiance, he made sure that Korzeniowski was sent instead to Vologda, in north Russia. Apollo's colleagues on the revolutionary committee then proposed to organize the poet's escape, but he rejected the offer, not wanting to compromise the existence of the organization for his own freedom.

At Vologda, where Ewelina Korzeniowska had accompanied her husband (taking the four-year-old Conrad despite her delicate health and his), Apollo received the news of the insurrection. It had not been expected by the leaders of the movement at the moment or in the manner in which it came. It had somehow escaped their hands. Apollo wrote to his friends: "This is not the right road! This is not the right road! . . . But look, it is always thus with us! Either we are too late or too early! But God is great!"[25]

All Polish historians of importance severely judge the movement of 1863 into which, as Bobrowski relates in his *Memoirs*, his brother-in-law had been tragically swept. The leaders of the move- ment, he wrote,

> thought to be able to make use of falsehood as an instrument: some consciously, for ends self-admittedly too high to be accessible to in- ferior spirits; others, without knowing it, in repeating the orders given and irresponsibly spreading information which came and went

---

[24] *Ibid.*, p. 71.
[25] *Ibid.*, p. 75.

from Paris to Poland and from Poland to Paris. They made un-
scrupulous use of false information which, originating in the neighborhood of Napoleon III and Prince Plonplon, spread across all the
spheres and bedchambers of Polish society; they penetrated thus
into the modest bedchamber of the little village steward [Korzeni-
owski], whom they attracted and incorporated into the movement.
They presented him with an illusory image of the powerful succor
that was coming from abroad. It is possible to affirm without exaggeration that the movement of 1861–1863 was conceived in falsehood (for one cannot call voluntary creation of illusions otherwise,
even the most noble), grew on falsehood, and finally died in falsehood.[26]

Bobrowski's bitterness against a poet who ignored the practical
circumstances of mundane politics is understandable when one
knows something of Bobrowski's life. He was by profession a lawyer, trained in the rationalism and relativism of the francophile
faculty of law at the University of St. Petersburg—the same university where Apollo Korzeniowski, like many other young Polish
poets, dabbled in oriental languages.[27] When Bobrowski was twenty-
one, his father died, leaving him at the head of his family and in
charge of his mother's large properties in the Ukraine. He felt
obliged to abandon his ambition to become a professor of international law as a result of what he later told Conrad was "that
duty which circumstances define." The years deepened his erudition

---

[26] *Ibid.*, p. 74.

[27] In *The Cambridge History of Poland*, II (Cambridge, 1941), 369, one finds contradictory information: "At [the University of] Kiev, where the 800 to 1000 Poles
formed two-thirds of the University population, there arose soon after the death of
Nicholas a Polish society, called The Trinity. Its moving spirit was Apollo Korzeniowski, the father of Joseph Conrad. At first its objective was purely spiritual: to nourish
resistance to the idea . . . that national emancipation could be achieved through
political cooperation with Russia. . . .

"Slowly and imperceptibly but inevitably 'The Trinity' became political. By 1858
its members had established contact with Polish students in all parts of the Russian
Empire as well as with General Mierosławski in Paris. They had formed a super-
organization that co-ordinated the activities of the isolated groups within university
walls. Alike in quiet Dorpat and in more agitated Petersburg and Moscow, one question in the late 'fifties was debated: what part shall youth play in the life of a state
ruled by a foreign master?"

None of Korzeniowski's biographers mentions Kiev as Korzeniowski's university, or
even the possibility that he was there for a time.

and his respect for French rationalist philosophy, which had flowered in Poland as a reaction against (among other things) political romanticism and obscurantism. Undoubtedly he compared Korzeniowski's intrigues and impecunious pursuit of poetry with his own austere regard for duty. Jean-Aubry describes Bobrowski's nature as the very antithesis of Korzeniowski's, calling his analytical zeal as different as possible from the romantic spirit of Conrad's father. Bobrowski's political prudence was well known even among the Russian authorities, and he was frequently called upon to "use his credit" in favor of compatriots less well-endowed.

Like many other members of the Polish nobility (which, according to George Brandes[28] was so numerous as to constitute an upper middle-class), Bobrowski dropped the title which he might have claimed, and did so on democratic principles, at the same time refusing to be called a democrat, because the name would identify him with revolutionary elements unpredictably festering in Russia and Europe.

Of his brother-in-law, who had sacrificed himself (and his wife) for the freedom of Poland, Bobrowski wrote bitterly, "I assert only that in general poets, men of imagination and ideals, are not capable of clearly formulating the concrete postulates of existence, and that they would do better not to mix in politics, leaving this task to souls less pure and elevated."[29]

This was the view of Apollo Korzeniowski which Bobrowski held before Conrad's eyes, from Korzeniowski's death in 1869 until Bobrowski's own death in 1894—twenty-five years, during which he was Conrad's closest friend as well as nearest relative. Korzeniowski could not debate the question, yet the impress of his nature (and the Pilchowski strain) upon Conrad appeared to be so strong that Bobrowski perpetuated the feud with Korzeniowski's spirit, dramatizing his romanticism and melancholia, his impulsiveness and inconsistency—possibly in this way nourishing the very thing he meant to kill. Conrad's fantastic decision to turn seaman, an im-

---

[28] Poland, p. 28.
[29] Miłosz, op. cit., p. 70.

pulse inspired by the novels of Victor Hugo and the literature of
exploration rather than by any direct knowledge of the sea, Bobrowski attributed to the romantic absurdity the father had instilled in
Conrad during their years together in exile. Making the most of
what was given him to work with, however, Bobrowski approved the
maritime profession for want of anything better to steady Conrad
on a course. Among other advantages, it served the purpose of taking Conrad out of Poland, the nation which his father had illuminated for him with an aura of fantastic illusions.

In 1878 Bobrowski was called upon to rescue Conrad from a web
of difficulties, nearly fatal, which he had brought upon himself in
Marseilles. Describing it to an old friend of the family, the uncle
wrote of Conrad, "he is not a bad boy—only exceedingly sensitive,
conceited—reserved, yet excitable. In short, I found in him all the
defects of the House of Nałęcz."[30] Thirteen years later, when Conrad was thirty-three, Bobrowski was still urging him to be on his
guard against one of the main defects of his father's family—the
idealizing of oneself and of Poland:

> Our country, as Słowacki well says (although he himself was not
> free from the reproach), is the "paw" [peacock] of the nations,
> which, in plain prose, means that we are a nation who consider our-
> selves great and misunderstood, the possessors of a greatness which
> others do not recognize and will never recognize. If individuals and
> nations would set duty before themselves as an aim, instead of
> grandiose ideals, the world would be a happier place.
>   . . . I have taken the motto "usque ad finem" as my guide, the
> love of the duty which circumstances define.[31]

"I think the proper wisdom is to will what the gods will," Conrad
writes in A Personal Record, "without, perhaps, being certain what
their will is—or even if they have a will of their own."[32] His thought,
as so often it does, seems like Bobrowski's in substance but with
an odd, flickering light shining below or above it.

[30] Letter to Stefan Buszczyński, March 24 (New Style), 1879, published by Jocelyn
Baines in the Times Literary Supplement (London), Dec. 6, 1957, p. 748.

[31] Letter to Conrad, Nov. 9, 1891, Life and Letters, I, 148. Jean-Aubry mistakenly
transcribed paw as pan.

[32] A Personal Record, p. xix.

On at least one occasion, nevertheless, we find Bobrowski himself reminding Conrad of what he owed to his national heritage, and significantly enough this was in response to Conrad's suggestion that he might settle in America—tantamount, in Bobrowski's opinion, to "going to hell."[33] In 1880, six years before Conrad became a British subject, Bobrowski wrote to him,

> I told you in my last letter that it would be wiser, in my opinion, to remain a sailor than to become an American politician. Nevertheless, I shall have nothing to say if you do otherwise, but on two conditions: that you always keep in mind that you have to take the consequences of your own acts, and that you never forget in the stormy confusion of American life what you owe to the nobility of the race [i.e., nation] to which you belong.[34]

Bobrowski's arguments against the reckless schemer in his nephew and in favor of the public-spirited workman bore fruit both in Conrad's dogged devotion to his two crafts, as seaman and as writer, and in the themes of his novels. But the driving power, in his life and art together, seems always to have welled up from the impulsiveness, "conceit," or "egoism" his uncle had proscribed. The avuncular correctives, offered and welcomed as a healing discipline, could hardly have inspired the values Conrad lived and wrote by. Discipline became a supreme value for him only because Impulse (both good and bad) was so dynamic a force. Discipline, in his sense of the word, is wanted not to quell impulse, but to channel energy into Purpose. For Purpose is the *raison d'être* of discipline. Conrad stolidly refused to admire "life force" in the raw, though he lived through the period of its apotheosis by Bernard Shaw and D. H. Lawrence, both of whom he disliked.

Bertrand Russell found Conrad's point of view "far from modern" for the curious reason that Conrad "despised indiscipline and hated discipline that was merely external."[35] In other words, ap-

---

[33] It is curious to compare this attitude with Dostoevsky's. Svidrigaïlov, in *Crime and Punishment*, talks of his plan to commit suicide as "a journey to America."

[34] Letter to Conrad, June 17, 1880, *Life and Letters*, I, 59.

[35] Bertrand Russell, *Portraits from Memory* (New York: Simon and Schuster, Inc., 1956), p. 89.

parently Conrad was, unlike modern man, neither an anarchist nor a totalitarian "type." And he was neither because he had an extraordinary knowledge of both, from within as well as from without.

There is a tendency today to regard the dark powers of original impulse as more antisocial than Conrad shows them to be in novels like *Heart of Darkness* and *Nostromo*. It is in the nature of egoism, he writes over and over again (examining the thought from many different angles), to assert a social context for its mirror. But the reflection tricks the hopes of its subject, and may suddenly flash upon his eye as loathsome. The image Kurtz has of himself is a case in point. Like the portrait of Dorian Grey, the projection of his ego into its social frame appears to keep an original beauty while changing, at first unnoticeably, according to a remorseless logic.

George Brandes, a Danish traveler to Poland in the late nineteenth century, who read Polish literature and knew most other European literatures as well, commented on this social consciousness (which we for some reason call "conservatism" in Conrad) as a characteristic of all Polish writers, attributing it partly to Poland's having been deprived of official political organs of expression:

> The schism between the great individual and the nation which is so characteristic of the life and poetry of Shelley and Byron, never manifests itself here [in Poland]; this is, indeed partly because the poets never exalted themselves so high above the average intellectual condition of their people, its religious and political daily life, as Shelley, for instance, but also quite as much because of their feeling of homogeneity with the people whose only organs they were.[36]

If Conrad was divided between two conflicting family strains, it must be remembered that both strains were politically active. In describing his two grandfathers to Edward Garnett, Conrad emphasized that "none of the members of the many families to which these two are related was a literary man; all made sacrifices of

---

[36] Brandes, *op. cit.*, pp. 244–45. In this connection it is worth noting that the cultural homogeneity of Poland was a subject for envy among several prominent Russian writers of the nineteenth century (including Soloviev and Paul Milyukov) who attributed it to the dispersal of education among all classes by the Roman Catholic Church.

fortune, liberty and life for the cause in which they believed; and very few had any illusions as to its success."[37] The cause was the liberation of the Polish Republic.

Rather curiously, Conrad never refers to the political differences between his father and uncle, and we must draw our own conclusions as to which, if either, had the greater effect upon his mind. A case could be made to support the idea that Conrad reconciled their differences on the basis of an idealized childhood memory of his father (perfectly resistant to adult reasoning) and his mature recognition of an uncle whose political thought and action were apparently irreproachable in every way. Thus Conrad the writer— the fully formed Conrad—is able to share his uncle's scorn for revolutionaries on the ground that they are fanatics guided by political ignorance and morbid self-righteousness; at the same time he seems impervious to the fact that Bobrowski ascribed just these qualities to Apollo Korzeniowski.

In 1919, when forced by one of his critics to defend his father against the charge of "revolutionist," Conrad protested: "No epithet could be more inapplicable to a man with such a strong sense of responsibility in the region of ideas and so indifferent to the promptings of personal ambition as my father." Making a careful distinction between "revolutionaries," who aim at the subversion of the "social or political scheme," and "rebels" like his father, who support a realized political existence against its oppressors, Conrad concludes that his father was not a revolutionary but a "patriot in the sense of a man who believing in the spirituality of a national existence could not bear to see that spirit enslaved."[38] The spirituality of national existence, perfectly expressing the nature of man in society, has deep sources in Conrad's past and far-reaching tributaries in his fiction. Like the African Congo that fascinated him, he came to it as an explorer, discovering it as if for the first time.

One of the many senses in which Conrad was *homo duplex* can be found in what he made of the two aspects of Polish liberalism—

---

[37] Letter to Garnett, Jan. 20, 1900, *Life and Letters*, I, 291.
[38] Author's Note to A *Personal Record*, pp. vii–viii.

very different from Western ideas of liberalism—handed down to him by his father and uncle. Both were liberals to the extent that they believed, however different their methods of action, in the moral and material emancipation of a whole society from the tyranny of any class within the society, as well as from any foreign oppressor. If Apollo Korzeniowski underestimated the importance of human rights, as Bobrowski charged, it was partly because he was devoted to what he considered two more pressing needs: the independence of Poland, without which he saw little hope for a vigorous political life, and the purgation of Poland's responsible leadership, without which the pressures for civil liberties might degenerate—as they had in Poland's nearest cultural relation, France—into a bloody struggle.

Remembering his father's reverence for the old Republic and his ideal of social cohesion, Conrad protested in some fairness that he must not be identified with revolutionaries whose aim was the liberation of one segment of a nation at the expense of any other. At the same time, profiting from his uncle's instruction, Conrad strengthened his guard against the idealization of society that had induced Korzeniowski to lose everything in a quixotic gamble. The central characters in Conrad's political novels are, or become, tragically aware of the menace lurking in political ideals.

Because of his awareness of the reactionary spirit that western Europe often associated with counterrevolutionaries, Conrad labored to dramatize his view of the malignant roots of revolutionary trends in Europe. *The Secret Agent* is not, however, the result of his thought on this important subject, as many readers take it to be. For this we must turn to *The Rover*, a work that deserves more notice than is usually acknowledged, which was rated by R. L. Mégroz as inferior only to *Nostromo* and *The Nigger* of the *"Narcissus."*[39]

In *The Rover* and the unfinished *Suspense* Conrad's intention was, in part at least, to express the historic effect on Europe of

[39] *Wiadomości* (London), July 10, 1949.

Napoleon I and the French Revolution. In 1907 he began reading for a long-projected Napoleonic novel and wrote "The Duel," into which he packed "as much of Napoleonic feeling as the subject could hold."[40]

If we pay attention to Conrad's use of "historical" perspective from the beginning of his writing life, particularly in The Rescue, "Youth," and Heart of Darkness, we find that historic matter always carries strong political and moral overtones and is never used merely for distance, glamor, or to make a good story. When he writes, therefore, that "The Duel" is his "first attempt at historical fiction," we may interpret it to mean that the Napoleonic material, with its political and moral perspective, was the first historical mat-ter that he used in more than an incidental way.[41]

He used history in The Rover (and Suspense, had he finished it, would have provided an even better example) to dramatize the ex-travagant hopes and brutal disillusionments that the French Revo-lution had brought upon Europe. As a Pole, Conrad was well situ-ated to see that play of forces. Napoleon had at one time promised the restoration of Poland's political identity. He had been hailed as one of the hard-sought Polish messiahs, and Polish legions went to slaughter in droves to serve his ambitions, never—even when the evidence of Napoleon's double-dealing was all too clear—completely withdrawing their devotion. "A Napoleon cult sprang up in Poland," Brandes writes, "in comparison with which that in other countries and other literatures is inconsiderable."[42]

Conrad's reaction to Napoleon I and the French Revolution gives us a strong hint as to what he made of his political inheritance. "We Poles," his uncle wrote,

> have an inborn liking for the French and the Republic; but he [Conrad] does not like them at all, and is for the Emperor. De

---

[40] Letters from Joseph Conrad, ed. Edward Garnett (Indianapolis: Bobbs-Merrill Co., Inc., 1928), p. 211.

[41] Notes by Joseph Conrad Written in a Set of His First Editions in the Possession of Richard Curle, ed. Richard Curle (London: privately published, 1925), p. 27.

[42] Brandes, op. cit., pp. 244–45.

gustibus non est disputandum—but I couldn't stand it upon several occasions and scolded him roundly.[43]

This was written, one should note, of the young Conrad in Marseilles. One of the impulses that had turned Conrad to the maritime service was patently the urge to master a useful craft under conditions which put his personal qualities to a test, detached from outward influences of his family and national tradition. Once engaged for a time as a steward aboard French freighters, the aristocratic advantages sacrificed to this ordeal must have presented themselves sharply. Hence, perhaps, his extracurricular dalliance with royalists and their causes in Marseilles (see Baines, *Joseph Conrad*, pp. 35–59). While admiring the rough and manly life of ordinary seamen, in this period Conrad evidently surprised his uncle by a sudden repudiation of republican ideals.

What Bobrowski took to be another display of the family flaw was in fact a display of Conrad's independence. Korzeniowski, the devoted translator of Victor Hugo, was no more in sympathy with "the Emperor" who had exiled Hugo from France than was Bobrowski.[44] Yet this was the emperor who was Conrad's "favourite modern ruler," according to Ford Madox Ford. Although Conrad saw Louis XVIII as "a bewildered figure, forced to sleep and receive petitioners in a corridor between two doors. . . . That was how we—or rather how Conrad—regarded restored Legitimacy,"[45] there was undoubtedly more to it than Ford allows. As we shall see, in 1916 Conrad seriously recommended a hereditary monarchy as the proper government for an independent Poland after the war.

In short, Conrad charted a course for himself which was neither his father's nor his uncle's way, though it combined his father's turn

---

[43] Letter from Bobrowski to Buszczyński (see above, note 30). Wiktor Weintraub points out that the original Polish reads ". . . he is an imperialist," not ". . . he . . . is for the Emperor." But Bobrowski's meaning obviously relates to the sovereign power, not to France's overseas dependencies.

[44] Korzeniowski's *Poland and Russia*, Wiktor Weintraub tells me, can be cited as an example of Korzeniowski's dislike of Napoleon III.

[45] Ford Madox Ford, *Joseph Conrad: A Personal Remembrance* (London: Duckworth, 1924), p. 60.

for prophetic historical insight with his uncle's fierce legalism. Conrad's thought depended on a sort of wry nostalgia for lost legitimacies. He could hold fast to his conceptions of evolutionary (rather than revolutionary) political values only by insisting on a gentle Götterdämmerung for what was passing out. Ford is proudly inaccurate as to facts, but he is often brilliant in striking hidden truths about his subject. When he says that for Conrad all revolutions "are an interruption of the processes of thought and of the discovery of the New Form,"[46] we may be amused but must remember too that for Razumov, in Under Western Eyes, this is a grave and finally a tragic matter.

The four works (including "The Warrior's Soul" in addition to "The Duel," The Rover, and Suspense) Conrad wrote on Napoleon's period and influence suggest the full range of Polish feelings on the subject, from romantic elevation through bitter humorousness to dry disgust. In the background of Suspense is the Polish memory that, as a result of Napoleon's escape from Elba, the Triple Alliance at Vienna rushed to insure its member nations against a repeated union of French and Polish nationalists and, after many months of argument, decided upon the fourth division of Poland. What Conrad dramatizes, however, are the colorful personalities involved in the whole European struggle: soldiers, seamen, aristocrats and servants, lovers and politicians—and not a Pole among them. Through them one finds his political ambivalence toward the Europe that preceded the French Revolution and the one that followed it. But his credo—so similar on this subject to Edmund Burke's—we find only in his essays:

> The degradation of the ideas of freedom and justice at the root of the French Revolution is made manifest in the person of its heir; a personality without law or faith, whom it has been the fashion to represent as an eagle, but who was, in truth, more like a sort of vulture preying upon the body of a Europe which did, indeed for some dozen of years, very much resemble a corpse. The subtle and manifold influence for evil of the Napoleonic episode as a school of violence, as a sower of national hatreds, as the direct provocator of

Ibid.

obscurantism and reaction, of political tyranny and injustice, cannot well be exaggerated.[47]

The French Revolution is thus, for the mature Conrad, the turning point of modern political history, an opening wedge, or model, for the forces of violence threatening in socialism and Russian "barbarism." Tsarism, producing a "democratic" reaction with the same demonic power it controlled itself, would use the procedures of the French Revolution to produce a Caesarism more awful than any preceding it in history—because disregardful of any human rights but those of a nonexistent, abstract "people." Little wonder that after the Russian occupation of Poland in 1945, Conrad's works (which had circulated freely until then) should be condemned as "bourgeois" and "decadent."

One should recall that what repelled Conrad most in the direction Western civilization was taking was not what repelled Henry James—that the social changes were ugly though inevitable—but that they were *wrong and unnecessary*. "The revolutionary spirit is mighty convenient in this," he wrote in *A Personal Record*, "that it frees one from all scruples as regards ideas."[48] The most serious errors of misinterpretation have been made by the failure of Conrad's critics to discover beneath the Conrad of "the dark powers," beneath the Conrad who protests in *Lord Jim*, *Heart of Darkness*, and *Nostromo* that ideas and principles are nothing if not worse than that, there hides a Conrad who believes that "scruples as regards ideas" may absolutely distinguish the good man and the good society from the bad.

It is often assumed that Conrad's sentimental regard for a Polish past that he had no need to cope with in his English life compelled him to deny on irrational grounds the political realities that faced him. The partial truth in this observation should not obscure the fact that Conrad's critiques of positivistic rationalism have a positive and progressive aspect insofar as he uses them judiciously as a foil against the pride of modern civilization in its "rational"

---

[47] "Autocracy and War," *Notes on Life and Letters*, p. 86.
[48] *A Personal Record*, p. xix.

solutions to problems which he sees as far from being solved. The label of "feudalism" that for many years has been applied to Conrad's social outlook is a case in point. One of the attractions of the sea life was, of course, that the organization of a ship presented Conrad with the model of a stable social order, based on a sensible reciprocity of services, with honors allotted on the basis of vocation and merit.

The "society" of a working ship was the realization of the society Apollo Korzeniowski had dreamed of, stripped of all romantic illusions. Miłosz writes that Korzeniowski's plays reveal

> certain illusions as to the relations between landlords and peasants traditionally based on feudal reciprocity of duties, rather than on the 'liberal' recognition of the essential rights of man. Across a Shakespearean mirage, the past took on for him all the colors of lost perfection.[49]

The sailing ship gave Conrad both his father's ideal reciprocity of services and the "facts, facts, facts," demanded in all his uncle's letters. Aboard ship, significantly, no value was put either on aristocracy or on material wealth, both highly suspicious institutions in Conrad's fiction and politics. In this connection one recalls his stern correction of John Galsworthy when Galsworthy referred in a critical essay on Conrad to the aristocracy of his family. "I would ask you at once to eliminate the word aristocracy, when you see the proof," Conrad wrote. "Land-tilling gentry is the most precise approach to a definition of my modest origin."[50]

At the other extreme, in the same letter, Conrad corrects Galsworthy's notion of the system of government aboard ships: "I may express the doubt whether ship-life, though pervaded by a sort of rough equality, is truly democratic in its real essence." The word "democracy"—even for Tadeusz Bobrowski, with his strong sense of human rights—had at the time the ring of "mobocracy" to the Polish ear. Like many other liberal-minded Poles, Bobrowski and Conrad considered that one of the greatest dangers to civil liberty was the kind of "democracy" that might result in eastern Europe

---

[49] Miłosz, op. cit., p. 71.
[50] Letter to Galsworthy, Oct. 29, 1907, *Life and Letters*, II, 63–64.

after either a revolution by the proletariat or a mismanaged revolt against Russian tyranny. "I have no taste for democracy—and democracy has no taste for me," he wrote in 1897 to a Polish noblewoman, formerly a childhood friend, the Baroness Jeanne de Brunow.[51] Such considerations were still strong in Conrad's mind when in 1910 he was finishing his comparison of Western democracy and Eastern autocracy in *Under Western Eyes*.

Conrad often refers to the "chivalrous" character of his heroes— men like Captain Tom Lingard—but such men have more in common with the seamen of the Viking *comitatus*[52] than with the aristocratic knighthood of medieval Europe. And even the *comitatus* was more aristocratic in practice than the ship of Conrad's days at sea. Adrian Green-Armytage aptly remarks that Conrad "had an ingrained dislike for anything institutional, abstract, and above all, inherited. He was almost fanatically a self-made man."[53] Tradition was not, for Conrad, basically institutional in character. His conception of loyalty demanded a power of individual discretion which his readers often miss in overstressing the irrational compulsions of his heroes.

Jacob Epstein writes in his *Autobiography* that the "report that Conrad refused a knighthood because it was offered by a Socialist Government would, if true, bear out my observation about his feudal cast of mind."[54] Conrad knew that his opinions were misinterpreted in England. When writing to Bruno Winawer on the subject of dramatizing *The Rover* in 1924, he said: "I do not think that the Labour Government would forbid the play on the ground that being both Poles we are 'horrid aristocrats' and enemies of the virtuous Bolsheviks."[55] The remark carries its own explanation—

[51] Letter to Baroness Jeanne de Brunow, Oct., 1897, quoted in Jean-Aubry, *The Sea Dreamer*, p. 260. For the early friendship see Baines, *op. cit.*, pp. 28–30.

[52] Thomas Moser has remarked on this similarity in *Joseph Conrad: Achievement and Decline* (Cambridge, Mass.: Harvard University Press, 1957), p. 18.

[53] Adrian Green-Armytage, "The Religion of Joseph Conrad," *The Tablet* (London), December 7, 1957, p. 501.

[54] *Autobiography* (London: Hulton Press, 1955), p. 74.

[55] Letter to Bruno Winawer, Jan. 31, 1924, *Life and Letters*, II, 335.

that Conrad's objection to the British Labour Party was its policy of pacifism in the face of the Russian Revolution.

His sympathy with the rising of the Russian moderates in 1905 reflects his uncle's as against his father's progressivism. In November, 1905, he wrote to Mrs. John Galsworthy:

> It's just a half century since the Crimean War, forty-two [forty-four?][56] years since the liberation of the peasants—a great civic work in which even we Poles were allowed to participate. In the words of my uncle's *Memoirs*, this great event opened the way to a general reform of the state. Very few minds saw it at the time. And yet the starting point of orderly rational progress in accord with the national spirit was there![57]

As to his class-mindedness, in 1922 he wrote Elbridge Adams:

> I don't know that the advent of class parties into politics is abstractly good in itself. Class for me is by definition a hateful thing. The only class really worth consideration is the class of honest and able men, to whatever sphere of human activity they belong—that is, the class of workers throughout the nation. There may be idle men; but such a thing as an idle class is not thinkable.[58]

To another American, John Quinn, he found it necessary in 1920 to dissociate himself from certain men among the Polish nobility, notably the magnates that resembled the American tycoon:

> I confess to some little gratification at the thought that the unbroken Polish front keeps Bolshevism off and that apparently the reborn state has one heart and one soul, one indomitable will, from the poorest peasant to the highest magnate. These magnates, by the by, have no more power and precious little more wealth than

---

[56] Although 1861 was the year of Russia's emancipation of the serfs, Conrad may be confused by remembering an order published in 1863 by the Polish revolutionary government in which his father participated. This act was intended to extend rather than to initiate the liberties of the peasants. The failure of the insurrection prevented enforcement of the order.

[57] Letter to Mrs. Galsworthy, Nov. 2, 1905, *Life and Letters*, II, 28.

[58] Letter to Elbridge Adams, Nov. 20, 1922, *Life and Letters*, II, 285.

the poorest peasant, with whom they fight shoulder to shoulder against moral and physical pestilence bred in Russia . . .[59]

That this is more than the color the chameleon novelist wears when put up against American opinion should be evident when one remembers Conrad's story "Il Conde," where historical reference links the aristocrat (suggested by the Polish Count Sigismonde Szembek who told Conrad the story), seeking refuge significantly in a sleeping car on the *train de luxe*, with the Roman nobles who ran away to health resorts and abandoned Rome to political chaos under the emperors.

Conrad's exact thought on his Polish past is a mystery that carries us away from his autobiographical remarks and deep into his non-Polish fiction, where it moves continuously among non-Polish shapes. Loyalty to one's homeland, as an issue raised in times of peace rather than war, is a hauntingly pervasive obsession in our century, and no one typifies as vividly as Conrad the elusive shadows that fall behind it. It is in regard to this issue that the *homo duplex* theme in his personal story asserted itself most vehemently. He recognized it explicitly, furthermore, as he did not the division in his thought between his father and his uncle's political influence.

Born a Pole who was legally a Russian citizen, Conrad became a Pole who was legally British. Although his British naturalization was wholly deliberate, and although it reflected a common Polish sympathy with the English way of life, Conrad was never allowed by the British to forget that he was an alien or allowed by Poles to forget that he was an émigré.

Since the publication of Gustav Morf's *The Polish Heritage of Joseph Conrad* in 1930, many readers have come to believe that the loyalty themes in Conrad's fiction had a direct connection with the public charge of disloyalty brought against him in 1899 by a Polish novelist. Although a careful consideration of dates should

---

[59] Letter to John Quinn, March 24, 1920, which appeared as an extract in a letter published in the *New York Herald Tribune*, April 5, 1920, p. 10.

reveal that Conrad's stories had pivoted on loyalty questions some time before Eliza Orzeszkowa's attack, the episode furnishes an illuminating case study of Polish sensitivities on political questions. It demonstrates, moreover, the perilous balance between private choice and political commitment that did become an increasingly important theme in Conrad's fiction between 1896, when he began *The Rescue*, and 1911, when *Under Western Eyes* was published. One can feel the gathering concern for this problem particularly in *Lord Jim*, a novel begun before Orzeszkowa's attack and finished in July of the following year. Gustav Morf, Jean-Aubry, and Jocelyn Baines again recently, assume that *Lord Jim* was tantamount to Conrad's self-defense against the charge of disloyalty. Under analysis, however, the novel is found to support rather than to deny the argument of the Polish "shrew" (as Conrad called her). If the novel provides any rebuttal at all, it is an answer to English readers rather than to Poles.

The discussion of Conrad's defection from Poland became a public issue as a result of the visit to Conrad in 1896 of another Polish émigré, Wincenty Lutosławski, a critic and philosopher who had lived for some time in Boston. In March, 1899—three years after their meeting—Lutosławski published an article in *Kraj* (*The Country*), a Polish weekly in St. Petersburg, entitled "The Emigration of Talents." It defended the thesis that Poles, either living abroad or naturalized in foreign countries, were able to serve the cause of Poland as well as people who remained at home. "The work produced is Polish," Lutosławski wrote, "even though it is published in a foreign language, for it is the fruit of the Polish spirit, differing from that of other nations." Lutosławski refused "to bring a charge of disaffection for their native country against those who could not remain in a suffocating atmosphere, who courageously went forth to take part in the universal struggle for the conquest of material or moral riches, a large part of which would be returned to their homeland."[60] Lutosławski named Conrad as an example of such émigrés and quoted Conrad's excuse for not writing in Polish

---

[60] Ujejski, *op. cit.*, p. 15. The translations from this work are mine.

as given during their visit together: "I should never have dared to foist my attempts upon the beautiful literature of Poland."[61]

The editors of *Kraj* felt it necessary to comment in the same issue on Lutosławski's opinions, and they drew attention to their agreement not with Lutosławski but with a riposte by Tadeusz Zuk Skarszewski which they published along with the other. Although the latter did not mention Conrad, he covered Conrad's case along with Lutosławski's in the statement that it would be better to be a school teacher in any out-of-the-way village in Poland than a Polish Plato in Boston.[62]

In the next issue of *Kraj* came Eliza Orzeszkowa's outcry in response to Lutoslawski, singling out Conrad in particular because he, like herself, was a novelist. Emotion carried her to assumptions far from true as to Conrad's literary success in England at the time. She referred to him as "this gentleman, author of novels written in English which are all the rage and lucrative as one could wish."[63] With female precision she had found her way to one of Conrad's most sensitive nerves. His inability to support his family by his pen was an embarrassment all the more acute because of his ingrained prejudice against money-making—a prejudice common among Polish nobles, who traditionally supported themselves from their lands, in professions, or by services to the state. Orzeszkowa went on:

> Is this the way creative artists should associate in the exodus? Till now [emigration] was a question only of engineers, public prosecutors, and opera singers. And now they are ready to absolve writers! If it were a matter of chemistry or even philosophy [jibing at Lutosławski], I might see certain reasons for editing them in foreign languages; but if it is a question of the novel, a fragment of creative effort, then I am involved. I know our commitments to the corps, obligations *fortes comme le mort*, and with all my strength I protest. Creative gifts are the floral crown, the crest of the tower, the very heart of the nation. And this flower, this crest, this heart, to see it torn from our nation and surrendered to the Anglo-Saxons,

---

[61] Jean-Aubry, *The Sea Dreamer*, p. 237.

[62] Ujejski, *op. cit.*, p. 16.

[63] *Ibid.*

who lack nothing among the goods of this world, and for the lovely reason that they pay better! . . . And to top everything, this gentleman has to bear what name? That of his direct ancestor, perhaps, that Józef Korzeniowski whose novels made me spill my first tears and feel the first flames of noble ardor and virtuous resolutions. No Polish girl will shed a generous tear or form a magnanimous resolution on the novels of Mr. Konrad Korzeniowski . . . but on reflection, this incident brings me only a moderate sadness, for I have faith in real creative genius and I do not suppose that ours ever wanted to respond to the call of a canteen girl or a saleswoman.[64]

No evidence has come to light that Conrad read the issues of *Kraj* in which his case was argued. But fearing that he might miss the agony of her appeal, Orzeszkowa addressed him in a letter directly, possibly enclosing her article. He harbored the memory of it fifteen years later when, in 1914, his cousin Aniela Zagórska unwittingly sent him one of Orzeszkowa's novels as a present. "Don't bring me anything from that shrew. . . . She wrote me a letter once," he replied.[65]

Conrad's dilemma becomes clearer when we recognize his tacit agreement with Orzeszkowa's premise: that whereas there might be good causes for emigration, the voluntary exile of a creative artist during a nation's time of need would be indefensible. Conrad protests too much for mere modesty's sake that he was ignorant of his creative abilities when he left Poland. He had not *chosen* to write in English: "English was for me neither a matter of choice nor adoption . . . there was adoption; but it was I who was adopted by the genius of the language . . ."[66] "If I had not known English I wouldn't have written a line for print in my life,"[67] he wrote Hugh Walpole in 1918—as Poland was about to win her independence. Furthermore, he had no idea of becoming a writer when he began his first novel: "My best remembered sensation about it is

---

[64] *Ibid.*, pp. 16–17. The novelist and dramatist Józef Korzeniowski (1791–1863) was not an ancestor of Conrad's, according to Conrad's own account. He mentions this to Garnett the following year, as if the subject were fresh in his mind. See *Letters from Joseph Conrad*, p. 165.

[65] *Ibid.*, p. 18.

[66] *A Personal Record*, p. v.

[67] Letter to Hugh Walpole, June 17, 1918, *Life and Letters*, II, 206.

the perpetual surprise that I should be able to do it at all."[68] To Retinger he made clear that his original reason for leaving Poland had been not to find a congenial land in which to do something he might have done as well in Poland but because of an impulse to enter a profession that did not exist in Poland. He had turned to writing because he could not make his living as a seaman. "I am not a political exile, who has duties toward his last acts. I am a voluntary emigrant who left in search of a career. My career now consists in writing in English."[69]

Ujejski reminds us that the moment of Conrad's birth decisively affected his attitude toward participation in Polish affairs: "Who knows . . . if Conrad would have had this evasive impulse if circumstances [when he left Poland] had been a bit less . . . prosaic —if he had matured before the year 1863 or much later, for instance in the period of The Union for Active Combat."[70] Given Conrad's temperament and parentage, there was for him no middle way. He was to be either a devoted rebel or a declared pacifist. Being by nature opposed to both of these alternatives, Conrad chose the only honorable course—emigration. When asked in later years why he took no part in Polish affairs, he used to answer (according to his son John), "It is not my watch on deck."

In *A Personal Record*, Conrad wrote his most direct answer to Orzeszkowa:

> I have the conviction that there are men of unstained rectitude who are ready to murmur scornfully the word desertion. Thus the taste of innocent adventure may be made bitter to the palate. The part of the inexplicable should be allowed for in appraising the conduct of men in a world where no explanation is final. No charge of faithlessness ought to be lightly uttered. The appearances of this perishable life are deceptive like everything that falls under the judgment of our imperfect senses. The inner voice may remain true

[68] *Notes by Joseph Conrad*, p. 15.

[69] Joseph Retinger, *Conrad and His Contemporaries* (London: Minerva, 1941), p. 118.

[70] Ujejski, pp. 25–26. The Union for Active Combat was formed by Józef Piłsudski at Lwov in 1908. Conrad's son John reports that Conrad had no use for Piłsudski, who spent some time in England during the Russo-Japanese War trying to raise a force of Poles to harass Russia from the rear.

enough in its secret counsel. The fidelity to a special tradition may last through the events of an unrelated existence, following faithfully too the traced way of an inexplicable impulse.

It would take too long to explain the intimate alliance of contradictions in human nature which makes love itself wear at times the desperate shape of betrayal.[71]

What Conrad could not explain to Orzeszkowa or to his readers was the "inexplicable impulse" that made him seek his career in a service (on the sea, so often associated with freedom) that required his departure from Poland. School children learn that Conrad went to sea, like the Marlow of "Youth," in search of adventure and romantic discovery. But for some years more sophisticated readers have remarked on the mood of desperation that shadows all the adventurers in his stories. In 1928 the French critic Daniel-Rops wrote:

> tant de personnages de Conrad—un Heyst, un Jim—se jettent dans l'aventure comme d'autres à l'opium, d'autres au jeu, comme d'aucuns se suicident. 'A l'aventure, s'était dit Heyst, délibérément' lorsque sa vie avait fini par se déssecher auprès de son père . . . L'aventure chez Conrad est-ce autre qu'un aspect du désespoir?[72]

In *A Personal Record* Conrad conveyed a strong impression that he suffered something like acute claustrophobia in Poland. Suggesting his early likeness to Don Quixote, another romantic adventurer who was supremely loyal although "he was not a good citizen,"[73] Conrad remarked that the "very unselfish fantasy" of the Don arose from his naïve desire to escape with his very body from the intolerable reality of things. Elsewhere in *A Personal Record* Conrad described his leaving Poland as a "jump," and one recalls in *Lord Jim* the hint that Jim's jump from the "Patna" was a sort of desperate reflex to his sensation that the ship was sinking. "He was not afraid of death perhaps, but I'll tell you what," says Marlow, "he was afraid of the emergency. His confounded imagination had

[71] *A Personal Record*, pp. 35–36.
[72] Henri Daniel-Rops, "Joseph Conrad," *Carte d'Europe* (Paris: Perrin, 1928), p. 69.
[73] *A Personal Record*, p. 36.

evoked for him all the horrors of panic . . ."[74] Having escaped with his life from the "Patna," which Weintraub associates with *patria* and Morf with *Polska* (Poland), Jim reflected on the shame of abandoning his charge and thereupon reacted similarly to Quixote in his divine madness. Jim's "keen sense of the Intolerable drove him away for good . . ."[75] Suicide as a way out is fearfully considered and rejected by both Jim and Marlow (in words that may excuse the reader for honoring reports of Conrad's attempted suicide after "jumping" from Poland and bungling his escape into adventure in France).[76] The question in Conrad's mind whether Poland and his duties there were really "sunk" haunted him through his writing life. It was this rather than uneasiness about his personal choices, as Pritchett pointed out, that attracted him into unfathomed depths in the problem of fidelity.

In adding these points to what Morf and others have already said concerning Jim's dilemma after leaving his ship and Conrad's after leaving Poland, I mean to stress that *Lord Jim* is less relevant as autobiographical comment than it is as a general comment on loyalty by a man who was absorbed creatively perhaps more than personally, and intellectually as well as emotionally, with the question of loyalty.

The center toward which Conrad draws the reader of *Lord Jim* is a long way from the little argument of whether or not he, Conrad, had sewn his talent up in a lining and flown from Poland to make his fortune. It is a question that hangs delicately and insolubly upon all loyalty issues—the nature of Jim's "Latin" sense of honor.

In the Author's Note to *Lord Jim*, Conrad protests that the lady who did not like the novel because it was "all so morbid" could not have been Italian. "In any case, no Latin temperament would have perceived anything morbid in the acute consciousness of lost

---

[74] *Lord Jim*, p. 88.

[75] *Ibid.*, p. 5.

[76] The most satisfactory discussion of this episode so far, I think, is by Jocelyn Baines: "The Young Conrad in Marseilles," the *Times Literary Supplement*, Dec. 6, 1957, p. 748. See also the same author in the *London Magazine*, Nov. 1957, p. 45.

honor."[77] (Conrad, like most other Poles, we recall, considered the Polish temperament "Latin" in its cultural origins.) English-speaking critics tend to credit only Marlow's Anglo-Saxon wisdom, as it were, and to disregard his other, often-conflicting opinions as something like empty "adjectival insistence."[78] They would thus have us place peak value on Marlow's annoyance that Jim "made so much of his disgrace while it is the guilt alone that matters,"[79] and overlook the fact that Marlow himself, and every non-English figure in the novel who thinks about Jim's guilt, thinks of it mainly in terms of the crippling disgrace it entailed.

In an early version of Lord Jim, Conrad stressed Marlow's unique understanding of Jim even more than in the published book, as if fearful that Marlow's English point of view would be thought the same as that of the other English officials at Jim's trial. In the early draft he had Marlow say (concerning the trial):

> I don't know what was the matter with me that morning but all the people there, the ex-officio stainless trio behind the desk, the natives in court, the people who did not understand anything, the few—besides myself—who understood the words read out; those who not having been tried were called to judge, and those who listened and did not care—they all seemed to me strange, foreign, as if belonging to some order of beings I had no connection with. It was only when my eyes turned towards Jim that I had a sense of not being alone of my kind, as if we two had wandered in there from some distant regions, from a different world. I turned to him for fellowship.[80]

Jim makes perfectly clear at the beginning of the trial that he is guilty of the legal charge and expects harsh punishment from his

---

[77] Lord Jim, p. ix.

[78] F. R. Leavis, The Great Tradition (London: Chatto and Windus, 1948), p. 177. V. S. Pritchett agrees in "The Exile," the New Statesman (London), Aug. 24, 1957, p. 229.

[79] Lord Jim, p. 177.

[80] Rosenbach Manuscript, discussed and quoted by John D. Gordan in Joseph Conrad: The Making of a Novelist (Cambridge, Mass.: Harvard University Press, 1940), pp. 151–52.

peers. Like the bad citizen Don Quixote, he is "condemned justly."[81]
But like the other characters in *Lord Jim* who win our sympathy,
Jim knows that his high sense of his own worth—the human value
which all social judgment supposedly protects—will survive his sentence and continue to demand objective proof while he survives.
Marlow's attachment to Jim is pure sentimentality, unless we recognize that he and Jim together have a stake in the outcome of
Jim's life after the "Patna" case is closed. Jim's acute sense of honor
has its source in another concern of his that would be more understandable to a Polish patriot than to English readers.

Marlow is plagued by what he calls the man-made doubt in the
power of "a fixed standard of conduct,"[82] and his interest in Jim
(beginning with a mere intuition that Jim is "the right sort") persists because Jim's very failure to maintain the seaman's code has
made him obsessively aware of its validity. The "partnership" Marlow forms with Jim is founded, as it were, for the sake of examining
a code of behavior under conditions that have brought it to its most
crucial test. Marlow fears that his untested liking for Jim may cause
him to relax his grip on a scheme of values which he has never put
to such a test. Worse still, Jim makes him suspect that "the very
fount and origin" of his sympathy with Jim lies in "the secret
sensibility" of his "egoism"[83]—that therefore the origins of the code
itself may lie in egoism! "I was made to look at the convention that
lurks in all truth and on the essential sincerity of falsehood."[84] If the
code is thus a sort of mirror of the ego, what "sovereign power"
can it hold over men like Jim, whose fatal weakness is enthroned
in the same ego that generates the power of the code? Jim is both
deviant and fanatic defender of the code. In Patusan he recreates
the code he lost through the sentence that closed the "Patna" trial.

The man-made doubt in the power of a fixed standard of conduct,

---

[81] *A Personal Record*, p. 36.
[82] *Lord Jim*, p. 50.
[83] *Ibid.*, p. 152.
[84] *Ibid.*, p. 93. The complex nature of falsehood, as it works privately and publicly, had
been in Conrad's mind for some time. It is almost a major theme in *Heart of Darkness.*
See chap. iv.

which is the ghost Marlow hopes Jim can lay, is not unlike the doubt Conrad's English life raised as to his fidelity to Polish tradition. If, as Morf and others have argued, Conrad wrote *Lord Jim* as an answer to Orzeszkowa, he would surely have leaned more heavily on Jim's innocence in jumping from the "Patna." The ground is firmer if we read the argument in the novel (and the question raised by the Polish woman) against the passage already quoted in *A Personal Record*. What made Jim carry on his "special tradition" in an alien land? This was the aspect of loyalty Conrad had in mind, apparently, when he first conceived the "Tuan Jim" story—the title itself suggesting that Jim was to be an expatriate—before the argument in *Kraj* appeared.

It seems evident from the "Tuan Jim" manuscript (in the Houghton Library at Harvard) that Conrad was interested, before Orzeszkowa's attack, in Jim as a case study in desertion. The manuscript shows, moreover, that Conrad began (possibly as early as 1896) by tracing Jim's moral lassitude to a crippling accident and his ensuing hospitalization, which cut loose an already overactive imagination. It was apparently after the Polish argument that Conrad accented Jim's longing for heroism. Jim's boyhood dream aboard the training ship is not in the manuscript, nor is the dream of heroism aboard the "Patna." Thus, the tendency toward detached dreaming, the original cause of Jim's desertion, later becomes a thirst for heroism, possibly suggested by Orzeszkowa's recalling to Conrad's mind the Polish romantic drive. Marlow's intense brooding on Jim's obsession, introduced after the "Tuan Jim" beginning, exaggerates Jim's romanticism all the more.[85]

Jim clings to a code very like the "special tradition" of nation and family to which Conrad called himself loyal "through the events of an unrelated existence"—a code derogated by all who scorn loyalty to a fixed standard of values. Jim and the quixotic Conrad are guilty of desertion but not of infidelity, of poor citizenship but not breach of faith to the spirit of unity with their native homes. In the Author's Note to *Lord Jim* Conrad points out that he was not able

---

[85] See my article, "Lord Jim: From Sketch to Novel," *Comparative Literature* (Fall, 1960), pp. 289–309.

to finish writing the pilgrim ship episode until he conceived it as part of "the whole 'sentiment of existence' in a simple and sensitive character." In other words, Conrad was interested as much as Marlow in what would happen to Jim's faithfulness to his code "through the events of an unrelated existence"—in Jim's case unrelated not to Poland and politics, but to England and the sea.

Jim fails to redeem himself, but he comes as close as humanly possible to redeeming Marlow's belief, in the only way belief can ever be proven, Conrad seems to say—by his willingness to die for it. "It is certain any conviction gains infinitely, the moment another soul will believe in it." Conrad uses the passage from Novalis as his epigraph for the novel.

The ethical or moral postulate that sovereign power can be enthroned in a fixed standard of conduct is axiomatic in the conduct of the French lieutenant and Stein, as well as of Marlow and Jim; whereas it is conspicuously absent in the motives of the "Patna" officers, Chester, Cornelius, and Brown. To Chester, Jim's certificate with all it represents is "a bit of ass's skin."[86] All these men are vigorous opportunists, "realists" determined like Chester to "see things exactly as they are" and "never to take anything to heart."[87] If, on the other hand, the power in a fixed standard of conduct is sovereign, it must be "real." The realism of the Chesters forces Marlow, with Stein, to insist upon a realism that can only be defined as romanticism.

Facing Stein, Marlow sees a man whose life had "begun in sacrifice" and who had traveled far "on strange paths . . . without faltering, and therefore without shame and without regret."[88] No one could have been more romantic than Stein, he remarks. But Stein shakes his head, implying that Jim is more so. "But *is* he?" Marlow demands, having just described the romantic as one like Stein, self-sacrificing, without shame and without regret. "*Gewiss*," Stein answers, standing and holding up the candelabrum—a figure of oracu-

---

[86] *Lord Jim*, p. 161.
[87] *Ibid.*, p. 162.
[88] *Ibid.*, p. 215.

lar truth who will appear again in *Heart of Darkness*, there in irony but here unquestionably to be taken seriously. He corrects Marlow's notion of the romantic element. It is not in the man who succeeds only but in all men who "follow the dream . . . *usque ad finem.*" Tadeusz Bobrowski's advice to his overromantic nephew Conrad! Stein, a curious combination of German romanticism, Polish realism, and the British naturalist Alfred Wallace (whom Conrad read avidly), is an example of Conrad's genius in recomposing life according to his own vision. We are suddenly made to see, with Marlow, that Jim's romanticism is in his ability to keep alive a standard (which can be defined objectively only as dream or illusion) *even when his own acts have belied it.* "What is it that by inward pain makes him know himself?" Stein asks. "What is it that for you and me makes him—exist?" For one fitful moment, which he unfortunately cannot sustain in cold reason but which is nonetheless surely the most substantial moment in Marlow's hunt for truth, he discovers in Jim, the romantic, "his imperishable reality." "We had approached nearer to absolute Truth, which, like Beauty itself, floats elusive, obscure, half-submerged in the silent still waters of mystery."[89]

The meeting with Stein reassures Marlow that Jim by his example has not weakened but strengthened the absolute power in a fixed standard of conduct. Instead of being mere unmanliness, as it had seemed to Brierly and Chester (both significantly English), Jim's suffering shows his ability to "swim" in the destructive element of human existence, with its dreamlike reality, which is all the more destructive to a man like Jim who repeatedly fails. Inability to bear the knowledge of failure had revealed the "sham" in Brierly's understanding of the seaman's code. The code lost its validity for him as soon as he saw that Jim, a man like himself, could break it. But for Stein the validity of the code and man's suffering in relation to it—taking the form of a concern for honor—are part and parcel of human reality, in an implied hierarchy of realities.

When Jim "goes away from a living woman to celebrate his piti-

---

[89] *Ibid.,* p. 216.

less wedding with a shadowy ideal of conduct," it is "at the call of his exalted egoism"—the same romantic call that Stein had admitted was "very bad" but "very good, too." For Marlow, Jim's last act is "a victory in which I had taken my part."[90] We have met this essential egoism before, in Conrad's expression of his political philosophy, based on the egoism which saves everything that we love as well as everything we abhor. Jim "achieved greatness" in the manner of Don Quixote, who ended with "his head encircled by a halo . . . spoiled or saved by the irresistible power of imagination."[91]

The code, so largely self-generated as it turns out to be, is on trial for Marlow till the end of the novel, and beyond the end. Characters like Chester, Robinson, and Jewel, who think of the code as simply a valid social convention that Jim has broken and been punished for, cannot conceive his continuing suffering in relation to it. They want what is left of him, closing off his past for their own sakes and what they think are his own best interests. In the last chapter, when Jim says to his servant, "I have no life,"[92] he implies that the one life he nearly regained through probationary achievement (himself being the probationer) has been lost—like Eurydice, because he let Brown turn his eyes back to the guilty past. Then to Jewel, who presses him to fight or fly for his life, he answers with deflecting irony: there is "nothing to fight for" and "no escape"—from the real enemy whom Jewel has never known, himself.[93] Only Jim, Marlow, and Stein remember what the real conflict was all about, and as in other Conrad novels such people cannot communicate their knowledge to "realists" like Jewel, who do not look deep into the truths behind social convention, into the all-important "shadowy ideal of conduct" which alone promises peace on earth, in politics or at sea.

Readers of the novel who interpret Jim's romantic egoism as the source of his guilt rather than as the despotic imagination ruling his

---

[90] *Ibid.*, p. 224.
[91] *A Personal Record*, pp. 36–37.
[92] *Lord Jim*, p. 409.
[93] *Ibid.*, p. 412.

conscience, identify his desertion of his wife Jewel with his jump from the "Patna" as two similar responses to his absorption in self. These readers often find the novel overlong, and with good reason, since according to their reading Jim's last act in Patusan was one more repetition of his first aboard the training ship. The difference, of course, is that in Patusan Jim saw his responsibility through to the end. "He could stay as well as spurt," Marlow stresses repeatedly,[94] the *usque ad finem* Conrad borrowed for all true romantics. Marlow leaves the reader with Stein's reflection that men are like butterflies, only they are not perfect. Absolute fidelity to unchanging moral law is a dream of perfection that cannot, however, be dreamed by butterflies. The dream is self-centered. It destroys as often as it confirms. But egoism saves everything.

If for "Jim" we read "Poland," the political analogy fits better than the analogy between Poland and the "Patna." Poland the pariah, a people, as Bobrowski lamented, who consider themselves great and misunderstood, "exists" (as Jim finally "exists" for Stein, while Marlow is never sure of his existence) only by her quixotic determination to follow an egoistical dream, the ancient and self-perpetuating code which is both her assurance of her integrity and a sign of her call to lead other nations on the right path. Conrad's ambivalence in accepting this myth, exaggerated by his uncle's feud with his dead father, is perfectly mirrored in Marlow's acute ambivalence toward Jim. Far from providing an answer to any Polish reader, *Lord Jim* does only a little more than present a riddle about life, suggested to him particularly by his own life. If there is any conclusion or answer, it is perhaps one phrased by Albert Guerard: "A man is what he does, which in Jim's case is very little that is not equivocal. But also he 'exists' for us by the quality of his feeling and the poignant intensity of his dream."[95]

Although Morf, Ujejski, and Jean-Aubry all date Conrad's concern for the imperatives of his Polish heritage from the writing of *Lord Jim*, certain aspects of the manuscript of *The Rescue* would

---

[94] *Ibid.*, p. 224.
[95] *Conrad the Novelist* (Cambridge, Mass.: Harvard University Press, 1958), p. 161.

seem to indicate that his mind turned decisively to questions of political values just after he wrote his second novel, *An Outcast of the Islands*. More than coincidentally, I think, this was the period of his marriage and increasing commitment to life ashore in England. Because of the lag in time required for his English publications to be known in Poland, news of his marriage and his new role as a writer reached Poland at about the same time. The impact of these two developments in Conrad's life was treated as a single shock, even by his relatives. On his honeymoon Conrad had a letter from his cousin Karol Zagórski:

> We heard of your literary début from Marguerite [Poradowska]. As I held your book in my hand, I felt, so to speak, a double sadness: first, I was sorry not to be able to get to know the work of your mind, and then I regretted that as a result of the exceptional conditions of your life your talent should be lost to our literature and become the fortune and heritage of foreigners, although they are not foreigners to you, since you have found among them the wife who loves you.[96]

On this question, the question of his English family, Conrad's conscience does not seem to have been easy, however much it may have been so on his reasons for leaving Poland. As late as 1920, Ujejski reports, he asked his cousin Karola Zagórska to "absolve" him for having raised his sons without knowing Polish. Although it was within the realm of possibility for him to carry on the spirit of his Polish past in his work, at sea or in writing, his marriage to an Englishwoman made a break with his heritage that could only widen with his English descendants. The common Polish example of a patriot living in exile but faithful to his heritage did not include the image of a man raising heirs in an alien political and religious tradition. One need only consider the importance Conrad's parents attached to his naming to visualize the strict limits with which the Polish patriot hedged the possibilities of a double life.

He was christened Józef Teodor Konrad Nałęcz Korzeniowski—the first two names for his grandfathers, and Nałęcz signifying the

---

[96] Jean-Aubry, *The Sea Dreamer*, p. 216.

branch of the Korzeniowski line from which he descended. The central name, Konrad, came not from his forbears but from a poem, Dziady (Forefather's Eve),[97] by Poland's greatest romantic poet, Adam Mickiewicz. Later, because Konrad, or Conrad, was the only one of his names that resembled an English surname and he badly needed a name that would not be misspelled or mispronounced a different way every time he joined a new ship, Conrad gradually simplified his name to this prénom. "Konrad" was the name by which he was called in his family, and it was logical that it should receive the stress as his surname—although he never dropped the Korzeniowski, and his legal signature was "K. N. Korzeniowski."

Like so many other incidents in Conrad's life, this simple choice of a name accrues deeper and deeper meanings when brought to examination. But as with other evocative incidents in his life, nowhere do we find Conrad himself encouraging our speculation.

In 1857, the year of his birth, Konrad was a name to conjure with in Russian Poland, among a people who could speak only in ciphers of their political past, present, and future. It was used by Mickiewicz at a crucial moment in his poetic development, when he decided to abandon themes of romantic love and personal passion and to dedicate himself to poems celebrating the nation. His complex, wandering poem Dziady dramatizes this decision by having the formerly love-stricken hero Gustav—also in prison—scratch on his prison wall: "Gustavus obit MDCCCXXIII Calendis Novembris. Hic natus est Conradus."[98]

Having before his transfiguration resisted God's efforts to chastise him, the new Konrad cries: "Now, my soul is incarnate in my country; I swallowed her soul with my body. I and the fatherland are one; my name is Million, for I love and suffer torment for the millions."[99]

Apollo Korzeniowski not only lived for the ideal of Polish mes-

---

[97] Jean-Aubry (The Sea Dreamer, p. 21) confirms that it was this poem rather than Konrad Wallenrod that gave the Korzeniowskis Conrad's name.

[98] Adam Mickiewicz, Forefather's Eve, translated by D. P. Radin (London: King's College, n.d.), p. 5.

[99] Weintraub, The Poetry of Adam Mickiewicz, pp. 257–61.

sianism—the idea that the Christlike nation would redeem the world —but in naming his only son, he marked him, too, as one who must realize the political vision. The debt he (and later Conrad) owed to Mickiewicz may have been more than Korzeniowski counted, however. As we consider Conrad's life in retrospect, he seems to have played the part of the fourteenth-century Konrad Wallenrod, hero of one of Mickiewicz's epic poems, more suitably than he filled that of the nineteenth-century hero of *Dziady*.

Wallenrod, like the other Konrad, lived a double life but in a realistic rather than a mystic sense. The closest approach we find to the *Dziady* theme in Joseph Conrad's imaginative life is in "The Secret Sharer," where one part of the new captain's selfhood has to be purged in order that the higher self (marked by its self-confidence in the matter of fitness for duty) can be born. At the end of the story the captain is ready to accept command of other men because he has "played out" his overconcern with his own self-command.

Konrad Wallenrod creates a culture hero much like the hero of *Dziady*; but since it was written in Russia while Mickiewicz was something of a darling in Russian literary salons, the story is given a medieval setting, seemingly irrelevant to nineteenth-century Poland. Brought up as an orphan among the German knights of the Teutonic Order, Konrad Wallenrod hides his loyalty to their enemy, his native Lithuania, so well that he is eventually elected Grand Master of the Teutonic Order, thereby achieving a strategic position from which to destroy the Order.

In thus creating a legend symbolic of his personal dilemma, that of the Polish poet in Moscow appropriated by Russian society for its own ornament while he secretly longed to assert his national enmity, Mickiewicz wove a pattern for succeeding generations of Polish artists—the only Poles in a nation deprived of public spokesmen who could represent their people to the world. Conrad was to be spoken of in Poland after his death as following the pattern of Mickiewicz, who carried the Polish gospel to foreign lands. In Cracow, where Conrad lived during the year of his father's death, the Poles have placed a placard that reads: "In the house which stood in this place lived, in his youth, about the year 1869, Józef Konrad

Korzeniowski—Joseph Conrad—son of an exiled poet. He brought the Polish spirit into English letters, whose ornament he became."[100]

An important subordinate theme in *Konrad Wallenrod*, and a theme that also strongly colored subsequent Polish literature, was the hero's brooding sense of remorse at having to play the part of conspirator, liar, and traitor—even though he must play it in service to a higher loyalty. This theme deserves particular notice for two reasons. It deepens our understanding of Conrad's tenderness on the subject of his father's revolutionary activities, reminding us of the scene Conrad sketches in *A Personal Record* of Korzeniowski's ritualistic burning of his papers—the accumulated store of his hatred for Russia—in the hours before his death. Fidelity, to the Polish mind, meant fidelity to the solidarity of all mankind; and a break in the bond with any part of it, however necessary, inflicted a sense of guilt.

In *Lord Jim*, speaking of England, Marlow says that Jim "would never go home now. . . . Woe to the stragglers. We exist only insofar as we hang together."[101] Jim had strayed away from English tradition by choosing a safe berth aboard the "Patna" in preference to the harder conditions of "the home service." But this was not the reason why he could not go home again. His critical failure was an act of cowardice against a motley crowd of Muslim pilgrims. In failing a little fragment of universal mankind, Jim forfeits his place at his own hearth.

While subtly tempering our impression of the "revolutionary" Korzeniowski, Mickiewicz's theme gives us reason for a richer appraisal of the infinite variations on the theme of remorse in Conrad's novels. We may expect to find in the majority of his tales, from the slight "Karain" and "The Lagoon" to the powerful *Under Western Eyes*—including most of the fiction written in the fifteen years after his marriage—that loyalty is an imperative in man's life which never comes with a clear call, and that any commitment, however conscientious, leads to some kind of betrayal. The word "duplicity"

---

[100] Photograph of inscription, translated from the Polish by Ilona Karmel Zucker.
[101] *Lord Jim*, pp. 222–23.

has its origin in the word "duplex"—man's dual nature, made up of matter and spirit, of good and evil. But man's ego is dominated by an imperative to reconcile the two natures, to keep faith with himself and his fellows. Loyalty is for Conrad what sincerity is for the "existentialist": a moral principle so basic to life that its mention may be utterly banal, but its significance is never exhausted. Conrad shies away from opposing spiritual and material values—even in *Heart of Darkness* and *Nostromo* where the two sets of values are waged against each other. He deliberately avoids solutions or reconciliations based on otherworldly values.

The Polish stress on fidelity, and Conrad's variations on the theme, might easily be connected with a yearning toward personal and political reintegration and a yearning to end deceptions suffered too long, a desire for peace and stability like the longing that is one force driving Jim away from the West. Deceit and the breaking of promises are, of course, primary causes of political disruption and unrest.

Another echo from Mickiewicz's poetry that reverberates in Conrad's fiction is the theme of Christian pilgrimage, played with variations. Wiktor Weintraub remarks in his book on Adam Mickiewicz that ". . . the word 'pilgrim,' rich in emotional overtones, played an important part in Mickiewicz's poetic vocabulary. . . . Every Polish émigré is a pilgrim since he made a vow to journey to the holy land, his free fatherland, until he finds it.' "[102] Weintraub writes that Mickiewicz stressed the unity of all wandering and exiled Polish pilgrims as "the soul of the nation."

Conrad's portrayals of the pilgrims in *Heart of Darkness* and *Lord Jim*, though very different from each other, ridicule without losing all sympathy, even where "pilgrim" is an ironically devastating epithet. Conrad's use of the word may, to some extent, reflect his opinion of Mickiewicz's political myth and the Polish fanaticism that derived from it. Marlow's words about Jim, that mankind's understanding of itself seemed to hang on his understanding of

---

[102] Weintraub, *The Poetry of Adam Mickiewicz*, p. 199.

Jim, is not very different from the idea that the future of mankind may depend on the fate of an individual nation.

Conrad's creative energy, as suggested earlier, so often seems to flow from the very things—ideas, situations, characters—he treats with searching distrust that one is reminded again and again of Tadeusz Bobrowski's sardonic objections to the Korzeniowski "generative myths" concerning Poland which had given Conrad his very name. "Konrad Korzeniowski" continued through his life to be his formal signature, the family names yielding place to the myth. But the power of the myth is so transformed by Conrad's alchemy that it is in effect a different substance, particularly as Conrad "increases" the tragedy of the individual's plight through an enlarged conception of his freedom as well as a deeper penetration of his commitments within the human community. This was only possible, perhaps, because he had received in youth a tradition in which the limits of freedom and bondage had already been intensely explored.

Conrad's rebellion against the tradition he received seems an important aspect of his art. Comparing him to his father, we find that he persistently secularized the material of Polish religion and universalized the material of Polish politics. Above all, he de-romanticized the role of the artist in society. The artist's job, he said, is to make men see and feel what is going on in the world around them, no more. "Fidelity to passing emotions,"[103] or a "passing phase of life,"[104] attention to every aspect of the visible universe—these mark the field of his labors. And he consciously confines his art "within the limits of the visible world and within the boundaries of human emotions."[105] Yet even here he has a dual role to fill. As a Pole writing in England, he is compelled to distinguish his idea of "realism" from what Englishmen mean by the term. "You stop just short of being absolutely real," he wrote to Arnold Bennett in

---

[103] Letter to Garnett, March 23, 1896, *Letters from Joseph Conrad*, p. 46.
[104] *The Nigger of the "Narcissus,"* p. x.
[105] *Typhoon and Other Stories*, pp. vii–viii.

1902, "because you are faithful to your dogmas of realism."[106] He is a symbolist—but not in the manner of "the Symbolist School of poets or prose writers. Theirs . . . is only a literary proceeding . . . I am concerned here with something much larger"—"a triple appeal covering the whole field of life."[107] (He does not elucidate this Dante-esque "triple appeal," but clearly he excludes from his meaning Dante's anagogical, scriptural level of meaning.) Though French symbolism is unrelated, Conrad depends on French to describe what he means: ". . . *en vérité c'est les valeurs idéales des faits et gestes humains qui se sont imposés à mon activité artistique.*"[108]

Curiously new to the English point of view also is Conrad's accent on conscience in his credo as an artist. If he abandoned his father's idea of literature as a political weapon, he seems to have stressed all the more the political nature of his work, in the sense of its use to society. His words remind one of his objection to Dostoevsky on the grounds that Dostoevsky cared nothing about the social effects of his representations of truth.

> I, too, would like to hold the magic wand giving that command over laughter and tears which is declared to be the highest achievement of imaginative literature. Only, to be a great magician one must surrender oneself to occult and irresponsible powers, either outside or within one's breast. We have all heard of simple men selling their souls for love or power to some grotesque devil. . . . I don't lay claim to particular wisdom because of my dislike and distrust of such transactions. It may be my sea training acting upon a natural disposition to keep good hold on the one thing really mine, but the fact is that I have a positive horror of losing even for one moving moment that full possession of myself which is the first condition of good service. And I have carried my notion of good service from my earlier into my later existence. I, who have never sought in the written word anything else but a form of the Beautiful . . .[109]

---

[106] Letter to Arnold Bennett, March 10, 1902, *Life and Letters*, I, 303.

[107] Letter to Barrett Clark, May 4, 1918, *Life and Letters*, II, 205.

[108] Letter to Sir Sidney Colvin, March 18, 1917, *Life and Letters*, II, 185.

[109] *A Personal Record*, pp. xvi–xvii.

Conrad's psychopolitical theory of art was fully formed when he wrote this letter (manuscript, The Berg Collection, New York Public Library) to his publisher T. Fisher Unwin on August 22, 1896. These reflections were evoked by a novel on which Unwin asked Conrad's opinion.

Much that Conrad resisted he resisted with only partial success. His biography makes evident that for many years he resisted not only his father's ideas but his father's profession as a writer, even when his uncle Tadeusz urged him to take up writing as a service to Poland. He always claimed, too, that he had a strong distaste for the theater—one of his father's passions. Yet something compelled him to write plays and even a film scenario. The one important activity of his father's, besides active politics, that Conrad resisted successfully was the writing of poetry. Poetry also, he said, he did not enjoy.

Ujejski is able to cite five ideological points, drawn from Conrad's essays after 1905 in *Notes on Life and Letters*, in which Conrad's defense of Poland's right to exist as a nation echoes his father's arguments and the romantic credo of many Polish émigrés. (1) Poland had never threatened any outside nation though she served as an obstacle to aggressors; (2) Polish wars were defensive only and took place only within Poland's frontiers; (3) Poland's territorial growth resulted from spontaneous unions with neighboring states who remained sovereign, not from conquest; (4) bloodshed and civil strife in Poland were always the result of excessive individualism and faith in freedom pushed too far; and (5) when heads were rolling on European scaffolds, only one political execution took place in Poland. The man responsible for it, furthermore, had no rest in his conscience even on his deathbed.[110] Utterly lacking in Conrad's essays, however, is the romantic's generative myth for the rebirth of Poland. To the contrary, Conrad singles out the passive features of Poland's political history in a manner that would not have disgraced Gandhi.

Politics turned from action to art: this was Conrad's achievement. His unique contribution to the English political novel was his response to a political imperative which was at the same time strange to English-speaking readers and universal in the modern

---

[110] Ujejski's source for this analysis is Julian Krzyżanowski, "The Sources of Conrad's Journalistic Studies," *Ruch Literacki* (Warsaw), 1932, no. 8. The title and article are both in Polish. See Ujejski, *op. cit.*, p. 57.

world. "What I was reading the day before my writing life began I have forgotten," Conrad wrote in *A Personal Record*. "I have only a vague notion that it might have been one of Trollope's political novels."[111] But it was not Trollope who gave him his psychopolitical theory of art: "Our captivity within the incomprehensible logic of accident is the only fact of the universe . . . while our struggles to escape from it—either through drink or philanthropy; through a theory or disbelief—make the comedy and the drama of life."[112]

The suggestion for Conrad's novels is more likely to have been the echo of a certain statesman's reflections than any of Trollope's. In the memoirs of one of Napoleon's aides-de-camp, which Conrad read and used for "The Warrior's Soul" and *The Rover*,[113] Philippe de Ségur, the author, recalls a supper on the eve of the battle of Austerlitz during which Napoleon led the conversation to the subject of dramatic poetry. Because the "glamour of the pagan religion no longer exists," Napoleon said,

> . . . our tragic stage requires another motive. Politics should be the great spring of modern tragedy. Policy should take the place in our theater of ancient fatality; that fatality which rendered Oedipus a criminal although he was not guilty; which causes us to feel an interest in Phaedra by throwing on the Gods part of the burden of her crimes and her weaknesses. . . .
> . . . in the exigencies of politics . . . one would find many advantages; it [is] only necessary to place your personages in opposition to other passions or other inclinations, under the absolute influence of this powerful necessity.[114]

---

[111] *A Personal Record*, p. 73.

[112] Unpublished letter from Conrad to T. Fisher Unwin, Aug. 22, 1896, in the Berg Collection, New York Public Library.

[113] Unpublished letter from Conrad to Sir Sidney Colvin, April 2, 1917, in the George T. Keating Conrad Collection, Yale University Library.

[114] Paul Philippe, comte de Ségur, *An Aide-de-Camp of Napoleon*, translated by H. A. Patchett-Martin (London: Hutchinson, 1895), pp. 240–41. I have edited it slightly.

"They had been in this vast and dark country only a very short time, and as yet always in the midst of other white men, under the eye and guidance of other white men, under the guidance of their superiors. And now, dull as they were to the subtle influence of surroundings, they felt themselves very much alone, when suddenly left unassisted to face the wilderness; a wilderness rendered all the more strange, more incomprehensible by the mysterious glimpses of the vigorous life it contained."

"An Outpost of Progress"

"What is it? The fascination of primitive ideas—of primitive virtues, perhaps. Something enticing and bitter in the life—in the thought around you, if you once step into the world of their notions. Very bitter. We can never forget our origin. . . . Don't give yourself up. Primitive virtues are poison to us—white men. We have gone on different lines."

The Rescue (British Museum MS Ashley 4787)

CHAPTER THREE

The Rescue

Most of Conrad's best work came out of the years, roughly 1896 to 1914, when he had most to say about the relationship between the nonconforming individual and the social forces that hedge him in. For Conrad these were the years of a new commitment to land ties of family and foster nation, years when at times the Polish émigré felt his alienation from the human community more acutely than ever he had during the free, wandering years at sea. In 1898, though it was less than two years after his marriage and on the eve of his first child's birth, he wrote to Garnett, "I went over the rise of forty to travel downwards—and a little more lonely than before."[1]

In this loneliness he faced the "stress and strife" within himself, probed into their general human relevance, and was compelled to make his living from their release in fiction. He began to explore more questioningly than he had in *Almayer's Folly* and *An Outcast of the Islands* the egoism which, in his own case, had made him an exile and adventurer. Permissively he followed in his imagination the distances a man could stray—a Jim, a Lingard, a Kurtz, or a Razumov—in isolation from the society with which he must ulti-

---

[1] *Letters from Joseph Conrad, 1895–1924* (Indianapolis: Bobbs-Merrill Co., Inc., 1928), p. 121.

mately make his peace. From the writing of *Heart of Darkness* through *Nostromo,* "Gaspar Ruiz," *The Secret Agent,* and *Under Western Eyes,* he gradually revealed a wide view of the ironic necessities imposed on nonpolitical individuals by political or quasi-political circumstances. The "surrender" that Thomas Moser has traced in Conrad's later writing—after 1914—was not only a lapse into the uncongenial subject of romantic love but also surrender to belief that it is history that shapes individual lives rather than men who shape history. The distance Conrad went along this path can be measured by the distance between *Lord Jim,* who did, after all, shape a little society according to his plans, and Razumov, whose life was taken out of his hands before it was really begun. Not that Conrad ever went so far as Tolstoy in imagining that the real power of history rests in the human atom. Conrad loved men as individuals as much as Tolstoy, but one of his objections to Tolstoy (and most other Russian writers) was that he could not face the logic of history. He retreated from plain reason into mysticism and obscurantism. Such people, Conrad prophesied, are used by ideas because they cannot use them. This was a ruling idea in his fiction until he had painfully objectified in *Under Western Eyes* his inmost thought upon the subject. After that there was nothing much left in him to say about it.

Conrad's Polish background made it easier for him to know, rationally, why men belong to communities or nations than why they cut their ties and go off on the loose. One of his first acts after marrying was to write *The Nigger of the "Narcissus,"* to "enshrine my old chums," he said,[2] but also to embody his idea of the basis of group cohesion in a ship that almost literally stands for England. The ship is imperiled by three different interests: half-humorously, by Christian religiosity in Podmore the cook; seriously, by socialist humanitarianism in Donkin the labor agitator; most seriously (because least clearly), by "the latent egoism of [the crew's] tenderness to suffering,"[3] the suffering of a dying man. What saves them all is

---

[2] *Ibid.,* p. 72.
[3] *The Nigger of the "Narcissus,"* p. 138.

not (here) *l'égoïsme* (for egoism saves only the imaginative man
who cannot live by honest toil and outward discipline alone), but a
vicious storm, recalling them to the necessity of hanging together,
and above all to the necessity of work.[4] The ship's captain "stands
for" government in the abstract, as someone must do, and ideally
men like the ship's officers, whose authority derives from ability.

Part of this magnificent novel's appeal lies in the cleanness of
its idea, the simple idea of good government, uncomplicated by
idealistic leaders. When dealing with this simple idea, Conrad
could write short, flawless works, as short as "Typhoon" or as long
as *The Secret Agent*. But complicate the idea ever so little by introducing a Tom Lingard, a Jim, a Kurtz, or a Charles Gould, and the
clean lines of the political fable blur, short stories turn into novels;
Conrad was helplessly borne past deadline after deadline; and his
critics still wonder what he "meant."

The Rescue was the first novel Conrad undertook in which his
principal character is a natural leader of men whose imagination
(or egoism) is both the source of his power for good and the source
of his destruction. Perhaps the subject took him before he was
ready to see, as he must have seen in *Lord Jim*, that it could bring in
review his own deepest personal and national concerns. He began
by visualizing Tom Lingard's story essentially as a picturesque tale,
appealing to readers of an island whose empire was reaching a dignified arm farther and farther around the "barbarous East."

"The East" is always for Conrad a conception relative to the
character he sends there, having its reality in the projection of the
Western man's purpose in going to the East. Conrad's Polish background greatly enriched the possibilities he could throw before his
English readers. Poles had for centuries considered themselves
guardians at the gate between East and West, fighting down the
"Slavo-Tartar Byzantine barbarism"[5] they thought alien to Poland's

---

[4] It is interesting—in the light of Conrad's stress on the healing power of work in
The Nigger and *Heart of Darkness*—to note that in Poland at the same time "the
nobility of work" was being hailed as a cure for the national ills of romantic self-
idealization and "the cult of sweet suffering." See *The Cambridge History of Poland*,
II (Cambridge: Cambridge University Press), 385–86.

[5] See Conrad's letter to George T. Keating, Dec: 14, 1922, *Life and Letters*, II, 289.

Roman heritage, but also attracted by the fabulous realms that tempted Napoleon beyond dreams of avarice, "the East of the ancient navigators,"[6] the Orient that Conrad's father had studied as food for poetry. Conrad wrests the image from its Polish frame and ascribes its appeal to the universal male ego that probably first conceived it. He makes this ego the driving power of nineteenth-century Englishmen, to the delight of readers whose idea of the horrors and wonders of the East derived from newspaper accounts of East India Company tribulations, opium wars, and such romantic daredevils as Rajah James Brooke.

At any rate, there was more to the geographic image for Conrad than the East, which according to Zabel he "always feared and disliked,"[7] or the East that Thomas Moser says for Conrad "resembles the coldness and fixity of death."[8] One must not lay an accent too heavily either on the wonder or the horror, for—since "East" in Conrad is a projection of the human spirit breaking away from the known and into the unknown—the geographic mirage is a mirror of both good and evil, the danger increasing the wonder, and the wonder the danger, until the spiraling image loses all definition.[9]

In his first two novels Conrad had begun to explore the moral and

---

[6] *Youth*, p. 41.

[7] Morton Dauwen Zabel, "Introduction," *The Portable Conrad* (New York: Viking Press, 1947), p. 22.

[8] Thomas C. Moser, *Joseph Conrad: Achievement and Decline* (Cambridge, Mass.: Harvard University Press, 1957), p. 46.

[9] As Baines has observed, Tymon Terlecki's "*Conrad w kulturze polskiej*" in *Conrad Żywy* (London, 1957) relates Conrad's interest in the Orient to a movement among Polish writers of his generation, following the tragic uprising of 1863. Summing up Terlecki's words, Wit Tarnawski—editor of the collection—writes in English: "Placed between the vanquished romanticism and the extreme negation of romanticism, they all sided with romanticism, although they also criticized it very strongly. . . . Conrad's decision to leave Poland and his choice of a seaman's career, is seen as the fulfilment of these two tendencies which were so characteristic of his generation. It is . . . paradoxical that these tendencies should have found their fullest expression in Conrad, who left Poland for ever.

"Mr. Terlecki supports his thesis by pointing out among other things that oriental exoticism played a considerable part in the literature of 'Young Poland,' although the writers (except Sieroszewski) had no personal knowledge of the East, as Conrad had. . . . [Terlecki] comes to the conclusion that 'the paradoxical opposition, so characteristic of the 'Young Poland' school: the flight from reality and the mastering of reality, has nowhere been so evident as in Conrad' " (p. 285).

dramatic suggestions of his memories as a European in the "un-civilized" corners of the earth he had touched in his travels. The matter was a rich source for many reasons. To begin with, it stressed his point of contact with his English audience: If as a Pole he was an outsider, as a merchant seaman he had gone to the tropics in the line of duty and "belonged" in the English branch of the European family. Furthermore, his original motives in going to sea merged well with his fictional themes. As the merchant service had given him both freedom and direction in life, the experiences he had in it gave his imagination both scope and a control for his writing.

The moral conflicts of Europeans escaping to, or thrust upon, "primitive" peoples had furnished ideas for both his first novels. When beginning *An Outcast of the Islands* in 1894, he wrote to Marguerite Poradowska that the characters and their moral plight were ready but he had no plot. All he had were "two human wrecks such as one meets in the forsaken corners of the world."[10] But the morality of his two wrecks, the white man Willems and the Malasian Muslim Babalatchi, interested him less than the contrast between them. In his scorn for the white man, Babalatchi measured the white man's code against the white man's practice. Conspicuously, however, Babalatchi also measured the white man's practice against the Muslim code rather than the Muslim practice. To him, the white men were "always the slaves of their desires," "always ready to give up their strength and their reason into the hands of some woman," and this was enough proof for Babalatchi that "they who worship many gods" would "destroy one another. . . . They know how to keep faith with their enemies, but towards each other they know only deception."[11] Conrad was enjoying the reverse image of Christian moralizers. He had no ax to grind for either the white or the brown race, in either *Almayer's Folly* or in *An Outcast of the Islands*.

---

[10] Letter to Marguerite Poradowska, August 18 [?], 1894, *Letters of Joseph Conrad to Marguerite Poradowska*, translated and edited by John A. Gee and Paul J. Sturm (New Haven: Yale University Press, 1940), p. 77.
[11] *Almayer's Folly*, p. 60.

When he turned to writing *The Rescue* in the summer of 1896, Conrad kept Malaya for his setting, but the scene subtly changed to one "ahead of civilization," as in *Lord Jim*; it was no longer "the forsaken corners of the world." For the first time he gave the principal role to a white man, built on heroic lines, with the admixture of a fatal flaw.

Also, for the first time in *The Rescue*, the East was to be an exact reflection of the hero, a Westerner who went there following a dream of freedom and power that he could not have realized at home. On the glassy surface of this mirage, Lingard finally sees himself chained by circumstance to his English compatriots and bound still more helplessly by psychic imperatives that conflict with his illusions of freedom and self-control. Lingard's conflicting loyalties to a Malayan political cause and to the Western intruders who foil it bring, perhaps force, Conrad for the first time to unleash certain bitter reflections on modern politics which he had kept under cover for many years.

Conrad's wife thought that his turn to political subjects after their marriage, first in the story "An Outpost of Progress" written in the summer of 1896, was occasioned by the sudden appearance of an old trunk carrying mementos of Conrad's Congo journey six years earlier. However that may be, there is a natural progression of thought between the Africa of "An Outpost of Progress" and the Malaya of *The Rescue*. Apparently in the novel, begun only a few months before the story was finished, Conrad decided to give wider play to certain ideas of a political cast which had been easy enough to handle in the short story.

"An Outpost of Progress" was a tale about two Europeans, an ex-civil servant and an ex-army officer, who went to pieces in the jungle when left alone together with nothing to sustain them but their schooling in "civilized" conduct. The story was quickly told, powerful, and ended neatly with a fillip. (Cunninghame Graham, the aristocratic, socialistic critic of British Empire delusions,[12] later

---

[12] Wishing to dedicate the "Youth" volume to Cunninghame Graham, Conrad felt it necessary to apologize for the socialist's political bias to the publisher William Blackwood: "I do not share his political convictions . . . but we have enough ideas in

read the story in *Cosmopolis* and wrote Conrad ecstatically, beginning their long friendship on the strength of it.) Conrad must have been confident that he could control the material when he decided to use it as an incidental theme, with variations, in *The Rescue*.

From the start, *The Rescue* was to be a contrast not between Westerner and Malay, as in the first two novels, but between two sorts of Westerner. Beginning the novel, Conrad wrote to Garnett of the "yacht people"—"the artificial, civilized creatures that are to be brought in contact with the primitive Lingard."[13] This is where his troubles began. Thinking he could use the story for visual contrasts, richly colored against the Malaysian background, he found himself dealing with a matter of much greater importance to him: the contrasting faces that Europe shows to the world; the effete, shallow pride in their cultural superiority of men like Martin Travers and the ungovernable energy of men like Tom Lingard who cannot live without challenge. Both Travers and Lingard as he pictured them first were men fired by a kind of egotism and a kind of ambition. But Travers was devoid of all the virtues for which he took pride in his cultural background. In the original manuscript, he first appeared to Conrad as more vile than he was finally allowed to be. In softening the edges of his character for the final draft, Conrad kept the point that Travers was a parasite on the cunning and daring of other Englishmen like Lingard.

Although the vicious aspects of Travers' morality suggest a point of view that could belong to any European living within an imperialistic society, Travers is a convincingly English figure. Lingard, on the other hand, is not. He has a sort of "Latin" obsession with honor like Lord Jim's, quite different from the cool correctness of his character in the first two novels he appeared in. In *The Rescue*, moreover, he has a very complex relationship with his land of origin, which he has to explain to himself and to others. This becomes important when the "yacht people" beg him, on the grounds

---

common to base a strong friendship upon." *Letters to William Blackwood*, ed. William Blackburn (Durham, N.C.: Duke University Press, 1958), p. 51. The volume was in the end dedicated to Conrad's wife.

[13] Letter to Garnett, August 5, 1896, *Letters from Joseph Conrad*, p. 63.

of their common nationality, to put their interests ahead of the Malay royal family's. Edith Travers reaches the core with her question:

> "What is there [in your English past] that you remember and love?"
>
> "Everything," he said. His eyes were tender, his voice defiant as though his indomitable affection were challenging all the obscure and cruel miseries of his youth to try his blind and heroic constancy.[14]

One may reasonably ask what "obscure and cruel miseries" Lingard could have met in his boyhood on the coast of Devon that tried his primitive soul to such an extent! Be that as it may, he is a man (Conrad tells us) who was true to some special tradition even "through the events of an unrelated existence," like Jim. Lingard "had not departed from his origins; he had only gone away from his beginnings."[15] This means, apparently, that his beginnings as the son of a Devon fisherman had lost their restraints upon him, but he had no thought of renouncing his origins, either his family or his English nationality. In going to the East, "he had retreated into a past so remote that it was the common property" of all men.[16] As with the Marlow of "Youth" (who reaches "the East of the ancient navigators") and of *Heart of Darkness* (remembering the Romans in the heart of England's former darkness), Lingard traveled back in history by going East, and the twofold journey is made for the purpose of moral assertion.

Falteringly in *The Rescue*, Conrad suggests that history is what it becomes most significantly in *Heart of Darkness*: an immense screen on which to throw larger-than-life-size shadows of men as they fundamentally are, regardless of time and change. Against this

---

[14] *The Rescue* (British Museum MS Ashley 4787). The political ideas developed in the published book were already fully formed in the manuscript which Conrad put aside in 1899. Throughout this chapter, I refer to manuscript and book by the same title. Although Guerard and Moser have most of the manuscript to support them in calling it "The Rescuer," the book title does appear as the title in the last pages of the manuscript.

[15] *The Rescue*, MS p. 581.

[16] *Ibid.*

shadow play on the screen of history, Conrad places the smaller figures of modern life, who move in the colors of their national dress, impelled by the motives of nineteenth-century men and women.

But in *The Rescue* he resists his instinct for using a second dimension as a means of moral inquiry. "I want to make it a kind of glorified book for boys . . . No analysis. No damned mouthing. Pictures—pictures—pictures,"[17] he wrote Garnett. The "primitive Lingard," he assumed, was the sort of figure his readers would recognize on sight, modeled on a man who had been much in the public eye earlier in the century.

Sir James Brooke, K.C.B., knighted by Queen Victoria in 1847 for his service to the Crown in carrying the fruits of British civilization to the primitive state of Sarawak in Borneo, was a man whose exploits were already legendary in the Malayan ports Conrad visited as a seaman in 1887–88, some twenty years after Brooke's death. To Englishmen he was a fabulous character because he had left the beaten path of British traders and missionaries who followed the safe mechanism of the East India Company in slowly colonizing lands needed for British industry.

Brooke's reasons for suddenly breaking his traditional family tie with the "John Company" in order to buy a brig (the "Royalist"), train a trustworthy crew, and sail off to Malaya, were far from clear and far from mundane:

> Could I carry my vessel to places where the keel of European ship never before ploughed the waters; could I plant my foot where white man's foot had never before been; could I gaze upon scenes which educated eyes had never looked on, see man in the rudest state of nature, I should be content without looking to further rewards.[18]

That was all he wanted at first.

John D. Gordan has documented the particulars of Brooke's life and Malayan intrigues that Conrad employed in all his Malayan

---

[17] Letter to Garnett, Oct. 8, 1897, *Letters from Joseph Conrad*, p. 110.
[18] Sir Spenser St. John, *Rajah Brooke* (London: Fisher Unwin, 1899), p. 9.

fiction.[19] The suggestions Conrad found in Brooke's journals and letters, as well as yarns and biographies about him, could be written about endlessly, but the sources referred to by Gordan are sufficient to show the main lines of Brooke's appeal both to the English and to Conrad.

It was not within Gordan's subject to inquire into the political significance of what Conrad used and what he left out or changed, or even to notice how highly these changes suggest Conrad's distance from his English readers. We can see from the use of Brookiana in *The Rescue*, however, the beginnings of Conrad's impulse to draw lessons for his English readers from their own political affairs.

Whenever Brooke appears in Conrad's fiction, he comes stripped of all connection with the educated, ruling classes in England. James Brooke set out to be a rugged individualist to be sure, but unlike any Conrad character (until Charles Gould, much later), Brooke very quickly resorted to the benefits of his family position and national heritage for help in his daring enterprise. He had to have money for his good works in Sarawak, and only England could fulfil all his demands for trained workers, construction materials, and armaments. He made England a party to his designs, first out of practical necessity, and in natural course returned to his nation part credit for Sarawak's stable economy, run according to British law and Christian ethics, keeping for himself and his heirs in Sarawak only the glorious title of rajah which had been the more or less voluntary gift of his grateful Malay friends.

At length the story of Brooke's exploits reached his fellow countrymen, carrying a suspicion of dark dealings. Brooke had perforce "gone native" to the extent that he had learned and used savage reprisals against Dyak head-hunters, Muslim pirates, and treacherous Chinese traders, some of whom would respect the democratic government he established in no other way. These contingencies suggested an aspect of Brooke's character that obviously

---

[19] John D. Gordan, "The Rajah Brooke and Joseph Conrad," *Studies in Philology*, XXXV (October, 1938), 613–34. See also Gordan's *Joseph Conrad: The Making of a Novelist* (Cambridge, Mass.: Harvard University Press, 1940), pp. 57–73.

transverse section of deck.

P.

S.

chain

big link

Lanyard. rope. Several turns,

ringbolt on the deck

deck

deck

P.S. Re - reading your letter -
That's how a stack would go
perhaps. And this would give
you an idea how to secure.
ik again {Here both lanyards to 5 have carried
away — say by a roll: the thing is then to
catch the ends of chains hook quick a
spare tackle into the big link and the ring
on deck and set taut. Should chains go
same principle of action must be followed}

Ah! Amigo! I've thought
of Rajah Laut in London and
if not in the W-H then next
thing to it. But I haven't
the heart. I haven't! not yet.
• I am now busy about his youth — a gorgeous romance — gorgeous as to feeling I mean. Battles and loves and
so on.

Conrad wrote to R. B. Cunninghame Graham on January 7, 1898 (manuscript,
Dartmouth College Library), illustrating at the latter's request how a smokestack
might be blown off a ship during a gale. In the last sentences Conrad refers to Sir
James Brooke, Rajah of Sarawak, the "white rajah" whose life served as a basis for
Tom Lingard's in *The Rescue*. Cunninghame Graham's suggestion that Brooke be
thought of as a character in the Western Hemisphere may have planted a germ for
the character of Charles Gould in *Nostromo*.

fascinated Conrad, even though he knew that Brooke's enemies, jealous of his power, had precipitated the humiliating Parliamentary inquiry that had dragged out all the gory details of certain tragic events in Sarawak; even though Conrad knew that Brooke was finally acquitted and knighted justly.

In life Brooke emerged as a hero. His biographers saw nothing sinister in his unwillingness at the end of his life to go back to England or to transfer his power as rajah to the heir he himself had chosen; saw nothing anachronistic in the Arthurian last farewell he took of his subjects, calling them together, "alluding to the long period he had spent in promoting [their] welfare,"[20] and promising to return if they should have need of him. Scarred by smallpox and with the signature of death written large on his wasted body, he could yet speak as an immortal, and his people wept as at the parting of a god.

Although Conrad fought to keep out of *The Rescue* every hint of maniacal tendencies in his hero, he tried to capitalize to the full on the tragedy of Brooke's interference in native politics, with its disastrously ironic reversal. In stabilizing the economy of Sarawak and beating off its enemies, Brooke had unwittingly brought to its doors the worst catastrophe it had ever known. Muslim pirates, made envious and bitter by the increasing power of the state Brooke had unified, in 1846 organized an attack during which "every member of the royal family known to favor the English alliance was massacred."[21] Conrad's royal couple Hassim and Immada, as well as most of the Malays and Muslims in *The Rescue*, are drawn straight from Brooke's life, as is the final scene of immolation. As unwitting traitors to their primitive friends, Brooke and Lingard are one.

To some extent Conrad must have identified himself with Brooke's character, in which there was a curious mixture of impulses toward clandestine adventures[22] on the one hand and toward the

---

[20] Gertrude Jacob, *The Raja of Sarawak*, II (London: Macmillan Co., 1876), 335–36.

[21] *Ibid.*, I, 321.

[22] Brooke's evasions of marriage and a settled life in England have been the subject of often-hilarious discussion. See Emily Hahn, *James Brooke of Sarawak* (London: Barker, 1953).

establishment of law and order on the other. Like Brooke too, Conrad had left his land of origin answering a dark impulse and had found fame abroad, raising suspicion of vile motives in the minds of his countrymen. (And Conrad's homeland also would later glorify his name.) Certainly, when he decided to form Tom Lingard of *The Rescue* on Rajah Brooke's mold, Conrad made the figure closer to his own pattern and purified him of all traces of imperialistic motivation. Tom Lingard was to be from beginning to end a perfectly disinterested sailor, admirable for unschooled virtues and a kind of virility, which—because Conrad denied to it any intellectual force—unhappily came to nothing more than a frustrated and frustrating sex appeal.

The dramatic episode Conrad imagined for the novel's plot was, he assumed, an incident of obvious appeal. Hoping to sell the story to *Blackwood's Magazine*, he wrote the publisher:

> The human interest of the tale is in the contact of Lingard the simple, masterful, imaginative adventurer with a type of civilized woman—a complex type. He is a man of tenacious purpose, enthusiastic in undertaking, faithful in friendship. He jeopardizes the success of his plans first to assure her safety and then absolutely sacrifices them to what he believes the necessary conditions of her happiness. He is throughout mistrusted by the whites whom he wishes to save; he is unwillingly forced into a contest with his Malay friends. Then when the rescue, for which he had sacrificed all the interests of his life, is accomplished, he has to face his reward— an inevitable separation. This episode of his life lifts him out of himself; I want to convey in the action of the story the stress and exaltation of the man under the influence of a sentiment which he hardly understands. . . . It is only at the very last that he is perfectly enlightened when the work of rescue and destruction is ended and nothing is left to him but to try and pick up as best he may the broken thread of his life. . . . I aim at stimulating vision in the reader. . . . The yacht, the shipwreck, the pirates, the coast —all this has been used time out of number; whether it has been done, that's another question.[23]

This is an admirable précis of the novel, as it was begun and as it was finished over twenty years later, with one notable qualifica-

---

[23] *Letters to William Blackwood*, p. 10.

tion. In writing to the publisher of a politically conservative magazine, Conrad omits altogether to mention the contrast which, as he had told Garnett, was the very essence of the plot: the accidental intrusion of a yacht full of "artificial, civilized creatures" into the chivalrous political intrigues of the "primitive Lingard."

In trying to simplify Lingard's character, Conrad apparently tried to reduce his complexity to two fundamentals. He would be first the paragon of a pure politician (I can find no better word): responsive to the appeals of friendship, wishing freedom for himself and therefore for anyone else who appealed to him in its name. Second, he would be, to his own surprise, a lover—also pure, of course. The conflicts he encountered would be powerful but not out of keeping with these simple characteristics. His consciously chosen loyalties would be subverted by his inherited loyalty; his integrated pattern of life, subverted by unrecognized erotic impulses. He would be like his brig, "floating between the wavering starlight of the pure and profound heaven, and these sudden mysterious lightnings" born "in the shallow serenity, in the smiling corruption of narrow waters."[24] The starlight above would correspond to the directions of his will, and the phosphorescent lights in the water to the unrecognized impulses ready in wait to deflect his consciousness. Like lightning (his brig is the "Lightning"), his story would be a frightening flash from the higher to the lower impulses.

His desire for power, Conrad tries to say again and again, is *not* malignant. He is merely a man "ready for the obvious, no matter how startling, terrible, or menacing, yet defenseless as a child before the shadowy impulses of his own heart."[25] "The opportunity to make war and to make history had been offered to him . . . a suggestion of power to be picked up by a strong hand."[26] Even before the thought has entered the reader's head, Conrad insists that Lingard's will to power is not Nietzschean but Emersonian, is in fact the very opposite of an oppressor's hunger: "above all it was himself, it was his longing to mould his own fate in accordance

---

[24] *The Rescue*, MS p. 581.
[25] *Ibid.*, pp. 15–16.
[26] *Ibid.*, p. 186.

with the whispers of his imagination."[27] If he wins power over others, it is because he recognizes in them the same need to be free from tyrannous pressures. This is

> the romantic side of the man's nature . . . that responsive sensitiveness to the shadowy appeals made by life and death, which is the groundwork of a chivalrous character. It was this unguarded generosity of heart recognizing the existence of mankind outside itself which more than his virtues or his foibles secured for him the affection of a strange and imaginative race.[28]

Even after writing *Heart of Darkness*, Conrad saw that the only way to carry out his plan for *The Rescue*, the only way to get it finished, was to maintain Lingard's primal purity—*even though he had ceased to believe in it*. For the final draft, adding introductory paragraphs to the novel that related Lingard to the famous Brooke, Conrad urged his readers to concentrate on the angelic natures of both men:

> Almost in our own day we have seen one of [the successors of the first adventurers in Malaya]—a true adventurer in his devotion to impulse—a man of high mind and of pure heart, lay the foundation of a flourishing state on the ideas of pity and justice. He recognized chivalrously the claims of the conquered; he was a disinterested adventurer, and the reward of his noble instincts is in the veneration with which a strange and faithful race cherish his memory.
>
> Misunderstood and traduced in life, the glory of his achievement has vindicated the purity of his motives. He belongs to history. But there were others—obscure adventurers who had not his advantages of birth, position and intelligence; who had only his sympathy with the people of forests and sea he understood and loved so well.[29]

In *The Rescue*, Lingard is so detached from his homeland and so personally disinterested that his motives are obscure, one suspects, even to Conrad. He had to be a true opposite to the English yacht people, and yet his dilemma had to result from the appeal of one of them—a highly civilized woman. Conrad presented himself with a

---

[27] *Ibid.*, p. 158.
[28] *Ibid.*, p. 133.
[29] *The Rescue* (book), pp. 3–4.

conflict which could not be resolved honestly, and for the first time in his writing life, he continued on a course that was alien to his vision.

The civilized man Travers is a beast, but his wife is a darling. Travers represents the sham of cultivated life; his wife its "flower."[30] Compared to her the Malay princess Immada is as "the cry" to the finished "phrase."[31] This conception balances well. The primitive Lingard is to be undone by the flower of civilization—both of them models in their way. But the conception has a deeper, political level on which Conrad can only be vague if he is to remain true to his effort to write a love story.

There is every evidence in the manuscript that when he began it, he expected the political fable to be as coherent as the love story, and to give him much less trouble. He was going to visualize (without "mouthings" or analysis) a rich assortment of Westerners, the Easterners, and then a group of middlemen—Westerners who, like Lingard, had crossed over to primitive lands more or less for good. In the book, finally, only Lingard and Jörgenson among these middlemen stand out. "Mosey"—the German Jewish spy—and the treacherous "New Englander"—who deals in Colt pistols—do not seem related to them. The reason is that Conrad excised from the manuscript a character—Wyndham—who was the piece that linked them all together.

If this group of Western strays, ranging from the chivalrous (who came to the East in quest of "virtues" not found in the West) to the despicable, had stayed in a pack, the moral to be drawn from their example would have accentuated still further the precariousness of the West's claim to superiority. And some strongly admirable image had to be kept if Conrad's heroine were to be one of its reflections.

The section of the novel where these problems arise is the flashback in Part II in which we are introduced to the crowd of adventurers drifting in and out of Malaysian ports, among whom Lingard moves gracefully and somewhat mysteriously. In the manu-

---

[30] *Ibid.*, p. 148.
[31] *Ibid.*

script, while Wyndham (later deleted altogether) and Jörgenson (even more pointedly than in the book)[32] find in the primitive tribes more manliness than in Western society, the "New Englander" (for which we might read "New World man," since "his people" live in Baltimore and he speaks with a drawl) is a loathsome caricature of what the ideal of manliness has become in the Western Hemisphere. His guns are "warranted to cure the worst kind of cussedness in any nigger."[33] Although this "new" Englishman remains in the published book, when Wyndham—with all his reflections on the beguiling and dangerous virtues of primitive races— is removed, the Negro-hater stands merely as an isolated figure, at most offering a contrast to the gentler racial prejudice of Lingard's simple but dutiful chief mate Shaw.

Without Wyndham, in the published book the primitive Lingard stands alone, remote from these supporting or contrasting characters, and thus makes a better head to the triangle which is to have civilization's sham and its flower at the two corners of its base. The love story is not overshadowed. Add Wyndham, and the West takes on a monstrous aspect, altogether out of keeping with the novel's heroine.

That Conrad was strongly attracted by the suggestions that would have made *The Rescue* a political fable of East and West, primitive virtue and Western overcivilization, seems to be clear from the coincidence that the excised portion of the manuscript dealing with Wyndham presents the entire theme of the novel in miniature, love story or no.[34]

---

[32] *The Rescue*, MS p. 164.

[33] *Ibid.*, p. 175. In the book the phrase appears on p. 96.

[34] Because this passage has controversial aspects, I here quote it in full from the manuscript, pp. 139–42: "A little professional jealousy was unavoidable, Wajo on account of its chronic disturbances being as yet untapped by the white traders. But there was no ill-will in the banter of these men who rising with handshakes dropped off one by one. The last who remained, a quiet distinguished looking little man, with iron-grey hair and steady black eyes, looked keenly at Lingard for a time. His visits to the settlements were rare, he was supposed to be a real gentleman and his reserved manner commanded respect. His name reposes in a musty shrine, within old official documents in the Dutch language and marked 'confidential,' where he is alluded to as 'the Englishman called Wyndham who has been living for many years with the Sultan of Solo, and whose great influence upon the turbulent chiefs is deplorable and

This reduction of the over-all theme seems to have been Conrad's intention when he had Wyndham, a sort of *alter ego* for Lingard, warn him against falling under the spell of primitive virtues: "Primitive virtues are poison to us—white men. We have gone on different lines. Look on, trade, make money . . . don't go further than that." Wyndham's lesson was that the primitive races

---

should be put an end to in the interest of our northern possessions.' Lingard puffed thoughtfully at his cheroot.—'I trust you will forgive my offering advice unasked, Captain Lingard, but I am an old hand out here,' began in a cultivated sad-toned voice the friend of turbulent Solo pangerans. 'Say on, Wyndham, we all know you,' exclaimed Lingard.—'I was going to say that with those people—I speak of the whole race—a man who once obtains their confidence and . . . and regard— I was going to say affection—that man can do no wrong. I've lived for years now in . . . a den of tigers,' he went on slowly while a nervous fine hand played absently with an empty tumbler. 'Yes, that's how the place has been described—a den of tigers. Well, today were I to stumble when walking along, half a dozen men who think themselves the salt of creation would be off their ponies in an instant to pick me up.'— 'That shows what kind of man you are,' interrupted Lingard with honest admiration in his eyes.—'I am afraid,' went on the other smiling sadly, 'that it does . . . and what's more I am afraid that you also are the kind of man to whom such unfortunate success would come—if you don't look out.'—'I don't follow you,' said Lingard staring hard.—'Don't go in too deep with them,' pursued the prince of adventurers. 'I say to you *don't!* Take a warning from me; I can't get away now.'—'Can't you!' exclaimed Lingard in surprise. 'Everybody thinks you've made a big pile there.' —'Oh! I've plenty of coin—and that kind of thing, but take a warning by me. I am ready to go—and I can't. I've given myself up to them. Never do that—never. Be loyal, be honest with them—but don't allow yourself to like anyone. You will regret it—too late. We are no better, perhaps, but we are different. There is about them a fascination. . . . What is it? The fascination of primitive ideas—of primitive virtues, perhaps. Something enticing and bitter in the life—in the thought around you, if you once step into the world of their notions. Very bitter. We can never forget our origin. Like no one. Don't give yourself up. Primitive virtues are poison to us— white men. We have gone on different lines. Look on, trade, make money. . . .'— 'What on earth do you think I am going to do?' exclaimed Lingard. 'I am going to trade—that's all.'—'Well—don't go further than that. Above all don't fight with them. That's how it begins. First you fight with them—then you fight for them— no closer tie than spilt blood—then you begin to think they are human beings . . .'— 'And aren't they?' asked Lingard seriously.—'They are—very. That's the worst of it— for when you begin to see it your ideas change. You see injustice and cruel folly of what, before, appeared just and wise. Then you begin to love them—that fascination you know; and then. . . .' He set his teeth.—'What?' asked Lingard breathlessly.— 'Damnation!' jerked out the real gentleman. 'Your friendship can only bring remorse to you, misfortune to them. Always. It's fatal. . . . Good bye. Probably never see you again.'—'Why! Are you going home at last?' inquired Lingard grasping the extended hand.—'I might; plenty of money; a certain welcome . . . Yes, I might—but I am going back to my den of tigers.' He gave a short laugh and disappeared in the night."

would make Lingard despise his own civilization. He would begin by discovering that the Malays were "very human," then "your ideas change. You see [the] injustice and cruel folly of what before appeared just and wise. Then you begin to love [the natives]." But "your friendship can only bring remorse to you, misfortune to them. Always. It's fatal." In the manuscript, before Edith Travers arrived to remind Lingard of any positive qualities in his land of origin, Wyndham was there telling him that there was nothing in England that *could* wean him back once he had yielded to the charms of a primitive people. Wyndham could not voluntarily go home but must return to his "den of tigers."

Although both Guerard and Moser have seen in this passage suggestions of sexual depravity and bondage to a people Conrad believed racially inferior, such a reading seems to me alien to the text of both manuscript and book. There is certainly some likeness between Wyndham and Kurtz, but not much more than between Kurtz and David Livingstone. All three were Europeans so attracted to life among "primitive" peoples that they could not return to life in Europe. If depravity were to be part of Wyndham's story, however, would it not have left its mark on his appearance as it did on the figure of Kurtz? Instead, Wyndham is described in the manuscript as "a quiet distinguished looking little man, with iron-grey hair and steady black eyes . . . he was supposed to be a real gentleman and his reserved manner commanded respect."

Even Wyndham's description of the primitive life as bitterly enticing, and of primitive virtues as "poison to us—white men," makes sense when read along with Jörgenson's remark (also cut out of the book), "Remember that unless you young chaps are like we men who ranged about here twenty years ago, what I could tell you would be worse than poison."[35] If one is man enough to meet the challenge of a culture in which one finds no support from civilization's accumulated sanctions and graces (everything from the corner policeman to clothes for one's nudity, as we shall see in *Heart of Darkness*), one may end by embracing as brothers the very

---

[35] See above, n. 32.

people one is supposed to think inferior, and finally, denying blood ties, to join them in war against one's countrymen. Something of the sort seems to have been the fate of the actual Wyndham,[36] an Englishman who in Conrad's words,

> had been living for many years with the Sultan of Sulu and was the general purveyor of arms and gunpowder. In 1850 or '51 he financed a very lively row in Celebes. He is mentioned in Dutch official documents as a great nuisance—which he, no doubt, was. I've heard several versions of his end (occurred in the sixties) all very lamentable.[37]

As I read the problematic episode, then, there is no hint that Wyndham and Lingard have anything to lose but their chance to live at peace with their own kind. They are not on their way to unspeakable depravities but rather on the track of some life genuinely preferable to the one they left behind. If taken seriously, this idea would make a logical absurdity of Conrad's attempt to create his heroine out of a society lady. She could offer Lingard nothing that he could not better by taking a noble savage in her place. Rather like his own hero, Conrad is caught by "sudden and mysterious lightnings" that lurk beneath the surface of his creative temperament.

Lingard's remorse, if it had followed the prediction Wyndham made, would have been the remorse of a man who had cut himself off from his cultural tradition and national loyalties; the remorse he would have felt had he abandoned the "yacht people" in favor of the Malays he was pledged to support.

---

[36] Baines has been unable to find documentary evidence of this man's activities beyond a reference in Sir Spenser St. John's biography of Rajah Brooke (see Baines, p. 420). I can add only that Najeeb M. Saleeby's *History of Sulu* (Manila, 1908) reproduces a letter from a William Windham, written from Sulu on May 28, 1849, to the Spanish governor of Zamboanga, announcing a treaty made the day before by Sir James Brooke with the Sultan of Sulu. Windham, who here describes himself as an intimate of the "residents" and the partner of a merchant in Singapore, writes to allay possible suspicion of Brooke's treaty and to warn the Spanish of the imminent arrival of Dutch troops with "the declared intention of taking possession of the entire coast of North Borneo, Sulu, and all its dependencies" (p. 237). The tone of this letter seems to support my impression of "Wyndham" as a man bound to the people of Sulu by strong sympathies rather than by unspeakable addictions.

[37] *Letters to William Blackwood*, p. 10.

By going primitive, Lingard and Wyndham had transcended their accidents of birth and found a sort of timeless culture, based on fundamental human virtues and vices that appealed to them both by the simplicity of its moral standards and by its preservation of primal virilities. It is supposedly these virilities that attract Edith Travers to Lingard, who contrasts so violently with her effete husband. For obvious reasons, Conrad hoped to maintain the contrast between the two Englishmen without having to pull down the whole edifice of Western civilization on which the contrast and the heroine stand.

The catastrophe Wyndham predicted Lingard would bring on his Malay friends does certainly occur. And Edith Travers has the lioness' share in causing it. But Conrad is disloyal to his nascent thought in that he finally had to save the civilized lady from the political incubus which, in spite of him, afflicts her as well as her husband.

Conrad tries to believe himself that the force of civilization, whatever it has done to men like Travers, has refined feminine character. Comparing Edith Travers with the primitive Immada, the aristocratic (significantly Spanish) d'Alcacer—supposedly a counterpart to the chivalrous Lingard, perhaps to show that a man can be chivalrous even if he is an aristocrat—explains to the reader why Mrs. Travers might appeal to Lingard. The Spaniard's only real argument is that she, unlike Immada, can express her full nature—in gestures and dress but above all in the subtleties of speech. This argument is equally strong in both manuscript and finished book.

But the idea of it is blatantly wrong in the novel. In the first place, Lingard is not and never can be a conversationalist. In the second place, the lady never does express herself clearly. The most we can believe is that she *reminds* Lingard of an aspect of civilized society that has definite charm. We cannot be convinced of this, however, unless Conrad himself believes it and therefore allows the argument some glimmer of truth. This he was constitutionally unable to do. In "The Return," in "The Planter of Malata," in the unfinished *Suspense*, and every other work in which society people cross his stage, they are hollow to the core. When Conrad chose his own "white woman" for a wife, she was not from "society," and it is doubtful if she could have been. Furthermore, his political novels all indicate most pointedly that discourse, verbal persuasion, is utterly ineffective as a tool. Men change one another's minds by talk in Dostoevsky, but not in Conrad.

In *Heart of Darkness*, Conrad took vengeance on the trap his heroine in *The Rescue* had set for him. In the Congo story the white woman remains "out of it" in more ways than one and is fully appropriate in character to the kind of world the West has made for her. The best Conrad could do in *The Rescue*, since he had promised his publishers a love story, was to develop the lady as a *femme fatale*, a woman who could maintain her heady appeal for Lingard in spite of her part in the disastrous intrusion of the Western civilizers.

Because she must be spared, or become a villainess (which, considering her attributes, might have shocked Conrad's conservative readers, and considering Conrad's gallantry would have shocked his own nerves), the whole point of the political fable is weakened almost out of existence. The dealer of the tragic blow is not Lingard's forgotten Western past as Wyndham had predicted it would be, but Venus in Victorian drapery. As a result, the sacrifice of Hassim and Immada dumbfounds us as a bloody holocaust, a dreadful mistake rather than the inevitable reversal of Lingard's politically criminal irresolution.

Conrad rejected one possible source of political interest in the novel by deleting from Lingard's influence with his Malay friends all benefits that an educated Englishman could have brought. He divided the character of Sir James Brooke between Lingard and Travers, made a sham of the representative of the British Empire, and then withdrew from pursuing the suggestions of the character. In the finished book Travers remains as he was in the manuscript, a man "whose life and thought, ignorant of human passion, were devoted to extracting the greatest possible amount of personal advantage from human institutions."[38] Leaning on the bulwark of England's imperial power, he has made a career for himself out of writing tracts to prove the rightness of England's imperial claims over all contenders. When his yacht goes aground in Lingard's waters, he is on his way to "expose" the Dutch colonial system. He is devoid of any of Brooke's human sympathy with the people caught in the wheels of the imperial juggernaut. He is utterly confident of the future of his own superior race.

> And if the inferior race must perish, it is a gain, a step towards the perfecting of humanity which is the aim of progress. Our duty to these regions lies in the ruthless, merciless repression of natural instincts.[39]

The last sentence of this passage disappears in the finished book. It made some sense in the manuscript, of course, because Lingard and Edith Travers are both seeking a rediscovery and reunion with the powerful instincts that Travers has suppressed in himself and wants to suppress in the expanding civilized world. But Conrad rightly perceived that Travers must not be allowed even to glimpse the lost power of natural instincts. The insight would have been, in the terms we use today, too Nietzschean or too Freudian. It would have brought Travers next door to discovering that his idea of "progress" depended on a denial of truth.

For Nietzsche and Freud (the latter almost Conrad's exact contemporary), "progress" in history and in civilization is a long story of sublimation and suppression of human instincts. Necessary but not in all ways good. In Nietzsche's terms, sublimation and repression are necessary to the herd of men because they cannot cope with the full powers of the human spirit. Heroes can. To them falls the glory of merging man's past actions and future hopes in one present insight of the whole human potential. Heroes do not progress; they are.

Similarly with Freud. The fortunate man is the man who can face his own past, however painful; the man who does not suppress

---

[38] *The Rescue* (book), p. 123.
[39] *The Rescue*, MS pp. 282–83.

painful memories only to express them neurotically with no memory of what he is expressing. Like Nietzsche's hero, Freud's enlightened "patient" will gain full control of himself and of his future. He will neither escape from primal instincts nor project false fantasies as to what he can do.

Progress, in its nineteenth-century economic and political sense, is suspect for Nietzsche, for Freud, and for Conrad, and for all three because the idea encourages a natural tendency men have to suppress important truths. Nietzsche thought the run of men have to be kept in the dark about these truths. Freud thought it would be better for a patient to remain in darkness than to have revelations forced upon him that he either could not accept or could not control. Conrad was not sure, when he wrote *The Rescue*, what he meant to say to his English readers about progress, civilization, and the suppression of primal instincts.

It can be argued that Conrad needed to write as much as he did of *The Rescue* before 1898, when he began (or resumed) *Lord Jim* and finished *Heart of Darkness*, in order to see what the Travers team really meant to him, in order to release for his full view all the phantoms in command of his mind. In *Heart of Darkness* the "yacht people" become what they are always threatening to be in *The Rescue*: images of European men and women whose history has passed on to them a torch of illusion which they carry into "backward" territories. These images are not only of the villains of Europe. They include gallant men like d'Alcacer and Lingard, who cannot see the unholy light that the torch throws on their own faces or recognize the nemesis which lies in wait because of all they have forgotten in their determination not to let the torch go out.

". . . a work of art should speak for itself. Yet much could be said on the other side; for it is also clear that a work of art is not a logical demonstration carrying its intention on the face of it."

Letter from Conrad to F. N. Doubleday, June 2, 1924

"[Written words] seem to talk to you as though they were intelligent, but if you ask them anything about what they say, from a desire to be instructed, they go on telling you just the same thing for ever. And once a thing is put in writing, the composition, whatever it may be, drifts all over the place, getting into the hands not only of those who understand it, but equally of those who have no business with it; it doesn't know how to address the right people, and not address the wrong."

Socrates, in Plato's *Phaedrus*

CHAPTER
FOUR

Heart of Darkness

After *Lord Jim*, none of Conrad's novels inspires so much critical furor as *Heart of Darkness*. And most of what has been written is of little use because it does not explain adequately why the story is so heavy, stylistically speaking, or—when the critic does give reasons, drawn from the substance of the story, for the opacity of Marlow's "yarn"—the philosophy or meaning discovered is often so extraneous to the narrative as to call in question Conrad's interest in the fiction.

If we listen to critics as generally reliable as F. R. Leavis and Marvin Mudrick, we may be persuaded that, in fact, this short novel is not a major work and is hardly worth the volumes of critical commentary that have been published on it. E. M. Forster may have been thinking of *Heart of Darkness* when he complained in *Abinger Harvest* that, alas, the casket of Conrad's genius contains not a jewel but a vapor.[1] This was exactly Leavis' lament when he could bring out nothing of value after searching for treasure in this elaborate tale of an English seaman's horrifying journey up the Congo. Leavis blames Conrad for his "adjectival insistence" on

---

[1] *Abinger Harvest* (New York: Harcourt, Brace, 1936), p. 138.

impressions that were intended to be "unspeakable," but turn out in the end, says Leavis, to be merely "unspecified."[2]

In the same vein, Marvin Mudrick calls Conrad's overelaboration of image and symbol in *Heart of Darkness* a sort of *reductio ad absurdum:* symbolism carried so far beyond the objective correlatives of significance as almost to discourage any other writer from ever using symbol and image extensively again.[3]

It has become so much the fashion to rake Conrad's imagery for exotic gems that the solid soil of the story is by now quite overturned. In 1948 Louis Halle suggested that the story be read as an intricately concealed protest against the tortures Conrad suffered in writing fiction.[4] More recently, Lillian Feder and Jerome Thale have interpreted the novel as an allegory of the soul's journey to salvation through purgatory and hell, as a new Dante's *Inferno* or a modern quest for the Holy Grail.[5]

Morton Dauwen Zabel comes to our aid by giving us simply a careful understanding of what the episodes, taken together, quite objectively say. Albert J. Guerard clarifies the tale by stressing Conrad's preoccupation with Marlow (as opposed to Kurtz's "revelation") and by questioning the completeness of Marlow's self-knowledge at the end of the story.[6] But even Zabel and Guerard leave room for further emphasis on the "public significance" of the story and its relevance to the time in which it was published, as opposed to the period in which Conrad himself went to the Congo.

It would be well for us to recall in some detail the political

[2] F. R. Leavis, *The Great Tradition* (London: Chatto and Windus, 1948), pp. 177–80.

[3] "The Originality of Conrad," *Hudson Review* (Winter, 1958–59), pp. 545–53.

[4] "Joseph Conrad: An Enigma Decoded," *Saturday Review of Literature,* May 22, 1948, pp. 7–8.

[5] Lillian Feder, "Marlow's Descent into Hell," *Nineteenth-Century Fiction* (March, 1955), pp. 280–92; Jerome Thale, "Marlow's Quest," *University of Toronto Quarterly* (July, 1955), pp. 351–58.

[6] Morton Dauwen Zabel's best appraisal is his recent introduction to *Youth* (New York: Doubleday Anchor Books, 1959); Albert J. Guerard's introduction to *Heart of Darkness and The Secret Sharer* (New York: Signet Books, 1950) should be considered as well as his *Conrad the Novelist* (Cambridge, Mass.: Harvard University Press, 1958), pp. 33–48.

milieu out of which the novel sprang—in England, almost a decade after Conrad's journey in 1890. For *Heart of Darkness*, as much as any other of his works, is a product of his reflection on "*la race, le moment, et le milieu*," as Taine would say, in which he found himself. "The subject is of our time distinctly," Conrad wrote, "though not topically treated."[7]

Like Melville warning Hawthorne that *Moby Dick* was essentially an iconoclastic book, Conrad wrote to Cunninghame Graham in February, 1899, after the first installment of *Heart of Darkness* had appeared in *Blackwood's Magazine*, that the novel's "idea" was "so wrapped up in secondary notions that you,—even you!—may miss it." The letter is ambiguous, particularly as the letter which it answers is lost. Apparently Cunninghame Graham had responded enthusiastically to the first part of the story, seeing it as another exposé of imperialism like Conrad's "An Outpost of Progress." Reading Conrad's answer, one assumes that there may be more to "the idea" of the Congo story than the obvious attack on King Leopold II's activities in the Belgian Congo. Conrad goes on to say:

> And also you must remember that I don't start with an abstract notion. I start with definite images and as their rendering is true some little effect is produced. So far the note struck chimes in with your convictions,—*mais après*? There is an *après*. But I think that if you look a little into the episodes, you will find in them the right intention, though I fear nothing that is practically effective.[8]

If *Heart of Darkness* were to have a practical effect, it would be to end forever the presumptions of all European "civilizers" wherever they were carrying their flags by force. But Conrad's readers, coming to the story in 1899, were poorly equipped to penetrate its whole meaning, especially for two reasons. First, they were English, and the author was English only in sympathy and by adoption. Second, the story was not exactly addressed to them. None of Conrad's novels was pointed at a particular readership, and this one least of all. He wrote "over their heads," not because he despised

---

[7] *Letters to William Blackwood*, ed. William Blackburn (Durham, N.C.: Duke University Press, 1958), p. 37.

[8] *Life and Letters*, I, 268.

them but perhaps the opposite: because of a conviction that men's instinctive loyalties must not be violated. In the year before beginning *Heart of Darkness*, in a letter to his publisher, Conrad included one of the most poignant statements ever made by a didactic artist: ". . . a sweeping assertion is always wrong, since men are infinitely varied; and hard words are useless because they cannot combat ideas. And the ideas (that live) should be combatted, not the men who die."[9]

Taking this statement as it was intended, we are able to imagine what it cost Conrad to write in *Heart of Darkness* a vehement denunciation of imperialism and racialism without damning all men who through the accident of their birth in England were committed to these public policies.

To a man for whom "race" meant "nation" more than "pigmentation," and for whom "nation" was a sacred image, the nineteenth-century cultivation of racialism[10] as a means of commercial profit through tyranny was history's most agonizing chapter. In conveying the effect upon his mind, he could only imagine the worst torments of hell, invoke Virgil and Dante who had seen hell as if with their own eyes (knowing it as a place where evil is not justified by the morality of the moment), and add to their testimony what he had seen with *his* eyes in the Congo.

Yet, like Virgil and Dante, Conrad lived in a historical moment and in a foster nation which, if it was not racked by civil war like

---

[9] *Letters to William Blackwood*, p. 14.

[10] William L. Langer discusses the subtle influence on English thought of the Pan-German League doctrines of racial superiority. "The idea no doubt went back to Count Gobineau's essay on *The Inequality of the Human Races*, which was first published in 1854, but the cult of this extravagant racialism and nationalism came only in the last lustrum of the nineteenth century. In England as in Germany it was carried to absurd heights." The significant point about Conrad's nationalism, as we have already seen, is that in his theory at least he disclaimed for it both a definition according to color and any argument for the right of one nation to influence or control other nations by force. The nation is defined by Conrad in purely cultural and historic terms. In addition to other embarrassments he faced as a British citizen, his profession as a British seaman continually exposed him to the argument, winning adherents in England at the time, that England's right to conquer most of the earth was manifest in her natural gift of naval prowess. See Langer's *The Diplomacy of Imperialism, 1890–1902* (New York: Alfred A. Knopf, Inc., 1951), pp. 417–23.

theirs, was threatened from within and without by powers that could turn to their use the criticism of even well-meaning citizens. Everything that was good in England had been thrown, along with the bad, into the "competition in the acquisition of territory and the struggle for influence and control," which according to William Langer, "was the most important factor in the international relations of Europe" between 1890 and 1910.[11]

From 1896 through the first years of the twentieth century, England passed through a crisis in south Africa which, from the point of view of the public at large, was at once the most dramatic trial of British imperial claims and the clearest test of the very idea of imperialism. The genesis of the war, as Langer describes it,

> had a long and complicated history, stemming from the fundamental antagonism of the English and Dutch in south Africa, from the conflict of British imperialist ideas and Republican aspirations, from the peculiar economic problems of the four south African states, from the revolution brought about by the discovery of great gold fields in the Transvaal, and lastly from the growing pressure of German competition in the colonial and commercial fields.[12]

In early 1897, at almost the same moment when Conrad's final papers certifying him as a British subject reached his hands, the British government was forced by the fabulous Cecil Rhodes to stray from a path of rectitude that England had carefully marked out for herself on the African continent. In his combination of titanic idealism with daemonic egotism, Rhodes appears the prototype of a Conrad character—of Martin Travers in *The Rescue*; still more, perhaps, of Kurtz in *Heart of Darkness*. Even his close friend William Stead described Rhodes in words Conrad seems to have echoed in presenting the despicable Travers.[13] According to Stead,

> the perfecting of the fittest species among the animals, or of races among men, and then the conferring upon the perfected species or

[11] *Ibid.*, p. 67.
[12] *Ibid.*, p. 213
[13] See above, p. 106.

race the title-deeds of the future; that seemed to Mr. Rhodes . . .
the way in which God is governing his world.[14]

Furthermore, like Travers and Kurtz, Rhodes drew his strength not
from himself as an individual but by identifying himself completely with his nation's rights in the Transvaal.

> Rhodes's was essentially a single-track mind. He built up a tremen-
> dous fortune with the idea of using the power which it brought for
> the aggrandizement and glorification of the British Empire. He con-
> fessed that history had taught him "that expansion was everything,
> and that the world's surface being limited, the great object of pres-
> ent humanity should be to take as much of the world as it possibly
> could." Returning from a visit to England in 1899, he was delighted
> to report to his friends in South Africa that all thoughts of a little
> England were gone: "They are tumbling over each other, Liberals
> and Conservatives, to show which side are the greatest and most
> enthusiastic Imperialists."[15]

Conservative or Liberal, it was Britain's assumption that, although the Boers owned the territory in the neighborhood of the
mines, British subjects should have not only fair treatment according to their investments in the mines but also voting privileges in
the government based on the large proportion of British citizens in
the area. British government policy in south Africa, as the Foreign
Office had stressed soothingly for some years, was pointed at the
suppression of the slave trade. To this end, the government would
staunchly support the Christian missions while protesting that protection was not to be used as an excuse for the acquisition of territory. The spirit was willing but the flesh was weak.

Cecil Rhodes meanwhile argued persistently that all interests in
Africa, including that of the African natives, could be advanced
fairly only if a railroad could be constructed from Capetown to
Cairo. The company he organized to build the railroad was in due
course chartered by the Crown, and little note was taken of Rhodes'
opinion that when the railroad materialized, the supremacy of the

---

[14] Langer, *op. cit.*, p. 94.
[15] *Ibid.*, pp. 78–79. Langer is quoting Rhodes.

British "race" would soon become apparent in Africa, as it was bound to be in the world. He held, moreover, that eventually Britain and the lost American colonies must reunite in a glorious condominium.

The Boers in the Transvaal, who had to live with the present threat of Rhodes and his henchmen, thousands of miles away from the well-meaning British home government, tried to obstruct the railway construction in a number of different ways. And the more political events threatened his wish, the more Rhodes labored for its fulfilment. Kruger, the president of the Boer Republic, rightly felt himself no match for Rhodes, who was not only prime minister of Cape Colony but also head of both the South Africa Company (by whose charter the British government gave him "almost unlimited powers of government in the huge area north of the Transvaal and west of the Portuguese possessions, without fixing any northern limit"[16]) and of the Consolidated Goldfields Company, largest of the goldmining concerns. In 1895 Kruger publicly announced that British policies were forcing him to ask support from the German emperor, and more or less in retaliation Rhodes and his sympathizers began to foment a revolution in Johannesburg, where—although the land belonged to the largely agricultural Boers—the commercial population had outnumbered the landowners. Rhodes and his friends bought arms, smuggled them into Johannesburg, and acquired the other provisions for an invading force.

In the summer of 1895 Lord Rosebery's Liberal government, which had represented the last gasp of the old Gladstonian liberalism and temperate imperialism, fell and was replaced by Lord Salisbury's Conservatives, of whom the colonial secretary, Joseph Chamberlain—the most ardent of the entrenched imperialists— was the figurehead. Despite their similarities (or possibly because of them), Chamberlain distrusted Rhodes as a man. He grudgingly turned over to the South Africa Company a strip of territory bordering the Transvaal, which was to be used for the railway north.

---

[16] *Ibid.,* p. 218.

Later, an agent of the company who had negotiated with Chamberlain for the land claimed that Chamberlain knew the land was to be used for an insurrection against the Boers. Whether or not this was true, Chamberlain allowed a British police force to be concentrated in the new strip. On December 29, then, Dr. Leander Starr Jameson, administrator of the South Africa Company, who was on the frontier of the strip with six hundred police, took it upon himself to hasten the day of the revolt. He and his raiders started on the 140-mile ride to Johannesburg, cutting the telegraph wires that might have warned them of the unpreparedness of their cohorts in the city and of the full readiness of the Boer defense force. The Boers gradually closed in, and on January 2, 1896, Jameson was forced to surrender.

The affair was humiliating in the extreme. Even mutually hostile continental powers met to plot suitable measures for checking the insatiable appetites of Great Britain. The German emperor turned the knife in the wound by telegraphing Kruger congratulations on "maintaining the independence of the country against attacks from without."[17] England forebore to recall that the independence of the Transvaal was conditional upon terms of an 1884 convention limiting the right of the Boers to make treaties with foreign powers (such as Germany). War was averted narrowly. To save face in Europe, Chamberlain denounced the raid, but he also refused to insist that Rhodes reveal the whole story before Parliament. The British press therefore glorified Jameson and his raiders as gallant defenders of helpless women and children in Johannesburg. And about the time Conrad began to write *The Rescue*, Alfred Austin, the poet laureate, contributed to the *Times* a poem called *Jameson's Ride:* "Not Heaven itself shall stay us/ From the rescue they call a raid."[18]

---

[17] *Ibid.*, p. 237.

[18] *Ibid.*, p. 230. The newspaper antics over this episode may have suggested two of Conrad's titles, *Lord Jim* and *The Rescue*. Jameson, a man who failed though activated by the noblest motives, was often referred to as "Dr. Jim." Although the episode was odious to Conrad, the popular hue and cry may well have shown him the advantage of calling a story "Tuan Jim," if—as I think likely—he laid out the early sketch for the novel in the summer of 1896.

Complaints and annoyances from the (mostly British) Out-
landers against the Boers became more and more aggravating, and
three years later in April, 1899, the Boers declared war on England.
The war that Rhodes had desired broke out.

This was the first of the wars in which England was engaged
during the years of Conrad's "English life." The other was World
War I, in which his elder son Borys fought and nearly died; out of
which, however, Poland regained her life. As we have noted, Conrad had been brooding for years over the shadows, "more or less
distorted," of European events, suggesting "the lurid light of
battlefields somewhere in the near future." While professing himself in "a state of despairing indifference," he had yet, as early as
1885, intimated to a fellow Pole living in England that "an anti-
Russian alliance [with Germany] would be useful, and even possible, for Great Britain."[19] War in itself was a terror he could face with
some hope even amid despair over Poland's fate and despite his
constitutional loathing for blood-letting as a cure for the body
politic. But Germany, it was plain a decade later, was developing
poorly as a friend of freedom in Europe.

Conrad trusted England's policy *faute de mieux.* Even while
Britain consistently labored to appease Russian threats and to pad
the concussion of Russian civil strife so that it would not shake the
delicate balance in Europe, and even while England herself began
to develop a posture in remote parts of the globe not wholly different from Russia's imperial posture in eastern Europe, Conrad
maintained the reticence appropriate to an immigrant enjoying the
hospitality of a fostering people.

To someone earning his living by the publication of his thought,
this reticence must have been excruciating at times. On the spring
day in 1897 when he received the formal confirmation of his British
citizenship, Conrad wrote his English friend E. L. Sanderson
describing this dilemma. He had received "the form of nationalization and its reality,—the voice of what is best in the heart of peoples." He went on to say:

---

[19] *Life and Letters,* I, 80.

> I feel horribly sentimental,—no joking matter this, at my age, when
> one should be grave, correct, slightly cynical,—and secretly bored.
> I am none of these things and, feeling my shortcomings, withdraw
> from the gaze of my fellow beings. Now, note the inconsequence of
> the human animal: I want to rush into print whereby my senti-
> mentalism, my incorrect attitude to life,—all I wish to hide in the
> wilds of Essex,—shall be disclosed to the public gaze! . . . Alas! I
> have been born too far East, where not many cultivate the virtue of
> reticence.

As if to show further "the inconsequence of the human animal," in
his next paragraph he makes a comment curiously out of keeping
with his remark that nationalization is "the voice of what is best in
the heart of peoples." Now he writes, "A lying prophet must ultimately die but the folly of nations is practically immortal."[20] And
this merely to express personal weariness with the difficulties of
being a writer!

If this letter discloses a radical ambivalence in Conrad's attitude
toward nationalism and toward his own involvement with the
Polish and British forms of it, a few months later, writing to
Sanderson's fiancée, he makes clear that he holds an attitude which
can reconcile these conflicts: "A man's duties are wide and complex: the balance should be held very even, lest some evil should be
done when nothing but good is contemplated."[21]

Whether or not this principle was vital to him in connection with
reports of British affairs in South Africa at the time, in the months
following the Jameson raid, it is evident from the struggle he was
having with *The Rescue* manuscript that his mind was full of the
perils Englishmen were inviting upon themselves by their intrusions in "the dark places of the earth." In 1895, meaning to praise
Almayer's Folly, a reviewer in *The Spectator* had predicted Conrad
would become "the Kipling of the Malay Archipelago."[22] Kipling!
an artist of superior intelligence who could nevertheless, like
Martin Travers, speak solemnly of "the white man's burden," who

---

[20] *Life and Letters,* I, 203–4.

[21] Letter to Miss Watson, June 27, 1897, *Life and Letters,* I, 205.

[22] G. Jean-Aubry, *The Sea Dreamer,* translated by Helen Sebba (New York: Doubleday & Co., Inc., 1957), p. 210.

went East, not as the perfectly disinterested trader Tom Lingard, but rather as the newspaper reporter whose accounts in a "home paper" were read blindly by the heroes of "An Outpost of Progress." This paper, according to Conrad, "spoke much of the rights and duties of civilization, of the sacredness of the civilizing work, and extolled the merits of those who went about bringing light and faith and commerce to the dark places of the earth."[23]

Conrad despised the rhetoric of the new journalism which was finding its voice in the same years when his own works were beginning to appear. Aimed as it was to excite as well as to reflect the emotions of a newly enfranchised populace, it often fortified the worst kind of nationalistic conservatism. "There is certainly some room for argument," writes Langer, "that popular pressure was more important in the growth of imperialism than was the action of the ruling classes. It must be recalled, for example, that the rise of imperialism was contemporaneous with the extension of the suffrage in 1867 and 1884."[24] Rudyard Kipling, who was a newspaper writer in India from 1882 to 1889, did much to frame the style of popular attitudes toward the Empire. A few months before Conrad began "An Outpost of Progress" in May, 1896, Lord Northcliffe began publication of the *Daily Mail*, introducing it with the announcement that it was "to be the articulate voice of British progress and domination. We believe in England. We know that the advance of the Union Jack means protection for weaker races, justice for the oppressed, liberty for the downtrodden."[25] The *Daily Mail* immediately became so popular that, says Langer, "even the best-established of the older papers were obliged to follow the same line."

In August, 1897, Conrad wrote a lame defense of Kipling to Cunninghame Graham—who had just introduced himself by letter to Conrad with an ecstatic eulogy of "An Outpost of Progress." Conrad replied:

---

[23] "An Outpost of Progress," *Tales of Unrest*, p. 94.
[24] Langer, *op. cit.*, p. 81.
[25] *Ibid.*, p. 84.

Mr. Kipling has the wisdom of the passing generations,—and holds it in perfect sincerity. Some of his work is of impeccable form and because of that *little* thing, he will sojourn in Hell only a very short while. He squints with the rest of his excellent sort. It is a beautiful squint: it is an useful squint. And—after all,—perhaps he sees round the corner? . . . It is impossible to know anything, tho' it is possible to believe a thing or two.[26]

About this time Conrad became acquainted with another of Kipling's "excellent sort," the publisher who had just accepted his exotic "Karain" for "Maga." William Blackwood—the kindly Conservative Scot to whom Conrad felt compelled to disguise his opinion of the "artificial, civilized creatures" in *The Rescue* and to apologize for his devotion to Cunninghame Graham—was a man whose political "squint" Conrad was willing to tolerate. Two years later, when he finally came to write his most probing work on the civilizers of dark lands, he would offer it as part payment of a debt, for the millennial issue of *Blackwood's Magazine*. And in offering it, he would use the phrase "civilizing work" that had one sort of ring in the passage just quoted from "An Outpost of Progress" and quite a different tone in this letter to Blackwood's:

> The title I am thinking of is *"The Heart of Darkness"* but the narrative is not gloomy. The criminality of inefficiency and pure selfishness when tackling the civilizing work in Africa is a justifiable idea. The subject is of our time distinctly—though not topically treated. It is a story as much as my "Outpost of Progress" was but, so to speak "takes in" more—is a little wider—is less concentrated upon individuals.[27]

This letter will be worth considering again in a later context.

It would not be hard to believe that Conrad, who had sunk all his meager inheritance in a south African mining venture and had lost it in the months after the Jameson raid, on the eve of his marriage, took a view of events in south Africa that harmonized well with the impressions of his Congo journey in 1890. From the beginning of 1896, when events occurred in south Africa that

---

[26] *Life and Letters*, I, 208.
[27] See above, n. 7.

finally brought on the Boer War, until the end of 1898, when Conrad began the actual writing of *Heart of Darkness*,[28] he was deeply absorbed in two questions: his loyalty, both as man and as writer, to England, and his acute mistrust of the way the "civilizing work" was being accomplished by the European powers in southeast Asia and in Africa. In letters he made little of either point; just what we have seen—a casually contorted reference to "the folly of nations" or Kipling's squint. He appears to have made no comment on England's affairs in south Africa until late 1899 when he complained to William Blackwood that the war was making it difficult for him to concentrate on his work, that the newspaper reports of British persistence in spite of military setbacks were "unseemly" and "expressed so stupidly that it is exasperating to a man whose faith is as deep as the sea and more stable."[29]

To Cunninghame Graham, two months earlier, he had said that the war itself was absurd:

The whole business is inexpressibly stupid,—even on general principles: for, evidently a war should be a conclusive proceeding, while this noble enterprise (no matter what its first result) must be the beginning of an endless contest. It is always unwise to begin a war which, to be effective, must be a war of extermination: it is positively imbecile to start it without a clear notion of what it means and to force on questions for immediate solution which are eminently fit to be left to time. . . . There is an appalling fatuity in this business. If I am to believe Kipling this is a war undertaken for the cause of democracy. *C'est à crever de rire!* However, now the

---

[28] Both Ford Madox Ford, in *Joseph Conrad: A Personal Remembrance* (London: Duckworth, 1924), pp. 99 ff., and Edward Garnett (ed.), *Letters from Joseph Conrad, 1895–1924*, p. 14, remark that Conrad related the Congo story to them, with certain scenes substituted for others, some time before *Heart of Darkness* was written. It was at least vividly in Conrad's mind in the summer of 1898, when he visited Garnett (for date see *Life and Letters*, I, 248). Garnett laments the loss in print of certain scenes which he says Conrad described as his own experience. Curiously, the one Garnett singles out for mention is, in fact, not from Conrad's life but from the life of Mungo Park. Conrad writes of the same eposode—the explorer deathly ill in a native hut, abandoned by whites but cared for by a native woman— in "Geography and Some Explorers," *Last Essays*, p. 15. It is possible that Conrad was trying out ideas for the story on Garnett and already transmuting fact into fiction.

[29] Letter of Dec. 26, 1899, *Letters to William Blackwood*, p. 80.

fun has commenced, I trust British successes will be crushing from the first,—on the same principle that if there's murder being done in the next room and you can't stop it, you wish the head of the victim to be bashed in forthwith and the whole thing over for the sake of your own feelings.[30]

This was as close as he ever came to a written denunciation of British imperialism, or to a denunciation of any British government policy. He maintained the same reticence later during the Labour government's policy of appeasement toward Russia in 1917. And shortly after writing Cunninghame Graham about the stupidity of the south African war, he jumped to defend British policy against the needling criticism of a Polish cousin. When answering a question raised in a letter from Aniela Zagórska, he argued, not that it was a war for democracy to be sure, but that it was at least a war to fend off a graver menace than British commercial expansion:

> Much might be said about the war. My feelings are very complex— as you may guess. That they—the Boers—are struggling in good faith for their independence cannot be doubted; but it is also a fact that they have no idea of liberty, which can only be found under the English flag all over the world. *C'est un peuple essentiellement déspotique*, as all the Dutch. This war is not so much a war against the Transvaal as a struggle against the doings of German influence. It is the Germans who have compelled the issue.[31]

To another foreigner, the Frenchman R. L. Mégroz, he presented a similar view. Recalling a much later conversation, Mégroz wrote:

> What really influenced Conrad was the knowledge that the Boer War was largely serving the purpose of an anti-British intrigue on the continent, led by Germany, and his imagination was aroused by the idea of the British dominions taking part in a war which could not influence their material interests.[32]

Thus, amid an embarrassed defense of Great Britain, expressing a characteristically despairing hope that this nation perhaps alone

---

[30] Letter of Oct. 14, 1899, *Life and Letters*, I, 284–85.
[31] Letter of Dec. 25, 1899, *Life and Letters*, I, 288.
[32] R. L. Mégroz, *Joseph Conrad's Mind and Method* (London: Faber & Faber, [1931]), p. 134.

STATION :—
SANDLING JUNCTION, S.E.R.

tary success. There is an
appalling fatuity in this
business. If I am to believe
Kipling this is a war undertaken for the came of democracy. C'est a crever de rire.
However, now the fun has
commenced, I wish British
successes would be will be
crushing from the first — on
the same principle that if there,
murder being done in the next
room and you cain't stop
the you wish the head of the
victim to be bashed in forthwith
and the whole thing over for
the same of your own feelings.

Letter from Conrad to R. B. Cunninghame Graham, October 14, 1899 (manuscript, Dartmouth College Library). Although this letter was written in the months
after *Heart of Darkness* appeared, it expresses feelings Conrad experienced concerning
the rhetoric of imperialism during his whole writing life.

among the living on earth was energized by a generous and just political vision, we find Conrad clearly opposed to two major arguments in support of the war. Most importantly, for Conrad the war was in no sense a "just war." Second, even if Britain was, of all the powers in Africa, the only one that had evolved and put in practice "the idea of liberty," still in no sense could these actions in Africa be interpreted as a movement for "the cause of democracy"—that is, the cause of self-government, which could only be government by the Africans themselves.

Ford Madox Ford, who persistently ridicules Conrad's sensitivities in matters of personal and public fidelity, offers as an object of wonder that, during the months of the south African war, when *Heart of Darkness* had just been finished and Conrad was helping him to write *The Inheritors*, never once did they discuss any political matter. Ford himself, he avows in the third person,

> was an active and sometimes uproarious Pacifist. Not a pro-Boer: he would have hanged President Kruger on the same gallows as Mr. Chamberlain. . . . Now and then on idle occasions after lunch he would declaim about either of these causes. Conrad would listen.[33]

In the same memoir, written just after Conrad's death, Ford recalled with customary jocosity that Conrad had debased himself to the extent of accepting membership in the British Academy, a "body without venerability, committed to courses of propaganda, and of a habit, to be destructive to the art by which Conrad had made his name, to which he owed fidelity."[34] Ford sums up this lapse by remarking that "if it was a question of his private principles against any honour he could show the English State, his private principles must go by the board."[35]

---

[33] *Joseph Conrad: A Personal Remembrance*, pp. 121–22.

[34] Election to the British Academy carried with it a stipend which Conrad desperately needed at this time in order to settle a terrible debt—a fact Ford does not consider, though he himself was one of Conrad's creditors, and not always a gracious one. On the connection between Conrad's extremity and his membership in the academy see *Letters from Joseph Conrad*, p. 150: "I've lost the last ounce of respect for my art. I am lost—gone—gone—done for—for the consideration of 50 gs."

[35] *Joseph Conrad: A Personal Remembrance*, p. 70.

Ford omits to mention that Conrad's feelings might have been infinitely complex, while Africa, as Poland had been, was being carved up by various European powers. He mentions that Conrad would become incensed against the Belgian imperialists in the Congo Free State "after he had been up to London and had met Casement who . . . was passionately the champion of the natives."[36] Conrad and Casement had met in central Africa in 1890, and Conrad had felt a powerful and immediate sympathy with this Irish patriot who was, like himself, employed by the infamous *Société Anonyme Belge* and later honored for his services to the British Crown, a man touched with the same quixotic ardor that ran in Conrad's own veins.[37] Ford remarks on Casement's compassion for the African natives, which might be the strongest of bonds between an Irishman and Pole whose people had suffered similar fates. But Ford does not conclude, as he might have in 1925, that Casement, hanged as a traitor to Britain in World War I, perhaps did not "let his private principles go by the board" when "it was a question of any honor he could show the English State."

Conrad, Ford asserts, "was certainly more Imperialistic" than himself.[38] On the other hand, in 1899, after writing *Heart of Darkness*, Conrad helped Ford to write a scathing novel about a foully imperialistic venture in Greenland in which English writers, publishers, statesmen, and capitalists were fooled into taking a part. Ford drew up the plot. Conrad tore it to shreds and had Ford put it together again. The work was nevertheless finished within a year and accepted early in 1900. Conrad then wrote to Garnett,

> I set myself to look upon the thing as a sort of skit upon the sort of political (?!) novel fools of the N[ew] S[tatesman] sort do write. This in my heart of hearts. And poor H[ueffer, i.e., Ford] was in dead earnest! Oh Lord. How he worked! There is not a chapter I haven't made him write twice—most of them three times over.[39]

---

[36] *Ibid.*, p. 122.

[37] *Life and Letters*, I, 325.

[38] According to Joseph Retinger, Conrad ". . . did not believe in the 'White-man's burden,' but neither did he feel much sympathy for the underdog . . . . if he was anything at all, he was . . . a 'Little Englander.'" *Conrad and His Contemporaries* (London: Minerva, 1941), pp. 65–66.

[39] *Letters from Joseph Conrad*, p. 168.

In the same letter Conrad refers cryptically to his private feelings concerning the novel: "And there's no doubt that in the course of that agony I have been ready to weep more than once. Yet not for him. Not for him. You'll have to burn this letter—but I shall say no more. Some day we shall meet and then—!"

I do not think it was Ford's politics that made Conrad want to weep, or he would hardly have agreed to collaborate in the first place. Garnett's politics were, moreover, no less imperialist than Ford's. There are ways and ways of expressing political principles, however, and from what Ford wrote after Conrad's death it appears that the *effect* of political criticism upon the national morale was uppermost in Conrad's mind. We have noted that this was a matter of special concern to Conrad in the months when *Heart of Darkness* was appearing in *Blackwood's Magazine*. He had written Cunninghame Graham in early 1899 that his pacifism and socialism were illusions which could not remedy the political disease of the time, particularly because they failed to account for the perversity of the political animal and its egoism. The worst aspect of the pacifists, including politicians from all sorts of parties and nations, in Conrad's view was not their ideas but their propaganda—the use they made of their ideas—which he said "tends to weaken the national sentiment, the preservation of which is my concern."[40]

As we have observed, throughout his life Conrad wrote as if his two nations, and in fact nationalism itself, were in a state of continual emergency. "We exist only insofar as we hang together." And, "Woe to the stragglers!"[41] As with Jim, so with Conrad, a straggler could *exist* only when a new people won possession of him, when its spirit had broken his personal freedom: all the "trust, the fame, the friendships, the love—all these things that made him master had made him a captive, too."[42]

In everything Conrad wrote touching the activities of Englishmen abroad, a strain of irony betrays his struggle to maintain the "national sentiment" while hinting strongly at the evils lurking

---

[40] See above, pp. 18–19.
[41] *Lord Jim*, p. 223.
[42] *Ibid.*, p. 247.

behind it. Thus, in his review of Hugh Clifford's *Studies in Brown Humanity*, published the same year that *Heart of Darkness* was begun, Conrad remarks on Clifford's concern over England's account in the Book of Judgment. Clifford hoped that England's "most excellent intentions" would count. Conrad remarks that the "intentions will, no doubt count for something, though, of course, every nation's conquests are paved with good intentions."[43] But Conrad refuses, even for the honorable Clifford, to allow a place in heaven for England's conquests. Whatever rewards are due in justice will be settled on earth, for it is at best, Conrad suggests, a matter of profit and loss—a commercial rather than a moral transaction: "it may be that the Recording Angel, looking compassionately at the strife of hearts, may disdain to enter into the Eternal Book the facts of a struggle which has the reward of righteousness even on this earth—in victory and lasting greatness, or in defeat and humiliation." Through the entire review there runs an acrid implication that even this English traveler perhaps cared less about brown humanity than about the exotic nature of its life and surroundings.

One is not wrenching phrases out of their context in taking such things from different works Conrad wrote at this time. *Lord Jim* and *Heart of Darkness*, at least, should be read together. Conrad himself wished it to be so. While finishing the story "Youth" in the spring of 1898, he seems to have had his first thought of making a single volume of which these "stories" would make the second and third part. Blackwood was asking for some stories to make a volume with "Youth," and Conrad (having only the bare motifs clearly in mind) evidently thought they could be tied together as three of Marlow's yarns. He planned the links to be even stronger than that, however.

"Youth" would come first in order, *Heart of Darkness* second, and *Lord Jim* third. Later, when Jim threatened to run too long and Blackwood suggested publishing the volume without it, with an-

---

[43] "An Observer in Malaya," *Notes on Life and Letters*, p. 58.

other story in its place, Conrad pleaded that *Jim* was not "planned to stand alone. H[eart] of D[arkness] was meant in my mind as a foil, and *Youth* was supposed to give the note."[44]

The "note" of innocent adventure gives the pitch for a theme that runs from the Marlow of "Youth" through the Marlow of the Congo (and through the Russian "harlequin" of the Congo) to the dreamer Jim. But in what sense *Heart of Darkness* is a "foil" for *Lord Jim* is less clear. We see, of course, that in both Marlow is a detective of the human soul. As in *Heart of Darkness* he follows clues toward solving the mystery of Kurtz, so in the longer work he pursues the mystery of Jim's conscience. In each Marlow suffers a mental crisis, in one through his encounter with Kurtz, in the other through catching sight of Jim. Kurtz's moral fiasco may "foil"—enhance by contrast—the moral disaster of Jim aboard the "Patna" and in Patusan: the dark "victory" of Kurtz, a delegate of Europe's cultural egoism, is a foil for the brighter "victory" of Jim, who "of all mankind had no dealings but with himself."[45] For the condition of Kurtz's soul is not, as in Jim's story, the essence of the plot. Kurtz is not interesting so much in himself as in what made him.

If the mystery to be detected is thus different in the two novels, the two Marlows are also dissimilar. It is the nature of Conrad's narrators to become only what the meanings of the novels require of them. They have, most crucially, quite different moral standards in certain points. Although both Marlows prove willing to lie for, or at least excuse, the moral failings of their mysterious "partners," the object of Jim's Marlow is to reveal his subject's "greatness," whereas Kurtz's Marlow ultimately strives to conceal it. We must conclude that the Marlow of *Lord Jim* believes that even dangerous knowledge is worthy of public examination, whereas the Marlow of *Heart of Darkness* believes the contrary: that dangerous knowledge must be suppressed.

[44] *Letters to William Blackwood*, p. 94. T. S. Eliot, apparently sensing this design in the relation of "Youth" to *Heart of Darkness*, uses the quintessence of Conrad's meaning in *The Waste Land*: "I will show you fear in a handful of dust" takes from "Youth" the "heat of life in a handful of dust" (p. 37) and inflicts on it the violent negation of feelings found in Conrad's hollow men of the Congo.
[45] Compare *Lord Jim*, pp. 224, 339, with *Heart of Darkness*, pp. 117, 151.

We may note in passing that Jim's Marlow appears to be of two minds on the capacity of his listeners to interpret Jim's story correctly. On the one hand he seems to credit them with more objectivity and perhaps more understanding than he has himself:

> He existed for me, and after all it is only through me that he exists for you. I've led him out by the hand; I have paraded him before you. Were my commonplace fears unjust? I won't say—not even now. You may be able to tell better, since the proverb has it that the onlookers see most of the game.

On the other hand, and in the same two pages, he suspects his listeners of obtuseness:

> My last words about Jim shall be few. I affirm he had achieved greatness; but the thing would be dwarfed in the telling, or rather in the hearing. Frankly, it is not my words that I mistrust but your minds. I could be eloquent were I not afraid you fellows had starved your imaginations to feed your bodies. I do not mean to be offensive; it is respectable to have no illusions—and safe—and profitable—and dull.[46]

This apparent indecision may be due to Conrad's effort, elsewhere evident in *Lord Jim*, to condition his readers in the matter (discussed in Chapter Two, above) of distinguishing different levels of "reality." In one paragraph he encourages them to see more than even Marlow can see; in the next he warns them at least not to see less.

In *Heart of Darkness* the case is very nearly reversed. Marlow is forever fussing about reality and unreality, but it is his own rather than his listeners faculties that he mistrusts. We are cautioned at the start that this Marlow will see the meaning of the episode "only as a glow brings out a haze."[47] And still this Marlow identifies himself with his English listeners to the point of assuming that they will see in the story neither less nor more than he sees himself. His listeners accept in silence. They are utterly inert, except for one trivial rejoinder.[48] Nothing is feared from them besides boredom,

---

[46] *Lord Jim*, pp. 224–25.
[47] *Heart of Darkness*, p. 48.
[48] *Ibid.*, p. 94.

and nothing is expected of them. And this makes sense because in fact the Marlow of the story is himself incapable of decisive moral insight. At no point is he granted the sight of "imperishable reality," the vivid conviction of "absolute Truth" that Jim's Marlow enjoyed.[49]

I have suggested that Conrad wrote *Heart of Darkness* with a sense of relief, as if taking revenge on his "love story," *The Rescue,* because it led him to gloss over or to evade certain issues—the nature of "Western superiority" in primitive lands and the appeals of primitive virtues and vices to men like Lingard and women like Edith Travers. If indeed *Heart of Darkness,* the very antithesis of a love story, provided him with a means for releasing ideas and feelings evoked by *The Rescue,* this might explain the speed, unequaled in any other story of comparable length and complexity, with which he wrote the Congo story, getting it down in little more than a month.

Frustrated for over two years by *The Rescue,* he sat down to *Heart of Darkness* in command of a new strategy. To begin, the simple exordium of "Youth"—first of the trilogy—would serve, later, the weaving of an almost impenetrable web. "Youth" had begun:

> This could have occurred nowhere but in England, where men and sea interpenetrate, so to speak—the sea entering into the life of most men, and the men knowing something or everything about the sea, in the way of amusement, of travel, or of breadwinning.

Thus again, aboard the "Nellie," the nameless narrator, about to introduce Marlow of the Congo, would reflect:

> The sea-reach of the Thames stretched away before us like the beginning of an interminable waterway. . . . A haze rested on the low shores that ran out to sea in vanishing flatness. The air was dark above Gravesend, and farther back still seemed condensed into a mournful gloom, brooding motionless over the biggest, and the greatest, town on earth.

---

[49] See above, p. 67.

This friend of Marlow's, wanting us to see Marlow the far-traveler in his English setting before we see through Marlow's eyes, uses in both stories the motif that has such different outgrowths. As the first accents the sea, the second accents the land, for as the first introduced a tale of youth breaking free, the second presents a tale of age and bondage—the aging of humanity (which may bring it wisdom or folly) and the bondage of men whose nature is to be possessed by what they love.

As if in spite of "the philosopher" Ruskin, whose work Conrad mentions derisively in the beginning of "Youth," the first narrator in *Heart of Darkness* dwells pensively on an immense pathetic fallacy: the haze and darkness "brooding" over London. He speaks of it three times in four paragraphs, reminding one of Conrad the Pole, native of a land where rough nature still had the ascendant in men's minds. It is also, however, Conrad the conscious artist, finding an exact correlative for the force, discernible in history but not in the moment, that turns men's actions on the wheel of an overriding logic. He had used this correlative of physical nature in practically everything he wrote.[50] History, according to the optimists of his time, was an evolving process, rationally understandable, heading toward moral and physical improvement. Nature, to the eye beholding it, despite the evolutionists, presented an aspect of cyclical constancy, heading nowhere in particular, predictable only in its eternal returns. Like the Japanese *Bunraku* puppeteer, whose effects Conrad seemed instinctively to apprehend,[51] he required for his art something like a metaphysical dimension behind the representational figures of men and women, but he would not go beyond the sphere of the physical world to achieve it. As the *Bunraku* puppeteer moves behind his marionette, immense and shrouded in black, Conrad has sky and jungle, geography and history, on the move behind Marlow in *Heart of Darkness*.

F. R. Leavis objected especially to the gloom "brooding" insistently through different parts of the narrative. But the gloom that is

---

[50] See above, p. 49.
[51] See *Life and Letters*, I, 213.

pendant over London is more than local color. It is pending in Africa, where Marlow is aware of "the stillness of an implacable force brooding over an inscrutable intention."[52] And he sees it again in the "half-shaped resolve" of Kurtz's native woman when her god is carried back dying to his people: "She stood looking at us without a stir, and like the wilderness itself, with an air of brooding over an inscrutable purpose."[53]

Leavis complains that throughout the story Conrad tries to make a virtue out of not knowing what he means."[54] The virtue is, in fact, in *Marlow's* not knowing what he means. We are meant to "see through" this narrator Marlow in both senses of the phrase. He can see but he cannot see clearly. Only Kurtz in the end could do that.

That we are allowed only occasionally to see glimpses of light through the Marlovian fog does not belie Guerard's point that the story is primarily about Marlow, though it calls in question the extent to which Marlow's night journey is congruent with Conrad's own journey to the Congo and its significance for him. Although Conrad seems to disappear into Marlow in the same way he does in "Youth," he remains detached. The best clues he gives to this separateness are in the incremental repetitions (as in brooding gloom) of which Marlow is not fully cognizant, and the self-contradictions into which Marlow stumbles again and again without noticing.

As the novel begins, both the first narrator and Marlow give voice to the same thoughts with subtle differences. "And this also has been one of the dark places of the earth," says Marlow, implying that this England, this London, are no longer dark, though the first narrator has just noted that they are quite hidden beneath the gloom. Then, looking at the Thames, Marlow puts in his own words what the other has just said about the "great knights-errant" of Elizabethan exploration, the "hunters for gold or pursuers of

---

[52] *Heart of Darkness*, p. 93.
[53] *Ibid.*, p. 136.
[54] Leavis, *op. cit.*, p. 180.

fame . . . bearing the sword, and often the torch . . . bearers of a spark from the sacred fire."[55] Answering, Marlow says,

> Light came out of this river since—you say Knights? Yes; but it is like a running blaze on a plain, like a flash of lightning in the clouds. We live in the flicker—may it last as long as the old earth keeps rolling! But darkness was here yesterday.[56]

Both voices give us the curious picture of torch-carriers issuing out of darkness. To the first voice it is "a spark from the sacred fire," which like the gloom this voice described over London will have a later resonance, for "sacred" in this story is a highly fraught word. Marlow, the English seaman, is modestly aware that the light of England's achievements and civilization was struck by men long dead, that he and his contemporaries bask in the reflection of their glory, but his unwary optimism proposes an absurdity: that the light shed by a grass fire or a flash of lightning might last to the end of time! Marlow seems little affected at this point by the experience he is about to recount.

Reading this story repeatedly, as we must for anything like its full effect, we know that the dark English coast before him recalls for Marlow the darkness of modern Africa, which is the natural darkness of the jungle but more than that the darkness of moral vacancy, leading to the atrocities he has beheld in Africa. In a second reading we may wonder even this early whether the moral darkness Marlow saw in Africa is, as he implies, the same as the precivilized darkness of England, or if Marlow's insight is incomplete. For the moral darkness of Africa, we learn later, is not the simple darkness of native "ignorance," but of white men who have blinded themselves and corrupted the natives by their claim to be light-bearers. If I am not mistaken, the reader must very early begin to question Marlow's ultimate "discovery," for we are from the start treated to several questionable examples of his wisdom, this Marlow who has been matured, supposedly, by his Congo experience.

---

[55] *Heart of Darkness*, p. 47.
[56] *Ibid.*, p. 49.

Compared with the English conquests, Marlow claims, the Roman conquest of England was "just robbery with violence, aggravated murder on a grand scale, and men going at it blind—as is very proper for those who tackle a darkness." In the original manuscript, we can see that Conrad originally had Marlow say of these Romans, "The best of them is they didn't get up pretty fictions about it," and make a sarcastic comparison with King Leopold's *Société Anonyme Belge.*[57] But comparisons further favor the Romans if we think of Conrad's reference (above, p. 122) to Britain's activity in South Africa as "on the same principle" as murder. One may easily wonder, too, if this very English Marlow, who says the Roman "chaps were not much account really," is not distinctly removed from the Conrad who insisted so often that Rome was the fountainhead of Western civilization and that Poland's culture derived directly from it.[58]

Although Marlow admits that English conquest, like all others, "means the taking [the earth] away from those who have a different complexion or slightly flatter noses than ourselves," he claims that the English form is redeemed by an idea: "An idea back of it; not a sentimental pretence but an idea; and an unselfish belief in the idea—something you can set up, and bow down before, and offer a sacrifice to."[59]

All critics have read this astonishing passage as a straightforward, unambiguous apology for British imperialism, spoken from Conrad's heart through Marlow's mouth. No one seems to hear the reverberations of Marlow's bitter emphasis later on figures of religious devotion, especially the worship of ideas. He will himself finally say that he had to lay the ghost of Kurtz's "gifts" with a lie, but it is left to the reader to perceive that Marlow must kill off a part of his own self-knowledge with lies in order to save the "beauti-

---

[57] MS "Heart of Darkness" (Yale University Library), p. 15.
[58] E.g., to George T. Keating in 1922: "Racially I belong to a group which has historically a political past, with a Western Roman culture derived at first from Italy and then from France; and a rather Southern temperament; an outpost of Westernism with a Roman tradition . . ." (*Life and Letters* II, 289).
[59] *Heart of Darkness*, p. 51.

ful world" of British civilization along with the beautiful world of Kurtz's Intended.

Before his last insight the cadaverous Kurtz will speak of right motives and redeeming ideas, too: "Of course you must take care of the motives—right motives—always." Marlow then wonders if Kurtz is preparing phrases for some newspaper as he speaks, even while dying, of "the furthering of my ideas. It's a duty."[60] At the beginning of the tale, Marlow's words about redeeming ideas must have a jarring effect if we follow his curious notion that the British "idea" has to become a sort of idol, reducing the minds that hold it to the posture of worshippers. The mind that masters the idea is to become its slave? Why this association of ideas and idols?

To his fellow Englishmen in this moment of wisdom early in the novel, Marlow resembles "a Buddha preaching in European clothes and without a lotus flower." Later, Marlow will repeatedly fret over the unsuitability of European clothes. As to the lotus, if it symbolizes incorruptibility, he will indeed be forced to do without it. One may reasonably recall here too the Buddha's flight into meditation, away from a decadent society.

At the first company station, Marlow is shown a picture painted by the remarkable Mr. Kurtz, "representing a woman, draped and blindfolded, carrying a lighted torch. The background was sombre —almost black. The movement of the woman was stately, and the effect of the torch-light on the face was sinister."[61] Stately *and* sinister, in Marlow's descriptive, unanalytical words—not stately *but* sinister. Only much later in the story will the reader learn that Kurtz saw his mission in Africa as that of torchbearer for white civilization. Was it not while painting the picture that Kurtz began, as Marlow might phrase it, to feel his nerves go wrong—to feel the attraction and the necessity of exacting from the natives human sacrifice to himself as God? At any rate, it was not long after he finished the painting that the natives began to adore him ritually, while his hatred for them plunged to the depth out of which came

---

[60] *Ibid.*, pp. 148–49.
[61] *Ibid.*, p. 79.

his prescription of the only method for dealing with primitive people: "Exterminate all the brutes!"

Marlow never interprets the allegory of the painting or asks why the face appears sinister. He does not connect the light of the torch-bearers that came out of England with the light on the lady's face. We remember, of course, that it was the first narrator who compared England's light to the brand of a torchcarrier. The reader may suspect that darkness—the black of the natives as well as of "ignorance" in uncivilized portions of the earth—is innocent; and hence the corollary holds, that light may have an evil influence.

We have, then, even in the first pages of the novel, repeated reversals or inversions of normal patterns of imagery, warning us to perceive that what appears to be bright and white may turn out to be dark or black in many different senses; that what seems holy and sacred may prove to be idolatrous and even diabolical; that what is clothed may be stripped. The reversal works both for the European whites and the African blacks. For Marlow will establish in his more lucid moments (and we must admit he has many) that what is black in Africa is what has a right to be there. If whiteness finally emerges as moral vacuity, blackness finally appears as reality, humanity, and truth.

The matter is more complex still, for along with the physical blackness of men and the metaphoric blackness of uncharted regions of the earth, the darkness Conrad has been suggesting all along is the forced expulsion of whatever is displaced by "light," whatever is displaced by civilization—the expulsion of Africa's native virtues by Europe's self-righteousness. Thus, "the savage who was fireman" (as Marlow phrases it)

> was an improved specimen; he could fire up a vertical boiler . . . upon my word, to look at him was as edifying as seeing a dog in a parody of breeches and a feather hat, walking on his hind-legs. A few months of training had done for that really fine chap.[62]

A few pages later Marlow notes that these servants of civilization

---

[62] *Ibid.*

were big powerful men, with not much capacity to weigh the consequences, with courage, with strength even yet, though their skins
were no longer glossy and their muscles no longer hard. . . . I
looked at them with a swift quickening of interest . . . it occurred
to me I might be eaten by them . . . though I own to you that
just then I perceived . . . how unwholesome the pilgrims looked,
and I hoped . . . that my aspect was not so . . . unappetizing.[63]

It is typical of Marlow's dilemma that while he claims to be concerned above all with self-knowledge and truth, he progresses toward deception and denial; while disdainful of the staves which all
the European civilizers carry in the Congo, he obsessively frets that
they and he himself lack anything to support them; and while
priding himself on the power of his English belief in an idea, he
can find no "real" idea in his head to support him when he needs it.

Marlow cannot interpret clearly the question of what supports a
man, though he can sense the different aspects of social life that
should put something solid "behind" a man. The European para-
sites in Africa are hollow, we are made to believe, because they have
no personal moral vision of their inhumanity and folly, but they
are also collapsible because they have nothing "behind them"—in
their society's institutions—to hold them up.[64] Marlow shares the
onus, and he is conscious of doing so. For his own reasons, he becomes a pretender like the others. He lets the brickmaker think he
is an important emissary of the company, higher in status than the
brickmaker, closer to Kurtz. "I became in an instant as much of a
pretense as the rest of the bewitched pilgrims. This simply because
I had a notion it somehow would be of help to that Kurtz whom at
the time I did not see—you understand." Instead of stopping the
foolish "papier-mâché Mephistopheles," Marlow says, "I let him
run on . . . and think what he pleased about the powers that were
behind me. I did! And there was nothing behind me!"[65]

---

[63] *Ibid.*, pp. 104–5.

[64] The general manager is made an archetype of bad government. His one hold over his
subordinates is his power to inspire uneasiness. His managerial genius is seen in the
round table he has had made to end quarrels over precedence at meals. In tacit contrast to King Arthur, "Where [the manager] sat was the first place—the rest were
nowhere" (*ibid.*, p. 74).

[65] *Ibid.*, pp. 82–83.

Just when men have most need of the institutions their civilization boasts of—particularly in "backward" lands—they find nothing available. The corner policeman and the reassuring pressures of public opinion are not only too far away, but their strength has been built on men's ability to forget the very things they would have to know in order truly to conquer a wilderness. Like one hydrogen-filled balloon tied to another, when Kurtz's diabolism is revealed to him, Marlow says Kurtz "had kicked himself loose of the earth. . . . and I before him did not know whether I stood on the ground or floated in the air."[66]

Marlow's sharpening awareness of "reality" suffers a bifurcation early in the story. On one side is his consciousness of what is real for the Africans, which turns out to be their natural lives and surroundings in Africa. What is real for the Westerners reduces itself quickly to their reasons for being there. "The word 'ivory' rang in the air, was whispered, was sighed. You would think they were praying to it."[67] But the ivory, which is white like the men, is the mean side of another aim that is at once more exalted and more pernicious. As ivory has become the idol of the foolish run of European pilgrims, the ideal of racial whiteness and all it supposedly stands for has become the idol of "superior" white men like Kurtz. Marlow was prepared to find Kurtz a man for whom the ivory was only the outward sign of an inward grace. The allegoric picture and the reports of Kurtz's artistic, intellectual, and persuasive powers whetted his appeal for the Marlow who described himself as a man that would offer sacrifices to an idea, as a man who imagined his best weapon against the jungle was his "voice," his power of speech[68]—"for good or evil mine is the speech that cannot be silenced."[69]

Progressively Conrad tangles the Marlow who will surrender to

---

[66] *Ibid.*, p. 144.

[67] *Ibid.*, p. 76.

[68] It seems to me that Conrad is here by insinuation recanting the notion presented in *The Rescue* that refinement of speech is a proof of cultural progress. See above, pp. 99, 104–5.

[69] *Heart of Darkness*, p. 97.

Kurtz in his own yarn. The irony is Conrad's, not Marlow's, when Marlow reveals that Kurtz had "appropriately" been entrusted with the job of giving guidance to the International Society for the Suppression of Savage Customs. ("All Europe contributed to the making of Kurtz," and likewise the society for suppressing the natives is "International.") Marlow's comment on the report is characteristically confusing: "eloquent . . . but too high-strung, I think." While he spins the yarn, the thought seems to occur to him that there was something a bit "ominous" in Kurtz's paragraph asserting that the white men must necessarily appear to the savages as "supernatural beings," who by the "simple exercise of our will" can exert practically unbounded power "for good." This same report, he says, made him "tingle with enthusiasm." And when he finally does express irony, he rises to it considerably later than the quick reader gives him credit for. It is only when he ironically calls the report's "valuable" postscript ("Exterminate all the brutes!") "the exposition of a method" that we know Marlow has at last reached Conrad's level of irony. Even now, however, Marlow (aboard the "Nellie," supposing himself freed of Kurtz's influence and "gifts") has missed an important aspect of the story he is telling. His perception that Kurtz in his madness was driven to an ultimate insight which was, in the report, the "exposition of a method" does not suggest to Marlow, even while he comments wryly on it, that all talk of method—efficiency—is in itself despicable in a report that from beginning to end is vicious by its premises that all savage customs should be suppressed and that there is something almost supernatural about white men.[70]

It is only on the level of animal reflex that Marlow makes a decisive move against his heritage. As the nightmare journey nears its climax, his very clothes (one thinks of *Sartor Resartus*), tokens of his European "reality," become irritating. After the blood of the native helmsman stains his shoes, he impulsively casts them overboard. His impulse, with one foot as it were, is to dissociate himself

---

[70] *Ibid.*, p .118.

from the blood-guilt; with the other, to strip away what will be of little use in facing "the wilderness." Guerard is right too, surely, that Marlow must divest himself of these tokens of his conscious mind, "tossed overboard" before the meeting with Kurtz. Guerard calls attention to the curious sentence: "Talking with . . . I flung one shoe overboard, and became aware that that was exactly what I had been looking forward to—a talk with Kurtz."[71] All these suggestions are wanted to explain Marlow's comment: "To tell you the truth, I was morbidly anxious to change my shoes and socks."[72]

Although Marlow repeatedly perceives with "relief" that what is "real" (and we must also read "right") in Africa is what needs no excuse for being there, we must observe that he never adequately judges the unreality of one aspect of his own culture which, along the trail of his journey, has afforded him other instances of "relief." This is the criterion of efficiency. It has been taken for granted too long that Marlow speaks of Conrad in his devotion to this Western standard of measurement. *Heart of Darkness* may be read in part as a profound inquiry into this very point of view.

Douglas Hewitt, among other discerning readers of the novel, flatly accepts the idea that Marlow's "immediate work gains for him the significance of a moral principle."[73] If so, it is a moral principle only for want of something better. The work that saved the ship and also the corps of men in *The Nigger of the "Narcissus"* had its proper eulogy there. But in the Congo all "work"—even Marlow's— becomes inexpressibly stupid. True, even here Marlow has the sense that through the work he was hired for comes the "chance to find yourself,"[74] some of the "self-knowledge" which, he says, is "the most you can hope for."[75]

---

[71] *Ibid.*, p. 113.

[72] The "slippers" Marlow later puts on might be associated with sleep or one's subconscious life, but anything which, after the fashion of tropical countries, slips on— as opposed to a European laced shoe—could be referred to when Marlow says he put on "a pair of dry slippers" (*ibid.*, p. 119). The accent seems to be on the clean, dry, and native rather than on the apparel of private life.

[73] *Joseph Conrad: A Reassessment* (Cambridge: Bowes and Bowes, 1952), p. 21.

[74] *Heart of Darkness*, p. 85.

[75] *Ibid.*, p. 150.

We remember Conrad had written his Conservative publisher that *Heart of Darkness* was a story ("not gloomy") about the "criminality of inefficiency and pure selfishness when tackling the civilizing work in Africa."[76] In the story Marlow makes much of the inefficiency and selfishness he sees everywhere along his journey in Africa. But it is the criminality of the civilizing work itself that receives the heaviest emphasis in the novel as a whole. Thus Conrad allowed his publisher to be as much deceived as was Marlow by the conflicting emphases of the story.

Until we see Marlow meet the Belgian company's chief accountant, we have only vague intimations that Marlow's point of view is in any way different from Conrad's on this matter. Here for the first time we discover that Marlow is capable of seeking relief not only in what is "natural and true" but also in what is merely familiar, even though he knows it to be, in the setting, unnatural and false. In typically misleading language Marlow remarks to his listeners—and one of them is an accountant, we remember—that he would not mention the chief accountant at all if it had not been he who had first mentioned the name of Kurtz. Still, Marlow goes on at some length about him. The accountant won his *respect*, he says, because "in the great demoralization of the land he kept up his appearance. That's backbone. His starched collars and got-up shirt-fronts were achievements of character."[77] Marlow partially recognizes this clerk as a sort of "hairdresser's dummy," another figure from a make-believe world like the "harlequin" and the "papier-mâché Mephistopheles" he will meet later on. The three are linked to each other and to the absurd ivory hunters who are like pilgrims with staves.

We remember that in his letters Conrad claimed that all his meanings in his fiction are brought out by lighting and *grouping* of characters. One naturally recognizes the grouping of the masqueraders in the Congo. What distinguishes *Heart of Darkness*

---

[76] See above, p. 120.
[77] *Heart of Darkness*, p. 68.

from, say, *Lord Jim, Nostromo,* and *The Secret Agent,* however, is that all the groupings of Europeans tend to become one group. They are all hollow men. There is in this novel, strikingly, no individual or fellowship that forces our sympathy out of the complex of prosecutions and appeals over which we are made to sit in judgment.

At the moment of greatest crisis, when Marlow is faced with "a choice of nightmares" and will side with the diabolical Kurtz against the flabbier devils of the European trading company, we may too quickly assume that there is some radical difference between the two nightmares. Reading more cautiously, we discover that Kurtz's characteristics can be found in diluted solution in all the other Europeans, and Marlow himself, in his own way, betrays his kinship. What Marlow with incomplete irony calls the accountant's "achievements of character" are revealed by the meticulously white linen he wears. Marlow, as marveler, registers but never questions or later recalls that when he asked the clerk "how he managed to sport such linen," the clerk answered "with just the faintest blush," that he had "been teaching one of the native women about the station. It was difficult. She had a distaste for the work." Kurtz, too, had influence with a native woman. Hearing the clerk's explanation, Marlow—the moralist who sanctifies Britain's efficient imperialism—comments, "Thus this man had verily accomplished something."

Clearly the accountant's devotion to his job is successful only because he can obliterate from his mind all conflicting intrusions from the African wilderness. When he tells Marlow about Kurtz, more efficient than all other agents in sending out ivory, a dying European who has just come out of Kurtz's territory is lying within earshot. His groaning distracts the accountant, but the sick man is too ill to offer any correcting information on the subject of Kurtz. The enchanted silence protecting Kurtz from the inquiries of his fellow workers is thus protected by the celebrated job sense of the efficient clerk, compartmentalizing himself against all disruptive knowledge.

This scene prepares us for the superbly dramatic last pages of the story when Marlow, too, will close off a sentimental lady—and not only a lady but himself and all Europe—against the disruptive truth of Kurtz's experience.

"Everything else in the station," of course, "was in a muddle—heads, things, buildings," except only this miracle of neatness, who significantly is the first to mention the name of Kurtz. He is in fact a clue to Kurtz, who is also a creature standing in the forefront of his kind, distinguished by special "virtues." Marlow insists that these superior individuals, to whom will be added the Russian "harlequin," in some way relieve the stupidity of the farce. Finally, taken together, they merely define the only alternative choice to the nightmare of delusion in which the manager of the company is the main figure.

In the design of the novel there are, thus, the extremes represented on one hand as efficiency and intellectual superiority, signaled by the accountant and the "harlequin" respectively, pointing to Kurtz as head, and on the other hand extremes of inefficiency and inanity, represented by the anonymous officials of the company, by the "brickmaker" and the manager. When Marlow chooses the nightmare dominated by Kurtz in preference to the nightmare of the inferior traders, he gravitates to the pole of his own values, without fully exploring his kinship with Kurtz.

A further exposé of Marlow's devotion to efficiency is built up around the handbook of seamanship which Marlow discovers in an abandoned hut, in front of which hung a "flag of some sort" and a "neatly stacked wood-pile"—the one a symbol of yet another nation planting its claim in Africa, the other a fine exemplum of good method. The manual, "*An Inquiry into some Points of Seamanship*, by a man Tower, Towson—some such name,"[78] inspires Marlow with its "singleness of intention, and honest concern with the right way of going to work." And he experiences another of his moments of relief, the "delicious sensation of having come upon

---

[78] The book is obviously suggested by Alfred Henry Alston's manual of seamanship, which Conrad kept from his own training days and is still saved by his son John as one of Conrad's favorite books. Alston probably also gave Conrad the name of Captain Allistoun in *The Nigger of the "Narcissus."*

something unmistakably real."[79] In the margins, however, are unreadable notes, which he learns only later are not ciphers but notations in Russian. It turns out that the owner of the book, like the accountant "wonderfully neat," is the son of an archpriest, who has run away to sea and then to Africa in search of experience and ideas. He reminds one a bit of Lord Jim and of Conrad himself at a certain stage. But like Marlow, this young man is capable of marveling without discernment and is a worshipper at the shrine of efficiency and ideas, which is the altar over which Kurtz, the most "successful" of all the ivory hunters, is God.

As the "hairdresser's dummy" accountant had some of the virtues that hallow Kurtz, so too this Russian "harlequin"—another figure from make-believe worlds, with whom belongs also the "papier-mâché Mephistopheles." The marvelously mended suit of the Russian might remind us of the patchwork talents of Kurtz, the "universal genius," whom Marlow thinks of as "draped nobly in the folds of a gorgeous eloquence,"[80] the Kurtz who is also the patchwork of all Europe. And the glamorous young Russian is indeed a thing of patches—a snatch of several different explorers (Mungo Park, as Conrad describes the fair youth in "Geography and Some Explorers," the quixotic Roger Casement, and Conrad himself), all possessed by the "absolutely pure, uncalculating, unpractical spirit of adventure."[81] Is he not, too, a remnant of earlier history and the earlier part of Marlow's tale, of those "knights-errant of the sea" who bearing "a spark from the sacred fire," had first opened the dark places of the earth? In him we see man's continuing expansive energy, gullibly innocent of its association with all the despotisms intruding on the integrity of Africa.[82]

---

[79] *Heart of Darkness*, p. 99.

[80] *Ibid.*, pp. 154–55.

[81] *Ibid.*, p. 126.

[82] Something of the Russian sycophant's relationship to Kurtz may have been put in Conrad's mind by Sir Henry Stanley's "prosaic newspaper stunt" in trailing David Livingstone—who, like Kurtz, was a "restless wanderer refusing to go home any more." (Conrad's description of Stanley's discovery and of Livingstone is in "Geography and Some Explorers," *Last Essays*, pp. 16–17.) The Russian would of course be a more ingenuous Stanley, and Kurtz a Livingstone wanting in all the sympathetic

When Conrad saw what the young Russian saw in Africa, it changed his life. ("Before the Congo I was just a mere animal."[83]) But in *Heart of Darkness* not one of these intruders is changed into a moral being by what he sees. Or rather, only Kurtz—ultimately, when it's too late—becomes a moral agent. Marlow then sides with him in his "victory" but only imperfectly: "I was within a hair's breadth of the last opportunity for pronouncement, and I found with humiliation that probably I would have nothing to say. . . . He had summed up—he had judged. . . . After all, this was the expression of some sort of belief."[84]

If taken as evidence of Marlow's moral enlightenment after meeting Kurtz, this is most unsatisfactory. Much earlier Marlow was convinced that Kurtz "had come out equipped with moral ideas of some sort."[85] Now Marlow has only been reassured, after frightful disillusionment, that indeed Kurtz achieved "some sort of belief."

Kurtz may in the end see himself even as he is seen. But Marlow? We watch him cling to Kurtz as a fugitive clings to a foothold above an abyss. Having clutched at one inadequate support after another among the hopeful symbols of his culture in Africa: the efficient accountant, the work he himself has been trained for, the manual of seamanship—all comforts having to do with good method—at perhaps the most critical moment in the story, when the general

---

qualities Conrad recognizes in the essay. The Wyndham of *The Rescue* manuscript, another who would not go home, was closer to Livingstone. Guerard has suggested Stanley as a model not for the Russian but for Kurtz, being "no mean example of a man who could gloss over the extermination of savages with pious moralisms which were very possibly 'sincere' " (*Conrad the Novelist*, p. 34).

If I have urged that Rhodes was a likelier model for Kurtz than Livingstone or the real agent Conrad met in the Congo, the Belgian Georges Antoine Klein (whose name appears instead of Kurtz through much of the Yale manuscript), it is partly because I think too much stress has been laid on these two elsewhere. Livingstone and Klein may have loomed large in Conrad's mind in 1890 when he went to the Congo, but Rhodes and other British imperialists must have troubled him more eight years later when he came to write the story. Jean-Aubry describes the autobiographical background of *Heart of Darkness* in *Life and Letters*, I, 119–43; in *The Sea Dreamer*, pp. 152–76.

[83] *Life and Letters*, I, 141.
[84] *Heart of Darkness*, p. 151.
[85] *Ibid.*, p. 88.

manager uses just this standard for judging Kurtz, Marlow is revolted.

In answer to the manager's remark that "Mr. Kurtz's methods had ruined the district" (for trading purposes), Marlow confusedly mumbles "No method at all,"[86] meaning what it is hard to guess, unless that at this point he refuses to think at all of Kurtz's methods in collecting ivory, this spokesman for British efficiency. Of course, it is because the manager cannot see that there is more than a question of method in Kurtz's madness that Marlow feels he has "never breathed an atmosphere so vile" and turns "mentally to Kurtz for relief."[87] Kurtz has discovered (in himself) evil unsimulated, though until his very last words he goes on posing as a standard-bearer of European superiority in matters of efficiency and ideas. Through his absolute possession by evil, Kurtz "exists in the moral universe even before pronouncing judgment on himself with his dying breath," Guerard points out.[88] But where does Marlow stand in this universe?

Identifying Marlow closely with Conrad, Guerard suggests that the novel expresses a deferred collision between "the adventurous Conrad and Conrad the moralist."[89] But surely *that* collision is conveyed better in Marlow's meeting with the Russian than in his meeting with Kurtz. Face to face with Kurtz, Marlow experiences a more serious collision, between Conrad the British subject and Conrad the moralist. The question left hanging is whether good work any more than evil work justifies the empire-builder in Africa.

In the iconography of the novel, Marlow's talk of "devotion to efficiency" has a religious overtone no less menacing than his reference to an "unselfish belief in the idea—something you can set up, and bow down before, and offer a sacrifice to." We cannot separate these images altogether from the "pilgrims," the ivory ("you

---

[86] *Ibid.*, p. 131.
[87] *Ibid.*, pp. 137–38.
[88] *Conrad the Novelist*, p. 36.
[89] *Ibid.*, p. 38.

would think they were praying to it"), the young Russian's worship of Kurtz's ideas, and Kurtz himself, self-apotheosized, "insatiable of splendid appearances, of frightful realities."

Of course I am speaking of the public or political logic of Marlow's narrative. As Moser and Guerard have shown, the same material lends itself to psychological analysis on a more private level. But whether or not the latter is "deeper" as far as the significance of the novel is concerned, it is unlikely that the tale's psychological content can contradict what Guerard calls the "more superficial" meanings of the story.[90] It is important to decide, most crucially, whether "the jungle" and all it signifies for Conrad in *Heart of Darkness* is evil in the sense of intrinsically alien to man's social instincts, as both Guerard and Moser imply, or whether primitive life represents the "existential" truth of human relationships which has had to be suppressed by racialist "civilizers."

Moser writes that "going into the jungle seems to Marlow like traveling into one's own past, into the world of one's dreams, into the subconscious." Finding the jungle described in the story as "lurking death," "profound darkness," and "evil" (all these separate from their contexts), he concludes that "the vegetation imagery means much more than female menace; it means the truth, the darkness, the evil, the death which lie within us, which we must recognize in order to be truly alive."[91] The implication is that in siding with Kurtz, Marlow is in some Freudian or Nietzschean way attracted into a revolt against the cage that society has made for him. But he makes plain that the savages in the jungle are as "virtuous" and humane in their society as he is in his own. His revolt is only against the falsehoods that are ruining his society. If he finally suppresses the truth he has seen, it is not because it is evil but because he is by nature conservative in the political sense and suppresses it for the good of white society, as Chamberlain suppressed the truth about Rhodes.

Cannibalism and sexual perversion exist in the jungle, as in dif-

---

[90] *Ibid.*, p. 34.

[91] *Joseph Conrad: Achievement and Decline* (Cambridge, Mass.: Harvard University Press, 1957), p. 80.

ferent forms they exist in cities. But one must read something foreign into Conrad's text (both here and in the excised Wyndham episode in *The Rescue* manuscript) if one is to conclude that familiarity with the "dark" races breeds contempt for one's "better" in the sense of "more social" instincts. Marlow puts it clearly, that "the wilderness" had found Kurtz out early, "had taken on him a terrible vengeance," had "echoed loudly within him *because he was hollow at the core*."[92] There is a condition. Freud, denying the possibility of moral hollowness, would say that primitive nature is "morally" dangerous to all men living in more advanced societies. In his tentative way, Marlow sees that it is dangerous only to the man who is not "at least . . . as much of a man as these on the shore."[93]

Time is treacherous. This is part of the truth that Marlow says is "hidden—luckily, luckily."[94] The river that carried Marlow back in time "to the earliest beginnings of the world" also carried him forward to civilization's superman, Kurtz. And this conquering genius, by the might of his Nietzschean will, had not conquered but surrendered to the savage customs he most hated. The implication is that he and the people that contributed to his making will disappear into the reality of Africa as torchlight disappears in sunlight.

Marlow, who will not allow that Kurtz's experience in the Congo is vitally relevant to Europe's future action, is yet aware that its "shadow" can follow him home. Into the lady's house with him goes the sound of savage drums, like the heartbeats "of a conquering darkness." In spite of the darkness, the wilderness is vibrantly alive and throbbing, while in her "radiance," the lady inhabits a "sarcophagus." She is a "familiar Shade," recalling Dido in Virgil's underworld. And it is her Europe that is the underworld. Marlow's interview with Kurtz's Intended, like everything else in the story, approaches allegory in its suggestiveness without depart-

---

[92] *Heart of Darkness*, p. 131. The italics are mine.
[93] *Ibid.*, p. 97.
[94] *Ibid.*, p. 93.

ing from the concrete experience a man like Marlow would have registered in such a situation.

Marlow has made too much of lying all through the story to convince us at the end that he lies only to save the woman. Guerard has suggested that in the scene much earlier, where Marlow is about to tell of his encounter with Kurtz but stops to tell about Kurtz's Intended instead, Conrad was "perhaps compelled to defer climax in this way."[95] The intrusion has another effect besides deferring the climax, however. The story, for all its length, is bound from start to finish by the repetitions in Marlow's random observations which Marlow is not himself able to correlate. In his half-awareness, at the beginning of the tale, Marlow informed his listeners that there was an aunt—the lady who pulled strings to secure his Congo job with the "Continental concern"—who lived in a make-believe world, "too beautiful altogether," that "would go to pieces before the first sunset"[96] if it were to be set up. Yet we learn, too, that the aunt is merely expressing illusions held by most people in the city like a whited sepulcher, particularly the people in the trading house where Marlow is hired, a house as still as the "city of the dead."[97] Then in the moment before Marlow's meeting with Kurtz, we are reminded again that there is a world, a woman's world, that must be kept inviolate "lest ours get worse"; that the knowledge of Kurtz we are about to gain is going to have to be killed with a lie so that the woman's world, now the world of the Intended, will remain intact.[98]

Shortly after Kurtz's death—far enough from this disclosure for Marlow's oversight not to seem absurd—we learn that Marlow feels compelled to lie about Kurtz not to a woman, to save a woman's world, but to men, representatives of commerce and finance who had a right to know about Kurtz but could not possibly, Marlow thinks, be allowed to know. He assures one of them that "Mr.

---

[95] *Conrad the Novelist*, p. 41.
[96] *Heart of Darkness*, p. 59.
[97] *Ibid.*, p. 57.
[98] Henry Steele Commager, Jr., has remarked on this. See chap. i, n. 28.

Kurtz's knowledge, however extensive, did not bear upon the problems of commerce or administration."[99] Not a direct lie, perhaps, but certainly an effort to keep them in a beautiful world which is not a real world.

It should be clear when Marlow's lies for Kurtz are considered together—and they are given us in good order for a proper perspective on the final scene with the Intended—that the male world of civilized Europe no less than the woman's world is entirely "out of it." The house of the Intended in the final scene (as the sun sets on it) is a good image for the "house" of all Europe. Morton Dauwen Zabel keenly observes that the Intended is merely "the vestal of the ideal to which [Kurtz's] genius has been dedicated."[100] As the allegorical female torchcarrier embodies more meaning than the painter intended, so his Intended is more than the representative of the woman's world that Marlow takes her for.

Thus critics conclude too hastily that she is only one more example of Conrad's ineptitude in treating the subject of romantic love; they do not trust Conrad to have seen the effect his words create. He had, however, chosen a similar image a few years earlier in alluding to his own state of mind when he felt creatively barren and enervated while writing *The Rescue*: ". . . my very being seems faded and thin like the ghost of a blonde and sentimental woman, haunting romantic ruins pervaded by rats."[101]

It is worth recalling that in *The Inheritors*, the idea for which was of course Ford's, the Woman is a peculiar kind of heroine, representing not only the feminism of her age (which Ford with Con-

---

[99] *Heart of Darkness*, p. 153. Marlow's refusal to admit that Kurtz's atrocious successes had anything to do with commerce and finance is an obvious evasion which amounts to a lie. In *The Rescue* MS, too, Martin Travers isolated "administrative and commercial problems" from their base in the moral condition of human life. Travers—in the MS; the passage is revised and sweetened in the book—made it his business "to study the impact of western progress upon the barbarous races, mostly from an administrative and commercial point of view where the pain, injustice, the violence, are out of sight and the profitable side of civilization may be seen . . ." (*The Rescue* MS, p. 224; p. 123 in the book).
[100] Introduction to *Youth*, p. 21.
[101] Letter to Garnett, June 19, 1896, *Letters from Conrad*, p. 59.

rad detested), but also the spirit of the age itself, which they pictured as arriving with a new menace and called "the fourth dimension."

Although Marlow is conscious that "sunlight can be made to lie,"[102] he is never able to see that darkness, too, may be deceptive, and that what is dark may not be kept so. He thinks it is only his own memory of Kurtz's "horror" that accompanies him like a living shadow into the European scene of death, as still as "a well-kept alley in a cemetery."[103] No wonder he has to kill this ghost with the lie which he said before, when lying for Kurtz to a man, has always for him "a taint of death, a flavour of mortality."[104] Anything so much alive as the dead Kurtz (and, we may add, as the "half-shaped resolve" beginning to mobilize in Africa) seems a threat to the "whiteness" of the lady's house, the "cold and monumental whiteness." Conrad plays intricately with his design. Against her white background, the lady is in black mourning, and the daylight begins to recede. Metaphysical darkness fades into the ordinary; metaphorical light into what can be precisely seen. The blonde and sentimental lady exerts her depressing radiance over the closing story. Almost aware of his impotence before this encroaching "radiance," this inversion of real light and darkness, "with a dull anger stirring" in him, as if repeating his spontaneous gesture when he blew out the candle on Kurtz's dying words, Marlow blows out the candle of truth in a final pretense of saving the lady from what "would have been too dark . . . altogether."[105] But he and his fellow Englishmen sit looking at the Thames, which ominously is a "tranquil waterway leading . . . into the heart of an immense darkness."

Marlow perfectly exemplifies one "normal" human response, which Conrad described elsewhere in a political essay:

And everybody knows the power of lies which go about clothed in coats of many colours, whereas, as is well known, Truth has no such

[102] *Heart of Darkness*, p. 154.
[103] *Ibid.*, p. 155.
[104] *Ibid.*, p. 82.
[105] *Ibid.*, p. 162.

advantage, and for that reason is often suppressed as not altogether proper for everyday purposes. It is not often recognized, because it is not always fit to be seen.[106]

But are we to assume that when the truth is not "fit to be seen," as in *Heart of Darkness*, Conrad (leaving aside Marlow) wants it suppressed for society's advantage, for—let us say—the good of "national sentiment"? This is one conclusion, and the one that is usually reached by readers trying to explain Marlow's last lie for Kurtz,[107] but still far from satisfactory.

In *Heart of Darkness* one major theme, if not the ruling theme, is that civilization depends for its conquest of the earth on a combination of lies and forgetfulness. Conrad's debt to Nietzsche (with whose thought his friend Garnett was at the time deeply occupied[108]) seems nowhere more apparent. One of Nietzsche's aphorisms would have made an excellent epigram for the story: " 'I did that,' says my memory. 'I could not have done that,' says my pride, and remains inexorable. Eventually—the memory yields."[109] Out of this profound and involuntary human perversity come all the devils and all the nightmares that Marlow encounters in Africa, as well as his own oversights or forgetfulness concerning Britain's activities in "the dark continent."

Marlow and his friends at the end of the novel sit looking at the Thames, seeming to see its course run back into the Congo, which Marlow compared to an immense snake uncoiled. The snake is motionless, perhaps, but venomous, ready to recoil in the heart of that immense darkness. Marlow continues to sit like a meditating

---

[106] "The Crime of Partition," *Notes on Life and Letters*, p. 133.

[107] As a possible interpretation of Marlow's motive in lying, Thomas Moser suggests that the "scene can be read . . . as an indictment of this woman, safe and ignorant in her complacent, Belgian bourgeois existence; she does not deserve to hear the truth" (*Joseph Conrad*, p. 81). Though this ascribes an uncharacteristic spitefulness to Marlow, the conjecture indicates the breadth of the scene's ambiguity. Marlow's tone of voice throughout the novel convinces me, nevertheless, that the irony in this scene is Conrad's alone, that Marlow behaves here, as before consistently, as a punctilious, well-meaning British conservative.

[108] See *Letters from Conrad*, pp. 157–58.

[109] Friedrich Nietzsche, "Beyond Good and Evil," *The Philosophy of Nietzsche* (New York: Modern Library, 1927), p. 451.

Buddha, but we are left to meditate on what he has failed to see: that England's efficiency and ideas will not save her from the half-shaped resolve in Africa which will hardly distinguish one white man from another when Africa's moment comes. All Europe contributed to the making of Kurtz, Marlow said. It seems the major burden of the story to reveal what Marlow has failed to see—that England is in no way exempt.

"All Europe contributed." But did Poland, which Conrad so often insisted was a part of Europe? The question is not impertinent if we consider that, according to his own testimony, Poland ("whose ideals are the same [as those of western Europe], but whose situation is unique"[110]) was the one nation that stood immune to the particular dangers of the European powers in Africa, the one nation that he believed had never lusted after empire or made up "pretty fictions" to condone political crimes. As I have already suggested (p. 79), Conrad's acceptance of the political premises of Polish romantic emigration prose demonstrates that he tacitly held in reserve a suspended ideal of political correctness, which—however removed from the arena of political conflicts in his day—served him in his fictional reflections on human affairs.

In his essay on "The Crime of Partition," published in the *Fortnightly Review* in 1919, Conrad allows the world its first complete view of the compartment in his mind devoted to Polish politics—only that year, when Polish independence, which for many years he imagined a sentimental dream, had become a reality in the Treaty of Versailles. Now, describing Poland's early political maturity, he mentions that she has never in her history added to her territory *by conquest* but only by "a spontaneous and complete union of sovereign states choosing deliberately the way of peace," and he adds that the "Polish State offers a singular instance of an extremely liberal administrative federalism which, in its Parliamentary life as well as its international politics, presented a complete unity of feeling and purpose."[111] Poland can boast, furthermore, that in "all

---

[110] "The Crime of Partition," *Notes on Life and Letters*, p. 129.
[111] *Ibid.*, p. 120.

the history of Polish oppression there was only one shot fired which was not in battle. . . . And the man who fired it in Paris at the Emperor Alexander II, was but an individual connected with no organisation."[112] To the envy even of Englishmen he could say that

> when heads were falling on the scaffolds all over Europe there was only one political execution in Poland—only one; and as to that there still exists a tradition that the great Chancellor who democratised Polish institutions, and had to order it in pursuance of his political purpose, could not settle that matter with his conscience till the day of his death.[113]

We cannot rightly distinguish the fixed point of vision in *Heart of Darkness* if we reckon without this heroic phantom that deliberately abstains from the making of Kurtz.

The vital paradox in Marlow's Congo experience points beyond Conrad's own conflicting sympathies to a didactic intention, neatly disguised so that only the wise English reader might profit from it. While the careless would miss it, the imprudent at least would fail to find in it material for destructive propaganda. As a method of writing fiction, Conrad's strategy reminds one of Leo Strauss's remarks on the behavior of certain Jewish philosophers, writing under conditions of persecution not unlike Conrad's family's conditions in Poland. Strauss reflects that,

> if an able writer who has a clear mind and a perfect knowledge of the orthodox view and all its ramifications, contradicts surreptitiously and as it were in passing one of its necessary presuppositions or consequences which he explicitly recognizes and maintains everywhere else, we can reasonably suspect that he was opposed to the orthodox system as such and—we must study the whole book all over again, with much greater care and much less naïveté than ever before. In some cases, we possess even explicit evidence proving that the author has indicated his views on the most important subjects only between the lines.[114]

---

[112] *Ibid.*, p. 130.
[113] *Ibid.*, p. 132.
[114] Leo Strauss, *Persecution and the Art of Writing* (Glencoe, Ill.: Free Press, 1952), p. 32.

So with Conrad in *Heart of Darkness*, we see an extraordinary example of political fiction, conveying its most important meanings through the evasions and self-contradictions of a narrator who is sympathetically one with his "orthodox" readers.

This is not to say that Conrad belongs with writers like Maimonides, who (according to Strauss) wrote primarily for the initiated reader who could decode his ciphers, for I think Conrad spoke sincerely (if wishfully) when he said he did not write for "a limited coterie . . . which would have been odious to me as throwing a doubt on the soundness of my belief in the solidarity of all mankind in simple ideas and sincere emotions."[115]

The Marlow of *Heart of Darkness* has a counterpart in *Lord Jim*, who is not however the Marlow of that novel. Jim's Marlow chooses this man to be receiver of a letter telling of Jim's last days. He is chosen because, says Marlow, he "alone showed an interest in [Jim] that survived the telling of the story." But this nameless sympathizer, like the Marlow of the Congo story, was a more typical Englishman than Jim's Marlow. He had contended that Europeans could live their lives in primitive lands only if they had "a firm conviction in the truth of ideas racially our own, in whose name are established the order, the morality of an ethical progress." He had said, "We want a belief in its necessity and its justice to make a worthy sacrifice of our lives." Jim's Marlow thereupon wonders if Jim—who lacked these convictions and relied on something other than the morality of ethical progress ("of all mankind Jim had no dealings but with himself")—"at the last . . . had not confessed to a faith mightier than the laws of order and progress."[116]

Heart of Darkness, no less than *Nostromo* (the next major novel, chronologically speaking, Conrad wrote after finishing, in 1900, the passage from *Lord Jim*), probes deeply into the insufficiency of trust in order and progress. As I suggested in Chapter Two, the Marlow of *Lord Jim* stands in judgment to some extent on the English so-

---

[115] Inscription in Richard Curle's first edition of *Chance* (George T. Keating Collection, Yale University).
[116] *Lord Jim*, pp. 338–39.

ciety from which Jim is justly an outcast. By contrast, the Marlow of *Heart of Darkness* is an Englishman entirely given over to reflection on the tangle of his commitments, which come to him largely through his racial and national heritage—what is "behind him" and "in him" and the choices allowed him as a European meeting the humanity of Africa.

And Conrad puts us inside this Englishman, with just enough difference so that we can perceive the inability to transcend his circumstances that blocks every man, which no man can disclose completely in himself because of the limitations of self-awareness. To confess this incompetence in one's own person is one thing. Marlow does it all through the story. But to discover it in another soul, as Conrad does in the sympathetic Marlow, is to remind us that even while confessing our limitations, we may be evading other serious deficiencies; that confession itself can be a kind of excuse for partial honesty, a bid for absolution that will purge sins rankling unrecognized along with the sins one is ready to admit. "The heavens do not fall for such a trifle," Marlow tells his listeners finally, waving aside the lie for Kurtz which is central to the story, the climax of his long and hazy confession aboard the "Nellie." But the heavens will fall because of the truth Marlow, along with the rest of the white race, has suppressed.

In *The Rescue* gropingly, but in *Heart of Darkness* fully and for the first time, Conrad used politics in literature after the manner prescribed by Napoleon when he said, "Politics should be the great spring of modern tragedy . . . it [is] only necessary to place your personages in opposition to other passions or other inclinations, under the absolute influence of this powerful necessity." And, "Policy should take the place in our theater of ancient fatality . . . which rendered Oedipus a criminal although he was not guilty."[117] Marlow's "descent" to Stanley Falls, "as if to the center of the earth," is the descent of a man, following the passion for innocent adventure, into guilt, though he is innocent. The extent to which

---

[117] See chap. ii, p. 80.

Marlow is aware of the guilt he shoulders in meeting the truth about Kurtz, the extent of his suffering for this awareness, is the measure of the novel's tragic power.

The work is not formally tragic, but I think this is for different reasons than those given, say, by Leavis. Conrad makes the story center in Marlow, who neither acts decisively nor suffers conclusively. Because the story's important revelation is Kurtz, and Kurtz does drink the whole cup of agony for his crimes, there is a tragic scene within the narrative. But Conrad is more concerned with a member of the audience whom he brings upon the stage in Marlow. Sophocles might have done the same with a member of his chorus of citizens. All modern tragedy, from at least as early as Shakespeare's *Hamlet*, has leanings in this direction, transferring our care from the men who perform the acts of villainy to an innocent bystander who is compromised and then expected to react in a manner appropriate to the evil discovered.

Marlow's response is superb, once we agree that he *is* compromised by Kurtz and that he does act appropriately. His guilt grows with his gradual submission to Kurtz, which is gradual submission to Europe's atrocious presumptions in "dark" lands. No less than Oedipus, he gouges his eyes out, inflicting the lie upon himself and then crawling back for shelter to the "beautiful world" that must, when the story ends, continue in blissful ignorance of waiting nemesis. It won't strike in Marlow's lifetime or in Conrad's. There is no single figure—like the "eminent and prosperous" Greek hero —to bear the whole burden of his society's crime and to expiate it with his own ruin. The ancient gods were sometimes satisfied with the sacrifice of a single hero, but modern politics is a hungrier despot and more inclined to take its revenges slowly.

"The ideas (that live) should be combatted, not the men who die."

Letter from Conrad to William Blackwood,
October 29, 1897

"Of course reason is hateful,—but why? Because it demonstrates (to those who have the courage) that we, living, are out of life,—utterly out of it."

Letter to R. B. Cunninghame Graham,
January 14, 1898

CHAPTER FIVE

Nostromo

Like other modern intellectuals, Conrad is haunted by the ghost of the Inquisition and ideological warfare in general. Like the others, whether he will or no, he inherits the premises of the Inquisition: that ideas distinguish and objectify good and evil in history, and there can be no escape from or muddling through the ideological issues. Conrad speaks to his English readers from the point of view of one who embraces their social equanimity but scorns their unreason and their complacency toward what is occurring in the world. His dilemma, as we saw in *Heart of Darkness*, is that he can find in practice nothing better than English society while feeling at the same time that its presumptions are not as righteous as they are made out to be. The English live, as it were, in a beautiful insular world which might not survive the first sunset if the truth were brought home to them.

The logic of ideas in history is discovered partly through Marlow's effort not to face it in *Heart of Darkness*. In *Nostromo* Conrad brings this logic to the surface. Out of a mood of empty-headedness and creative impotency before his passively waiting English readers[1]

---

[1] See Author's Note to *Nostromo* (New York: Modern Library, 1951), p. 1. Because this edition more closely follows the manuscript of the novel in the library of the Rosenbach Foundation, and because in certain important passages (see below, pp.

came the idea of offering them a novel in which historic process could be seen (as it could not in *Heart of Darkness*) as the real subject of the story, more important than any of the people in it. Silver is the real hero,[2] he pointed out, because what the silver stands for—material interests—have become the rationale of modern economics and politics. Conrad asks how it happened and what will happen next. Ideas are to be combatted.

Conrad the political analyst comes to the fore. Modern history began with the revolt against religion and monarchy. First (in the purview of the novel) came the failure of wars for abstract Liberty, and we are given a remnant of that cause in Viola the Garibaldino, "undecayed, like an old oak uprooted by a treacherous gust of wind."[3] English sympathy, combined with cool immunity, is indicated deftly: Mrs. Gould sharpens Viola's vision with a gift of eyeglasses; with them he reads the present of another Englishman, an English Bible, which sustains him in his Republican, anticlerical idealism.

England has now to call the tune and pay the piper. Rejecting abstractions, for the honorable reason that ideas by themselves can neither impose justice nor fill men's stomachs, Charles and Emilia Gould cast their lot for an earthly paradise to be built from the earth up, from the mining of silver in Costaguana (an imaginary country on the west coast of South America) to securing justice and morality for a nation. Begin with tangibles, get them working in a just and orderly manner, "and they are bound to impose the con-

---

181, n. 41, 207, n. 126) it throws additional light on the novel, I use it in preference to the Dent Collected Edition, and all references are to this text, first copyrighted by Doubleday & Co. in 1904.

[2] Letter to Ernest Bendz, March 7, 1923: ". . . Nostromo has never been intended for the hero of the Tale of the Seaboard. Silver is the pivot of the moral and material events" (*Life and Letters*, II, 296).

Garnett was trying to write a book, called *London*, touching the same subject but never finished it. Reading part of it in 1897, Conrad wrote, "It is good—wonderfully good. 'The material . . . gripped, moulded . . . by man' and the sudden disclosure in the following sentences that man after all hardly masters and marks its surface while the material grinds, smashes men into chips." (*Letters from Conrad, 1895–1924*, ed. Edward Garnett [Indianapolis: Bobbs-Merrill Co., Inc., 1928], pp. 84–85.)

[3] *Nostromo*, p. 630.

ditions on which alone they can continue to exist."[4] As it turns out, the conditions required by the material interests are not justice and freedom for the men whom they employ, but perfect obedience to economic demands which are more inhuman and arbitrary than any human despot of the past. As Dr. Monygham will say, "the material interests will not let you jeopardize their development for a mere idea of pity and justice."[5]

Gould is only an early and imperfect model of the real capitalist, the American financial wizard with a missionary's zeal, Holroyd, whose motives in South America Mrs. Gould questions and her husband (already committed to the conditions of his investment) chooses prudently to overlook. Wishing only to cultivate his own garden, Gould can ignore the expansive impulse behind Holroyd's passion for reform. Together the Goulds and Holroyd lay the foundations for future disaster. The oppressed people, whom Gould plans to deliver from cruel authority and want, care nothing for his idealism (which is firmly grounded for the Goulds in Britain's early political maturity). It is the Goulds who unknowingly teach "the people" to associate their welfare with the mine, and "the people" learn their lesson without any digression through amorphic principles. The mine is universally coveted. "The rich must be fought with their own weapons," says the hater of capitalists at the end of the novel.[6] After all he has principles and a justice to establish, too. We are left knowing that the next chapter in history will not be written by the Goulds or anyone like them. They are childless historically as well as personally. The next contest will be between Holroyd and the Marxist, who hates, for their association with Holroyd, the only men who have a clear understanding of political justice. "Comrade Fidanza . . . you have refused all aid from that doctor. Is he really a dangerous enemy of the people?"[7]

A naïve but brilliant page in a wholly political novel. "The people," whom Nostromo represents, are little concerned about class

---

[4] *Ibid.*, pp. 92–93.
[5] *Ibid.*, p. 569.
[6] *Ibid.*, p. 627.
[7] *Ibid.*

warfare. Nostromo refuses the doctor's help for the same reason he refused the help of priests—and the help of the Marxist. His war, spiritual or physical or both, is a matter of interest to him alone.

Nostromo is the first of the great novels Conrad wrote from inspirations provided by books more than personal experience. To some extent, perhaps, its overriding vision of men trapped within circumstances not of their own making is a reflection of the closing of his own frontier, of his knowledge that the years had run out in which life yielded to his impulses and that there would be no more escapes by sea. The great consolations now lay in the mooring provided by a small circle of vivid friends—Cunninghame Graham, Edward Garnett, John Galsworthy, Henry James, Ford Madox Ford, and later Norman Douglas and W. H. Hudson—and in such meditations upon life as only a man newly committed to life ashore could conjure.

Virginia Woolf saw this as an inevitable running aground:

> He never believed in his later and more highly sophisticated characters as he had believed in his early seamen; because when he had to indicate their relation to that other unseen world of the novelists, the world of values and convictions, he was far less sure what those values were. . . . There are no masts in drawing rooms; the typhoon does not test the worth of politicians and business men.[8]

Although she meant this judgment to apply only to works after "the middle period" (which she does not define), clearly she would include *Nostromo* in the middle period only as a tale about a "simple seaman." It may have been for "common readers" like herself that Conrad encouraged the public to think Nostromo's story had inspired the novel, as he implies in the Author's Note. In point of fact "the world of values and convictions," the world of politicians and businessmen, was his whole concern. If English readers, even at his death when Virginia Woolf wrote this criticism, missed the thematic insistence, it was not because Conrad was unsure of his values but more likely, as in the case of *Heart of Darkness*, because they were slightly bored with his insistence on values that were at once so obvious and so impracticable.

---

[8] "Joseph Conrad," the *Times Literary Supplement* (London), Aug. 14, 1924, pp. 493–94.

That only a man newly committed to life ashore could have undertaken to write *Nostromo* is suggested by the astonishingly fresh virulence of Conrad's attack on social failings already very old in 1902 when he began the novel. The disease of a society sacrificing itself for material interests had been portrayed by Flaubert, Zola, James, and Hardy (to mention only a few), but as Conrad saw, the blight had before it vast stretches of virgin ground to devastate.

His Polish tenderness to mercenary activity,[9] which we noted (pp. 58–59) in the storm created by Orzeszkowa, and in the nagging accusation that he may have chosen to live in England for its creature comforts, possibly sharpened the taste of bitterness in contemporary events: England's deepening involvement in "doublethink" for the sake of her empire, and the pious moralizings of Carnegie and Rockefeller as civil disorder in America progressed from crisis to crisis and the United States stumbled along on the old path of her "manifest destiny" in the "development" of Latin America.

As we focus our eyes on Conrad the writer, it is curious to remember that when he was twenty-two, he had contemplated giving up the Merchant Service and settling in America, as assistant to a Canadian named Lascalle, who had political as well as financial interests in railroads.[10] Here had been an instance of Conrad's youthful hunger for adventure in lands "ahead of civilization" (as he

---

[9] Conrad called *Nostromo* one of his two best novels (along with *The Secret Agent*) only in speaking to a fellow Pole, Retinger, with whom he started on a stage adaptation of the novel. (Retinger, pp. 91, 120–25)

[10] Our sources here are Tadeusz Bobrowski's letters to Conrad, dated May 30 and June 17, 1880. Although Jean-Aubry's translation was cited above (p. 45), Baines's is sometimes more correct, if less felicitously expressed. Bobrowski wrote in the first letter: "You would not be a Nałęcz, dear boy, if you didn't have constant occupation with some enterprise and if you didn't chase after ever new projects. This refers to what you wrote about Mr. Lascalle's proposal that you become his secretary and make money later in connection with railways!" And in the second letter: "I do not reject all your plans to become a Yankee. I stated what I think in this connection in my last letter—that I would not be in favour of giving up your maritime career to enter the service of an American politician though it would not scandalise me if you insist on acting counter to this view—but on two conditions: (1) that you bear in mind our proverb: As you make your bed, so you must lie on it, and (2) that you never forget what is due to the dignity of the nation and families to which you belong amidst the *businesses* [sic] of American life" (Baines, *Joseph Conrad*, pp. 64, 66).

conceived civilization); an instance also of his appetite for politically charged action that might prove a substitute for the moribund Polish conspiracies stigmatized by his guardian. Bobrowski, of course, recognized the proxy. He had seen another form of it in Conrad's smuggling arms for Spain two years before. Now—twenty years later—when Bobrowski is long dead and Conrad is engaged in writing *Nostromo*, his attraction to America has been thoroughly purged. One was already aware of the growing revulsion, expressed in the Negro-hating Yankee gun-monger of *The Rescue* (probably written into the manuscript sometime in 1898). In *Nostromo* this antipathy reaches its full growth.

The reasons are not far to seek. Clearly, Conrad offers but one more example of a man in whom time deepened the dye of family convictions he had resisted in youth. It also becomes increasingly clear that in the decade following 1896, when Conrad married and settled down to land life and work, his preoccupation in politics was the struggle for empire being waged among European powers, with the upstart United States entering as gadfly to the hospitable Great Britain, as well as to the more sinister imperial designs of Russia and Germany. In his "An Outpost of Progress" (1897), *Heart of Darkness* (1899), *The Inheritors* (1900—with Ford), *Lord Jim* (1900), and the unfinished *Rescue*, Conrad contented himself with ironic commentaries on the European forms of imperialism. It was the Spanish-American War of 1898 which turned his glaring monocle on the hypocrital aggressiveness of the apostles of New World freedom.

On July 30, 1898, Conrad wrote to Cunninghame Graham expressing concern over their mutual interest in Spain. For some reason a crucial paragraph in the manuscript letter (at Dartmouth) is omitted, without sign of ellipsis, from the letter published by Jean-Aubry.[11] The paragraph appears just after Conrad has referred to the review of an English edition of *Don Quixote* and has been reminded in turn of the policy toward Spain's activities in South America expressed by *Blackwood's Magazine* (which in the follow-

---

[11] Jean-Aubry, *Life and Letters*, I, 243–44.

ing months would be bringing out "Youth," *Heart of Darkness,* and *Lord Jim*). "I do like the attitude of the Maga on the Spanish business," Conrad writes in a one-sentence paragraph. It is the next paragraph that is deleted from the Doubleday edition of the *Letters:*

> If one could set the States and Germany by the ears! That would be *real fine.* I am afraid however that the thieves shall agree in the Philippines. The pity of it!

The printed text continues from here, "*Viva l'España!* Anyhow." And then comes the paragraph asserting Conrad's (wishful) faith in Spain's invulnerability and power "to keep the Yanks capering around for an indefinite time."

Was the deletion a mere oversight by typist or printer? Or was it a deliberate proceeding? One leans toward the latter view, picturing Jean-Aubry (perhaps together with F. N. Doubleday) nodding over the wise suppression of Conrad's little acknowledged hostility. Better still, one sees a stoutly patriotic stenographer, galled into a supraprofessional act of censorship.

We might dismiss the omitted paragraph as unimportant and, in effect, summed up in what follows were it not for the curious fact that there seems to have been an unintentional conspiracy among French, English, and American critics and biographers to tone down or ignore Conrad's insuppressible antipathy to American politics, institutions, and character. Only Conrad's wife Jessie, in a few wonderfully graphic anecdotes, manages to convey the depth of it; and her biography was unfortunately depreciated (quite unjustly) by some of the literati—Graham Greene and H. L. Mencken most notably—when it appeared in 1935.

When Conrad refers in the Dartmouth letter to the likable attitude of *Blackwood's Magazine* "on the Spanish business," he refers undoubtedly to articles that had appeared in February and May, weighing the respective merits of Spanish and American motives.[12]

---

[12] "The Spanish Crisis," *Blackwood's Magazine* (Edinburgh), Feb., 1898, pp. 238–53; and "Spain and the United States," *Ibid.,* May, 1898, pp. 702–3.

The main points of these articles were that, although Spain had recently fallen from the glorious heights of her former heroism in dealing with the peoples of her far-flung colonies, the belligerency of the United States in Cuba savored less of real sympathy for the oppressed insurrectionists than of provocation in the interests of a new imperialism. Faced with this situation, the editors of "Maga" —normally so disposed to favor friendly relations with America if these could stanchion British commercial interests—for the first time turned a jaundiced eye on the whole contest for empire, in which Britain was no small contender. To the "Little Englanders" Cunninghame Graham and Joseph Conrad, this new editorial policy was a cause for rejoicing.

Conrad's letters to Cunninghame Graham remind us, then, that he was, above all, absorbed by the activities of a number of different modern *conquistadores* between 1898 and 1903 (when he wrote, ". . . what do you think of the Yankee Conquistadores in Panama? Pretty, isn't it? *Enfin!*"[13]), the year in which he completed *Nostromo*. His quondam attraction to such adventurers merely sharpened his scent for the audacious commercial titans intruding in lands where "tradition," "order," and "legality" were new words, produced on the spot to serve whatever interest happened to be asserting itself at the moment. Unless Conrad had grappled with some such early sympathy, we can hardly explain his appetite for whatever book came to hand on Spanish conquest, English travel in South America, or on the wars of "liberation" in that region. His interest was guided, it is true, by Cunninghame Graham, who had lived and traveled in South America for years. But "Don Roberto's" passion for Spanish America was quickly met in Conrad by a more highly charged repugnance, not only to the politicians and magnates of the new conquest, but to the whole theory of history they invented, or at any rate used, to justify their exploits.

A striking illustration is evident in Conrad's response to three of the documentary sources he employed in creating his South Ameri-

[13] Letter to Cunninghame Graham, Dec. 26, 1903, *Life and Letters*, I, 326.

can republic in *Nostromo*. According to Jocelyn Baines, the "points of view of the authors, particularly that of Eastwick, would have been sympathetic to Conrad."[14] This remark might serve as a caution to all of Conrad's English and American readers. Edward B. Eastwick's conservative English voice may be "sympathetic," but it is certainly less in tune with Conrad's own than with the voice of stodgy Captain Mitchell, who "prided himself on his profound knowledge of men and things in the country—cosas de Costaguana."[15] According to Eastwick, "the worst possible government is perhaps better than civil war and a restless appetite for change, which grows with every fresh revolution. Slavery and the inquisition are monstrous evils, but rebellion and scepticism are as bad, if not worse."[16] One cannot conclude from *Nostromo* that Spanish imperialism was preferable to civil war, even though there are contrasts in this novel as elsewhere in Conrad's fiction suggesting that the old monarchies (forgetting for a moment their foreign plunder) were more appealing and sometimes more efficient than the present forms of democracy.[17] It is in reading just such passages as this from Eastwick that one appreciates the novelist's finer brush in defining the issues. Conrad's point is that the new politics in Latin America are merely the old in modern dress, and his accent is on

---

[14] *Joseph Conrad* (London: Weidenfeld & Nicolson, 1959), p. 296.

[15] *Nostromo*, p. 11.

[16] Edward B. Eastwick, *Venezuela* (London: Chapman and Hall, 1868), p. 318. This book was in Conrad's library when he died.

[17] In "Autocracy and War," written in 1905 (less than two years after he finished *Nostromo*), Conrad wrote of the wars he saw ahead in the present century: "They will make us regret the time of dynastic ambitions, with their human absurdity moderated by prudence and even by shame, by the fear of personal responsibility and the regard paid to certain forms of conventional decency. For if the monarchs of Europe have been derided for addressing each other as 'brother' in autograph communications, that relationship was at least as effective as any form of brotherhood likely to be established between the rival nations of this continent, which, we are assured on all hands, is the heritage of democracy. . . . No leader of a democracy, without other ancestry but the sudden shout of a multitude, and debarred by the very condition of his power from even thinking of a direct heir, will have any interest in calling brother the leader of another democracy—a chief as fatherless and heirless as himself" (*Notes on Life and Letters*, p. 105). This essay is as useful (as non-fictional background) to our reading of *Nostromo* as "The Crime of Partition" was useful in reading *Heart of Darkness*.

plunder. As to scepticism, there is the castigated Decoud but also the approved scepticism of Dr. Monygham.

More than Eastwick's *Venezuela*, which gave Conrad the character and Christian name of the beautiful Antonia, G. F. Masterman's *Seven Eventful Years in Paraguay* provided Conrad with history, scenery, situations, and suggestions for characters, as well as most of their names.[18] But Masterman is far less relevant as a "source" than as a reminder that its author's point of view belongs to the target of Conrad's attack in *Nostromo*. The essence of the novel's meaning—that progress, leashed to faith in material interests, is inhuman, without rectitude, continuity, or force—could be a

---

[18] G. F. Masterman, *Seven Eventful Years in Paraguay* (London: Sampson Low, Son, & Marston, 1870).

In Masterman one finds a British chargé d'affaires named Gould (Conrad supplies the name Charles for reasons that will appear), a Creole named Decoud (three of them, in fact, if the Spanish edition is consulted), a priest named Romàn (two of them, one a torturer, the other a simpleton), suggestions for the priests Berón and Corbelàn, an English gunboat captain named Michell, a drunkard General Barrios, and (not to speak of the names for many of *Nostromo's* minor characters) an Italian merchant marine captain named Simon Fidanza who contradicts his name by turning out a traitor. Of course, the symbolic theft of the silver, we now know, was from a tale about a scoundrel named Nicolo, which Conrad found in "Frederick Benton Williams' " *On Many Seas*. See John Halverson and Ian Watt, "The Original Nostromo: Conrad's Source," *Review of English Studies* (February, 1959), pp. 45–52.

From Masterman also Conrad drew several small episodes and suggestions: Guzman Bento's alternate fits of intoxication and devotion; the mysterious disappearance of his body from the church, ascribed to the work of the devil; a prophetic parrot; and Pedrito Montero's delusions of grandeur as inspired by the atmosphere of Paris.

I am grateful to an unpublished M.A. thesis by Edgar Wright (London University, March, 1955) for a fairly detailed discussion of Masterman and some other sources used for *Nostromo* as well as to Jocelyn Baines's biography, pp. 293–97. I had begun on the same trail Wright followed—the "ur sources" Cunninghame Graham used and possibly passed on to Conrad—when I discovered Wright's thesis. The arguments I would raise on a few points are worth mentioning. Wright and Baines somewhat miss Conrad's detachment from, and even criticism of, Masterman himself. According to Wright, Dr. Monygham is evidently Masterman, an apothecary employed by the dictator, who was imprisoned and made to produce a false confession under torture. Nothing could be farther from Masterman's equanimity, however, than Monygham's obsession with disloyalty and his "special conception of the political crisis." It is even significant that Conrad took the name Monygham from a sculptor in Masterman. No one who has written about Masterman as a source for *Nostromo*, furthermore, has pointed out Masterman's sweeping condemnations of Catholicism in South America. Conrad greatly tempers this view, presenting only one vicious priest among Masterman's many and creating some sympathy for the Church where in Masterman there is none.

direct answer to Masterman's conclusion, that the moral depravities he witnessed under the dictatorship of Francisco Lopez in
Paraguay were bound to provoke a reaction of humane interest,
especially among the materially advanced nations of the earth: "The
Teuton and Anglo-Saxon will soon find the void this war of extermination has made, and permanent prosperity will banish all
trace of its devastations."[19]

Another major "source" was the Latin American statesman (ambassador from Colombia to England and Spain) S. Perez Triana,
whose character and writings Conrad used to the extent of fearing
himself a fraud.[20] Perez Triana may have given Conrad the idea of
using a fictional Latin American republic as a microcosm fore-
shadowing the fate of mankind. Conrad chose to name it Costaguana after the bird excrement used in making explosives. A guano
island, we remember, was where Chester offered to "busy" Jim. In
a book published during the year before Conrad began writing
Nostromo (a book for which Cunninghame Graham wrote the
introduction), Perez Triana wrote of this coast:

> On the surface of the globe no more favorable spot exists for the
> home of mankind. Along the coast of the Pacific Ocean runs the
> mighty backbone of the Cordillera like a bulwark, high, immense,
> stately; above it, like the towers and turrets in the walls of a for-
> tified city, rise the hundred snow-capped peaks that look east and
> west, now on the ocean, now on the everspreading undulating
> plains.[21]

Proud of his homeland (which he views as a nest of democracies),
Perez Triana like Masterman throws his faith into reason, education, and the hopes of material progress:

---

[19] Masterman, *op. cit.*, p. 300.

[20] "I am compunctious as to the use I've made of the impression produced on me by
the Ex. Sr. Don Perez Triana's personality. Do you think I have committed an un-
forgivable fault there? He'll never see or hear of the book probably." Just before
this he had written: "For in regard to that book I feel a great fraud" (Letter to
Cunninghame Graham, Oct. 31, 1904, *Life and Letters*, I, 337–38). It was in regard
to *Nostromo* as a whole, however, and the use he had to make in it of all the written
sources, that he felt himself a fraud.

[21] S. Perez Triana, *Down the Orinoco*, introduction by R. B. Cunninghame Graham
(London: William Heinemann, 1902), p. 102.

In the midst of the daily turmoil and agitation and sanguinary struggle which constitutes the life of these democracies, these problems [the development of river and railroad communications in Colombia and Venezuela], urgent and vital as they are, pass unheeded; and the more the pity, for in their solution lies the basis of permanent peace.[22]

Still, Perez Triana's optimism and idealism are irrepressible:

If the power of things ideal, of things that have in them the divine charm of undying force, overcomes time and distance, why should not the ideal of righteousness, of liberty, and of justice prevail? And the vast continent of South America, why should it not be the predestined home of a happy and regenerate humanity? The tradewinds which come from the old world and across the ocean are purified on the heights of the Cordilleras. Even so humanity in that pilgrimage that is bound to take place ere long, as the ancient world begins to overflow, may regenerate itself and establish liberty and justice in that new world. If these be dreams, awakening were bitter.[23]

Bitter but imperative. To Conrad the Pole, Masterman's cool optimism combined with Triana's passionate oratory may have suggested an alliance both humorous and likely. The aristocrat of Spanish blood, impoverished and futureless, honorably anxious to make good his country's foreign debts (which torment Eastwick to such a degree), would embrace with all his heart the scion of Englishmen, promising prosperity and a dependable constitution. The businessman would compensate for the diplomat's verbosity and impotence with silence and power. Thus the friendship of Charles Gould and Don José Avellanos in *Nostromo*. Out of it come events that kill Don José, dehumanize Gould, and forecast a new era of slavery in the New World, justifying Conrad's estimate of the current dream:

Progress leaves its dead by the way, for progress is only a great adventure as its leaders and chiefs know very well in their hearts. It is

[22] *Ibid.*, pp. 246–47.
[23] *Ibid.*, pp. 114–15.

On page 345 of the manuscript of *Nostromo* (The Philip H. and A. S. W. Rosenbach Foundation), Conrad sketched a relief map of the coast of Costaguana—his imaginary republic on the west coast of South America.

a march into an undiscovered country; and in such an enterprise the victims do not count.[24]

He implies that the novelist has a special duty to perform in keeping one truth before the revelers celebrating technological and scientific miracles, the truth that "life and the arts follow dark courses, and will not turn aside to the brilliant arc-lights of science."[25] In our time, he suggests in an essay on Henry James, written the year after *Nostromo* was published, only the novelist can render convincing the old truth that for every gain "a sacrifice must be made, . . . something has to be given up." For whether he stands "at the beginning or the end of things, a man has to sacrifice his gods to his passions or his passions to his gods."[26]

Nostromo, indeed, argues a theory of history almost at the cost of its felt life and characterization. Guerard, comparing it with *Lord Jim*, calls *Nostromo* less "an 'interior' novel, either for the characters or for the reader." Its psychology, he points out, "is classical rather than Freudian. Reason and folly play a larger part than unconscious or half-conscious compulsion; reasoning on political affairs occupies more pages than solitary introspection."[27] There is a tendency in the novel, I would add, to see character as politics in action rather than the other way around—politics as character in action (Guerard's prescription for a successful political novel). Everything illustrates the author's theory of history,[28] from the anecdote of the damned treasure-seekers that opens the novel to the characters of its heroic doubles, Gould and Nostromo, who but illustrate the anecdote.

In Part I (of three), "The Silver of the Mine," we are given scenic background and a teeming world of characters in the most

---

[24] "The Crime of Partition," *Notes on Life and Letters*, p. 118.

[25] "The Ascending Effort," *Notes on Life and Letters*, p. 74.

[26] *Notes on Life and Letters*, pp. 15–16.

[27] Albert Guerard, *Conrad the Novelist* (Cambridge, Mass.: Harvard University Press, 1958), pp. 176–77.

[28] It does not seem to me that the operations of chance, which Guerard sees as a conception of history in the novel (which should be there, if Conrad's own intention were carried out) *do* function independently from what Guerard calls "the vast predetermined economic movement" (*ibid.*, p. 195).

fragmentary fashion. Guerard has given good reasons for the technique: the evocation of a country ruled by anarchy, of the apparently timeless, "absurd rhythm of exploitation and misrule, of revolution and counterrevolution" in Latin America.[29] He mentions Conrad's creative temperament "that refuses to give the normal, logical, expected emphasis."[30] And Guerard finds this remarkable effect achieved (though I do not): "that more persons, events, and forces exist than these few we are allowed to glance at," an effect that in fact " 'creates' them."[31]

Jocelyn Baines echoes Guerard's main point when he writes that the "elimination of progression from one event to another . . . has the effect of implying that nothing is ever achieved." He adds that "it seems to have been Conrad's aim to approach the simultaneity of visual experience which a painting offers."[32] One can argue just as well that the chronological involutions of Part I have rather the reverse effect to that of ordinary painting, since they break all the pictures (not just the surfaces as in *pointillisme*) into fragments. It would be just as true to say that abstractionist painters are endeavoring to approach the *concatenation* (as opposed to simultaneity) of disconnected visual effects achieved by Conrad in *Nostromo*.

In short, I find that this disorderly presentation of material contributes greatly to the novel's "dramatic impenetrability" (as Morton Dauwen Zabel calls it) and its "hollow" reverberation (F. R. Leavis). It has not the chronological suggestiveness of *Lord Jim*, where all fragments relate perceptibly to Jim, where the reader need not wonder distractedly for two hundred pages whether his human interest—the only worthy interest in a novel—is to be given anywhere a worthy object.

"Life and the arts follow dark courses," but political history, one would judge from *Nostromo*, is predictable. In comparison with *Nostromo*, Tolstoy's *War and Peace*, using realistic chronology

[29] *Ibid.*, p. 178.
[30] *Ibid.*, p. 182.
[31] *Ibid.*, p. 214.
[32] Baines, *Joseph Conrad*, p. 301.

and character development to arrive at the opposite conclusion—
that history is *not* predictable—seems a far better illustration of
Conrad's "theory" concerning the mysteries of human nature.

If *Heart of Darkness* was a "foil" for *Lord Jim* in the contrast it
offered between the illusion of a man concerned with personal conduct and the illusion of a man obsessed by race superiority, *Nostromo* brings other, even more startling contrasts. The modern
political novel, so well typified by *Nostromo*, is on the whole a
foil to the modern novel centering on private experience, of which
Lord Jim is perhaps the finest example.

The political novel, which is a child of the mid-nineteenth century, represents the antithesis of the old picaresque tale. Whereas
the latter celebrated the wit and mastery of the individual at the
expense of society, the political novel laments the loss of individual
self-control and the defeat of will power by anonymous social
forces, whether blind or directed by the menacing ingenuity of
"representative" leaders. *Lord Jim* is Conrad's picaresque in the
modern key, the story of an individual's self-assertion in the face
of an uncomprehending society and incomprehensible fate. His
"victory" is measured by his ability to convince Marlow, who maintains the strength of the social code even while finding Jim's appeal
to his personal vision of integrity "irresistible."

The irrational faith which Conrad calls Jim's "illusion," and in
"Youth" the "heat of life in a handful of dust," seems to be as
much the motivating force in *Nostromo* as in *Lord Jim*. But now,
in *Nostromo*, it expresses motives which, when unveiled, appear
consistently unworthy. Illusion becomes, in Dr. Monygham's
words, the "vanity which makes the world go round."[33] He alone,
with his concern for personal integrity, is allowed the illusion that
is romantically "the imaginative exaggeration of a correct feeling
. . . in its force, influence, and persistency, the view of an eminently loyal nature."[34]

I would suggest that Conrad's reflection on the evils of rampant

---

[33] *Nostromo*, p. 353.
[34] *Ibid.*, p. 418.

materialism (partly because of his family and national background, as I have said) to some degree unhinged his creative judgment. Only in *Nostromo* does he concentrate on the antinomies between matter and spirit, which on the philosophical plane are risky for one who declared himself

> penetrated by an invincible conviction that whatever falls under the dominion of our senses must be in nature and, however exceptional, *cannot differ in its essence from all the other effects of the visible and tangible world of which we are a self-conscious part.*[35]

This generalization might fit the unmaterialistic world of a ship at sea, but does it hold up in *Nostromo*?

Conrad evidently began the novel with an uneasy feeling that the adamant logic of his conception would rob his characters of their interior interest as individuals. The disorderliness of Part I (which might better have appeared in Part II, after the reader's grasp on the complex scene and interest in its people had been established) is partly an effort to stave off discovery of the obvious lesson which must follow the anecdote of the treasure-seekers on Azuera. Until Decoud's letter in Part II securely establishes the connections between people and interests, we are continually frustrated in our inclination to reflect to some purpose either on Nostromo's affairs or on the sequence between the Goulds' youthful hopes and their commitments to corrupting forces. There is no good reason for the inversion of sequence between Chapter V, in which the Goulds celebrate the preparations for opening a National Central Railway to serve the mine, and the flashback (which is not really that since no present time has been established) to their courtship and the invention of their plans to save the mine. The sequence is further evaded, of course, by the mysteriously fitful appearances of Nostromo at different times and places in the first four chapters.

Guerard, Baines, and others have speculated sufficiently on the distortions of Part I, Douglas Hewitt most sympathetically. I will add only this summary of my criticism: It may be the conception of

---

[35] Author's Note to *The Shadow Line*, p. v. The italics are mine.

evil Conrad meant to reveal in the novel—evil in a far more concrete and exterior form than anywhere else in his "moral dramas"
—that accounts for many of the novel's idiosyncrasies of style as
well as its failure to reverberate richly. In the words of Ramon
Fernandez, "*Enfin, quelque beau que soit un roman comme
Nostromo, il me semble d'une tenue artificielle, un peu pénible.*"[36]

Surprisingly enough, the novel's virtues seem to proceed from
this concentration on one aspect of evil and even from Conrad's
unmitigated fatalism. Tolstoy's philosophy of free individual wills
and the indeterminacy of historic leadership presents a finer
and "rounder" view of human nature in the flow of history. But
Tolstoy's subject, the miraculous balking of Napoleon's invasion
at Moscow, was after all a subject for delight in "the people" of
Russia, for celebration of the victories of unknown inner resources
over the known. With equal truth, Conrad's subject stresses the
impotence of individual wills in the face of tragic events no less
historical than Russia's defeat of Napoleon but, indeed, the reverse
of flattering to any of the egos represented. If the Russian novel
points to a nation's expanding political horizon, the novel of the
Polish exile points with equal justice to the loss of any horizon at
all.

Appropriately, in *War and Peace* apparent design shifts continually into the unforeseen. In *Nostromo*, apparent disorder is
disciplined progressively into the fulfillment of prophecy: that the
treasure-seekers are fated to be eternally hungry and thirsty, "where
a Christian would have renounced and been released."[37] The prophecy binds everything on earth and in heaven, too, and thus makes
Nostromo larger in its presumption than *War and Peace*. Conrad's
achievement is that the pattern of lives he conceives as bearing
out the prophecy in his imaginary republic does fully cover the
cloth of historic material. The nations involved are successfully
represented or evoked, without any absurd attempt at analysis of
their individual histories. While each personality evokes a national

[36] Ramon Fernandez, "*L'Art de Conrad,*" *Nouvelle Revue Française* (December,
1924), p. 737 n.
[37] *Nostromo*, p. 5.

character, it manages to express a complex of human traits that render the individual reasonably distinct even in the act of serving the argument from which the novel is never free. The interest created by the *pattern* of these individual lives interacting together compensates to some degree for our increasing failure to hope, as the novel progresses, for the emergence of any lasting spark in the handful of silver dust.

V

The most important figure in the pattern is, of course, the parallel between Nostromo and Charles Gould. These two men are intended, the Author's Note tells us, to be "racially and socially contrasted." Conrad maintains that his interest in making Nostromo a "Man of the People as free as possible from his class-conventions and all settled modes of thinking" was "not moral but artistic."[38]

Yet there is a moral as well as artistic point to Nostromo's willingness (unlike the Anglo-Saxon, Conrad says) to stay out of politics, "to feel himself a power—within the People." One of the main contrasts in *Nostromo*, no less than in *Heart of Darkness*, is between the men who have "an insatiable imagination of conquest" and the rest of humanity who are their victims. And the distinction Conrad makes is geopolitical. Geography is a key to politics as well as to personal qualities. It is the author, not Decoud, who says, "There is always something childish in the rapacity of the passionate, clear-minded southern races, wanting in the misty idealism of the northerners, who at the smallest encouragement dream of nothing less than the conquest of the earth."[39] We remember in *Heart of Darkness* the hybrid imagination that was given to Kurtz, that patchwork of all Europe. In *Nostromo* it is the American Holroyd who has this carefully mixed national background: "his parentage was German and Scotch and English, with remote strains of Danish and French blood, giving him the temperament of a Puritan and an insatiable imagination of conquest."[40] As in *Heart of Darkness* the attractive Russian youth innocently pre-

---

[38] *Ibid.*, "Note," pp. 5–6.
[39] *Ibid.*, pp. 370–71.
[40] *Ibid.*, p. 84.

figured new conquests for his "race," the American (young for his years) suggests the helplessness of *his* people to resist the call of their manifest destiny. Russia's name (like Poland's) is never mentioned in *Nostromo*, but this perhaps makes all the more sinister the nameless, nationless "photographer" posted at Nostromo's deathbed, keeping count of the enemies of the people. We are not to forget, however, that Charles Gould, the central political figure of *Nostromo*, has the same gift as the English Marlow of the Congo, the gift of viewing the development of backward areas in terms of efficiency and redemption.

As an upperclass Englishman, technically a Costaguanero like the Frenchified Decoud, Charles Gould has the gift Nostromo lacks of idealizing his undertakings. Nostromo idealizes only himself. Conrad here makes some distinction between ego and action in a variation of the distinction Stein made (see above, pp. 66–68) between Jim's behavior and his romantic sense of existence. (And one recalls that only Latins, perhaps, understood Jim's "morbid" sense of personal honor.) Of course, Nostromo is no Jim. He is emphatically unintellectual,[41] and amoral. Both are described as "simple," but

---

[41] Conrad's original impulse was evidently to exaggerate the contrast between Gould and Nostromo to the point where the latter had no intellectuality at all. He later softened this, fearing justly that it would further undermine interest in an already shaky characterization. Thus, the Rosenbach MS (chap. viii, part ii, p. 7) has two sentences that appear with slight correction in the Modern Library text (copyright by Doubleday, 1904, but not used in Doubleday's collected editions, which follow the revised version). On p. 417 of the Dent and Doubleday collected editions, these two sentences (found on p. 466 of the Modern Library edition) are missing: "And no wonder—with no intellectual existence or moral strain to carry on his individuality, unscathed, over the abyss left by the collapse of his vanity; for even that had been simply sensuous and picturesque, and could not exist apart from outward show. He was like many other men of southern races in whom the complexity of simple conceptions is much more apparent than real." And three pages later, the Modern Library text has "unintelligence" where the others have "intelligence." Hence: "The word had fixed itself tenaciously in his unintelligence." This reading, too, follows the original manuscript in the Rosenbach collection.

Evidence might be cited for Conrad's strong disapproval of the Modern Library edition, if a letter concerning his works in general, written to Reginald Leon in February, 1917 (now in the Berg Collection, New York Public Library), is applicable: "The only edition in which I take interest is the Collected Edition (limited to 1000 sets in England and in the U.S.) which Doubleday, Page in New York and Wm. Heinemann here are going to publish after the war. I've settled the format, the bindings, the fount, and the paper. For the text, it will be exactly the text of the

Nostromo cannot exist without other men's adulation, whereas "Jim had no dealings but with himself," however necessary the respect of others in confirming his sense of honor. Nostromo's sluggish recoil from insult and still more sluggish progress into temptation adds to rather than detracts from the virility of his action in rallying the rioters and hurtling to retrieve the Sulaco forces. And the point is won that Gould, significantly without ever coming into effective contact with this elemental man, is the cause of Nostromo's corruption, by virtue of so magnifying the silver in Sulaco that even the incorruptible capataz cannot resist it. From simple sailor, Nostromo is elevated to being the savior of the material interests—an apparent rise but in reality a great fall, planting the root of evil in a life where not even the roots of morality existed before. *Nostromo* is not unlike *Lord Jim* rewritten, with materialism substituted for moral concern in the egoistical title figure.

Inevitably this tale of temptation and corruption has some reverberations from the original Fall of Man. By taking our sights from the biblical prototype we can see the political fable most distinctly. The creation of man, in *Nostromo*, is the creation of a quasi-political consciousness in a figure (representative of the people) who was previously not much different from a happy animal. When Nostromo is entrusted with sole responsibility for the silver, he does not pluck the apple but has it forced upon him by supposedly responsible men. And in the moment of realizing what has been done to him, he changes from one who is "as natural and free from evil . . . as a wild beast" to a full man, with the knowledge of good and evil that is said to have corrupted the first man in Eden: "Then, in the suddenly steadied glance fixed upon nothing from under a forced frown, appeared the man."[42] (One must remember, though, that here it is *bad* politics which corrupts, not *all* politics as Irving Howe implies by his reading of *Nostromo*.)

Gould is not God—or the devil—dealing out the choice, or tempting the man. He is Nostromo's double as well as the initiator of

English first editions freed from misprints and with, perhaps, a few (very few) verbal alterations."

[42] *Nostromo*, p. 458.

his fall. That is to say, Gould's corruption is the model for Nostromo's, and Gould himself is an Adam, disturbing creation in the "paradise of snakes" where the mine slept until he resolved to use it for human salvation. Evil (one cannot tell about good, since there's very little of it in the novel) is exterior and is not, even, moral. The evil is the silver.

There is something very touching, if one thinks of Conrad's own childhood, in Gould's fatal temptation in the scenes (forgotten too easily later) where the boy is seen growing up, away in England, respectful but incredulous of the seemingly perverse passion burning out the stub of his father's life.

> To be told repeatedly that one's future is blighted because of the possession of a silver mine is not, at the age of fourteen, a matter of prime importance as to its main statement; but in its form it is calculated to excite a certain amount of wonder and attention.[43]

Gould resolves to disobey his father's command to stay out of Costaguana and have nothing to do with the mine. The motive for his disobedience, however, is rehabilitation—the desire to transvalue the father's command into a higher service. Not refusal of the difficult task but a boyish determination to make it good in a way the old man was unable to see. (No one, I think, has called attention to the relevance of this passage to Conrad's decision against his Polish past and its intimate connection with memories of his father.)

> That irreparable change a death makes in the course of our daily thoughts can be felt in a vague and poignant discomfort of mind. It hurt Charles Gould to feel that never more, by no effort of will, would he be able to think of his father in the same way he used to think of him when the poor man was alive. His breathing image was no longer in his power. This consideration, closely affecting his own identity, filled his breast with a mournful and angry desire for action. In this his instinct was unerring. Action is consolatory. It is the enemy of thought and the friend of flattering illusions. Only in the conduct of our action can we find the sense of mastery over the Fates. . . . It was imperative sometimes to know how to disobey

---

[43] *Ibid.*, p. 63.

the solemn wishes of the dead. He resolved firmly to make his disobedience as thorough (by way of atonement) as it well could be.[44]

To measure Charles Gould, as most do, by his wife's later disappointments and by the paltriness of the rich man's fate, which must finally bring him the ass's ears of a Midas, is to forget that Gould, no less than his wife, is victim and standard-bearer of the best hope their culture held out for the future. Together and equally, the young couple set out in quest of the moral possibilities in amoral things. Silver mines might have been "worthless, but also they might have been misunderstood."[45] Gould does not hoodwink his bride; she fools herself, loving Gould for "his unsentimentalism, . . . that very quietude of mind which she had erected in her thought for a sign of perfect competency in the business of living."[46] It was in the "voiceless attitude of this man towards the world of material things" that "her delight . . . found a pinnacle from which to soar up into the skies."[47]

Gallantly, as in *The Rescue*, Conrad offers the English wife a succoring hand—even, now, suggests that she is a secular saint, able to maintain in the face of nullifying experience her hold on the existential values which compensate for, though they cannot mend, the moral disaster in which she has played her part. She is endowed with "delicate shades of self-forgetfulness," and puts others at their ease by an attitude of "universal comprehension."[48] In the end, because of these qualities, Nostromo will make her his confessor, giving her the chance to annihilate, emblematically and without disloyalty to her husband, the silver that has ruined her husband's life and her own: "No, capataz . . . . No one misses it now. Let it be lost forever."[49]

---

[44] *Ibid.*, p. 72. Fanatic devotion to Polish freedom, in Conrad's case, would be the command he would disobey. Following a different path, he might not only redeem his father's futile sacrifice but also, perhaps, conquer the evil destiny that seemed to lie in wait for him as his father's only heir. Of course the mature Conrad sees that destiny is not conquered but only driven into a new channel.

[45] *Ibid.*, p. 65.

[46] *Ibid.*, p. 54.

[47] *Ibid.*, p. 65.

[48] *Ibid.*, p. 50.

[49] *Ibid.*, p. 625.

But it won't do to imply, as many do, that there is any important moral standard for the *politics* of the novel in Mrs. Gould's responses, or that affairs might have been better if left in "her unmercenary hands."[50] Irving Howe makes one of his brilliant points when he objects that

> she has sealed herself off in an enclave of disciplined suffering. The court she holds for the Europeans and a few chosen "natives" is merely a mirror to her loneliness; the life of the country on which her comfort depends remains a secret forever closed to her. All Costaguanans, she admits, look alike to her—she means no malice, not even unfriendliness yet how fatal an admission it nonetheless is. The rhythms of Costaguana are alien to her racial conventions, and because she cannot transcend those conventions—because she lacks the boldness of Mrs. Moore in *Passage to India*—her life narrows into a ritual of controlled deprivation.[51]

Like a remarkably similar character in a later novel, Mrs. Ramsay in Virginia Woolf's *To the Lighthouse*,[52] Mrs. Gould seems very much the earth-mother figure, providing relief rather than solutions, warmth rather than light. She is not, however, as with Mrs. Ramsay, an end in herself. If she does not fully see the great issues, she is nevertheless an instrument through which they are seen: the sterility of the enterprise to which she has given up her husband will be the sterility of a society to which he has given up the people of the country. Her personal reflections are fraught with high political significance.

> It had come into her mind that for life to be large and full it must contain the care of the past and of the future in every passing moment of the present. Our daily work must be done to the glory of the dead, and for the good of those who come after.[53]

This is an answer mainly, perhaps, to her husband's and her own disobedience to the order of the dead father, but it may also be

---

[50] *Ibid.*, p. 118.

[51] *Politics and the Novel* (New York: Horizon Press, 1957), p. 110. It is only Howe's *political* analysis of *Nostromo* that suffers from his reliance on the totally inadequate corroborations of Marx and Trotsky.

[52] This novel seems to spring from the form suggested in *Nostromo*, the tripartite analysis of past, present, and future, with a lighthouse symbolizing the main character's personal qualities and significance to his fellow men.

[53] *Nostromo*, p. 582.

taken as a reflection on the pattern of revolt against the errors of past generations in Europe, which she and Gould have followed, thus instigating the beginnings of a worse revolt in the future. How one is to be faithful to the past without confirming its errors never becomes quite clear, though it is a strong theme in all Conrad's political novels. We must recall again, however, that he came from a country that had a past and no present. His best answers appear in "Autocracy and War," where he appeals for a form of government that, unlike the old monarchies, has the power "to be adaptive from within,"[54] but has, unlike the modern democracies, the virtue of continuity according to coherent principles.[55]

The tragedy of the Goulds' lives—which is vitiated more perhaps than Conrad intended by Decoud's convincing raillery and the shift of our interest in mid-novel to Gould's "unintelligent" double, Nostromo—seems meant to provide a genuinely tragic perspective on "the spirit of an epoch in the history of South America," in which Conrad conveys the dilemma of an era in our world. If Gould is a sentimentalist, he has in English fashion become so through honest effort to rectify the sentimental errors of the past, not so much his father's as Europe's. And one may view from the tragic side as well as the satirical Decoud's observation that Gould can only act as he does by not thinking logically about it: "It's part of solid English sense not to think too much; to see only what may be of practical use at the moment."[56] The "solid English sense," Decoud points out, is fortified by the Englishman's moral illusions: "illusions . . . somehow or other help them to get a firm hold of substance."[57] Decoud's aggravation may be seen partly as a confession of his own deadly failure to grasp "substance." Once isolated from the social world on which his satirical nature depends for life, he cannot survive. We see in *Nostromo* the same dichotomy later explored in *Victory* (1914), where Conrad considers the "destructive process" in Heyst of his father's scepti-

---

[54] *Notes on Life and Letters*, p. 101.
[55] *Ibid.*, p. 105.
[56] *Nostromo*, p. 209.
[57] *Ibid.*, p. 265.

cism: "It is not the clear-sighted who lead the world. Great achievements are accomplished in a blessed, warm mental fog, which the pitiless cold blasts of the father's analysis had blown away from the son."[58]

Like the political philosopher Michael Polanyi, now at Oxford—another exile in England from an eastern European country—Conrad is torn between admiration and perplexity on the subject of Britain's (and Polanyi would say America's) political achievements, their way of succeeding morally as well as materially by refusing to drive either their principles or actions to logical conclusions.[59] If Gould thought too deeply about his policies, he could not have put them into practice, we are told repeatedly by both Decoud and the distant authorial voice. Even if he *talked* about his actions, he could not have proceeded, for speech imposes consecutive thought on the sane mind. Hence Gould's gradual retreat behind his wall of silence, where his wife, too, seeks shelter.[60]

Conrad brilliantly suggests this growing dilemma in a series of scenes (Parts I and II) between Gould and his wife. Before they set foot together in Costaguana, Emilia—speaking of Charles's father—"wondered frankly that a man of character should devote his energies to plotting and intrigues." And Charles, implying personal immunity, answers, "with a gentle concern that understood her wonder, 'You must not forget that he was born there.' "[61] Not long afterward, in the early days of their life in Costaguana, Emilia protests again about the "comedy of naïve pretenses" in the public affairs of the country, which are now beginning to involve their lives. And Charles answers, reprovingly this time, "My dear, you seem to forget that I was born here."[62]

In the next of these scenes, having just closed the deal with Holroyd, Gould tells his still partly approving wife that whatever

[58] *Victory*, p. 92.
[59] Michael Polanyi, *The Logic of Liberty* (London: Routledge & Kegan Paul, Ltd., 1951).
[60] *Nostromo*, p. 183.
[61] *Ibid.*, p. 66.
[62] *Ibid.*, p. 54.

else happens, "The great silver and iron interests shall survive, and some day shall get hold of Costaguana along with the rest of the world." The words are overheard by their pet parrot, who shrieks out "Viva Costaguana!" Mrs. Gould is alarmed by the "awful materialism" in her husband's words, but Gould (still like the parrot using words without real knowledge of their meaning and catching at things "belonging to his vocabulary,") merely answers, "My dear, it's nothing to me . . . I make use of what I see."[63]

Gould himself shies off, somewhat prudishly considering the coolness of his negotiations with Holroyd, when it becomes necessary for him to enlist the services of the bandit Hernandez—the God-fearing Robin Hood of the *campo*, who has been put outside the law not by the criminality of his impulses but by the criminalities of the "legal" authorities.[64] While going to whatever lengths of bribery are required for advancing the interests of the mine in government circles, Gould prudishly if not puritanically resists allying his mine with any political "policy," thus making it necessary for Decoud to plot secretly for "separation" from the chaotic central government of Costaguana, and, after the suicide of Decoud, for Dr. Monygham to send Nostromo after General Barrios without telling Gould. In Gould's refusal to commit his mine to any politically responsible line, Conrad evidently means to

---

[63] *Ibid.*, p. 91.

[64] The original of Hernandez seems to appear in the travel memoir by Captain Basil Hall, *Extracts from a Journal written on the coasts of Chile, Peru, and Mexico in the years 1820, 1821, 1822,* I (Edinburgh, 1824), 315–69. Conrad was apparently struck greatly by Hall's analysis of the wars of liberation from Spanish rule, and especially by the effect of this rebellion on the peasantry, which had no understanding of, and nothing to gain from, the change of power. In Hernandez to some extent, and much more in "Gaspar Ruiz," written shortly after *Nostromo,* Conrad applies Hall's political generalizations to the story of a poor soldier, victimized by the changing revolutions. This soldier, in Hall, is a man of fabulous strength who makes the incredible escape from prison and then the firing squad (vividly portrayed in "Gaspar Ruiz") and then defects to the Royalists, thereafter becoming a sort of Chilean Tamerlane. By supplying the religious motif in *Nostromo* and the love motif in "Gaspar Ruiz," Conrad elevates Hall's Benavides from a pitiless bandit to a figure who heroically avenges himself for the wrongs a lawless society has inflicted on him. Schiller's *Die Räuber,* Wiktor Weintraub points out, offers a striking analogy with, if not a source of, the Hernandez story.

demonstrate (and does so most credibly) the essential anarchy of capitalist societies in which politics is directed by business interests. ("By Jove!" he later wrote Cunninghame Graham, "If I had the necessary talent, I would like to go for the true anarchist, which is the millionaire. . . . But it's too big a job."[65])

Gould, now turning his silence against his wife as well as the outside world, refusing even "to discuss the ethical view," trusts that she will "be intelligent enough to understand that his character safeguarded the enterprise of their lives as much or more than his policy."[66] Even his character will not support him, however. Antonia Avellanos, displaying the unfounded idealism she shares with her father, begs Gould to descend from his prejudice against Hernandez, and echoes Gould himself in saying, "It is your character that is the inexhaustible treasure which may save us all yet— your character, Carlos, not your wealth."[67] But in the ensuing crisis, it is the mine that saves them—and saves Gould, character and all— against the murderous wrath of Pedrito Montero, who cannot destroy the goose that laid the silver egg.

To do justice to this vast psychopolitical theme, Conrad invented a new form of emotional drama. He calls it a "tragic farce,"[68] a contradiction in terms which the subject itself imposes on the fiction, alternately choking our mockery with pity, and stifling our pity with satire. Denying us—and denying himself, too—the inclination to despise Gould, Conrad upholds the strength of Gould's honesty as a man and his stature as the new king in the land. There is something heroic in Gould's willingness to bear the brunt of adverse fortune when his utopian dream turns to ashes. He is no foreign exploiter, like Holroyd, nor does he even intellectually repudiate his country as Decoud does. When the foreigner Monygham scornfully says of Costaguana, "It is a fine country, and they have raised a fine crop of hates, vengeance, murder, and

---

[65] Letter of Oct. 7, 1907, *Life and Letters*, II, 60.
[66] *Nostromo*, p. 158.
[67] *Ibid.*, p. 402.
[68] *Ibid.*, p. 405.

rapine—those sons of the country," Gould answers (in words very like Conrad's own response to a jeer about Catholics[69]), "Well, I am one of them."[70] On the last occasion when Gould and his wife are able to communicate at all—coming significantly only a third of the way through the novel—Gould reminds his wife of their irrevocable commitment: "There is nothing to say now. There were things to be done. We have done them; we have gone on doing them. There is no going back now. I don't suppose that even from the first there was really any possible way back."[71]

No way out is suggested, furthermore. Even Dr. Monygham, who hates Gould for "his subtle conjugal infidelity" and foresees that the mine will "weigh as heavily upon the people as the barbarism, cruelty and misery of a few years back,"[72] sees that there is no possibility (now) for "pity and justice" in Costaguana apart from the order that the mine has imposed. The beautiful Antonia and her uncle, Archbishop Corbelàn, a sort of New World Ignatius Loyola, long to "annex the rest of Costaguana to the order and prosperity of Sulaco," which has separated itself. The doctor reminds them that, as this might jeopardize "the material interests," it cannot happen. The archbishop protests, "We have worked for them; we have made them; these material interests of the foreigners." Monygham retorts, "And without them you are nothing."[73]

At this point in the third-to-last chapter, the future is revealed by Corbelàn in one of the continual surprises which turn out to be inevitabilities not only in the novel but in history, though Conrad did not live to see his words fulfilled. Although I agree with Guerard that Corbelàn is a man like Hernandez and General Barrios, who under Gould's "regime find themselves in paradoxically respectable positions or as trusted old men," it seems to me that Conrad suggests through this priest one of the tragic move-

---

[69] Jessie Conrad, *Joseph Conrad and His Circle* (New York: E. P. Dutton & Co., Inc., 1935), p. 228.

[70] *Nostromo*, p. 344.

[71] *Ibid.*, p. 230.

[72] *Ibid.*, p. 571.

[73] *Ibid.*, p. 569.

ments ahead. When Monygham reminds Corbelàn that all his good works are now dependent on the material interests, Corbelàn returns menacingly, "Let them beware, then, lest the people, prevented from their aspirations, should rise and claim their share of the wealth and their share of the power."[74] One thinks of the "priest workers" in France and Germany, who had to be suppressed by Rome after the last war because in their ardor to support "the people" they crossed too far over the line between Christian charity and class warfare. But Conrad also quite clearly makes the matter originate long before the time of the novel's setting, in the alliance between Christianity and secular power. Before the opening of the novel, the Church in Latin America let itself be identified with the Spanish Empire. When in the novel the power has shifted to the interests of the San Tomé mine, Corbelàn devotes himself to regaining from the new order Church properties confiscated during the various "liberations" of Costaguana. The hierarchy of the Church, Conrad predicts, will thus continue to play its role in the "really very relentless warfare" which is the fate of man.

In *Nostromo* we find no successor to the heroic nonpolitical Jesuits of Paraguay whose short-lived utopia Cunninghame Graham had just commemorated in a book called *A Vanished Arcadia*.[75] Opposed to Corbelàn there are only the vicious police tool Father Berón and the elemental, saintly Father Romàn.[76] Related to Corbelàn somewhat as Nostromo is related to Gould, Padre Romàn is Corbelàn's equal in heroism but is a better priest in that he is above politics, caring only for the spiritual good of his flock. He is "incapable of fanaticism to an almost reprehensible

[74] *Ibid.*, pp. 569–70.

[75] The work was first published by William Heinemann in 1901. Conrad reread it while writing *Nostromo* and commented admiringly upon it in a letter to Cunninghame Graham on March 19, 1903. Interestingly enough, the latter in his final chapter quotes words from St. Ignatius Loyola exceedingly like the epigraph for *Nostromo* which Conrad took from Shakespeare. According to St. Ignatius, "No storm is so insidious as a perfect calm, and no enemy so dangerous as the absence of all enemies." Quoted in *A Vanished Arcadia*, p. 259.

[76] A harmless simpleton of a priest named Romàn appears in Masterman. Conrad ennobles him and, one may note in passing, fastens on a memorable Polish name later used for the autobiographical short story "Prince Roman."

degree."[77] Guerard, who finds "intelligence" a transcendant virtue in Conrad's political fiction as elsewhere in his works, interprets Romàn's cynicism concerning politics as "nihilistic" and his uninformed intelligence as Conrad's way of expressing prudent disapproval along with his sympathy for this "nihilism." To some, Romàn's "clear-mindedness . . . [although] served by an uninformed intelligence" may rather suggest the survival value of a form of Christianity which goes about its business independently of the current Caesar, stolidly careless or defiant of all the lurking menaces. An informed Padre Romàn, after all, might have questioned the altar painting of the Resurrection presented by Mrs. Gould, protesting that her mind was on the resurrection of the mine.[78]

If my subject were Conrad's religion, I should argue that, far from finding "the Christian faith the most cruel and grotesque" of all faiths,[79] Conrad is himself no mean advocate of "a purer form of

---

[77] *Nostromo*, p. 444.

[78] *Ibid.*, p. 114.

[79] V. S. Pritchett, "The Moralist of Exile," the *New Statesman* (London), Jan. 30, 1960, pp. 157–58. Pritchett makes too much of Conrad's remarks to Garnett (see *Letters from Conrad*, pp. 99, 185), which are not borne out in Conrad's life and other writings.

When considering the now common description of Conrad as an atheist or agnostic, one should take into account his conduct when faced with choices. Houghton Library at Harvard owns a letter, dated October 8, 1923, in which Conrad speaks to the point. He is answering an invitation from Gordon Gardiner to join an unnamed London club: "I am sending back the pamphlet of the rules of the Club. It is very interesting, but it occurs to me, my dear Gardiner, unless all these words are printed for nothing and the scheme of it has no meaning—mere verbiage as it were—I can not very well belong to this Club by the mere fact that I was born a R. C. and though dogma sits lightly on me I have never renounced that form of Christian religion. The booklet of rules is so, I may say, theological that it would be like renouncing the faith of my fathers.

"Of course you will understand, my dear, that it is not with me any question of the principles but merely a matter of correct conduct. I do not think it would be correct for me to ask you to put my name down, and indeed I do not think it could be done since one of the conditions of membership is to be a Protestant.

"This is my inner feeling, but as a matter of fact I perceive that I simply could not be elected since election to the Club is based not on any assurance of sentiment but on a clear matter of fact—member of the Church of England, for which in truth I have a great regard and sympathy. I think that you will agree with the reflections that prompt me in what I have said.

"I am afraid I am a lost soul. Some years ago I received an invitation to join a R. C.

Christianity" and that his religious scepticism goes little deeper
than the impasse many reach when finding that the presumptions
and commitments necessary to maintaining an active faith, especially in respect to men outside the faith, are odious. Certainly
Nostromo does not support Masterman's trust in the restorative
powers of a religious Reformation in South America. One hardly
looks forward to the arrival in Romàn's flock of "the Protestant
invasion of Sulaco" financed by the American pope Holroyd.[80]

Padre Corbelàn, Conrad suggests, has something in common
with the atheist Decoud. Both are committed to political action
for ulterior reasons, reasons that have nothing to do with the right
purpose of politics, which is the benefit of the secular community.
"Those two men got on well together, as if each had felt respectively that a masterful conviction, as well as utter scepticism, may
lead a man very far on the by-paths of political action."[81] Corbelàn
goes into politics for the Church; Decoud for Antonia Avellanos.

For her Decoud throws himself into the Sulaco revolution, com-
mitting himself to a patriotism he abhors and the capitalist dream
in Sulaco for which he has only contempt. His chances for success

---

Association, presided by the Duke of Norfolk, the secretary of which was W. S.
Lilly, for whose writings I had always a certain sympathy. The proposal itself was in
a sense complimentary. We exchanged several letters but when the articles of the
Association were sent to me in due course I discovered that the members engaged
themselves with all their might and power to work for the restoration of the temporal
power of the Pope. Conceive you that imbecility! Of course I pointed out that this was
a political object, that the accomplished fact had all my sympathy and that I certainly would not lift a finger to re-establish temporal power; upon which Lilly lectured me with great severity and that was the end of it. So you see now I have got to
stand between the two, a prey to the first inferior devil that may come along. My
only hope of escaping the eternal fires is my utter insignificance. I shall lie low on the
Judgment Day, and will probably be overlooked."

[80] *Nostromo*, p. 568. Again one thinks of Cunninghame Graham's reflections on
religion in South America. He once wrote in a letter advising the United States
government on care of the Indians: "I would exclude all missionaries except those of
the Roman Catholic faith, for in my experience of missionaries and Indians, the
Roman Catholics alone have seemed to understand them." (A. F. Tschiffely, *Don
Roberto* [London: William Heinemann, 1937], p. 253.)

[81] *Ibid.*, p. 221. Decoud is then compared with a man of purely political faith,
Garibaldi. Conrad remarks on the difference between the apostle of Italian republican-
ism and Decoud, who had "no faith in anything except the truth of his own sensations" (p. 254).

in politics, again like the archbishop's, are better than those of men who take these causes seriously in themselves.

One trouble with Decoud as a character is that we do not really believe in his "passion" for Señorita Avellanos, which, we are told repeatedly, he "frankly" recognizes as his motive for every action. This passion, supplemented by his pose of intellectual superiority, is Decoud's particular illusion, even if he is able to consider it objectively. Opposed to Guerard's impression that Decoud is a man really "very much in love,"[82] we have Conrad's assertion that "even his passionate devotion to Antonia" had been "worked . . . up out of the depths of his scepticism."[83]

If Antonia Avellanos was indeed based on a girl from Conrad's Polish boyhood, as the Author's Note tells us, nothing besides her austere patriotism seems to have survived in his mind. What little else there is to her character is straight from Eastwick, altered only by a slight change of light on her predominantly masculine qualities. In Eastwick's admiring portrayal, as Baines has remarked, she "talked like a bookworm, like a politician, like a savant, but so little like a señorita of eighteen years of age, that at times I almost forgot I was speaking to a girl."[84] As if questioning Eastwick's analysis of charm, Conrad says—not of Antonia but of Mrs. Gould —"A woman with a masculine mind is not a being of superior efficiency; she is simply a phenomenon of imperfect differentiation."[85] Conrad was, however, drawn to Eastwick's intellectual heroine rather than to the simple Paraguayan Carmelita whom Masterman describes as the *novia* of "Don Carlos Decoud." This Decoud was slaughtered by the despot of Masterman's story, and Carmelita thereupon went insane.[86]

Conrad's Decoud is theoretically a man made up of atheism,

[82] Guerard, *Conrad the Novelist*, p. 200.
[83] *Nostromo*, p. 296.
[84] Eastwick, *op. cit.*, pp. 185–87.
[85] *Nostromo*, p. 73.
[86] Masterman, *op. cit.*, pp. 53–54.

"imaginative materialism,"[87] and factitious intellectuality; possessed of "a Frenchified—but most un-French—cosmopolitanism, in reality a mere barren indifferentism posing as intellectual superiority." In personal appearance he is "of medium height, rather thick," and in general rather unprepossessing: "The fluffy moustache and the short curly, golden beard did not conceal his lips, rosy, fresh, almost pouting in expression. His full round face was of that warm, healthy Creole white which is never tanned by its native sunshine."[88] Something in Decoud was suggested by the treacherous nephew of Conrad's glamorous Marseilles companion, Dominic Cervoni. In A Personal Record Conrad describes how this nephew was drowned by the weight of money he had stolen.

Decoud sees through the poses of all the other characters in the novel (thereby providing a principal source of psychological analysis) and claims to be ruthlessly honest in self-knowledge as well. The one insight he lacks concerning himself, and by implication concerning everyone else too, is into "the genuine impulses of his own nature."[89] These, one finally realizes, are the moral rather than the intellectual or biological impulses. Only a moment before his suicide does he achieve "the first moral sentiment of his manhood."[90] But then it is too late. The only virtue he has previously recognized was intelligence, and intelligence alone will not stand up against solitude, where there is nothing to entertain or occupy it. "Both his intelligence and his passion were swallowed up easily in this great unbroken solitude of waiting without faith."[91]

For once Conrad distinguishes between faith and illusion. Decoud has the "illusion" which always in Conrad energizes the imaginative man. But unlike Jim, Marlow, Lingard, Heyst, the

---

[87] Decoud and Nostromo are both described as imaginative materialists, the main difference between them being that the former has intellectual pretensions, and the latter distrusts intellectuality as a tool of deception used by "los hombres finos" (Nostromo, pp. 405, 461).

[88] Ibid., p. 168.

[89] Ibid., p. 169.

[90] Ibid., p. 557.

[91] Ibid.

intellectual Razumov, or Dr. Monygham in *Nostromo*—all characters whose illusions are saving graces even when they threaten to destroy them—Decoud is wanting in the insuppressible quixotic element which all Conrad's fully compelling characters possess, even such unimaginative ones as MacWhirr and Singleton. Conrad abortively suggests that Decoud has the appealing quixotic idealism but then effaces it with a conflicting trait. Decoud himself describes the conflict as endemic in the Latin American temperament. "There is a curse of futility upon our character: Don Quixote and Sancho Panza, chivalry and materialism, high-sounding sentiments and a supine morality, violent efforts for an idea and a sullen acquiescence in every form of corruption."[92]

The quixotic drive for Conrad comprises, among other things, faith in a difficult moral commitment, in an impossible standard of conduct, or in the job that gives men their moorings in an incomprehensible universe. It is, as we have seen in *The Rescue*, likely to be associated with elemental men such as the "primitive Lingard." It is hard to agree with Robert Penn Warren that Decoud is related in Conrad's mind with "the natural man in that he erected passions into duties."[93] As we have seen in *Heart of Darkness* as well as *The Rescue*, there is nothing more materialistic or less moral about "primitive" man than "civilized" man. In fact, it is only the civilized man, like Kurtz or Decoud, who will intellectualize his passions and make duties out of them.

For all this, through roughly half of *Nostromo*, Decoud is curiously the still point of the turning whirligig of Sulaco. Guerard, more searchingly than any other, has speculated on the reasons for Decoud's major role in illuminating characters and events, for his performing, even, a number of the crucial political actions.

> The characterization obviously belongs with those in which a writer attempts to separate out and demolish a facet of himself; attempts to condemn himself by proxy. But there are certain signs of an even more special relationship than this; *there is, generally, a marked*

---

[92] *Ibid.*, p. 189.
[93] Robert Penn Warren, Introduction to *Nostromo*, p. xxiv.

discrepancy between what Decoud does and says and is, and what the narrator or omniscient author says about him. . . . To put matters bluntly: Conrad may be condemning Decoud for a withdrawal and scepticism more radical than Decoud ever shows; which are, in fact, Conrad's own.[94]

To be fully understood, Guerard's comment must be read in the context of his whole chapter on *Nostromo*. It presents a concise picture both of the novel's technical composition and the meanings as achieved through its dramatic effects and characterizations.

Into the making of Decoud there may have gone, as Guerard holds, "a deeply patriotic and even excited feeling toward Poland doubled by intellectual distrust of fanaticism."[95] One is continually reminded, however, that it was probably Conrad's Polish sensibilities which were most exasperated by the quixotic Sancho Panzas in South America and that the discrepancies in Decoud's character (which finally make it unconvincing) result largely from Conrad's effort to view the situation in Costaguana with seriousness and sympathy. He infuses into Decoud sensitivities both solemnly critical and derisively detached, and ends by creating a monster—a man who professes scorn for his country yet remains on the scene to take a part in its development. Decoud never loses his contempt for his national origin. If Poland gave Conrad the ligaments of Decoud's mind, only the politics of Latin America could produce the extremity of Decoud's self-contempt.[96]

Jocelyn Baines, once more agreeing with Guerard but pushing the case a bit further, concludes that "Costaguana is . . . primarily a prototype of a politically inexperienced nation, and it is tempting to see an analogy between it and Poland."[97] This is rather a fantastic

---

[94] Guerard, *Conrad the Novelist*, p. 199.

[95] *Ibid.*, p. 201.

[96] Alvan Hervey in "The Return" is another monstrous character whom Conrad endowed with qualities he himself admired and possessed. Hervey lectures his wife: "Restraint, duty, fidelity—unswerving fidelity to what is expected of you. This—only this—secures the reward, the peace. Everything else we should labor to subdue—to destroy" (*Tales of Unrest*, p. 156).

[97] *Joseph Conrad*, p. 313.

assertion coming from anyone who has read Conrad's essays and *obiter dicta* on Poland's political history, "great and misunderstood" like Jim. I have tried to present the essence of these writings in Chapter Two. When Baines calls to his aid Conrad's essay on "Autocracy and War" (1905)[98] in which Poland is never mentioned even by implication, he ignores such essays as "The Crime of Partition" (1919) and the Polish idealism which Conrad had locked away, the key to a mausoleum where the possibilities of political wisdom lay buried, to be released only when the "politically inexperienced" nations seemed ready to recognize the ancient Polish rights and virtues. Nowhere in Conrad's writings about Poland do we find even a hint of the imperious soldier-clowns Guzman Bento and Pedrito Montero, or the plague of materialism which in "Autocracy and War" infects Europe as in *Nostromo* it infects Costaguana. Had there been more of Poland in Latin America, Conrad's hallowing sympathy might have flowed more freely with his corroding judgment into *Nostromo*—and into the character of Decoud—as they flow together into *Lord Jim* and its title character.

In the development of Conrad's rigorous scheme for *Nostromo*, Decoud's day rises as Gould's wanes. Decoud first appears in Part II ("The Isabels") only a third of the way into the narrative, bringing his sardonic analysis to bear on the Goulds and the political chaos of his native land at the point where we are already losing the brief romantic moment of hope for the rehabilitating powers of the mine. The fine mechanism of a rationalist mind suddenly halts

---

[98] Baines finds this passage applicable to Costaguana (and Poland): "The intellectual stage of mankind being as yet in its infancy, and States, like most individuals, having but a feeble and imperfect consciousness of the worth and force of the inner life, the need of making their existence manifest to themselves is determined in the direction of physical activity. . . . Action, in which is to be found the illusion of a mastered destiny, can alone satisfy our uneasy vanity and lay to rest the haunting fear of the future—a sentiment concealed, indeed, but proving its existence by the force it has, when invoked, to stir the passions of a nation. It will be long before we have learned that in the great darkness before us there is nothing that we need fear" (*Notes on Life and Letters*, pp. 108–9). The subject of the essay is, of course, the threat of Russia (just defeated in the Russo-Japanese War) and the increasingly warlike atmosphere of all European nations.

the wild veerings of scenes brought before us in the days of the mine's reopening: "America is ungovernable," Decoud asserts. "Those who worked for her independence have ploughed the sea."[99] But someone later points out that "everything merely rational fails in this country."[100] And Decoud's mind is caught in its own analysis: Don Quixote and Sancho Panza, the "curse of futility." A few pages later we hear him say with dreadful meaning he cannot see, "No occupation is serious, not even when a bullet through the heart is the penalty of failure!"[101] And not long afterward, seeing the fanatic religious commitment of Father Corbelàn and blind to his own Achilles heel, he imagines himself to derive aesthetic pleasure from reflecting that Corbelàn's "sacred conviction . . . is like madness. It must be because it's self-destructive."[102] It is not Corbelàn, however, who destroys himself.

Decoud is the only entirely convincing nihilist Conrad ever created, and as such is missed as much in his absence from the Geneva of *Under Western Eyes* as he is valued for his presence in the Costaguana of *Nostromo*. His cosmopolitanism is lethal—to himself and probably to the Conrad who considered "the preservation of national sentiment" one of his concerns. As with the Russian nihilists, it is *moral* revulsion against social injustice that leads Decoud, ironically, to deny the grounds of morality itself. Beginning with contempt for bad institutions, he ends by despising the humanity in whose name he is indignant.

> "Señor, I refuse to fetch a priest for a dying woman . . ."
> Decoud was heard to stir.
> "You did, capataz!" he exclaimed. His tone changed. "Well, you know—it was rather fine."
> "You do not believe in priests, Don Martin? Neither do I. What was the use of wasting time? But she—she believes in them. The thing sticks in my throat."[103]

[99] *Nostromo*, p. 206.
[100] *Ibid.*, p. 350.
[101] *Ibid.*, p. 195.
[102] *Ibid.*, p. 225.
[103] *Ibid.*, p. 297.

In the artistry of the novel, Decoud snaps off our emotional interest in Gould. He brings before our eyes, in a letter to his sister, the riot following the collapse of Sulaco's government when word comes that Pedrito Montero has overthrown Ribiera and is on his way with his *llaneros* to usurp the mine. Decoud then sets up the third and last division of the novel by accompanying Nostromo on the desperate journey to save the silver from the invading forces. Part I of the novel, through kaleidoscopic images, gave us the past, both of the Gould romance and of the early opening of the "scar" of the San Tome mine, with glimpses of Costaguana's past history of Spanish conquest, colonization, rebellion, and finally military dictatorships. Part II, mainly through Decoud's eyes, establishes the present, developing the reader's excited attention and holding it through long scenes in which Decoud talks with Mrs. Gould or makes love to Antonia in the same breath as jeering at the *"gran bestia"* of the farce. It is Decoud who will lead Nostromo forward, first by visualizing his activity during the riot, then by experiencing alone with him the long night in the Golfo Placido. This accidental partnership between Decoud and Nostromo prepares us to accept Nostromo's domination over Part III, "The Lighthouse," which makes up nearly half the novel.

Now Decoud's day will set, if not technically till the twelfth chapter of Part III at least dramatically, when Nostromo abandons him on the island where the silver is buried. Decoud's death is vividly foreshadowed just before this when, aboard the lighter in impenetrable darkness, Nostromo puts out the candle and it seems to Decoud "as if his companion had destroyed by a single touch the world of affairs, of loves, of revolution, where his complacent superiority analyzed fearlessly all motives and all passions, including his own."[104] The death of the "imaginative materialist" Decoud is a variation on the novel's theme, "the menace of death" in materialism. Although in his intellectual materialism he maintains a philosophical contempt for the "material interests" (no hardship for an independently wealthy man), Conrad's rhetorical reitera-

---

[104] *Ibid.*, p. 305.

tions[105] urge the reader to compare his suicide with the more human death of Nostromo.

Appropriately it is Nostromo who snuffs out Decoud's world of affairs. In Part III Decoud's form of scepticism is no longer wanted as a source of light, for Nostromo—as suspicious of Decoud as Decoud was of him—must come into his own as title figure. If Decoud's overriding consciousness comes between Gould's story in Part I and Nostromo's in Part III, it serves the principle that the two pillars upholding the affairs of the novel must be separated for the strength of the whole. Gould's corruption is the corruption of a system; Nostromo's the fall of a man. They could not be related more closely because the corruption of Nostromo by Gould must be seen as an indirect reaction long delayed, entirely unforeseen by Gould.

And Decoud must go. In his "complacent superiority," he alone might have guessed the secret of Nostromo's new life in Part III. "One must pay in some way or other for such a solid thing as individual prestige,"[106] he had maintained against Mrs. Gould's trust in Nostromo's integrity. Dr. Monygham, the sceptical realist who continues the lifeline of political insight to the end of the novel, fails in lucidity when he must judge Nostromo. "The doctor's misanthropic mistrust of mankind (the bitterer because based on personal failure) did not lift him sufficiently above common weaknesses. He was under the spell of an established reputation."[107]

Decoud's opinions, furthermore, posited a timeless—or rather endless—cycle of vile rebirths in Latin American politics. In Part III, not forgetting Decoud's assessments, we are made to look seriously to the future, and for this vision we are offered the sight of Captain Mitchell, of Dr. Monygham, of Mrs. Gould, of Padre Corbelàn, and finally of the little "hater of capitalists." Nostromo looks to no future but his own, of course. He is "the people," non-

---

[105] *Ibid.*, pp. 560–61.
[106] *Ibid.*, p. 244.
[107] *Ibid.*, p. 483.

political,[108] concerned with himself alone. But after his death, the Marxists will recreate him in their own image.

Even readers who, like me, do not find with Guerard and Baines that the novel falls off sharply in the latter half, when Decoud drops from the scene, may feel that Nostromo is insufficiently compelling as a character to hold together the rich situations that follow coherently from the hiding of the treasure, the disappointed greed of the Monterist forces, and the ambiguous victory of the forces of prosperity.

If Conrad fails in the characterization of Nostromo, it is at least a daring enterprise. The stealing of the silver, which Conrad says in the Author's Note gave him his idea for the novel, plainly held nothing of the fascination for him that, say, the desertion of a pilgrim ship held in setting him on the trail of Lord Jim. *Nostromo* is the very opposite of a free and wandering tale, growing out of anecdote as oak from acorn. The novel is rather a tightly organized political fable, whose burden was fully preconceived in Conrad's mind, whose anecdotes and characters—even while they form infinitely complex patterns, rich in suggestion—seem to illustrate rather than to explore the theme, as character explores theme in *Lord Jim* and *Under Western Eyes.*

As Jocelyn Baines puts it, the main figures in *Nostromo* "exist for what they represent rather than for what they are."[109] The silver is "the real hero"; therefore, Nostromo's secret life is a symbol for the silver. This intentional inversion of subject and object is what creates the novel's artificial manner as well as matter. Nostromo's worth, like the value of the silver, is determined more by what people say about him than by his intrinsic qualities. Through Nostromo we learn the truth about the silver rather than the other way around. As silver is incorruptible by rust and always valuable, Nostromo's character to the end is uncorroded in the eyes of the

---

[108] At this point, admittedly, one may argue against my assertion that for Conrad man is a political animal. I would answer that in *Nostromo* Conrad is, as usual, distinguishing between two kinds of politics: between the natural association of men for mutual benefit and the power politics of men who intentionally or unintentionally tyrannize over nations or races, according to some power ideal.

[109] Baines, *Joseph Conrad*, p. 299

world. Only Decoud reflects that he is "made incorruptible by his enormous vanity, that finest form of egoism which can take on the aspect of every virtue."[110] But Decoud dies too early to see the effect on this vanity of an indifferent world. Here is where Nostromo's humanity will out. Unlike the silver, he is susceptible to unseen changes. He is never devalued, but his nature is finally corrupted absolutely.

Thus Nostromo, and this explains his name in the title, emerges as the great manifestation and test of Gould's proposition—that the silver can be made an agent of moral reform. Gould cannot make morality out of silver, and Nostromo cannot make himself in the image of a material thing.

Gould, "*el rey de Sulaco*,"[111] in choosing his god, determines the aspirations of his people, as typified by Nostromo. *Cuius regio, eius religio.* As the man on whom the safety of the silver is made to depend, Nostromo asks only the recognition from his employers that they give to the silver. He does not resent being "lent out" like money by Captain Mitchell. He merely responds to the forces driving his moral and intellectual superiors. Under varying provocations, Decoud, the devout Teresa, and Dr. Monygham (with the high moralist's oversubtle scorn for his own practical wisdom) all taunt Nostromo about the uselessness of prestige alone as a reward for sacrifice.

Decoud credits Nostromo with a scepticism concerning the world of Sulaco which is in fact merely the egoism of his nature: "that Genoese sailor who, like me, has come casually here to be drawn into the events for which his scepticism as well as mine seems to entertain a sort of passive contempt."[112] Later we learn from Conrad that Nostromo's mind, like the "popular mind is incapable of scepticism; and that incapacity delivers their helpless strength to the wiles of swindlers and to the pitiless enthusiasms of

[110] *Nostromo*, p. 333.
[111] Guerard has remarked on the way Conrad subtly juxtaposes the figure of Charles Gould on horseback and the equestrian statue of Charles IV of Spain (*Conrad the Novelist*, p. 180).
[112] *Nostromo*, p. 273.

leaders inspired by visions of a high destiny."[113] Brought to the crucial test, Nostromo's sustaining veneer of detachment cracks, revealing a strong man pitifully at the mercy of the weak leaders who depend on him. Nowhere does Conrad's attack on *all* the false gods of modern politics show more clearly his preoccupation with the fate of ordinary men.

The infinitely slow pace of Nostromo's fall gives us the hebetude of his "unintelligence" but also suggests the strength of his resistance to corruption by the treasure. We imagine him to be tempted long before he thinks of stealing, when he first wakes up from his swim ashore, leaving Decoud stranded on the Great Isabel. (Decoud dare not use the small boat for escape while Montero is at large.) Now two more ominous birds, like the Goulds' parrot, presage disaster. And the unintellectual Nostromo, unlike the Goulds, is attentive to their warnings. A vulture, "patient watcher for signs of death and corruption," circling above his sleeping form, hops away as he wakes, and Nostromo mutters, "I am not dead yet."[114] Not dead but weak from exertion, destitute of "all worldly possessions" which however few had bought him prestige with the humble folk of Sulaco, and—worst of all—alone, he feels for the first time "the collapse of his vanity . . . [which] could not exist apart from outward show."[115] He feels betrayed without a definite idea of his betrayer. Teresa had been right when she said, "They have been paying you with words. Your folly shall betray you into poverty, misery, starvation."[116] He had refused her a priest; to safeguard the silver, had incurred her dying curse. But had she died? "As if in answer to this thought, half of remorse and half of hope, with a soft flutter and oblique flight, a big owl, whose appalling cry— 'Ya-acabo! Ya-acabo!' (It is finished! It is finished!) announces calamity and death in the popular belief, drifted vaguely . . .

---

[113] *Ibid.*, p. 470.
[114] *Ibid.*, pp. 459–60.
[115] *Ibid.*, p. 466.
[116] *Ibid.*, p. 285.

across his path."[117] She is dead, then. He has been betrayed by the *hombres finos* Giorgio Viola had told him to mistrust (for it is in part the memory of Viola's abstract stigmatization of "the rich" that persuades Nostromo he has been betrayed by the representatives of the mine).[118] With this thought, Nostromo shifts his loyalty from these men to the silver itself—"made up his mind that the treasure should not be betrayed."[119]

Still he has no thought of stealing it. Only the owl's cry suggests the certain fall of this Adam, the fulfilment of passion for this suffering servant of the material interests. (The same ironic consummation seems implied for Decoud, who shoots himself and mutters, "It is done."[120]) Even the renewal of trust on the part of Nostromo's superiors, confirmed when Monygham sends him on the daredevil mission to Barrios' forces, cannot compensate for Nostromo's sense of having been made to betray both Teresa and Decoud: ". . . he knew the part he had played himself [in Decoud's death]. First a woman, then a man, abandoned each in their last extremity, for the sake of the accursed treasure. It was paid for by a soul lost and by a vanished life."[121] Not till now, almost a hundred pages and several weeks after hiding the silver on the Great Isabel, does Nostromo decide to possess the silver. The decision is based on a moral bargain: he has bought the treasure with his own soul, forfeited when he betrayed Decoud and Teresa to save it.

The guilt for these betrayals belongs at the door of his superiors. When Nostromo's vanity crumpled, he "was ready to feel the burden of sacrilegious guilt descend upon his shoulders."[122] Guilt

---

[117] *Ibid.*, p. 468.

[118] Thus there meet in the corruption of Nostromo the vicious influence of the French Revolution (motivated by abstract ideas) and the materialist principles of the next Revolution, still under preparation when *Nostromo* was written. The ironic confluence is further dramatized by Viola's contempt for material things and "all personal advantage" (*ibid.*, p. 34).

[119] *Ibid.*, p. 469.

[120] *Ibid.*, p. 560.

[121] *Ibid.*, p. 561.

[122] *Ibid.*, p. 470.

itself is sacrilegious when thrown on the shoulders of an innocent man. Yet, like Decoud's first sense of moral responsibility at the hour of his death, Nostromo's moral awareness is born just in time to be sold for the silver.

Or rather those few weeks intervene before his decision to "get rich slowly." He is still, as it were, innocently carrying the burden of guilt when he leaves the beach and stumbles into Dr. Monygham in the dark, at the foot of the customhouse stairs, just after seeing the shadow of the hanging Hirsch. Perhaps because of his own guilt, he subtly perceives Monygham's indirect responsibility for "betraying" Hirsch. To win time, Monygham had planted in Sotillo's mind the idea that Hirsch was lying when he told of the silver's being sunk. Nostromo drives the point home: "Perhaps if you had not confirmed Sotillo in his madness he would have been in no haste to give the estrapade to that miserable Hirsch."[123] Freshly endowed with knowledge of good and evil, the fruit of his temptation, Nostromo can now see this moral flaw in the *hombre fino.* Quite justifiably, then, he withholds his knowledge of the silver's safety from the one man he has a chance to inform, further maintaining his innocence till after he has saved Sulaco as well as the silver and returned to the island to learn of Decoud's death. Then it is not so much the fact that conditions are right for the perfect crime as awareness of his partial responsibility for Decoud's death that turns him into a thief.

In the end, we see the measure of Conrad's unrelenting judgment against the material interest in Nostromo's failure, even when he tries, to renounce and be saved. The death scenes, like the earlier temptation scenes, remind one strongly of Marlowe's *Dr. Faustus.* "O Ile leap up to my God: who pulles me downe?" cries Faustus. Nostromo confesses everything to Mrs. Gould but still is not free. "It holds me yet!" he tells her.[124] The folk legend, Nostromo remembered, had called the foreign treasure hunters "gringo ghosts suffering in their starved and parched flesh of defiant heretics,

---

[123] *Ibid.*, p. 490.
[124] *Ibid.*, p. 624.

where a Christian would have renounced and been released."[125] But Nostromo cannot even fully renounce. He finally perceives that it is the silver that has killed him, not the *hombres finos*, and his last gesture is one of lofty defiance against the Marxist. Nostromo will not bequeath the silver so that the rich may "be fought with their own weapons"; neither will he label even the untrustworthy Dr. Monygham as "a dangerous enemy of the people."[126]

Dr. Monygham becomes, as I have implied, the governing intelligence as well as the most forceful political actor (apart from Nostromo himself) in the last third of the novel. Like Decoud, but for the opposite reason, Monygham now shakes off his sceptical detachment from the political conflict. Though both men are motivated by love, Decoud had to "erect passion into a duty" worthy of his complacent superiority, whereas Monygham's love for Mrs. Gould urges him to self-sacrifice without altering his almost abject humility. He had said to himself, "I am the only one fit for that dirty work."[127] He does not, moreover, sacrifice his intellectual detachment but quite the reverse. He sacrifices his respect for the solidarity of the human community to the necessities of saving his own "team."

> To lie, to deceive, to circumvent even the basest of mankind was odious to him. It was odious to him by training, instinct, and tradition. To do these things in the character of a traitor was abhorrent to his nature . . . . He had made that sacrifice in a spirit of abasement.[128]

Shades of the Polish epic *Konrad Wallenrod* and of Conrad's own father![129] Only by deceiving Sotillo, by indirectly bringing on the

---

[125] *Ibid.,* p. 5.

[126] *Ibid.,* p. 627. At this point again the collected editions differ from the Modern Library edition. According to the latter, Nostromo turns to the Marxist a glance of "enigmatic and mocking scorn" (p. 627); in the former, Conrad has corrected it to read "enigmatic and profound inquiry" (Dent, p. 563), having perhaps decided that Nostromo would not have known enough about the Marxist to do more than wonder at him.

[127] *Ibid.,* p. 491.

[128] *Ibid.*

[129] See chap. ii, pp. 72–73.

murder of Hirsch, has Monygham succeeded in dividing the forces of the enemy until Barrios can be brought back by Nostromo.

Quite apart from his action, it is Monygham, "with his special conception of this political crisis,"[130] who in Part III gives us our final assessment of Gould's politics. He reflects:

> The administrador had acted as if the immense and powerful prosperity of the mine had been founded on methods of probity, on the sense of usefulness. And it was nothing of the kind. The method followed had been the only one possible. The Gould Concession had ransomed its way through all those years. It was a nauseous process. He quite understood that Charles Gould had got sick of it, and had left the old path to back up that hopeless attempt at reform. The doctor did not believe in the reform of Costaguana. And now the mine was back again in its old path, with the disadvantage that henceforth it had to deal not only with the greed provoked by its wealth, but with the resentment awakened by the attempt to free itself from its bondage to material corruption. That was the penalty of failure. What made him uneasy was that Charles Gould seemed to him to have weakened at the decisive moment where a frank return to the old methods was the only chance. Listening to Decoud's wild scheme had been a weakness.[131]

In this difficult passage, Monygham is blaming Gould for not using the silver ingots to "buy off" Sotillo and Montero, as he had been buying off the corrupt officials from the beginning of his venture. Monygham sees that in putting the safety of the silver first, Gould has shifted his policy to suit the interest of the mine, thus destroying his integrity as a man with a consistent and trustworthy political aim. Even the resolution to separate Sulaco from the rest of Costaguana, while taken in the name of good government, has been carried by considerations for the safety of the mine rather than by regard for the future of the country, which is now doomed to civil war.

A realist in politics, a personalist in human relationships, Monygham comes as close as any character in Conrad's fiction to proposing the marriage of politics and morality which Conrad saw

---

[130] *Nostromo*, p. 411.
[131] *Ibid.*, p. 412.

as the perhaps unattainable goal of human history. Although definitions are perilous in criticizing an artist with Conrad's bias against the formulation of psychic and moral experience, it seems fair to distinguish a rather clear division in *Nostromo* between *ideas* and *moral principles* as guides for political action.

We have seen in *Heart of Darkness* the confusion of "ideas" and morality in both Kurtz and Marlow, each defending white supremacy in undeveloped countries according to his own lights. We have seen, too, that Decoud—perhaps the greatest of Conrad's intellectuals in that he most clearly analyzes a complex society and its members—is yet described as a moral paralytic. In *Nostromo* Monygham, the realist, whose only quirk is an exaggerated notion of his own frailty, epitomizes the political "message" of the novel:

> There is no peace and rest in the development of material interests. They have their law and their justice. But it is founded on expediency, and is inhuman; it is without rectitude, without the continuity and the force that can be found only in a moral principle.[132]

It is left to Mrs. Gould to recognize that other general truth concerning *ideas* in politics, which she and her husband have learned too late: "There was something inherent in the necessities of successful action which carried with it the moral degradation of the idea."[133]

"Moral degradation of the idea" is an odd phrase, calling attention to the way ideas (as figured here in the capitalist utopia) can be morally degraded even when they retain their ideological force. Although in "a prophetic vision" Mrs. Gould foresees her heirless husband overcome by the mine, and herself "surviving alone the degradation of her young ideal of life, of love, of work—all alone in the Treasure House of the World,"[134] there *will* be an heir to Gould's idea in the unfolding master plans of the American Holroyd.

Irving Howe interprets Monygham's remark about moral prin-

---

[132] *Ibid.*, p. 571.
[133] *Ibid.*, p. 582.
[134] *Ibid.*

ciples as a retreat from politics "to the resources of private affection and gentleness."[135] Since Conrad is as vague as anyone about moral principles, it is hard to argue the point, but obviously Monygham at least thought he was making a positive statement about good politics (possessing continuity and force because founded on moral principles), not just retreating from the bad. I would argue, moreover, that a man with a distaste for politics could never have begun to write *Nostromo*; that only an artist imagining somewhere a mature or maturing audience could so intensely explore the gaps between the ideals and oratory of the politicians and their achievements. It is a fully absorbed mind, compact of Decoud and Monygham, that immediately after finishing *Nostromo*, distrusts the power of art to convey political wisdom:

> Direct vision of fact, or the stimulus of a great art, can alone make [imagination] turn and open its eyes heavy with blessed sleep; and even there, as against the testimony of the senses and the stirring up of emotion, that saving callousness which reconciles us to the conditions of our existence, will assert itself under the guise of assent to fatal necessity, or in the enthusiasm of a purely esthetic rendering. In this age of knowledge our sympathetic imagination, to which alone we can look for the ultimate triumph of concord and justice, remains strangely impervious to information, however correctly and even picturesquely conveyed.[136]

Only an artist stimulated by the complex manifestations of political activity in history could create a microcosm of international intrigues as convincing as Costaguana. If there is anything like a retreat to the resources of private affection, it must be recognized as a movement to raise political consciousness to the level of personal awareness, where "the worth and force of the inner life"—Dr. Monygham's moral principles—might yet prove to be effective. "Autocracy and War," Conrad's first political essay, written as a sudden excited response to the defeat of Russia by Japan in 1905, is full of thoughts that ride in the wake of *Nostromo*:

> The intellectual stage of mankind being as yet in its infancy, and States, like most individuals, having but a feeble and imperfect con-

---

[135] See above, pp. 14–15.
[136] *Notes on Life and Letters*, p. 84.

sciousness of the worth and force of the inner life, the need of making their existence manifest to themselves is determined in the direction of physical activity. . . . Action, in which is to be found
the illusion of a mastered destiny, can alone satisfy our uneasy vanity and lay to rest the haunting fear of the future . . . Let us act
lest we perish—is the cry. And the only form of action open to a
State can be of no other than aggressive nature.[137]

Both *Nostromo* and this political essay stress the intellectual
moralist's resort, not to private affection, but to a frail hope in the
triumph of "the inner life" on a public level over all the various
forms of aggression that powerful states engage in to console themselves for their failures to achieve an earthly paradise. "*Il n'y a plus
d'Europe*—there is only an armed and trading continent, the home
of slowly maturing economical contests for life and death, and of
loudly proclaimed world-wide ambitions."[138] This is no aestheticist's
jeremiad against ugly industrialization but a philosophical analysis
of the *radix malorum*, "the incredible infatuation [with material
interests] which could put its trust in the peaceful nature of indus-
trial and commercial competition."[139] Conrad's indignation with
democracy, in its Western Hemisphere manifestations particularly,
may be seen in his novels repeatedly. Democracy went wrong, it
would seem, when in the eighteenth century its theory was founded
in the anarchic warfare of economic doctrines drawn from *The
Wealth of Nations* and later outgrowths of utilitarian thought.

Conrad's only practical suggestion is of course personalist: that
"some statesman of exceptional ability and overwhelming prestige"
might succeed "in carrying through an international understanding
for the delimitation of spheres of trade all over the earth," an
understanding, Conrad bitterly adds, "on the model of the territorial spheres of influence marked in Africa to keep the competi-
tors for the privilege of improving the nigger (as a buying machine)
from flying at each other's throats."[140]

Preferably, in other words, every nation should cultivate its

---

[137] *Ibid.*, pp. 108–9.
[138] *Ibid.*, p. 112.
[139] *Ibid.*, p. 106.
[140] *Ibid.*, p. 107.

private garden. But apart from controlling the present archvillainy of commercial competition, the political goal of the future is almost indistinguishable in the dark of man's emotional and intellectual immaturity: "it must be confessed that the architectural aspect of the universal city remains as yet inconceivable—that the very ground for its erection has not been cleared of the jungle."[141]

In *Nostromo* we have Conrad's most comprehensive and vivid portrayal of that jungle—and of one misguided effort to clear it. Notably, the only real foreigners who may be said to be in Costaguana for political purposes are the American Holroyd, the Marxist photographer, and the Englishmen of the railway, who illustrate as much as Gould does that the new imperialism of capital investment, through its refusal to jeopardize itself by political commitment, is inviting not only anarchy and war but a rabid xenophobia. Conrad, the foreigner in England, makes most of Costaguana's foreigners out to be refugees or innocent drifters.

There is more than one moral to be drawn from *Nostromo*, and now that readers are acclaiming its prescience, they will probably go on drawing different conclusions for many years to come. One conclusion *not* reached by Conrad has recommended the novel to a very acute British writer on modern history. It is entertaining to think what the author of *Heart of Darkness* would have thought while reading D. W. Brogan's appreciation of *Nostromo* as apparently the best example in modern literature of some "neglected truths" about imperialism. Brogan concludes:

> Under imperial rule, British or French, Khedives and Beys were not allowed to plunder and waste the public assets as they had done on their own. . . . It is not mere bravado that makes me pose the question, would not some South American states have been less exploited "imperialistically" if they had lost their independence?[142]

Brogan's practical wisdom, however Eastwickian,[143] is today good political morality, similar to what I have called "the normal human

---

[141] *Ibid.*

[142] D. W. Brogan, "Re-thinking Imperialism," *Encounter* (May, 1960), p. 77.

[143] See above, p. 169.

response" of Marlow in the Congo. Conrad's alienation from it, even while he pleads through Decoud and Monygham for reason against religious and political fanaticism, for "fidelity" against revolutionary "short cuts,"[144] reminds us that we cannot end with calling Conrad "a critic [in the sense of assailant] of the ideal" (Morton Dauwen Zabel's phrase[145]). Admittedly this is the side of Conrad we see best in our "moment," when ideology has become the bugbear of American and British writers, haunted by—among older specters—Nazi Germany and Communist Russia; when social scientists, particularly, are initiating a valiant quest after the fugitive political value which one of Polanyi's colleagues has termed "civility."

> Civil politics are based on civility, which is the virtue of the citizen, of the man who shares responsibly in his own self-government, either as a governor or as one of the governed. Civility is compatible with other attachments to class, to religion, to profession, but it regulates them out of respect for the common good.
>
> Civil politics do not stir the passions; they do not reveal man at the more easily apprehensible extremes of heroism and saintliness.[146]

Edward Shils, here, and many of Polanyi's admirers have Conrad on their side to some extent. Raymond Aron, who is one of them, agrees with Conrad that the violence of modern ideological warfare originated in the French Revolution. Notably, however, it is not the ideology that Conrad stresses but the "obscurantism" of ideologies schooled by the French Revolution, the tendencies of revolutionaries from then on to be *irresponsible* "in the region of ideas."[147] Ideologies are often villainous in Conrad's political *Weltanschauung*, but he never attempts to visualize a society in which they are kept in close rein. Edward Shils argues *against* the very force that, in *Lord Jim*, is the object of Marlow's search—

---

[144] "A revolution is a short cut in the rational development of national needs in response to the growth of world-wide ideals" ("Autocracy and War," *Notes on Life and Letters*, p. 101).

[145] Introduction, *The Portable Conrad*, p. 8.

[146] Edward Shils, "Ideology and Civility," *Sewanee Review* (Summer, 1958), p. 470.

[147] Cf. chap. ii, p. 52.

against (in Shils's words) "the romantic—and ideological—insistence on the universal application of a single set of standards."[148]

Though Conrad often pictured a future in which men may be
made aware of the consequences of their social action,[149] he never
implied that any radical change in human nature (such as a purging
of ideologies would entail) could be achieved, or that warfare could
cease. Monygham's "moral principles" strike one, rather, as the
good man's bulwark against an undiminishing barrage of evil
forces, "since from the duality of man's nature and the competition
of individuals, the life-history of the earth *must in the last instance
be a history of a really very relentless warfare.*"[150]

Nostromo is primarily a novel of *ideas*, and its theme (seen
especially in the contrast between the materialisms of the idealistic
Gould and the simple Nostromo) evolves as a revelation of the
logic of ideas in history. With the demise of Martin Decoud and
the ascent of Dr. Monygham in the last part of the novel, however,
we mark a rejection—characteristic with Conrad—of ideas, of intellectuality, and an invocation of moral sensibility (not devoid of
intelligence, of course, as Monygham shows) as the proper guide
for political action. For all his perspicacity, Martin Decoud lacks
Monygham's conviction that there can be law and justice which
are founded not on material interests but on moral principles. And
in Monygham's moral principles one infers a refusal to shift and
compromise as Gould had done.

What is most curious and most often missed about Conrad's
creative genius is his extraordinary dread of being caught in a fixed
moral posture, when indeed his whole energy is expended in the
effort to arrive at one. Among intellectuals the great objection to

---

[148] Shils, *op. cit.*, p. 479. Cf. chap. ii, pp. 64–68.

[149] E.g., to H. G. Wells in 1903: "The future is of our own making—and (for me)
the most striking characteristic of the century is just that development, that maturing of our consciousness which should open our eyes to that truth—or that
illusion. Anything that would help our intelligences toward a clearer view of the
consequences of our social action is of the very greatest value . . ." (*Life and Letters,*
I, 323). This hope for increasing awareness is, after all, one motive for writing
serious novels.

[150] "Henry James," *Notes on Life and Letters*, p. 15. The italics are mine.

Conrad is not his difficulty (which discourages the unintellectual
reader) but his moralizing, the one thing that would have recommended him most highly to unintellectual readers, if he had not
made his novels so difficult for them.

Amusingly, when Conrad chose to lecture his contemporaries,
Wells, Bennett, Galsworthy, and others, on the shallowness or
falseness of their morality, he told them it was their "literary truth"
rather than their general truth he found objectionable. Of course,
moral untruth is aesthetically as well as morally unpalatable, but
Conrad went to the further extreme of implying that the two kinds
of truth were at odds—that in order to be aesthetically pleasing, one
had to vitiate the morality. What he really wished, it seems apparent, was that they would curb their questionable moralizings and
penetrate to the true morality. Thus, although he complained of
Wells's "tendency to emphasize the moral at the expense of
artistic finish and complained about his fondness for preaching at
the expense of literary truth,"[151] Conrad gave Wells a moral rather
than artistic reason for the "fundamental" difference between them:
"You don't care for humanity but think they are to be improved. I
love humanity but know they are not."[152]

Later, without visibly straying from aesthetic criteria, Conrad
will write Bennett a criticism that can only be taken as an objection
to his limited range of values: "You stop just short of being absolutely real because you are faithful to your dogmas of realism. . . .
And your art, your gift, should be put to the service of a larger and
freer faith."[153]

Then, after lecturing Galsworthy on his tendency to identify
himself too closely with his characters' moral points of view
("Scepticism [is] . . . the agent of truth—the way of art and
salvation" and "You seem . . . to hug your conceptions of right
and wrong too closely"),[154] some seven years later, finding Gals-

[151] Joseph Retinger, *Conrad and His Contemporaries* (London: Minerva, 1941), p. 106.
[152] Rupert Hart-Davis, *Hugh Walpole* (London: Rupert Hart-Davis, 1952), p. 168.
[153] Letter of March 10, 1902, *Life and Letters*, I, 303.
[154] Letter of Nov. 11, 1901, *Life and Letters*, I, 301–2.

worthy immovable in his course, Conrad will abandon talk of technique and point of view, coming down to the essentials which give us a more intimate view of his own deep concerns. He still tries to discourage Galsworthy from moralizing, on the ground of its being poor art, but now he undertakes to define the *kind* of morality, the bad morality, that is bad for art:

> A moralist must present us with a gospel—he must give counsel, not to our reason or sentiment, but to our very soul. Do you feel in yourself the stature for that task? That you must meditate over with great seriousness . . .

He goes on to say that it is "impossible to read a book like that without asking oneself,—what then?" How is life to be lived, if this "gospel" is true? In a confusing sentence that follows, his meaning is nevertheless clear. The shallowly sentimental artist will pervert life as well as art by not rendering our "humanity . . . imperative enough and . . . elementary enough." And the cynical artist will make a "mere declaration, not of the vanity of things (that would be a too optimistic view), but of the utter futility of existence. Pessimism can go no further. This is the danger of the moralist who has not a faith, however crude, distorted or extravagant, to present to his audience."[155]

In *Nostromo*, that "tragic farce," Conrad appeals more to our heads than to our hearts, but even here, almost in spite of himself, he ends with the highly disorganized appeal heard in *Lord Jim*, *Heart of Darkness*, and in the two novels we turn to next—beyond head and heart, "to our very soul."

---

[155] Letter of 1908, *Life and Letters*, II, 77–78.

"This looks like mere fanaticism. But fanaticism is human. Man has adored ferocious divinities. There is ferocity in every passion, even in love itself. The religion of undying hope resembles the mad cult of despair, of death, of annihilation. The difference lies in the moral motive springing from the secret needs and the unexpressed aspiration of the believers. It is only to vain men that all is vanity; and all is deception only to those who have never been sincere with themselves."

"Prince Roman"

"The true greatness of a State does not spring from such a contemptible source. It is a matter of logical growth, of faith and courage. Its inspiration springs from the constructive instinct of the people, governed by the strong hand of a collective conscience and voiced in the wisdom and counsel of men who seldom reap the reward of gratitude."

"Autocracy and War"

CHAPTER SIX

The Secret Agent

"Are we on the eve of great changes or are we not? Is everything that's gathering underground, in the dark, in the night, in little hidden rooms, out of sight of governments and policemen and idiotic 'statesmen'—heaven save them!—is all this going to burst forth some fine morning and set the world on fire? Or is it to sputter out and spend itself in vain conspiracies, be dissipated in sterile heroisms and abortive isolated movements? I want to know à quoi m'en tenir . . . ."[1]

In *The Secret Agent*, Conrad answers the cry of the Princess Casamassima in an unexpected manner. The revolutionists of Conrad's novel—published in 1907 some thirty years after James's *Princess Casamassima*—neither set the world on fire nor rise to sterile heroisms. Their conspiracies are worse than vain; they achieve disaster inadvertently: the gory destruction of a feeble-minded boy, the suicide by drowning of a conscientious cockney woman.

Concerning the genesis of the novel, Conrad wrote in the Author's Note that an "omniscient friend"—that is, Ford Madox Ford—had given him the idea first in a conversation and that it was a matter of days only before "the story of Winnie Verloc stood out complete."[2] Since Ford and Conrad met at the house of Stephen

---

[1] Henry James, *The Princess Casamassima*, I (New York: Macmillan Co., 1948), 195.
[2] *The Secret Agent*, p. xii.

Crane[3] in February, 1898, one might imagine the two discussing at that time the abortive "anarchist outrage" of four years before. There seems little excuse, however, to look for an inspiration earlier than late 1905, when the Conrads were tenants at "the Pent" and Ford, according to Conrad's own testimony, could still be called "a sort of lifelong habit—of which I am not ashamed, because he is a much better fellow than the world gives him credit for."[4]

" 'The Secret Agent'—I mean the tale—came to me in the shape of a few words uttered by a friend in a casual conversation about anarchists or rather anarchist activities," Conrad recalls in the Author's Note. The friend's most striking remark was: "Oh, that fellow was half an idiot. His sister committed suicide afterwards." This, Conrad writes, remained merely an "illuminating impression" for "a considerable time."[5]

After Conrad's death, Ford wrote, "That passage is curiously characteristic Conrad. For what the writer really did say to Conrad was: 'Oh, that fellow was half an idiot! His sister murdered her husband afterwards and was allowed to escape by the police.'"[6] If not characteristic, it is significant that Conrad singled out and attributed to another the one incident that gives the story its essential originality and difference from the events that occurred in 1894.

For to an extraordinary extent, *The Secret Agent* shimmeringly reflects the newspaper attitudes as well as the factual hints provided in the accounts of "the Greenwich Observatory outrage." There is no ground whatever for the inference that Conrad transformed a melodramatic and tragic incident into a humorous, ironical tale about farcical secret agents and revolutionaries. He supplied only— besides the characters of Winnie, her mother, her brother, and their fates—the intrusion of Mr. Vladimir and the foreign embassy, and

---

[3] See Jessie Conrad, *Joseph Conrad and His Circle* (New York: E. P. Dutton & Co., Inc., 1935), p. 58. Baines doubts that they met before the following September at Garnett's, but Conrad was at Ford's house, Pent Farm, in May, when he addressed a letter from there (*Life and Letters*, I, 237).

[4] Letter of Oct. 20, 1905, to H. G. Wells, *Life and Letters*, II, 25.

[5] *The Secret Agent*, pp. ix–x.

[6] Ford Madox Ford, *Joseph Conrad: A Personal Remembrance* (London: Duckworth, 1924), p. 231.

even this was hinted as a possibility in the early newspaper reports, which xenophobically looked for all kinds of political treachery to come from the facts behind the fantastical death of the "foreigner" Martial Bourdin.[7] Thus, the *Times* first described "the deceased" as "a young man of about 30, supposed to be a foreigner. The only evidence of identification was a card bearing the name of 'Bourbon.' "[8]

Although it was quickly established that Bourdin (his right name) was the twenty-six-year-old brother-in-law of Henry Samuels, editor of the *Commonweal*, "A Revolutionary Journal of Anarchist-Communism," and probably a member of "an anarchist conspiracy," the *Times* hints darkly that an anarchist conspiracy, culminating in an attempt on the Greenwich Observatory, "does not fit in with the known facts." The reporters stress that the police are uninformative because (1) Parliament is sitting, (2) their duty is to give information to the Home Office, and (3) it is the duty of the Home Secretary to give the public, through the House of Commons, only "as much information as advisable from the point of view of the public interest."

As to the character of the anarchists, Conrad had the opinion of the journalists to support his own. The bomb-carrier was described in the same paragraph as "one of the most intrepid spirits" in the "dove-cote" of London anarchists, and at the same time as "notoriously indigent," an "out-of-work French tailor." A Paris informant (identity undisclosed) reported to the *Times* that the explosion was "a mistake"; that the London anarchists have been determined not to commit outrages for fear of losing their refuge and center of operations. Gladstone is the prisoner of demagogues, as of all the

---

[7] *The Secret Agent* either reminded British readers of foreign skulduggery in England or struck them as accentuating Conrad's foreign point of view, for in October, 1907, he wrote Garnett, revealing his own sensitivities as a foreigner: "I've been so cried up of late as a sort of freak, an amazing bloody foreigner writing in English (every blessed review of S[ecret] A[gent] had it so—and even yours) that anything I say will be discounted on that ground by the public . . ." See Edward Garnett (ed.), *Letters from Joseph Conrad, 1895–1924* (Indianapolis: Bobbs-Merrill Co., Inc., 1928), p. 205.

[8] *The Times* (London), Feb. 16, 1894. This and the other quotations from the *Times* are taken from the daily reports published Feb. 16–20, 1894, *passim*.

Radical sections, and can't move. The Home Secretary (Asquith) has tried to back out of blame by pleading the principle *de minimis non curat praetor*. After talking with police and legal advisers, the Home Office still feels that the anarchists are unlikely to do much. But, says the paper, it is unlikely that Bourdin went all the way to Greenwich Park just to bury his bomb. He was probably going to dispose of it in a useful way and then leave the park from the Maize Hill Station (point of departure for the park in *The Secret Agent*).

From February 19 on, the *Times* took a position as defender of the public against the efforts of government and police to minimize the incident. Against the insistence of the police that the explosion was not from a scientifically tested bomb, the reporters say Bourdin's contrivance was obviously the work of many hands—no sardine tin. The police show criminal inefficiency in not having had Bourdin under surveillance. Meanwhile, in the anarchist organ edited by Samuels,[9] a tone of middle-class sensitivity predominates. The poor victim had not intended harm to anyone or anything. He had merely gone to the park with his package in order "to put to the test a new weapon of destruction." Sympathy for the unfortunate comrade at first prompted the group to arrange a small private funeral, but a public funeral at St. Pancras Cemetery accompanied by a demonstration was finally agreed upon, perhaps after it was perceived that the press was incensed more against the government and police than against the anarchists themselves. The funeral cortège, far from being attacked by an irate populace, was given sympathetic encouragement by a group of medical students who tried to incite the crowds in Fitzroy Street. (One thinks of Conrad's former medical student Ossipon.)

The fidelity with which Conrad registers the tone of casual British opinion is further evident when one compares the *Times* reports with a résumé of the event written half a century later for the Greenwich Observatory's *Castle Review*.[10] Here one sees in

---

[9] If Ford was right, this may have been the brother-in-law murdered by Bourdin's sister, Samuels' wife.

[10] The *Castle Review*, Journal of the Royal Greenwich Observatory Social and Sports Club (March, 1955), pp. 9–12.

operation the same effect of humor-seasoned-by-distance in the normal English perspective which Conrad himself employs in the novel written twelve years after the event. And Conrad was blamed for callousness!

Considering the event in retrospect, the observatory's journal (without any apparent knowledge of Conrad's version) savors every macabre and gory detail in this splendid interlude interrupting the routine life of the institution. Possibly the account is a reprint of the one (which I have been unable to trace) sent in pamphlet form to Conrad by Ambrose Barker in 1923, for it is a dramatic résumé of Bourdin's story, touching lightly on all the "juicy" bits but reflecting a natural recession of interest in the roles played by police and government as compared with the newspaper reports, a satisfied unconcern over the government's adequacy in meeting the exigencies of the affair. Nothing could better illustrate Conrad's objectivity than this *arrière pensée* from the English themselves. Like Conrad, the author centers, to begin with, on Bourdin (Verloc *and* Stevie in *The Secret Agent*) and the events in his life leading up to the moment when he either "was priming his bomb with the customary glass phial containing acid or . . . tripped over a protruding tree-root" (Stevie's feeble-mindedness decides this question) and "his undistinguished career came to an abrupt conclusion." Like Conrad, the author records both the gory medical details and the incongruous reactions of the last viewers of Bourdin's remains. A park keeper is quoted: "The sight gave me a very queer turn, I can tell you." A methodical doctor announces that "Bourdin's liver, kidneys and stomach yielded seven . . . pieces of iron, while the biggest fragment was found in the base of his spine," and "that these weighed three and a half ounces." The public's stomach was far from queasy. "One of the Park-keepers stated that 'in all his experience he had never known so many people in the Park in a single day, except on Bank Holidays, even when the band was playing in the summer months.'" The jury is described as enjoying the outing it was obliged to make to the scene later. And finally, "photographs of the 'remains,' consisting of an old boot (complete with foot), bits of rag and cats' meat" were "hastily produced by

local private enterprise bent on satisfying public demand." Against
this, one may question how callous and morbid, charges which
Conrad said he had to meet, is his account of the same thing in
Chapter V of the novel. How well this demonstrates the point that
in general readers of daily papers expect less in the way of moral
responsibility from the press than they expect from the novelist,
who must review the human case from a point of view both omniscient and *sub specie aeternitatis!*

Since Conrad supports it to some extent, we may cautiously consider Ford's assertion in *A Personal Remembrance, Portraits from
Life,* and *Return to Yesterday* that he supplied Conrad with "most
of the material" for *The Secret Agent.* In *Portraits from Life*
(1930), Ford claims that Verloc was based on the Russian double
agent Azef, "whom I knew well," and that Conrad made him "even
more loathsome than [he] really was."[11] In *Return to Yesterday*
(1932), Ford gives a fuller account:

> I remember between 1893 and 1894 going home for longish periods
> almost every night from London University to a western suburb
> with Stepniak, Volkhovsky or Prince Kropotkin who were then the
> most prominent members of the Russian extreme Left and who
> were lecturing at the university on political economy, Russian litera-
> ture and, I think, biology respectively. And behind us always lurked
> or dodged the Russian spies allotted to each of those distinguished
> lecturers . . . .
> [Russian espionage] caused at one time a very considerable fric-
> tion between the British and the Russian courts. The redoubtable
> Azef, who was the Russian chief spy-master and agent provocateur,
> conceived the fantastic idea that an outrage in England might in-
> duce the British Government and British public opinion to decree
> the expulsion of all political exiles from their shores, the exiles
> themselves being remarkably law-abiding. He accordingly persuaded
> a half-witted youth to throw a bomb into Greenwich Observatory.
> The boy, however, stumbling over a tree-stump in the Observatory
> Park was blown to pieces and the whole matter came to light. For
> diplomatic reasons, the newspapers made very little of it. But the
> Home Secretary, Sir William Vernon Harcourt [in fact, Sir Herbert

---

[11] Ford Madox Ford, *Portraits from Life* (Boston: Houghton Mifflin Co., 1930),
p. 66.

Asquith], made such caustic remarks over it to the Russian First Secretary of Embassy that Russian activities on the Afghan border became very marked for a considerable period . . . .[12]

Ford goes on to say that Azef had sent him "by one of his emissaries a volume of the diary of the late Tzar; he imagining that I might like to publish it—which I didn't." Hurriedly ridding himself of the document, Ford notified the police. Thereafter, he allegedly came "a good deal in contact with the Scotland Yard Inspector who had charge of that sort of case and he told me a great deal about not only the activities of the Russian spies but gave me an—I daresay highly colored—account of what the Home Secretary had said to the Secretary of the Embassy."[13]

Zabel, in his excellent introduction to *Under Western Eyes*,[14] describes the activities of the vicious Azef as they bear on the plight of Razumov in that novel. Sensibly, no doubt, Zabel omits to mention either of Ford's claims: that Azef was the mind behind Martial Bourdin's exploit in Greenwich Park or that he was the original of Conrad's Adolf Verloc.

To credit Ford's words, one must begin by supposing him intimately involved with the "great many anarchists of the Goodge Street Group,[15] as well as a great many of the police who watched them"—his avowal in *A Personal Remembrance*:

Acquiring such knowledge is the diversion of most youths. . . . There are few English boys of spirit who have not at one time or other dressed up in sweaters and with handkerchiefs round their

---

[12] Ford Madox Ford, *Return to Yesterday* (New York: Liveright, 1932), p. 135.

[13] *Ibid.*, p. 136.

[14] Morton Dauwen Zabel, "Introduction," *Under Western Eyes* (New York: New Directions, New Classics Series, 1951).

[15] According to Ford, "the young Rossettis ran a printing press and an Anarchist journal called *The Torch* in the basement of William Rossetti's house—which belonged to his wife, my Aunt Lucy." After the latter's death, Rossetti ordered "the children" to move the press and its journal from the house. "It removed itself to Goodge Street, Tottenham Court Road—a locality as grim as its name. There it became a sort of club where the hangers on of the extreme Left idled away an immense amount of time. . . . I did not myself like it much and only went there I think twice—to see about the printing of my first poem" (*Return to Yesterday*, pp. 111–12).

necks gone after experience amongst the cut-throats at Wapping Old Stairs. . . . But Conrad, when he met the writer after the publication of *The Secret Agent* with preface in 1920, remarked almost at once and solicitously: 'You know. . . . The preface to *The Secret Agent*. . . . I did not give you away too much. . . . I was very cautious.''. . . . He had wished politely to throw a veil of eternal respectability over the writer. And he had been afraid that the suggestion that the writer had once known some anarchists, thirty-five years before, might ruin the writer's career![16]

I am unable to find any evidence, apart from Ford's testimony, that Azef was under suspicion as a Russian *agent provocateur* in London in 1893–94, or even that he was in England during this period. His most dramatic activities occurred not in England but Russia, and not in the nineties (when he was working his way upward in the confidence of revolutionaries and police agents in Germany, Switzerland, and Russia) but between 1904 and 1906.

In the year and a half before Conrad began *The Secret Agent*, Azef, who had been serving as a spy for the Russian state police (Okhrana) and at the same time as head of the terrorist section (Battle Organization) of the Socialist Revolutionary Party, engineered the assassination of V. K. Plehve, Russian Minister of the Interior and of the Grand Duke Sergei. While Conrad was in his third month of writing *The Secret Agent*, this "best-paid and most valued secret agent of the Okhrana"[17] brought off the bombing of the carriage in which Dubasov, the governor general of Moscow, was riding.

Although Burcev, editor of the St. Petersburg journal *Byloye* (*The Past*), published his astounding exposure only in 1908, and indeed began to suspect that the terrorist Azef was the same as the police spy "Raskine" only in May, 1906,[18] it is possible that Ford and Conrad, discussing the assassinations, posited the notion of a double agent and the possibility of a similar set of circumstances

---

[16] *Joseph Conrad: A Personal Remembrance*, pp. 231–32.

[17] Zabel, "Introduction," *Under Western Eyes*, p. xxi.

[18] See Marc Aldanov (pseudonym for Marc Aleksandrovich Landau), "Asef," *Les Oeuvres libres* (November, 1930), pp. 353–55, for an account of Burcev's dawning suspicion.

in the Greenwich Park mystery of a decade before. It is conceivable that Azef did cross Ford's path in those ten years and in London, although "thirty-five years" before 1920 (when Conrad wrote the preface to *The Secret Agent*), Ford was not yet in his 'teens, and Azef himself only four years older!

The whole passage in *A Personal Remembrance* is questionable, if for no better reason than Ford's remark that his "first poems were set up" by "one Anarchist young lady who figures in *The Secret Agent*."[19] Since no one of this description is in *The Secret Agent*, the lady referred to can only be the upper-class young English-woman, possibly a Rossetti, who appears in Conrad's story "The Informer" (finished sometime in 1906 while he was engaged with *The Secret Agent*). Indeed, all this mystery might seem unworthy of pursuit were it not for the curious suggestion in Conrad's preface, so in keeping with what we know of his loyalties, that he was trying to protect Ford from possible suspicion:

> I am sure that if he [Ford, the "omniscient friend"] had seen once in his life the back of an anarchist that must have been the whole extent of his connection with the underworld. He was, however, a man who liked to talk with all sorts of people, and he may have gathered those illuminating facts at second or third hand, from a crossing-sweeper, from a retired police officer . . . or even, perhaps, from a Minister of State met at some public or private reception.[20]

In the same preface Conrad implies that he, as well as Ford, knew in some detail the newspaper accounts of that episode in the un-impressive history of anarchist activities in England. Conrad re-members

> remarking on the criminal futility of the whole thing, doctrine, ac-tion, mentality; and on the contemptible aspect of the half-crazy pose as of a brazen cheat exploiting the poignant miseries and pas-sionate credulities of a mankind always so tragically eager for self-destruction. That was what made for me its philosophical pretenses so unpardonable. . . . a blood-stained inanity of so fatuous a kind that it was impossible to fathom its origin by any reasonable or even

[19] *Joseph Conrad: A Personal Remembrance*, p. 231.
[20] *The Secret Agent*, p. x.

unreasonable process of thought. For perverse unreason has its own logical processes. But that outrage could not be laid hold of mentally in any sort of way, so that one remained faced by the fact of a man blown to bits for nothing even most remotely resembling an idea, anarchistic or other.[21]

Many years later, in September, 1923, when Barker sent Conrad the pamphlet describing the Greenwich Park incident, Conrad replied that he "never knew anything" about the actual event.

I was out of England when it happened, and thus I never read what was printed in the newspapers at the time. All I was aware of was the mere fact—my novel being in intention the history of Winnie Verloc. I hope you have seen that the purpose of the book was *not* to attack any doctrine, or even the men holding that doctrine. My object, apart from the aim of telling a story, was to hold up the worthlessness of certain individuals and the baseness of some others. It was a matter of great interest to me to see how near actuality I managed to come in a work of imagination.[22]

In point of fact, Conrad *was* in England, and in London, on February 15, 1894, when Martial Bourdin stumbled with his bomb and blew himself to death.[23] Tadeusz Bobrowski's death had occurred on February 10, 1894, five days before Martial Bourdin's disastrous visit to the park. Conrad wrote his cousin Marguerite Poradowska that he was, when the news of his uncle's death reached him February 11, in bed just recovering from an illness.[24] One can picture him in the following days assailed more than ever by the impression of his loneliness in England, perhaps also of the alien ugliness of London streets in February and the rented rooms he lived in, far from his uncle's house and native land. When writing *The Secret Agent*, he tells us, "I had to fight hard to keep at arms-length the memories of my solitary walks all over London in my early days, lest they should rush in and overwhelm each page of

---

[21] *Ibid.*, pp. ix–x.

[22] *Life and Letters*, II, 322.

[23] See Jocelyn Baines, *Joseph Conrad* (London: Weidenfeld & Nicolson, 1959), p. 133.

[24] *Letters of Joseph Conrad to Marguerite Poradowska*, translated and edited by John A. Gee and Paul J. Sturm (New Haven: Yale University Press, 1940), p. 63.

the story."[25] In that month of 1894 he was, moreover, jobless, having sailed the last voyage of his mercantile career, though he was waiting for another to offer itself.

If, in these circumstances, he read reports of the explosion, it is not surprising that he forgot later where he was or what he read. But one might imagine the mood of those days leaving its stamp in a sensitive mind on whatever was later recollected of contemporary events: the futile death of an indolent anarchist, the feelings of simple or pathetic individuals, removed as far as possible from imagining such violence.

Following the sound habit of testing what Ford writes about Conrad against the interior evidence of Conrad's works, one may recall Ford's comment, several times repeated, that Conrad always wanted to write about "the life in great cities."[26] Hugh Walpole corroborates this testimony when he remembers Conrad to have said that Verloc was a sign "of what he might have done in letters had the sea not swept over him."[27] What sort of thing? Certainly not the plotting of half-baked revolutionaries, whose characterization reflects little of the creative energy in which the novel abounds. One marks a fuller engagement in the novel with the subject of the Russian agent sowing his seeds of discord on the barren ground of English soil. But above all, it is the dramatization of London that gives *The Secret Agent* its surprising pre-eminence among the seven or eight (out of fourteen) novels by Conrad which critics usually allow to be master works. In the Author's Note, Conrad specifies the alternatives he suggested to Walpole:

> One fell to musing before the phenomenon—even of the past: of South America, a continent of crude sunshine and brutal revolutions, of the sea . . . the reflector of the world's light. Then the vision of an enormous town presented itself, of a monstrous town more populous than some continents and in its man-made might as if indifferent to heaven's frowns and smiles; a cruel devourer of the

[25] *The Secret Agent*, p. xiii.

[26] Ford Madox Ford, "Tiger, Tiger," *The Bookman* (New York; January, 1928), p. 496.

[27] Note, dated Jan. 26, 1927, written by Walpole in a volume of *The Secret Agent* (Keating Collection, Yale University).

world's light. There was room enough there to place any story . . . darkness enough to bury five millions of lives.[28]

On the title page of the first edition of *The Secret Agent*, published in 1907 by Methuen, Conrad is named as "Author of 'The Nigger of the "Narcissus." ' "[29] This may well have been Conrad's choice and not the editors'. Methuen had published nothing of Conrad's before but *The Mirror of the Sea*, which had appeared the previous year. The relevance of *The Nigger of the "Narcissus,"* though not obvious to the reader, seems to have been clear to the author himself. Conrad's most intense and extended novel centering on life at sea looks forward in several respects to his most intense and extended novel centering on life in a city. In the middle of writing the first bedroom scene between Winnie and Adolf Verloc, on p. 160 of the Rosenbach manuscript,[30] Conrad stopped to sketch a small boat at the top of the page, as if once more contemplating a voyage.

"Let the earth and the sea each have its own"[31]—one might have guessed in *The Nigger of the "Narcissus,"* as early as 1896, that this polarization of sea and land in Conrad's mind was waiting for another theme to complete its tale. Compare the closing paragraphs of the two novels, so wide apart in times of writing. First: "Haven't

---

[28] *The Secret Agent*, p. xii.

[29] The title page also bears a note attesting that the novel is "based on the inside knowledge of a certain event in the history of active anarchism." Methuen has clearly used Conrad's own words, as written in a letter to him (Nov. 7, 1906, *Life and Letters*, II, 38), although Conrad specifically protests against being asked to supply such a note. ("I still think that the author is not the proper person for that work.") What is not clear from the words on the title page, out of context of the letter, is that Conrad is anxious to have the sensational and factual aspects of the novel publicized as subordinate to the author's special point of view on them, and even then used merely as the starting point for a purely imaginative work. The printed note avoids, as possibly too technical a question, the "ironic treatment" stressed by Conrad, thus of course neglecting the main feature of the novel's appeal.

[30] The manuscript, in 637 pages, is complete and essentially the same as the serial version that appeared in *Ridgeway's; A Militant Weekly for God and Country*, October 6, 1906—January 12, 1907. The murder scene and end were expanded for the book. See W. F. Wright, *Romance and Tragedy in Conrad* (Lincoln: University of Nebraska Press, 1949) and H. E. Davis, "Conrad's Revisions of *The Secret Agent*," *Modern Language Quarterly* (September, 1958), pp. 244–55.

[31] *The Nigger of the "Narcissus,"* p. 172.

160

extremely well cared for *(white)* ~~buthe~~
hand shining to the left
forefinger and thumb together
in subtle demonstration.

(luminous and mutilated) *(physically)*
This vision was so ghastly that
Mr Verloc started away from ~~the~~
window., letting ^{down} the veneti-an
blind ~~down~~ with a great rattle
~~and as a disconposed violence~~
~~watched his wife return and~~
~~go into bed~~ ~~XXXXXXXXXX~~
~~He watched his wife enter the room~~
~~and get into bed~~
Disconposed and speechless
with the apprehension of more such
visions he ~~XXXXXXXX~~ beheld
~~his~~ wife re-enter the ~~room~~
~~XXXXXXXX~~ and get into bed in
a ^{calm} ~~aut~~ businesslike manner which
made him feel hopelessly lonely
in ~~the~~ world. ~~Mrs Verloc ex—~~
~~pressed her surprise at seeing~~
~~him up~~

Conrad's difficulties in writing *The Secret Agent*—the first of his novels in which there are no escapes by sea—are suggested by this page and its drawing, perhaps wishfully sketched. (The Philip H. and A. S. W. Rosenbach Foundation, Philadelphia)

we, together and upon the immortal sea, wrung out a meaning from
our sinful lives?" asks the seaman of the "Narcissus." The story of
London life leaves no soul even to ask for a meaning, only two men
walking disregarded: one obsessed by a riddle of "madness or despair," the other "averting his eyes from the odious multitude of
mankind."[32] To what degree, we ask, was Conrad like Singleton
reading Bulwer Lytton: one of

> those beings who exist beyond the pale of life stirred by his tales as
> by an enigmatical disclosure of a resplendent world that exists
> within the frontier of infamy and filth, within that border of dirt
> and hunger, of misery and dissipation, that comes down on all sides
> to the water's edge of the incorruptible ocean?[33]

A crucial difference between the handling of affairs aboard ship
and ashore is made in *The Mirror of the Sea:*

> In her handling a ship will not put up with a mere pretender as, for
> instance, the public will do with Mr. X, the popular statesman, Mr.
> Y, the popular scientist, or Mr. Z, the popular . . . anything from
> a teacher of high morality to a bagman—who have won their little
> race.[34]

This passage might point to the philanthropic society "developing" the Congo—founded, managed, and staffed by "mere pre-
tenders," or the strutting Montero brothers who gave the course of
progress its usual turn in South America. But Donkin, the one
member of the "Narcissus" who belonged to earth, is Conrad's
only character before *The Secret Agent* who would fit as well here
as in his original setting. He is the sort of sham who tries to use
his own delinquency as proof of the need to rebuild society bottom-
side up. He is the "man who can't do most things and won't do the
rest." Like Donkin, Michaelis: "The pet of philanthropists and
self-seeking land-lubbers."[35] A failure at sea, Donkin is a success
ashore. "Donkin, who never did a decent day's work in his life,

---

[32] *Ibid.,* p. 173; *The Secret Agent,* pp. 310–11.
[33] *The Nigger of the "Narcissus,"* p. 6.
[34] *The Mirror of the Sea,* p. 28.
[35] *The Nigger of the "Narcissus,"* p. 11.

no doubt earns his living by discoursing with filthy eloquence upon the right of labor to live."[36]

When Conrad finally created an element native to the Donkins of the world, it had to be a city. (One cannot survive long without employment or a family in the country.) And it had to be an element fed, from one source or another, by Russia. Revolutions were brewing everywhere. To a degree, Conrad even defended the ones foreshadowed as *Heart of Darkness* and *Nostromo* ended. The French Revolution, breeding terror and obscurantism under the guise of abstract rights, seemed to Conrad to have drawn a fatal pattern for social change in the modern era. But the peculiar lawlessness of Russian autocracy had provided the only favorable spawning ground for men and women surrendering themselves wholly to the dogmas of revolution. Conrad's much-discussed "conservatism" (frequently ascribed to some sort of Oedipal hostility to his father's radicalism) was above all a revulsion against the kind of society existing in Russia (and Russian Poland) where revolution was the normal reaction to government.

Conrad's "escape" to the "hospitable sea," we must at the same time remember, was no more a total revulsion against *politics* than it was a total revulsion against Poland. He "moved" to sea as one moves from an impossible house (in Conrad's case a haunted house) to a better dwelling, where one expects to find a set of conditions not entirely new but only free of the limitations which made normal life impossible in the other. Boris Pasternak "escaped" from politics without moving. If political life is like a house, in *Doctor Zhivago* Pasternak escaped to the woods, denying the possibility of survival inside a roof and four walls. In the move from Poland to the "Narcissus," on the other hand, there is no forswearing of allegiance to the conditions of society. There is even an insistence on the original contract, sometimes in a light vein, as when Podmore the cook is checked in his assumption of pastoral authority. (Sensitive to his abuse of power, the "captain's cold

---

[36] Ibid., p. 172.

eyes, high up on the poop, glittered mistrustful."[37]) But the burden of the story is in the graver assumption of secular authority by a diseased impostor, who nearly destroys the ship as a society of freely associated men. The dying Negro is "like a sick tyrant overawing a crowd of . . . slaves," and the crew serves him as "the base courtiers of a hated prince."[38]

Thus it is not an antipolitical obsession in Conrad that divides sea from land, or *The Nigger of the "Narcissus"* from *The Secret Agent*. Between the two novels Conrad developed perforce into a landman himself, and while we find him no way closer in sympathy to the Donkins, we find him, curiously, less alarmed by the problems of government in the openly political *Secret Agent* than he was in the nonpolitical sea story.

Surprisingly, we will be forced to conclude too that in *The Secret Agent*, where Russian politics become part of Conrad's subject for the first time in a novel, despotism is a remoter menace than it was in his first and greatest sea story. He had to write *Under Western Eyes* afterward, perhaps, to use up the greater part of his thought on the subject skimmed lightly in *The Secret Agent*.

One is struck, indeed, by the very un-Russian character of the "simple tale." It is almost a parody of Dostoevsky in that Winnie and Adolf Verloc are, each for a different reason of course, heavily disinclined to explore moral and political questions—any kind of questions for that matter. If Conrad had wanted to rewrite *Crime and Punishment*, *The Possessed*, and *The Idiot* all in one, he could not have succeeded better than with this story of three desultory London revolutionists and a craven nihilist, an accidental murderer like Adolf Verloc, two down-to-earth women such as Winnie and her mother, and the really convincing idiot Stevie.

Conrad waited twenty years after requesting his release as a Russian subject to write this novel. In most of those years, perhaps, his hatred of things Russian was too bitter to allow fictional handling

---

[37] *Ibid.*, p. 38.
[38] *Ibid.*, pp. 35, 37.

except in the obliquest references—a young Russian in *Heart of Darkness*, a "hater of capitalists" in *Nostromo*—and the consuming suspicion of expansionist motives we have marked in all the works considered so far. The "change in . . . fundamental mood" which he thinks "had already stolen over me unawares"[39] in 1906 may have been helped by two decades of uneventful English life. It was certainly helped by the radical changes in Russia's fortunes toward the end of this time.

Henry James, eight years before the Greenwich Park explosion, had wondered in *The Princess Casamassima* if the revolutionary movement of which such events were symptomatic would set the world on fire or spend itself in vain conspiracies. By the time Conrad was ready to write *The Secret Agent*, he obviously thought the second alternative most likely, as far as England was concerned at least. It had been a different matter twenty years earlier, in 1885 (when James was writing *The Princess*), when hardly acquainted with England, Conrad had predicted that she was hurtling toward "the abyss" of socialism, which "must inevitably end in Caesarism." He had in that year written Kliszczewski that

> England was the only barrier to the pressure of infernal doctrines born in continental back-slums. Now, there is nothing! . . . The destiny of this nation and of all nations is to be accomplished in darkness amidst much weeping and gnashing of teeth, to pass through robbery, equality, anarchy and misery under the iron rule of a military despotism! Such is the lesson of common sense logic.[40]

In 1904–5, the miraculous defeat of Russia by the tiny power of Japan, in which lay an image of Poland, inspires Conrad to write not only his first and most searching political essay but his first public assessment of Russian politics. A few months later, after the October Revolution in St. Petersburg, he glimpses for the first time the possibility of political reform and "rational progress" inside Russia. Only now does Conrad begin to think of Poland as in any respect alive in the tomb. "I am greatly moved by the news

---

[39] *The Secret Agent*, p. ix.
[40] *Life and Letters*, I, 84.

from Russia," he writes Ada Galsworthy on November 2, 1905. "Certainly, a year ago, I never hoped to live to see all that." In the same letter we sight one of the few points of difference between Conrad's lifelong outlook and that of his uncle Tadeusz Bobrowski. Recalling the emancipation of the Russian serfs in 1861, Conrad writes Mrs. Galsworthy that Bobrowski had thought "this great event opened the way to a general reform of the state."[41] Bobrowski, however pessimistic, had remained in Poland, persuaded that political reformation was possible even in Russia. Conrad had left, persuaded (as he would be again when writing the Note to *Under Western Eyes* in 1920) that "the tiger cannot change his stripes nor the leopard his spots."[42]

The degree of relief Conrad felt, politically, in 1905–6, is one measure of the comedy in *The Secret Agent*. My reading fully supports Guerard's point that "the turn to comedy" implies "a normalizing of interest" and for Conrad a newly "objective interest in behavior."[43] *The Secret Agent* shows us the political novelist moved to levity and betraying a new garrulousness, a new willingness to talk politics with the crowd, as if for the first time there appeared a comfortable corner for conversation.

The novel delivers its wisdom on law and the seeds of social disintegration entirely from the perspective of a man securely confident that the ship of state is not and perhaps never can be seriously threatened. Surely Conrad sees himself, proposing this, as part of the irony. He might be caricaturing himself in the unlamented, presumably German Ambassador Stott-Wartenheim,[44] whom the

---

[41] *Ibid.*, II, 28.

[42] *Under Western Eyes*, p. x.

[43] Albert J. Guerard, *Conrad the Novelist* (Cambridge: Harvard University Press, 1958), p. 219.

[44] Conrad seems unwilling to forego any of the conventional forms of humor in the immense range of this novel's comedy. Stott-Wartenheim's name suggests in German a stuttering stay-at-home; Verloc's, in French a syphilitic; the German Chancelier d'Ambassade Wurmt, a worm; the medical student Ossipon, in Latin old bones. In the same vein, the papers exhibited in Verloc's window are *The Torch* (possibly a reference to the young Rossettis' paper but perhaps also to Lenin's *Iskra*—*The Spark*) and *The Gong* (Alexander Herzen's paper was *The Bell*). That both papers should lie in the same window indicates how indiscriminate the revolutionary camaraderie was. The two papers appear again in "The Informer" as the *Alarm Bell* and the *Firebrand*.

presumably Russian First Secretary Vladimir of the presumably German Embassy[45] in London remembers as woefully pessimistic and gullible. Stott-Wartenheim

> had the social revolution on the brain. He imagined himself to be a diplomatist set apart by a special dispensation to watch the end of diplomacy, and pretty nearly the end of the world, in a horrid democratic upheaval. His prophetic and doleful despatches had been for years the joke of Foreign Offices. He was said to have claimed on his deathbed (visited by his Imperial friend and master): "Unhappy Europe! Thou shalt perish by the moral insanity of thy children!"[46]

The serious "appeal to our very soul" which I have suggested does come through *The Secret Agent* is a less political appeal than any we have met in the novels previously considered. Henry James in *The Princess Casamassima* was far more involved with anarchism than Conrad in *The Secret Agent*, though the theory of revolution is maddeningly vague in James's novel and maddeningly precise, though caricatured, in Conrad's. James impresses us as sensitive to Hyacinth Robinson's state of mind but not to any other of his characters in *The Princess*. The "lives of quiet desperation" (which Thoreau, in *Walden*, said most men were leading) are far more present to our senses in Conrad's London than in James's, in (for example) the oft-quoted scene between Winnie Verloc and her charwoman Mrs. Neale.

James, like his Hyacinth Robinson, was hypersensitively concerned about the aesthetic texture of the social fabric, whereas to Conrad in *The Nigger* especially, and more lightly in *The Secret Agent*, the important question is only whether the social structure

---

[45] Because of Vladimir it is usually assumed that the embassy which employs Verloc is Russian. The two German members—particularly as the deceased Stott-Wartenheim was a roving ambassador—put one in mind rather of a German Embassy masterminded by a Russian employee. This would accord with Conrad's growing dread of the turn being taken by Prussianism since the years of the Boer War. Before that, we have noted, he once thought Germany might serve as an ally to Britain in caging the Russian bear. Now he visualizes Germany as falling into the treacherous Russian trap. Professor Weintraub remarks, on the other hand, that many Russian officials in this period bore German names; therefore, there may be no good reason to question that Vladimir's embassy is Russian.

[46] *The Secret Agent*, pp. 27–28.

serves the necessities of life. As a result, although *The Princess* is a deeply serious novel and *The Secret Agent* (despite its serious content) as frolicsome as any melodrama ever composed, James's final effect is a little frivolous, while Conrad's is profoundly disturbing. It is the nonpolitical Winnie, deprived of life's necessities, who makes the difference. In her unphilosophical way, Winnie is "one of us," and as a result *The Secret Agent*, with all its irreverence to the gravity of anarchism, is to me a more disturbing book than Dostoevsky's philosophically probing *The Possessed*, which presents no such compellingly normal victim.

Though Conrad has been accused by Howe, Daiches, and others of insensitivity to human misery in *The Secret Agent*, he represents himself thus only because the grim facts of modern life have become material for quack theorists like Yundt, whose task was to sniff the "air of social cruelty, to strain his ear for its atrocious sounds."[47] Once again, Conrad's subject is the parasite, the revolutionary who is to Kropotkin what Martin Travers of *The Rescue* was to Rajah James Brooke. This is not to say, of course, that Conrad respected Kropotkin even as much as he admired Brooke. His concern here is not to expose the demonic strain in "the imagination of conquest" but rather the contagion of madness spreading from inferior spirits who make a business out of wretchedness. His irony falters, losing its detachment, whenever it touches this point: Yundt "took the part of an insolent and venomous evoker of sinister impulses which lurk in the blind envy and exasperated vanity of ignorance, in the suffering and misery of poverty, in all the hopeful and noble illusions of righteous anger, pity, and revolt."[48]

In both "The Informer" and *The Secret Agent*, as again in *Under Western Eyes*, Conrad writes about a double agent. We have noted that he considered the theme of *homo duplex*, with its multiple meanings (political, philosophical, psychological) peculiarly applicable to himself, and we shall see it asserted in personal terms once again. But in the story and novel dealing with anarchism, the

---

[47] Ibid., p. 48.
[48] Ibid.

double agent is offered with monocular vision, fastening on a curiosity symptomatic (as Zabel has remarked) of Europe's malaise but not in itself the centripetal force of Conrad's plots. Verloc originally was to be the title character of the story, but the novel shifted emphasis while Conrad was writing it. Neither Sevrin (in "The Informer") nor Verloc is a Jim, Lingard, Marlow, or Decoud, split by the truth that lurks in convention and the falsehood in sincerity, all of them seeking reintegration. Neither Verloc nor Sevrin cares the least about integrity. Not coincidentally, it is their women —Verloc's wife, Sevrin's fiancée—who register the central experiences of the story. (In "The Informer" the well-bred girl, as Irving Howe notes, is a counterpart to the narrator—both seeking thrills among the smoldering rubbish of a revolution they would like to believe in as a consolation for their own sense of futurelessness.) Verloc's wife Winnie—backed by her obscure and immemorial origins—introduces the new element that distinguishes the novel not only from the short story but from the *Princess Casamassima* and Dostoevsky's *Possessed*, novels to which *The Secret Agent* is in some measure a response.

Like these novels, Conrad's two tales examine the attraction of anarchy and revolution to nineteenth-century aesthetes or aristocrats. James fashioned a sort of *homo duplex* in Hyacinth Robinson, divided between aristocracy and "proletariat" by the very conditions of his birth and finally destroyed by the conflict in himself between the aesthetic appeals of society's old order and the obvious justice in the demands of the forces gathering underground. This was James's own dilemma projected. Neither of Conrad's tales about anarchism suggests any such projection of the author's involvement. Aristocrat and aesthete are as removed from the center of his sympathy as the apostles of discord. Not being able to accept at face value this twofold detachment, Howe imagines Conrad himself as an aesthete gulled by the "joke" anarchist X plays on the collector of Chinese bronzes in "The Informer."[49] One has only to think of

---

[49] Irving Howe, *Politics and the Novel* (New York: Horizon Press, 1957), p. 85.

"Il Conde," however, to recall Conrad's objective interest in the theme.

George Steiner, singling out *The Secret Agent* and *Under Western Eyes*, repeats the misleading half-truth first suggested by Orwell: that Conrad's novels *after* 1900 were the ones which so unexpectedly and so presciently revealed what Steiner calls "the impulses towards disintegration, the cracks in the wall of European stability."[50] The truth of the matter is that, apart from the few tales that have no public reverberations, Conrad was concerned with these "impulses" and "cracks" in everything he wrote. Furthermore, he was exploring the impulses toward disintegration and the precariousness of Europe's assumptions more deeply in *Lord Jim*, *The Rescue*, *Heart of Darkness*, and *Nostromo* than in the two novels Steiner refers to. In fact, the unequivocal handling of ambiguous material and ideologically debatable questions in *Nostromo* and the novels after it seems to me to point again to what Guerard calls a normalized point of view. Guerard does not agree with me in the case of *Under Western Eyes*, but even there we find Conrad far more confident, both of what he has to tell his readers and what their reactions will be to it, than he was or meant to be in *Lord Jim* and *Heart of Darkness*.

The change we are observing does not represent, of course, a *bouleversement* of Conrad's basic political philosophy. In a way, *The Secret Agent* expresses his fundamental political convictions with greater clarity and simplicity than any other novel he wrote. "*L'homme est un animal méchant. Sa méchanceté doit être organisée. La societé est essentiellement criminelle,—ou elle n'existerait pas.*"[51] Chief Inspector Heat, the coolest and wisest political head in the book, pays tribute "to what is normal in the constitution of society (for the idea of thieving appeared to his instinct as normal as the idea of property)."[52] He pays tribute, in a word, to

---

[50] George Steiner, *Tolstoy or Dostoevsky* (New York: Alfred A. Knopf, Inc., 1959), p. 40.

[51] See above, p. 23.

[52] *The Secret Agent*, p. 93.

méchanceté—perversity. And this is just why he makes his distinction between "the world of thieves—sane, without morbid ideals," and the communist, anarchist, nihilist, and police spy he is forced to deal with in the Greenwich Observatory scandal. When perversity becomes depravity, when normal human impulses turn against themselves, "the game" (which is life in society) cannot go on. If all men were angels, there would be no game—"*il n'existerait pas*"—but neither could there be a game if all men were depraved.

In the letter to Cunninghame Graham, written in February, 1899, Conrad had distinguished between the anarchist, who desires the extermination of organized society, and the "peace man" who pretends that all men are loving brothers, or some day can be. He then said that of the two he preferred the anarchist position because it was both appropriate and clear, while the other was neither. Now, in *The Secret Agent*, we might expect to find the anarchist position further rectified. But instead a new distinction is made: between the "perfect" anarchist Professor, who would destroy anything, including himself, but is in fact seeking shelter from a humanity he fears and distrusts, and the mere shams who would not dare to lift a finger against the social edifice. Brought to the test, Conrad will not defend anarchism as a political stand, nor will he invent a Kropotkin or Gandhi, who sincerely trusted the goodness of individual "light," undisciplined rigorously by institutions and law. Of course, he would not class such idealists with the malcontents among revolutionaries but with "peace men" like Cunninghame Graham himself, who by 1906 is no longer enthusiastic over international peace meetings.

Thus one may question Hewitt's point when he identifies the irony of *The Secret Agent* with the irony in, say, *Heart of Darkness* and *Nostromo* (both so different themselves), as "a weapon to undermine comfortable assumptions and to make us scrutinize more deeply our beliefs and values"—a weapon which, he says, Conrad dropped in the later works, where irony "underlines an obvious sneer" or "acts as a shield for personal intrusions, cutting short investigation by the striking of an attitude."[53] The English-man who was not discomfited by the Greenwich Park explosion would not rethink his position after reading *The Secret Agent*. Nor, I suspect, would Conrad's jibes at the British aristocracy elicit much concern or surprise. There is nothing in the least offensive about the character of Lady Mabel ("an old woman who had es-caped the blight of indifference"),[54] or of the socialistic Sir Ethelred with his ridiculous secretary Toodles. One has only to compare them to *The Rescue's* Martin Travers, with his phony airs and menacing theory of empire, to realize that in Chapters VI and VII of *The Secret Agent* Conrad is poking a gentler kind of fun at the harmless, even foolish, political sentimentalities of London's high society. Again, one notes here that Conrad's irony turns corrosive not on the political or structural aspects of society but on the more homely features of city life and modern thought.

His eye is severely scornful as it falls on the fetish of science,[55] a major motif in the novel. We have met Conrad's jests over "scien-tific" presumptions before—in his mockery of Martin Travers or Kurtz as the evolutionists' improved man, in Marlow's revelations concerning technological "improvements" in Africa, and in the sentimental or religious fervor masking the dialectical materialism of Gould and Holroyd in *Nostromo*. Now science furnishes a wide range of targets for this humorous view of English life. "The fetish of today," Mr. Vladimir tells Verloc, "is neither royalty nor re-ligion. Therefore the palace and the church should be left alone." Not for the last time in the novel, the caricature of Russian autoc-

---

[53] Douglas Hewitt, *Joseph Conrad: A Reassessment* (Cambridge: Bowes and Bowes, 1952), p. 88.

[54] *The Secret Agent*, p. 110.

[55] "Autocracy and War" reminds us that Conrad closely associated science with economic and political maladjustments in the twentieth century: "Industrialism and commercialism—wearing high-sounding names in many languages (Welt-politik may serve for one instance) picking up coins behind the severe and disdainful figure of science whose giant strides have widened for us the horizon of the universe by some few inches—stand ready, almost eager, to appeal to the sword as soon as the globe of the earth has shrunk beneath our growing numbers by another ell or so" (*Notes on Life and Letters*, p. 107).

racy assumes Conrad's voice, to compound the fun of seeing present life in a fresh light. "The sacrosanct fetish of today is science." He elaborates:

> "A bomb in the National Gallery would make some noise. But it would not be serious enough. Art has never been their fetish. . . . Artists—art critics and such like—people of no account. Nobody minds what they say. But there is learning—science. Any imbecile that has got an income believes in that. He does not know why, but he believes it matters somehow. . . . All the damned professors are radicals at heart. . . . They believe that in some mysterious way science is at the source of their material prosperity."[56]

Vladimir proposes an attack on Greenwich Observatory because such an outrage would combine "the greatest possible regard for humanity with the most alarming display of imbecility. I defy the ingenuity of journalists to persuade their public that any given member of the proletariat can have a personal grievance against astronomy."[57] Science is universally worshipped. It has provided even the revolutionists with a handle for getting hold of society's faults. But like religion in the old days, science admits of many and contradictory uses. With the disappointed medical student Ossipon, science—particularly the social theory of the Italian criminologist Cesare Lombroso—provides an easy explanation of why all men apart from revolutionaries are criminals. Ossipon has "that glance of insufferable, hopelessly dense sufficiency which nothing but the frequentation of science can give to the dullness of common mortals."[58] He "submitted to the rule of science," but paradoxically insists,

> There is no law and no certainty. . . . What the people knows does not matter, were its knowledge ever so accurate. The only thing that matters to us is the emotional state of the masses. Without emotion there is no action.[59]

---

[56] *The Secret Agent*, pp. 30–33.
[57] *Ibid.*, pp. 34–35.
[58] *Ibid.*, p. 46.
[59] *Ibid.*, p. 50.

Ossipon is, incidentally, bringing light in the form of lectures on "the socialistic aspects of hygiene" to "workingmen's associations." Hygienic streets and hygienic babies, Verloc has noticed approvingly, are properties of the middle classes in the neighborhood of the embassies. Michaelis was kept in "a highly hygienic prison." Verloc's dim political "theory," an apology for his personal disinclinations, emerges from the pleasure he takes in the sense of London's "opulence and luxury," and a whole "social order favorable to . . . hygienic idleness" which has to be "protected against the shallow enviousness of unhygienic labour,"[60] Conrad's irony in *The Secret Agent*, no less than his elegiac sympathy in *The Nigger of the "Narcissus,"* is an instrument designed "before all, to make you see"—in this case, to see modern city life.

Verloc and Michaelis are impressed by the aspect of London which is hygienically sterile. To the Assistant Commissioner—and to Winnie before her death—London appears repeatedly as a slimy tank from which the water has been drained. (Winnie's suicide by drowning, then, is not only an escape but a return.) *Ideally*, a city should be a reservoir where the stream of human lives is profitably collected. "The murmur of town life" has for the life-affirming Heat "a precious familiarity and an appealing sweetness. He was human."[61] But *The Secret Agent* emphasizes the abandonment of the city's supposed function by an impressionable portion of its human element.

In simple quantity, of course, the element is plentiful. We are made here, as in *Heart of Darkness*, to see vacuity without loss of physical mass. To the Assistant Commissioner's jaundiced eye, the street below his office lay "wet and empty, as if swept clear suddenly by a great flood."[62] Later, his descent into the street is like "the descent into a slimy aquarium from which the water has been run off."[63] And to the "very friendless" Winnie in her despair, "the whole town of marvels and mud . . . rested at the bottom of a

---

[60] *Ibid.*, p. 12.
[61] *Ibid.*, p. 94.
[62] *Ibid.*, p. 100.
[63] *Ibid.*, p. 147.

black abyss from which no unaided woman could hope to scramble out."[64]

The "air of moral nihilism" Conrad scents in Adolf Verloc is a different thing entirely from the nihilism Dostoevsky dignified in *The Possessed,* for Conrad's is mainly "the air" or atmosphere "common to keepers of gambling hells and disorderly houses; to private detectives and inquiry agents; to drink sellers and, I should say, to the sellers of invigorating electric belts and to the inventors of patent medicines."[65] In Dostoevsky we are elevated above the symbols of this very real captivity, which Conrad relates to the moral nihilism of his drama: "photographs of more or less undressed dancing girls . . . books with titles hinting at impropriety . . . obscure newspapers, badly printed, with titles like *The Torch, The Gong*—rousing titles."[66] Such is the frame of anarchist apologetics in *The Secret Agent.* In this class of objects belongs, too, the "semi-grand piano" at the Silenus cafe which "executed suddenly all by itself a valse tune with aggressive virtuosity."[67] That the times are out of joint is not blamed on the revolutionists alone. We "see" the general idiocy of our condition when Ossipon— stunned by the superior nihilism of the Professor—leaves the pub, and the "lonely piano, without as much as a music stool to help it, struck a few chords courageously, and beginning a selection of national airs, played him out at last to the tune of 'Blue Bells of Scotland.' "[68]

Conrad's most pervading observation, that man hardly exists, or seems to exist in a dream only,[69] particularly when seen against the

---

[64] *Ibid.,* pp. 270–71.

[65] *Ibid.,* p. 13.

[66] *Ibid.,* p. 3.

[67] *Ibid.,* p. 61.

[68] *Ibid.,* p. 79.

[69] "La vida es sueño" ("Life is a dream") was a phrase often quoted by Conrad from Calderón's play, translated into Polish by Conrad's favorite romantic poet, Juliusz Słowacki. Conrad's own wording in *Lord Jim* (p. 214) typically stresses the destructiveness of the dream and the necessity of ceaseless effort to keep oneself balanced in it: "A man that is born [says Stein] falls into a dream like a man who falls into the sea. . . . The way is to the destructive element submit yourself, and with the exertions of your hands and feet in the water make the deep, deep sea keep you up."

unassailable "truth" of physical nature and artifact, lends to the wry scenes of *The Secret Agent* the same quality of tenderness shattered by hard facts found in *The Nigger*, *Lord Jim*, and *Nostromo*.

Another aspect of urban life which Conrad's irony doggedly scorns is sensational journalism. Thanks to newspapermen who irresponsibly exploit the emotions of their readers, Michaelis (when "young and slim") had fallen victim to the furious indignation of a crammed court and had received a long prison sentence for promoting an assassination he knew nothing about. On his release, "some emotional journalists in want of special copy"[70] turned the obscure incident into a cause for celebration. And, given a bit of scandal to chew on, Chief Inspector Heat smugly reflects, the same writers "who had written him up with emotional gush would be ready to write him down with emotional indignation."[71]

Against this kind of exploitation, the irrelevancies of Lady Mabel's enchantment with a nonexistent anarchist movement and Sir Ethelred's absorption with nationalization of the fisheries come across in a spirit of pure fun. The lady "was not an exploiting capitalist herself; she was, as it were, above the play of economic conditions." After all, the

> humanitarian hopes of the mild Michaelis tended not towards utter destruction, but merely towards the complete economic ruin of the system. And she did not really see where was the moral harm of it. It would do away with all the multitude of the "parvenus," whom she disliked and mistrusted, not because they had arrived anywhere (she denied that), but because of their profound unintelligence of the world . . . universal ruin (providing it was universal, as it was revealed to Michaelis) would leave the social values untouched. The disappearance of the last piece of money could not affect people of position.[72]

---

[70] *The Secret Agent*, p. 121.
[71] *Ibid.*, p. 122.
[72] *Ibid.*, pp. 108–11.

In the same vein, Sir Ethelred is made an image of the British State (mighty if a bit weak in the eyes—a point wrapped up in secrecy) next to whom a mere career policeman like the Assistant Commissioner looked "more foreign than ever" and "had the frail slenderness of a reed addressing an oak."[73] And indeed the unbroken record of [Sir Ethelred's] descent surpassed in the number of centuries the age of the oldest oak in the country."[74] Partly because of this oaklike frame and partly because his rooms are kept dark

---

[73] In the Author's Note (p. xi), Conrad implies that a book of recollections by the Assistant Commissioner of Police, Sir Robert Anderson, titled *Side Lights on the Home Rule Movement* had been like "the tiniest little drop of the right kind, precipitating the process of crystallization" for the novel. Anderson's book was published only in May, 1906, so unless Conrad had access to the book before publication, we may assume that he was already well into the story "Verloc" when the book came to hand. Possibly he had progressed somewhere near the fifth chapter of the novel, where both Chief Inspector Heat and the assistant commissioner are introduced, and had been hunting for concrete suggestions upon which to build not only the characters of the police department and ministry responsible in the Greenwich Observatory case, but also the character of the British legal system in general.

Anderson, who was as interested in the Bible and its beneficial influence in England as he was in the prevention and cure of crime, presents a marvelous view of the frustrations hounding a detective of political crimes. Unlike Conrad's diffident assistant commissioner, Anderson zealously pursues his job in the secret service, lamenting only that in England "everything must be done openly and above board," and arguing that "a mine can be reached only by a countermine" (pp. 127–28). Anderson had served under Sir William Harcourt from 1880 to 1885, when the latter was Home Secretary, and had provoked Sir William's quick temper often by maintaining a policy of secrecy when it was necessary to the interests of the Criminal Investigation Department. In 1889, when he was Liberal Opposition Leader, Sir William took revenge, publicly denouncing Anderson for dealing privately with a certain "informer" without the consent of the Home Secretary, then Henry Matthews. Loyally, Anderson avers that Sir William "was the 'biggest' man with whom I have ever had close personal dealings in the public service" (p. 89). Conrad applies this to Sir Ethelred as a physical characteristic, taking from the same page in Anderson the remark quoted (in Conrad's own words) from Sir William in the preface to the novel.

Both Chief Inspector Heat and Conrad's Assistant Commissioner seem modeled on Anderson, Heat coming closer to his personality, Heat's superior resembling him most strongly in looks. To judge from the photograph in Anderson's *Lighter Side of My Official Life* (1910), he was indeed a "Don Quixote of the Scotland Yard" and might pass as a twin to Conrad himself. He had the same disgust for Lombroso's "criminal type" theory that Conrad makes so evident in *The Secret Agent* (see Anderson's *Criminals and Crime*, 1907, p. 94). One suspects, too, that his refusal to discuss the Greenwich Park bombing or any other political crime involving conspirators of foreign countries, is evidence of the British determination to avoid any strain in diplomatic relations with Russia. The scantiness of official comment, of course, gave *carte blanche* to the novelist Conrad.

[74] *The Secret Agent*, p. 136.

to shade the haughty but weak eyes, the Assistant Commissioner feels in his office as if in "the greenish gloom" of a forest.

With such strokes as these Conrad makes us "see" the politics of *The Secret Agent*. Lady Mabel, behind her screen, banters intimately with the treacherous embassy official Vladimir. "He's been frightening me," she says caressingly, ". . . threatening society with all sorts of horrors."[75] But her obliviousness contains nothing lethal, as did the ignorance of Kurtz's Intended in *Heart of Darkness*. The secret evil is perfectly under control, not so much by the efficiency of the Special Crimes Department (which is very human and imperfect) as by the stolid impregnability of the island empire and the obsolescence of the Russian autocracy. Mr. Vladimir is caught between contempt and fear in the face of the London police.

> Descended from generations victimized by the instruments of an arbitrary power, he was racially, nationally, and individually afraid of the police. It was an inherited weakness, altogether independent of his judgment, of his reason, of his experience. He was born to it.[76]

Discovering that the contemptible commissioner has laid his finger on the heart of the Greenwich Park mystery (". . . we don't intend to let ourselves be bothered by shams"), Vladimir turns pleading—". . . we ought to be good Europeans,"[77] not just good Englishmen or Germans or Russians. And the Assistant Commissioner retorts with perhaps the only indelicate jest discoverable in Conrad: "Yes. . . . Only you look at Europe from its other end."[78]

---

[75] *Ibid.*, pp. 223–24.

[76] *Ibid.*, p. 224.

[77] We see in this episode, as also in the history of Verloc's activities in France, a gentle insistence on Conrad's theme in "Autocracy and War" (p. 103): "Since 1870 (as a distinguished statesman of the old tradition disconsolately exclaimed) *'il n'y a plus d'Europe!'* . . . The idea of a Europe united in the solidarity of her dynasties, which for a moment seemed to dawn on the horizon of the Vienna Congress through the subsiding dust of Napoleonic alarums and excursions, has been extinguished by the larger glamour of less restraining ideals. Instead of the doctrines of solidarity it was the doctrine of nationalities much more favorable to spoliations that came to the front, and since its greatest triumphs at Sadowa and Sedan there is no Europe."

[78] *The Secret Agent*, p. 227.

If Conrad's caricature of the British aristocracy as a class is sheer fun, his caricature of the anarchists is less so only because Conrad could not resist making them repulsive. "A certain simplicity of thought is common to serene souls at both ends of the social scale."[79] The revolutionaries Ossipon, Michaelis, and Yundt are pathetic enough in their general unfitness for survival but still more so in the way each contradicts himself while promoting the theories of the "supermen"—Nietzsche, Nechaev, and Marx. Ossipon rests all his hopes in science but preaches that social change can be wrought only by playing on the emotions of the masses. Similarly, Michaelis—gloriously optimistic as to the future of the masses— preaches economic determinism but describes chaos as he argues for caution "in our ignorance of the effect that may be produced by any given economic change . . . For history is made with tools, not with ideas; and everything is changed by economic conditions— art, philosophy, love, virtue—truth itself!"[80]

Of them all, Yundt has the most terrifying "philosophy" of social progress and yet is the most inoffensive. His violent language paralyzes the half-wit Stevie, but Yundt "had never in his life raised . . . his little finger against the social edifice."[81] So much for the man who has, like Nechaev, "always dreamed of a band of men ab-

---

[79] *Ibid.*, p. 42.

Irving Howe objects that Conrad dabbled in a medium of which he had no such knowledge as, say, Dostoevsky, Malraux, and Koestler—all of whom saw revolution at some time or other from the inside. Yet surely *not* to have seen it from the inside, but nevertheless in a real sense to have *seen* it, furnished Conrad with a valid perspective. For most of the city is outside. His subject in *The Secret Agent* is not revolution (as is the subject of Dostoevsky in *The Possessed*, Malraux in *Man's Fate*, or Koestler in *Darkness at Noon*) but rather the concussion produced in our everyday world by one small, not untypical incident in the annals of anarchist activity. Deliberately he chooses "a blood-stained inanity." No one, including Howe, could dignify Martial Bourdin's fiasco with a better name. When Conrad denied ever having intended to treat anarchism seriously in this novel, he sometimes implied that it might be treated seriously by another hand. But I think he was closer to the truth of his convictions when he doubted, in a letter to Galsworthy, that a grave (as opposed to ironic) study could be sensibly made at all. "As to attacking Anarchism as a form of humanitarian enthusiasm or intellectual despair or social atheism, that—if it were worth doing— would be the work for a more vigorous hand . . ." (*Life and Letters*, II, 37).

[80] *The Secret Agent*, p. 50.

[81] *Ibid.*, p. 48.

solute in their resolve to discard all scruples in the choice of means, strong enough to give themselves frankly the name of destroyers."[82]

Yundt speaks for the Professor[83] since someone must represent the nihilist position in the Brett Street symposium. The Professor himself is so much the perfect nihilist that he despises everyone including the revolutionists. "You revolutionists," he tells Ossipon who twice seeks him out for comfort in the course of the novel, "are the slaves of the social convention, which is afraid of you; slaves of it as much as the very police . . . It governs your thought, of course, and your action, too, and thus neither your thought nor your action can ever be conclusive."[84] Yet the terrorist Professor is terrified by the London crowds:

> . . . he became disagreeably affected by the sight of the roadway thronged with vehicles and of the pavement crowded with men and women. . . . They swarmed numerous like locusts, industrious like ants, thoughtless like a natural force, pushing on blind and orderly and absorbed, impervious to sentiment, to logic, to terror, too, perhaps.[85]

"Such moments," Conrad reminds us with his solemn mockery, "come to all men whose ambition aims at a direct grasp upon humanity—to artists, politicians, thinkers, reformers, or saints."[86] What distinguishes the Professor is that in his dread of the very thing he desires to grasp, he has resorted to a dependence on death and delights in his superiority over men like Ossipon who have a normal desire for life. As the visual contrast between Sir Ethelred and the Assistant Commissioner extends beyond physical description, so the Professor is contrasted with Heat:

---

[82] *Ibid.*, p. 42.

[83] The Professor also appears in Conrad's "The Informer," where he again wears the large round spectacles but where he blows himself up inadvertently, hidden away in his secret laboratory. This incident and the character himself may have been suggested by Marc Schweitzer, the young chemist who made a slip while charging bombs in his St. Petersburg hotel room and blew himself to pieces on March 11, 1905. See Boris Nikolajewsky, *Aseff the Spy* (New York: Doubleday, Doran, 1934), pp. 107–8.

[84] *The Secret Agent*, p. 69.

[85] *Ibid.*, pp. 81–82.

[86] *Ibid.*, p. 82.

To the vigorous, tenacious vitality of the Chief Inspector, the physical wretchedness of that being, so obviously not fit to live, was ominous; for it seemed to him that if he had the misfortune to be such a miserable object he would not have cared how soon he died. Life had such a strong hold upon [Heat] that a fresh wave of nausea broke out in slight perspiration upon his brow. The murmur of town life came . . . to his ears with a precious familiarity and an appealing sweetness. He was human.[87]

This contrast between what is fully human and affirmative toward life and what is wretchedly less than human and revolted by life gradually emerges as the central theme of *The Secret Agent*.

Guerard remarks that the "degenerate Stevie in his morbid horror of pain and in his indiscriminate compassion is a symbolic extreme both of the visionary and of his victim."[88] This warrants further notice. Stevie (who "was not mad" though half-witted)[89] accentuates the craziness of the "humanitarian" revolutionists by offering a genuine case of feeling to offset their sham sympathies. His horror at the spectacle of a beaten horse is so much more normal and direct than the sympathy for human suffering exhibited by the theorists that one finds the comedy humanized through his absurd agonies. Because he and his sister and mother are so delightfully and nobly sensitive in their desperate circumstances, the difference between them and the "humanitarians" finally prepares us for a tragic dimension when the three of them are unexpectedly victimized. It is not they who characterize the "madness and despair" which the novel explores. They are even a bulwark against it, which unfortunately proves too human to hold.

Conrad's Dickensian tenderness for lower-class nobility shows nowhere so clearly as in his potent and discriminating use of the mock-heroic hyperbole. In contrast to Swift, Fielding, and Pope, Conrad reserves this comic device for characters who come by our sympathy honestly, however absurd they may be in the excesses of their degradation. The cockney cabman, "like Virgil's Silenus, who, his face

---

[87] *Ibid.*, p. 94.
[88] *Conrad the Novelist*, p. 225.
[89] *The Secret Agent*, p. 167.

smeared with the juice of berries, discoursed of Olympian gods to the innocent shepherds of Sicily . . . talked to Stevie of domestic matters and the affairs of men whose sufferings are great and immortality by no means assured."[90] Winnie's conversation with Verloc is "as artfully adapted, no doubt, to the circumstances of his return as the talk of Penelope to the return of the wandering Odysseus."[91] And the poor charwoman, Mrs. Neale, takes her daily wage "round the corner to drink ardent spirits in a mean and musty public house—the unavoidable station on the *via dolorosa* of her life."[92]

The effect of the ironic voice used here seems to me just the opposite of what Irving Howe calls an irony so "peevish" that it "must have its source less in zeal or anger than in some deep distemper."[93] Like David Daiches, Howe misses most of the novel's power by not seeing the flexibility of Conrad's ironic range, which has more than the arrows of "zeal or anger" to its bow. With Conrad, irony can reach sympathetic intimacy whenever Winnie, Stevie, or their mother is about, or it can simply poke cool and gentle fun at a lazy secret agent's lovemaking. For it is the ironic voice alone, as Conrad said, that enabled him to say all he felt in pity as well as in scorn.[94] Without the ironic voice, allowing him above all to ennoble the plight of Winnie and her lower-class kin, the story would be as stiffly caricatured and falsely melodramatic as the scenes dominated by Mr. Jones and Ricardo in *Victory*.

To Conrad's chagrin, this is just what happened to the novel when it was adapted for the stage and had to go without the inexhaustible play of the storyteller's wit, flickering over character, scene, and dialogue. He foresaw what the audience's reaction would be when he wrote Pinker in November, 1919 (three years before the play was performed unsuccessfully):

As I go on in my adaption, stripping off the garment of artistic expression and consistent irony which clothes the story in the book, I

---

[90] *Ibid.*, p. 75.
[91] *Ibid.*, p. 183.
[92] *Ibid.*, p. 185.
[93] *Politics and the Novel*, p. 98.
[94] *The Secret Agent*, p. xiii.

perceive more clearly how it is bound to appear . . . a merely horrible and sordid tale, giving a most unfavourable impression of both the writer himself and of his attitude to the moral aspect of the subject. In the book the tale . . . was not treated sordidly. . . . The peculiar light of my mental insight and of my humane feeling . . . gave to the narrative a sort of grim dignity.[95]

We have noted often that, as an outsider in England, Conrad was splendidly endowed to develop the ironic mood and voice. Fiction gave him a means with which purposively to withhold or reveal information or viewpoints his readers lacked; in fiction also he found a means—through ironic hyperbole—to ennoble without sentimentality and to debase without distemper. Guerard describes the novel's "prevailing tone" as "one of ironic hauteur and control"[96] while David Daiches, like Howe, finds the ironic effects uncertain and liable to leave the reader "wondering whether Conrad in writing this novel was more concerned to reveal something or to suppress something."[97] The difference expressed may, of course, divide readers eternally: between whether or not the irony was successfully controlled for the effect of entertainment or whether it is largely the eruption of an uncontrolled psyche. Artistically speaking, at any rate, none of the ironic effects in the novel seem disproportionate to the ends they reach in revealing the inner necessities of character and plot.

Although the point from which Conrad views England's political institutions and law is deliberately amusing and lower than eye level, one can fairly apply to Winnie and her kin what Mme de Staël somewhere said, that "Political institutions alone can form the character of a nation." English character shows in the lesson Winnie teaches Stevie when he asks her to define the function of the police: "They are there so that them as have nothing shouldn't take anything away from them who have." Quite sensibly Stevie

---

[95] *Life and Letters*, II, 233–34.
[96] *Conrad the Novelist*, p. 226.
[97] *The Novel and the Modern World* (Chicago: University of Chicago Press, 1960), p. 57.

puts the question of the revolutionary: "What? . . . Not even if they were hungry? Mustn't they?" And she answers, "Not if they were ever so."[98] This rock-bottom social justice is really the standard on which the melodrama rests and turns. Winnie's eye for justice, along with her brother's and their mother's, is only funny because it is so true. Winnie and her relatives are not merely vivid characters in a tale; they vivify the side of society which stands as a bulwark against the "manifestation of discontent and imbecility"[99] represented by the anarchists. And British institutions, however susceptible to caricature, give Winnie and her family their solid characters. The almshouse to which her mother consigns herself, however depressing, is as trustworthy as the corner policeman.

The meaning of justice is a question that weaves in and out of the novel, but the subject discussed explicitly has no relevance to the poetic justice that asserts itself finally in the last pages. Concerning social justice in the abstract, Conrad reminds us that it is an unstable quantity, determined by the ratio between individual expectations and the ability of society, at a given moment, to meet them. Thus the Professor's struggles

> to raise himself in the social scale, had filled him with such an exalted conviction of his merits that it was extremely difficult for the world to treat him with justice—the standard of that notion depending so much upon the patience of the individual.[100]

This is Conrad's only novel in which England comes off as what the deceased Poland had tacitly been to him before—the highest example of political rectitude. The British genius for overlooking what was inconvenient to an ideal or a plan, which Marlow exhibited in the Congo and Decoud exposed as a radical failing in Charles Gould, is found in *The Secret Agent* to have redeeming virtues. England's superiority over the United States is unambiguous. "America is all right," says the Professor. "It is this country that is dangerous, with her idealistic conception of legality."[101]

---

[98] *The Secret Agent*, p. 173.
[99] Letter to Galsworthy, Sept. 12, 1906, *Life and Letters*, II, 37.
[100] *The Secret Agent*, p. 75.
[101] *Ibid.*, p. 73.

Even the gibes at the hierarchy of British officialdom for its habitual reticence in acknowledging or revealing sinister facts between one officer and another add up to a tenderly fond view of British character. Heat's reluctance to tell all he knows to the Assistant Commissioner and the latter's reticence before Sir Ethelred reflect the nature of their general institutions:

> By a benevolent provision of nature no man is a hero to his valet, or else the heroes would have to brush their own clothes. Likewise no department appears perfectly wise to the intimacy of its workers. A department does not know so much as some of its servants. Being a dispassionate organism, it can never be perfectly informed. It would not be good for its efficiency to know too much.[102]

Nothing is more characteristic of Conrad's extraordinary virtuosity in this novel than that this playful motif should become the bond between the very different characters who are in the end found to constitute the English people and everything that the sham revolutionaries oppose. Because of it we see the otherwise hidden kinship between Winnie (whose surrender to Verloc for her brother's sake is only possible because she is able to maintain her resolution of "not looking too deeply into things") and the official protectors of the society which she obscurely and immemorially represents. Her mother, of course, is just such another thoroughbred in fortitude, reticence, and self-denial.

This studied refusal to go to the bottom of things does make England a refuge for scoundrels (and Winnie a refuge for Verloc), but as the Professor points out, a refuge of freedom is utterly demoralizing to anarchists or cranks who need something politically vicious to nourish their hatred. The Assistant Commissioner elaborates this latter point and, as Mégroz remarks, seems almost to assume Conrad's voice[103] when he discourses to Sir Ethelred upon

---

[102] *Ibid.*, p. 91.

[103] Mégroz goes too far, however, when he suggests that Conrad has identified himself with the personality of the Assistant Commissioner to such an extent "that one of the artistic faults of *The Secret Agent* is the unimportant role necessarily allotted to that very interesting man, a veritable Marlow of Scotland Yard" (*A Talk with Joseph Conrad* [London: Elkin Mathews, 1926], p. 79). Even when he is described as "like the vision of a cool, reflective Don Quixote" (p. 147), we know that Conrad, as fre-

the necessity of putting an end to the intrusion of secret agents in England. His philosophy is motivated, however, by base impulses —the wish to cut the ground from under his more illustrious subordinate Heat and to divert suspicion (which might spoil his wife's intimacy with Lady Mabel) from Michaelis. The truth he expounds, therefore, reaches us less with the impact of an insight than with the force of an obvious truism:

> In principle, I should lay it down that the existence of secret agents should not be tolerated, as tending to augment the positive dangers of the evil against which they are used. That the spy will fabricate his information is a mere commonplace. But in the sphere of political and revolutionary action, relying partly on violence, the professional spy has every facility to fabricate the very facts themselves, and will spread the double evil of emulation in one direction, and of panic, hasty legislation, unreflecting hate, on the other. However, this is an imperfect world——[104]

To Americans of our period, Conrad's keen perception of the dangers in counterespionage and heresy hunts may seem more important to *The Secret Agent* than it actually is. The mechanics of the spy story and the unraveling of the mystery by the police, absorbing as they are, are carefully controlled to lead to the climax in Chapter IX where the real discovery is not Heat's but Winnie's in the peripeteia, or reversal, which changes her, through her questions about Stevie's overcoat, from a woman who carefully avoids "the inwardness of things" to one for whom there is no longer any external or objective substance to cling to. There is no finer evocation of tragic realization and revolt against the inevitable in all the writings of Conrad, though every one of his novels develops toward such a point as this. Of course the power of this scene and the ones that follow to the conclusion derives partly from the extreme reversal in the phlegmatic Winnie's character. The girl who sacrificed her love for a romantic butcher boy has taken instead a

---

quently he does, is infusing some of his favorite characteristics into an essentially different personality. For the Assistant Commissioner, with all his feelings of dislocation in London and his look of "a queer foreign-looking chap," is a man whose imagination is barely big enough to fill the demands of his job.

[104] *The Secret Agent*, p. 139.

man who inadvertently butchers her brother. The ferocious humor of the situation in some strange way determines its strength to move us. Winnie does not mean to murder her husband any more than Jim means to desert the "Patna." Verloc's sickening "Come here" (like the voices yelling, "Jump, George! Jump!" to Jim) forces Winnie to act on an unformed and unconscious resolve which the web of earlier choices and dispositions had rendered inevitable. Then, immediately, like Jim again, though here the likeness ends, Winnie's perception of justice sentences her instantly. Her terrified certainty that she has earned the gallows carries no dram of remorse—only revulsion against the idea of being hanged, an obstinate hold on life which perversely asserts itself in "the resolution to go at once and throw herself into the river."[105] But suddenly the ingratiating Comrade Ossipon appears to promise a lease on life, and one of Conrad's most suspenseful and harrowing scenes ensues. It brings a second peripeteia as Ossipon's expectation of falling heir to both Verloc's fortune and his wife, turns to appalled discovery that Verloc was not blown up in Greenwich Park but lies on his living-room sofa, murdered by the "widow" clinging now to Ossipon's arm like "death itself—the companion of life."[106]

Conrad told someone that the end of *The Secret Agent* came to him as "an inspiration." That Winnie should have been forced to suicide—the most convincing and pathetic suicide of the many in Conrad's works—is evidence of how immersed he was "in the absolute necessities of the case—Mrs. Verloc's case." When he told Retinger that his best works were *Nostromo* and *The Secret Agent*, "because in those books I accumulated the most difficult technical obstacles and I overcame them most successfully,"[107] Conrad referred partly, no doubt, to the problem he faced in making the futile brutalities of revolutionist and counterrevolutionist, as he pictured them in London, meaningful in a city which was largely

---

[105] *Ibid.*, p. 268.

[106] *Ibid.*, p. 291.

[107] Joseph Retinger, *Conrad and His Contemporaries* (London: Minerva, 1941), p. 91.

impervious to them. If my appraisal is correct, he could not have said at the time he wrote the novel that there was anything politically menacing in them as far as England was concerned. It was probably only in the course of writing the novel that he perceived the extent to which the activity of political shams could ricochet into the very heart of "the masses" they pretended to champion.

The two men directly responsible for Winnie's horrible end— Verloc and Ossipon—are aiming their malice in an opposite direction. Verloc, in his torpid way, has sheltered Winnie and her unfortunate family as he has pictured himself sheltering society in the abstract. The homeless Ossipon, Casanova of the anarchist "dove-cote," has permitted himself to be sheltered in her house and is ready, in her moment of greatest need, to offer his masculine charms for what they will bring. As with Verloc and the other shams, "the instinct of conventional respectability was strong within him, being only overcome by his dislike of all kinds of recognized labour . . . For obviously one does not revolt against the advantages and opportunities of [a] state, but against the price that must be paid for the same in the coin of accepted morality, self-restraint, and toil."[108]

Thus the two characters, Winnie Verloc and Tom Ossipon, run parallel courses and suffer parallel awakenings, which are awakenings into nightmare. We have met this phenomenon before in Marlow's awakening at Kurtz's station. The whole comic form of *The Secret Agent*, however, as well as its incidental techniques of playful irony and satire, is so different from *Heart of Darkness* that we wonder how it is we can suddenly be so moved, so ready to accept this descent into an element which is not fake in its pretences but truly destructive. Winnie is no Marlow, accumulating ominous insights as she progresses toward the revelation of realities below the surface in her experience. For in this story the detective work and the discoveries that matter are separate activities, registering on minds that never communicate.

The Assistant Commissioner's remark that "we are here in the

---

[108] *The Secret Agent*, p. 53.

presence of a domestic drama"[109] is clinical. He and Heat are personally unconcerned with the fate of the Verlocs. But this is just the point, in *The Secret Agent*, where we first begin to care more about Winnie than we would care about the accidental victim of a family melodrama reported in the newspapers. No one cares, least of all the police who have discovered the most intimate facts of her life. The tragic hero, Northrop Frye reminds us, "is only somebody who gets isolated from his society."[110] One of the novel's multifold ironies is that we have known all along how isolated Winnie was from her husband and, through him, from society itself. But *she* has taken no notice of it. To think how different this novel is from *Lord Jim, Nostromo,* and *The Nigger of the "Narcissus,"* we have only to realize that there is no one in the story (no Marlow, Monygham, or narrator who is "one of us") to sympathize or lament as Winnie rushes to her merciless fate.

Ossipon is there when the moment comes for help. The few pages left explore his abilities as a man who would save the world. His part in the "simple tale" accentuates the void, if we are sensitive to Conrad's expectations, of human courage and compassion which in large part "the city" has killed, first by isolating the only courageous characters and then by ignoring, in the midst of its crowds, their desperate extremities. Ossipon is one of Conrad's most immediately felt villains, but only for a moment. He has come to typify all the main characteristics of the revolutionary and counterrevolutionary crowd—their egotistical dependence on women (who in this story dramatize the grim fortitude of urban humanity), their worship of science ("He gazed at her, and invoked Lombroso, as an Italian peasant recommends himself to his favourite saint"),[111] their insufficiency as individuals, and above all their ignorance of politics and society.

In the parallel design that Conrad uses to finish the tale, Win-

---

[109] *Ibid.,* p. 222.
[110] Northrop Frye, *Anatomy of Criticism* (Princeton: Princeton University Press, 1957), p. 41.
[111] *The Secret Agent,* p. 297.

nie's terrible death touches off a reverberation. As a sort of coda, Comrade Ossipon closes the political comedy with his reflections on the private tragedy of Winnie Verloc.[112] Like Winnie, Ossipon changes from one with little or no insight into his own life to one who sees too much. The unsuccessful medical student is Winnie's opposite, of course, in having pretended to know more than he did. The farcical character of the story grew on this ground. Conrad now tries a difficult feat, which is to make Winnie's suicide a means of coalescing the absurd farce with tragedy into a single vision and form.

The Professor reappears to assert what he and the other revolutionaries have posited, with varying degrees of conviction and self-deception, all along: "Madness and despair! Give me that for a lever, and I'll move the world."[113] Ossipon is the only character in the story who has come into the presence of real madness and despair. He has himself, for the first time in his life, effectively exploited it, not meaning to but stumbling into it, and in a state of terror himself. The result, far from moving the world, has been merely to drive a simple woman to suicide. Ossipon is left to drown in drink his unique knowledge of the reasons for Winnie's drowning, of the "impenetrable mystery destined to hang forever over this act of madness or despair," in the journalists' resounding phrase.

If this conclusion impresses one, unfortunately, as too cerebrally just, it is perhaps because Conrad has too successfully cultivated his tragic characters in isolation from their farcical fellow men. The stimulus to a change of awareness in Tom Ossipon is adequate, but the receptor is not.

The Professor's part is more felicitously conceived. He is neither harmful nor harmed because he deliberately (and to protect himself from life and the crowd which he fears) cuts himself off, fabricating a *raison d'être* out of his scientific work on "the perfect deto-

---

[112] We saw in *Nostromo* and *Heart of Darkness* a similar mixing of tragedy and farce.
[113] *The Secret Agent*, p. 309.

nator." He is self-sufficient, and the master irony is in his fantasy that he will move a world by force of science which he dare not touch with his human hand or personality.

The perfect detonator is a timing device. The Professor, like the other anarchists, is dreaming of destroying history as well as society; he will use a scientifically clocked bomb to demonstrate his contempt for the accumulated experience of the past. His conception, thus, bears a resemblance to that of the archconservative who is his opposite number in the story—Mr. Vladimir, who saw an attack on the perfectly gauged timing devices of Greenwich Observatory as the solution to his problem.

Vladimir's sole ambition had been to shatter the British public's faith in liberal institutions. The only means to this end, he told Verloc, was to perpetrate an outrage "so absurd as to be incomprehensible, inexplicable, almost unthinkable; in fact, mad. Madness alone is truly terrifying, inasmuch as you cannot placate it either by threats, persuasion, or bribes."[114]

This exactly describes the Professor's conception of what is required: "The world is mediocre, limp, without force. And madness and despair are a force."[115] The unity of the novel emerges in the course of Winnie's progress from the English woman's basic soundness to a kind of madness that is utterly unavailing to either Vladimir or to the Professor. In a totally unforeseen manner, their bomb *has* moved the world, but it is the little world of Winnie Verloc. Society in the mass, their target, is as unaffected as the clocks at Greenwich (which tell the world's time), and it is surely one of Conrad's jests at science that the bomb invented for the cause of anarchy was by the easiest change of hands sent to serve the cause of autocracy. Unconscious to all of this, protected by the shadow of a city he hates and fears, the Professor is the last one off the stage as he plods on, "unsuspected and deadly" but also unsuspecting.

The fun is gone; at the end the novel hardly entertains us as it did so well in the scenes where Mr. Vladimir employed his wit to

---

114 *Ibid.*, p. 33.
115 *Ibid.*, p. 309.

make the lumpish Verloc squirm, where Heat before the Assistant Commissioner felt like a tightrope artist whose manager in mid-performance had rushed out to shake the rope, or where Winnie schooled Stevie in the methods of making her husband's life more comfortable. The ironic author, whose readers know all there is to know, leaves no question hanging as did the author of *Heart of Darkness*. He leaves only a mood of scorn at the futilities of conspiracy, a scorn increased by wonder at the inexhaustible capacity for resistance, suffering, and despair in a cockney breast.

". . . *Under Western Eyes*—that finest novel in the English language . . .

". . . the greatest, wisest and most poetic of all Mr. Conrad's works *Under Western Eyes* . . ."

Ford Madox Ford, *Thus to Revisit*

"You know there are about 30,000 words more than the printed text. Revising while ill in bed, I am afraid I have struck out whole pages recklessly. The other day I looked at the MS.—1357 pp. averaging about 120 words per page. There are passages which should have remained. I wasn't in a fit state to judge them. Well, it's done now, and let the critics make what they can of it."

Letter from Conrad to Galsworthy,
October 15, 1911

CHAPTER
SEVEN

Under Western Eyes

A year or so before he died in 1869, Apollo Korzeniowski wrote to a friend:

> I carry in my head a great Polish novel on the corruption that has come to us from Moscow, through Asiatic extravagance, "bureaucratic honors," the disbelief propagated by public education, by the false brilliance of the Russian "great world," and finally by the Russification of families under the guise of mixed marriages.[1]

This great Polish novel was never written, but an English novel very like it—and also very different—was the last great political novel to be written by Korzeniowski's son, Joseph Conrad. The fact that it was Conrad's last important political work in fiction suggests both that Conrad delayed in getting down to it and also that, once having written it, he had fully unburdened himself of a subject which had in some measure inspired the other political novels we have considered in this study.

Apollo Korzeniowski was concerned, as Czesław Miłosz points out, not only with the relations between Poland and Russia but with

> the slow but constant march of the Russian Empire toward the West. [Korzeniowski] justifies the aim of his life—the struggle

---

[1] Czesław Miłosz, "Apollo Nałęcz Korzeniowski," *Kultura* (Paris, February, 1956), p. 79.

against the imperial Moloch—by the imminent destruction of European civilization of which only the countries absorbed by Russia are aware. This criticism of the monstrous oriental organism resembles that which Karl Marx sketched in the same period in his history of Russian diplomacy.[2]

In a language even more passionate than that of Adam Mickiewicz, Korzeniowski echoes the words with which his romantic predecessor had lectured his audience at the Collège de France in Paris in the 1840's. Miłosz further summarizes the arguments Korzeniowski presented in the pamphlet *Poland and Russia*,[3] written and smuggled out of Russia during his exile in the 'sixties:

> The Tartar yoke formed Muscovy. It has always maintained the regime of the horde. All belongs to the Tsar. Each subject can, from one day to the next, be lifted to the summit of creation or hurled into the abyss. The form of government in Russia is despotism bounded by no other limit than assassination or a palace revolution. The Tsar unites in his person the functions of chief, legislator, and priest. Religion there is official and idolatrous; it spreads fatalism and fanaticism. The Russian people are not capable of being free; they feel that exposed to the fire of liberty, they would "go up in smoke like dry dung" and that they would cease to exist as a state.[4]

In Korzeniowski's words,

> Being what it is, in order to avoid annihilation Russia is obliged to pursue the struggle beyond her border. Although Europe can for a long time postpone this struggle, the time will come when it will be impossible to escape the crisis. However, this decisive moment will be selected in Moscow—a disadvantageous moment for Europe, and in it Europe will lose half her strength.[5]

When Conrad turns, in late 1907, to writing a novel on "the very soul of things Russian,"[6] as he described it to Galsworthy, we

---

[2] *Ibid.*, p. 76.

[3] The pamphlet was published anonymously in Dresden, in the émigré journal *Ojczyzna* (*Fatherland*), Nos. 44–46, 1864.

[4] Miłosz, "Apollo Nałęcz Korzeniowski," p. 76.

[5] *Ibid.*

[6] Letter of Jan. 6, 1908, *Life and Letters*, II, 64. Baines mentions a letter of Dec. 30, 1907, on the same subject, addressed to Pinker, which I have not seen. See Jocelyn Baines, *Joseph Conrad* (London: Weidenfeld & Nicolson, 1959), p. 345, n. 149.

would expect him to alter radically certain aspects of the vision of Mickiewicz and of his own father.[7] Most importantly, he would eradicate the mystical obsession both men had had with Polish messianism, their idea that Poland was a mystical reincarnation of Christ and that through communion with Poland's crucifixion, the other nations of Europe would be saved. That Conrad omitted all references to, and even the very name of, Poland from *Under Western Eyes* might be taken as a sign either that he repudiated this romantic nationalism altogether or that he wished merely to empty it of absurd mysticism and to concentrate on those aspects of Polish experience which would be acceptable and persuasive to readers ignorant (or suspicious) of Poland's peculiar experience and testimony in European politics.

The latter alternative seems to me the obviously right one. Still, there are critics (Baines is the most recent) who think repudiation of all Polish politics was evident in Conrad's novels as well as in his emigration from Poland. Against this, I would argue that the "jump" from Poland, the tortured defense of Jim's romantic egoism, and all Conrad's political scrutinies in the novels considered in this study, are manifestations of a mind laboring to distinguish, among the ashes of a dying, self-preoccupied and self-annihilating national tradition and spirit, those sparks of genuine and universal truth which make "fidelity" a rational principle, not simply a gesture of blind defiance in the face of terrible odds. (At times, of course, a reasonable principle may be defended blindly, as when a man fights for his life in the dark.)

Another important change had just recently occurred in Conrad's perspective to distinguish it from the visions of the Polish romantics. By 1907, when Conrad gave up writing *Chance* to develop the story "Razumov," out of a suggestion given him many years before in Geneva,[8] he no longer shared his father's fixation with the ex-

---

[7] See above, pp. 36, 71–75.

[8] Jean-Aubry writes confidently that the "novel with the preliminary title of *Razumov*, afterward called *Under Western Eyes* [was] first suggested by an anecdote told him in 1895 by a chance acquaintance in Geneva and recalled to his memory by his recent visit to that city" in 1907 (*The Sea Dreamer*, translated by Helen Sebba [New York: Doubleday & Co., Inc., 1957], p. 253). The manuscript of the novel at Yale has the

pansionist tendencies of the Russian state. He was in a better position to see the decay of the autocracy and not yet convinced that the revolution ahead could resuscitate the Bear to its former ferocity. Germany, for the moment, seemed to take the place that Russia had held in his father's mind. And by 1919, whatever he may have thought of the Bear revived by bolshevism, his speech was modified by the necessity (fatality, he would have called it) —evident in his essay "The Crime of Partition"—of recognizing Russia as one of the nations, victorious over Prussianism, which must be dealt with civilly if Polish independence was to be realized. There is only an implicit suggestion, in his letters and the preface (1920) to *Under Western Eyes*, that post-revolutionary Russia had reverted to the lethal potency it commanded before 1905. In the preface he argues that *Under Western Eyes* is "an attempt to render not so much the political state as the psychology of Russia,"[9] and, of course, this relieves him of any imperative to reveal Russia's political influence on Europe or her political future at home. On the other hand, by hindsight in 1920, he observes that "the general truth which underlies [the novel's] action" is as true under a regime of "Utopian revolutionism" as it was under the autocracy.

V. S. Pritchett and Gustaw Herling-Grudziński (an émigré Pole living in Italy) have called special attention to the fact that Conrad's view of "the corruption that has come . . . from Moscow (in Korzeniowski's words) has a generalized quality in *Under Western Eyes*, emphasizing that Conrad's experience of it was a distant childhood memory when he came to write the novel."[10] Pritchett finds in this terrible but remote experience the origin of Conrad's conception of evil in all his novels, of which *Lord Jim* is the best

---

title *Razumov* throughout, but on the last page the title *Under Western Eyes* is substituted. On the same page Conrad wrote "January 22, 1910," the date on which he finished the manuscript.

[9] *Under Western Eyes*, p. vii.

[10] V. S. Pritchett, "The Exile," the *New Statesman*, Aug. 24, 1957, p. 229. Gustaw Herling-Grudziński, "W oczach Conrada" ("Under Conrad's Eyes"), *Kultura* (Paris, October, 1957), pp. 16–32. The latter was translated for me by Mrs. Stanislas Wellisz.

example. Herling-Grudziński remarks that, considering its genesis, this certitude of evil must rouse suspicion, especially when in *Under Western Eyes* Conrad attempts to model the whole character of a people on experience drawn from the first ten years of his life and beyond that on reading he undertook in English much later for the novel. According to Herling-Grudziński, Conrad's interpretation of events in the time of Russia's 1905 revolution shows a very poor understanding of the revolutionary psychology of the period and reflects, rather, his gleanings from Dostoevsky, Bakunin, and other politically outdated theorists of the nineteenth century.

The objection is undoubtedly worth arguing. Herling-Grudziński refers Conrad's readers to Albert Camus' *The Rebel* as a more trustworthy guide to the political motives behind Igor Sazonov's assassination of de Plehve (Russian Minister of the Interior) in 1904. Victor Haldin, a character Conrad frankly modeled on Sazonov, is not endowed in *Under Western Eyes* with a very explicit political ideology, nor do his comrades in St. Petersburg add anything substantive to the few exalted but vague words Haldin pours out to Razumov in the latter's rooms. Conrad fortifies Haldin's short speech in defense of terrorism and murder with the more detailed arguments of Natalia Haldin, Sophia Antonovna, and the *dame de compagnie* Tekla in the second and third parts (out of four) of the novel, but all taken together are insufficient for Herling-Grudziński, who echoes Camus' conviction that the revolutionaries of the period in which *Under Western Eyes* is set were characterized by a noble humanism and political principles both sound and concrete: we could not ask them any questions concerning political principles today which they did not ask themselves then.[11] Herling-Grudziński refers particularly to one revolutionary who made the sign of the cross with one hand while he threw his bomb with the other, who left a lasting impression on Camus, not so much because of his religious faith as because he conscientiously dedicated his act to the realization of a political system free of tyranny.

One would like to answer Herling-Grudziński at this point that

---

[11] Herling-Grudziński, "W oczach Conrada," p. 26.

one could find no better instance than the very gesture in question
—the terrorist invoking the cross—of the mysticism combined with
despair which Conrad attributed to the historical character of Russian politics: ". . . the autocracy in mystic vestments, engendered
by the slavery of a Tartar conquest."[12] As we have seen, Conrad
confessed to Garnett several years earlier that his own father, Apollo
Korzeniowski, had "degenerated" into this same sort of "mysticism
and despair"—qualities Conrad claimed were not native to the
Polish character but caught like a disease from Russia.[13]

Considering Conrad's antipathy, one must argue with Herling-
Grudziński that Victor Haldin does express an exalted and prin-
cipled dedication to the best hopes of man with extraordinary
poignancy. "The Russian soul that lives in all of us . . . has a
future. It has a mission, I tell you, or else why should I have been
moved to do this—reckless—like a butcher—in the middle of all
these innocent people—scattering death—I! . . . I wouldn't hurt a
fly!"[14] With these words Haldin suddenly bursts into tears. The
gesture expresses compassion for the tragic human paradox far
more adequately, I should say, than would the sign of the cross
on such a day. Haldin's whole conduct during his two interviews
with Razumov, especially in the second when Razumov returns
supposedly from arranging Haldin's escape but actually from betraying him to the police, must convince the reader of his acute
human sensitivity. Suddenly aware that he has made Razumov an
accomplice against the latter's will, Haldin's dejection returns. He
knows that in view of Razumov's radically different ambitions and
ideas, he, Haldin, has in a manner betrayed Razumov by coming
to him. Razumov is most horrified by his own plight; Haldin, for
the plight of his friend. He leaves Razumov's house in such a
wretched frame of mind that one sees him half-resigning himself

---

[12] *Under Western Eyes*, p. 142.

[13] It is interesting in this connection to note that Towiański, from whom Mickiewicz
"caught" his most virulent political mysticism, was rumored to have been a secret
agent for Russia, spying on émigré Poles in Paris.

[14] *Under Western Eyes*, p. 22.

to his arrest as to an inevitable consequence of injustice to Razumov. Haldin initiates the human identification which will haunt Razumov until he can render the justice to Haldin that Haldin rendered to him. And it is a tough, unsentimental justice, free of the malign influences which through most of the novel plague all the sympathetic characters. Haldin's revolutionary ideal, and his ideal of human solidarity, remain pure through torture until his execution. And Razumov, who will submit himself to a correspondingly "just" torture, never falters in *his* original convictions. Thus, while people as different as Herling-Grudziński and D. H. Lawrence accuse Conrad of weakness in the conception of his "heroes" and of always "giving in"[15] to conventional norms in his novels, one must argue that the ideals that really matter to his tragic victims are never sacrificed or even compromised. The doctrines of revolution are not conveyed, in *Under Western Eyes,* simply as weakness or as insanity. Natalia Haldin's words hallow the lives of the conscientious revolutionaries (as opposed to the shams, Peter Ivanovitch, Madame de S—— and Nikita): "Destruction is the work of anger. Let the tyrants and the slayers be forgotten together, and only the reconstructors be remembered."[16]

In the strategy of the novel, Haldin's assassination of a minister seems to have the effect of an act against the individual Razumov as much as against the Russian autocracy. In Part III Razumov makes fully explicit an identification between himself and his nation which has been implicit throughout.

> "I don't want any one to claim me. But Russia can't disown me. She cannot!"
> Razumov struck his breast with his fist.
> "I am *it.*"[17]

Because Razumov's hatred for and betrayal of the revolutionary Haldin is based, moreover, on what Conrad clearly considers the

---

[15] D. H. Lawrence, *The Letters of D. H. Lawrence* (New York: Viking Press, 1932), p. 68.
[16] *Under Western Eyes,* p. 331.
[17] *Ibid.,* p. 209.

ordinary citizen's rightful loyalties to, and expectations from, his government, the question of justice or injustice in any revolution, in any state, becomes an abiding question in the novel.

In *The Secret Agent* the Professor argued that the "terrorist and the policeman both come from the same basket. Revolution, legality—counter moves in the same game; forms of idleness at bottom identical."[18] But Chief Inspector Heat persuaded us that the revolutionary is utterly outside "the game" and holds society in such contempt that indeed "the game" cannot be played successfully in his presence. Perhaps because of his very contempt for revolutionaries as well as organized society, the Professor was described as typical of revolutionaries in general. Son of "a delicate dark enthusiast" who "had been an itinerant and rousing preacher of some obscure but rigid Christian sect—a man supremely confident in the privileges of his righteousness," the Professor had inherited

> a frenzied puritanism of ambition. . . . To see it thwarted opened his eyes to the true nature of the world, whose morality was artificial, corrupt, and blasphemous. The way of even the most justifiable revolutions is prepared by personal impulses disguised into creeds.[19]

It was evident in *The Secret Agent* that, even when speaking abstractly of revolution, Conrad had in mind primarily the socialist revolution[20] seething underground in eastern and western Europe during his whole life. The methodical brutality and ideological obscurantism produced by the French Revolution (examined in "Autocracy and War" and *The Rover*) were only preludes, in Conrad's opinion, to the two most unprincipled political movements in the modern world: communism and New World democracy (which like communism "has elected to pin its faith to the supremacy of material interests"[21]). Both socialism and democracy, *The Secret Agent* made clear, might be intelligently controlled in nations pos-

---

[18] *Ibid.*, p. 68.
[19] *The Secret Agent*, pp. 80–81.
[20] For his rapport with his father on this matter, see above, pp. 38, 40, 47.
[21] *Notes on Life and Letters*, p. 107.

sessing a long history of organic political development, but both are anathema to the new nations in Africa, Latin America, and to non-Russian "Oriental despotisms" like China.[22]

In the original manuscript of *Under Western Eyes*, as we shall see, Conrad implied that socialism as represented by the Russian revolutionaries might be challenged by the utopian democracy of the New World, which—explosively combined with Russia—would act as models and instigators of revolutions all over the world.

Part of the poignancy of Razumov's tragedy derives from his illusion of becoming

> a great reforming servant of the greatest of States . . . of the mightiest homogeneous mass of mankind with a capability for logical, guided development in a brotherly solidarity of force and aim such as the world has never dreamt of.[23]

The reason his vision could not possibly succeed is given succinctly in "Autocracy and War."

> The truth is that the Russia of our fathers, of our childhood, of our middle age; the testamentary Russia of Peter the Great—who imagined that all the nations were delivered into the hand of Tsardom—can do nothing. It can do nothing because it does not exist. . . . being a fantasy of a madman's brain, [it] could in reality be nothing else than a figure out of a nightmare seated upon a monument of fear and oppression.
>
> The true greatness of a State does not spring from such a contemptible source. It is a matter of logical growth, of faith and courage. Its inspiration springs from the constructive instinct of the people, governed by the strong hand of a collective conscience and voiced in the wisdom and counsel of men who seldom reap the reward of gratitude.[24]

In this same essay, where Conrad is obliged by the historic subject of the essay to speak of revolution in measured terms, he tries momentarily to adopt a permissive attitude to certain forms of

---

[22] See Bertrand Russell's essay on Conrad in *Portraits from Memory* (New York: Simon and Schuster, 1956), where Russell describes a talk with Conrad on socialism in China and admits Conrad's superior political prescience in that case.

[23] *Under Western Eyes*, pp. 301–2.

[24] *Notes on Life and Letters*, p. 91.

revolution. But on close examination, we must conclude that his definition of a justifiable revolution implies such a modified form of warfare, involving emergencies so far from extreme and resistance so far from tyrannous, that "evolution" is a more appropriate word for it.

> The revolutions of European States have never been in the nature of absolute protests *en masse* against the monarchical principle; they were the uprising of the people against the oppressive degeneration of legality. But there never has been any legality in Russia; she is a negation of that as of everything else that has its root in reason or conscience. *The ground of every revolution had to be intellectually prepared. A revolution is a short cut in the rational development of national needs in response to the growth of worldwide ideals. It is conceivably possible for a monarch of genius to put himself at the head of a revolution without ceasing to be the king of his people.* For the autocracy of Holy Russia the only conceivable self-reform is—suicide.
>
> The same relentless fate holds in its grip the all-powerful ruler and his helpless people. Wielders of a power purchased by an unspeakable baseness of subjection to the Khans of the Tartar horde, the Princes of Russia who, in their heart of hearts had come in time to regard themselves as superior to every monarch of Europe, have never risen to be the chiefs of a nation. *Their authority has never been sanctioned by popular tradition, by ideas of intelligent loyalty, of devotion, of political necessity, of simple expediency, or even by the power of the sword.* In whatever form of upheaval Autocratic Russia is to find her end, it can never be a revolution fruitful of moral consequences to mankind. It cannot be anything else but a rising of slaves.[25]

In *Under Western Eyes*, the English narrator (who is quick to assign characteristics to Russia exclusively) analyzes the nature of revolution as if it were a phenomenon that might occur anywhere: Natalia Haldin has just said to him, "You shrink from the idea of revolutionary action for those you think well of as if it were something—how shall I say it—not quite decent." And he answers,

> "The last thing I want to tell you is this: in a real revolution—not a simple dynastic change or a mere reform of institutions—in a real

---

[25] *Ibid.*, pp. 101–2. The italics are mine.

revolution the best characters do not come to the front. A violent revolution falls into the hands of narrow-minded fanatics and of tyrannical hypocrites at first. Afterwards comes the turn of all the pretentious intellectual failures of the time. Such are the chiefs and the leaders. You will notice that I have left out the mere rogues. The scrupulous and the just, the noble, humane, and devoted natures; the unselfish and the intelligent may begin a movement—but it passes away from them. They are not the leaders of a revolution. They are its victims: the victims of disgust, of disenchantment— often of remorse. Hopes grotesquely betrayed, ideals caricatured— that is the definition of revolutionary success."[26]

Natalia—like her brother, perhaps one of the "unselfish and intelligent" who "may begin a movement" but "do not come to the front"—responds in accord with her nature:

> If I could believe all you have said I still wouldn't think of myself.
> . . . I would take liberty from any hand as a hungry man would
> snatch at a piece of bread. The true progress must begin after. And
> for that the right men shall be found.

We see from this exchange, as well as from Conrad's other reflections on revolution, that he has a tendency to base his objections on the moral character of the revolutionaries and the historic character (also moral) of the people from whom they spring. (None of the London revolutionaries in *The Secret Agent* is given an English name. Though their language is English, their exact origins are unspecified, and their names sound vaguely Russian or German. The terrorist Professor is not named at all.)

One can hardly generalize simply on Camus' more searching analysis of revolution in *The Rebel*, but it is interesting to note that he has very little interest in the "organic" growth of political institutions, taken apart from the specific ideas they embody. Camus considers revolution to be a peculiarity of the Western world's paradoxical aspirations toward freedom on one side and toward control on the other. He considers the personal integrity and character of rebels and nations less relevant to the history of revolution than the precise revolutionary idea that leads to disas-

---

[26] *Under Western Eyes*, pp. 134–35.

trous solutions if the idea is false; to a progressive realization of political freedom if the idea is sound.

Probably correctly, Herling-Grudziński charges Conrad with refusal to discriminate carefully among the ideological claims of a number of very different revolutions in eastern and western Europe, and invokes not only Camus but Dostoevsky as subtler minds on Conrad's own subject. Thus, Camus sees the faults of both the French Revolution and the Russian Revolution of 1917 in their leaders' dedication to the abstract ideas of equality and absolute freedom. The Russian revolutionaries of 1905, Camus points out, had no attachment to the society envisaged by Dostoevsky's Shigalov: "Starting from unlimited freedom, I arrive at unlimited despotism."[27]

I have called attention to Conrad's stress on the necessity of scrupulosity as regards ideas and principles in the conduct of political affairs. *Heart of Darkness* and *Nostromo* should stand as major and undisputed achievements in political analysis as well as in the whole range of human experience they undertake to fictionalize. It seems fair to admit that, compared with these, *Under Western Eyes* is less rigorous, relying on several political generalizations ("Western eyes," for example) that do not bear intense scrutiny. Conrad has become so much an Englishman for the sake of "seeing" Russia that he even develops Charles Gould's and Winnie Verloc's characteristic of not looking too deeply into certain troublesome matters. In spite of these problems, the breadth of historic knowledge and the depth of experience—even if acquired more through reading than through personal encounters with Russians in the author's mature life—concentrated in *Under Western Eyes* should make it, for all but the most biased reader, one of the most significant novels of the twentieth century.

When, in October, 1911, Garnett wrote warning Conrad that his review of *Under Western Eyes* was appearing in *The Nation* and would mention Conrad's Polish prejudice against Russia, Conrad answered in words that reveal a mordant anger, which had been

[27] Fyodor Dostoevsky, *The Possessed*, II, translated by Constance Garnett (London: Dent, 1931), 55.

developing, at least since publication of *The Secret Agent,* against this "Russian Embassador to the Republic of Letters" who was also his literary godfather. (Most of the English intellectuals among Conrad's friends in that period were admirers of Russia.)[28]

> There's just about as much or as little hatred in this book [he wrote Garnett] as in the Outcast of the Islands for instance. Subjects lay about for anybody to pick up. I have picked up this one. And that's all there is to it. I don't expect you to believe me. You are so russianised my dear that you don't know the truth when you see it—unless it smells of cabbage-soup when it at once secures your profoundest respect. I suppose one must make allowances for your position of Russian Embassador to the Republic of Letters. Official pronouncements ought to be taken with a grain of salt . . . But it is hard after lavishing a "wealth of tenderness" on Tekla and Sophia, to be charged with the rather low trick of putting one's hate into a novel. If you seriously think that I have done that then my dear fellow let me tell you that you don't know what the accent of hate is. Is it possible that you haven't seen that in this book I am concerned with nothing but ideas, to the exclusion of everything else, with no arrière pensée of any kind. Or are you like the Italians (and most women) incapable of conceiving that anybody ever should speak with perfect detachment, without some subtle hidden purpose, for the sake of what is said, with no desire of gratifying some small personal spite—or vanity.[29]

The letter shows us the Conrad (*homo duplex*) who throughout his life had to look charges of hate, desertion, or disloyalty full in the face and had settled such matters with his conscience before his accusers articulated them. As in the case of *Lord Jim, Under Western Eyes* was itself a better reply to the accusing critics than were Conrad's protests in self-defense, for his free-ranging thought

---

[28] Conrad had been smarting for some time after the accusation by a reviewer for the *Daily News* that he was a man "without country and language." Upon reading this, Conrad wrote Galsworthy, "The . . . genius exclaims that my novels would have been much better if translated by Mrs. Garnett. That's an idea. Shall I send her the clean type of *Razumov?* But why complicate life to that extent? She ought to write them; and then the harmless reviewer could begin something like this: 'Mr. Conrad's latest novel written by Mrs. Garnett is a real acquisition for our literature, not like the others previously written . . .' " (Letter of July, 1908, *Life and Letters,* II, 70–71).

[29] *Letters from Joseph Conrad, 1895–1924,* ed. Edward Garnett (Indianapolis: Bobbs-Merrill Co., Inc., 1928), pp. 232–33.

had taken into account, in the process of creating the novel, more of the evidence against his personal convictions than any of his critics were able to see. He made it clear, even in beginning the novel, that it was to be written for Western readers and therefore was not to be a novel designed to influence Russians, whose psychology and ideologies by their very nature were impervious to outside criticism. I said earlier, in speaking of *Heart of Darkness*, that Conrad never consciously wrote for a specific audience. In the case of *Under Western Eyes*, there was one specific reader the novel was *not* for. Readers like Garnett who chose to read the novel from the Russian point of view thereby lost the freedom from the subject which Conrad claimed with some justice he had himself achieved through arduous discipline.

In the Author's Note he allows that "the general truth which underlies [the novel's] action" and his own "honest convictions as to the moral complexion of certain known facts more or less known to the whole world" may not be one and the same thing. He speaks of his aim to express both "together."[30] In order to see how these two subtly different testimonies are given their full justice in the novel, one must take into account first the enormous body of written materials Conrad had at his disposal and used in shaping character and event and, second, the extraordinary subtleties of technique he employed in expressing the encounter of alien ideologies, alien personalities, and alien points of view. The hostilities he had to deal with were, of course, more than the hostilities of "East" and "West." Conrad allowed that particular counteraction to become rather naïve and questionable in the novel. I have already mentioned this and the weakness in his conception of different revolutionary ideas in the Russian history of the period. It is his intention, however, to see the decay of autocracy and rise of revolution in the nineteenth and twentieth centuries as a small passage in the history of Russia as a whole, and in view of his success with the over-all vision, one may excuse his lack of finesse in some details of the foreground.

---

[30] *Under Western Eyes*, p. vii.

A sturdier reader than I may one day trace all the characters, allusions, and episodes in *Under Western Eyes* to books, newspapers, and magazines that Conrad read in French and English. As he says of Nikita in the Author's Note, almost all his characters have been exhibited to the public eye for (now) at least a century in "newspaper articles, in secret histories, in sensational novels."[31] One may add that more scholarly works, from authors of widely different points of view, express insights very similar to Conrad's. But what discouraged me most was discovering hints for "sources" almost everywhere I looked—in the memoirs of Alexander Herzen, where there are several romantic and "noble" Natalias and and not a few sham as well as sincere revolutionaries; in E. H. Carr's *Romantic Exiles*[32] and studies of Bakunin and Dostoevsky; and in the Menshevik Boris Nikolajewsky's *Aseff the Spy*, to mention only the most striking. By comparison with the biography of Azef (or Aseff), whose author attempted only "to paint a historically true picture of his activities in both the revolutionary and the police worlds,"[33] Conrad's novel presents a picture of the Russians as paragons of sanity and civility. His Nikita is certainly no more monstrous than Azef, the police tool and terrorist, though "Necator," as his nickname suggests, was an expert killer in his own right, whereas Azef delegated the "weary work" (Haldin's phrase) to others.[34]

---

[31] *Ibid.*, p. ix. The "sensational novels," one suspects, were mainly the novels of Dostoevsky and Tolstoy. See letters to Galsworthy and Garnett, *Life and Letters*, II, 77 and 140.

[32] In *The Romantic Exiles* (London: Gollancz, 1933), p. 262, one reads of a Russian exile named Madame Shelgunov who preached free love. There may also have been a suggestion for Madame de S——in the character of Zöe Obolensky, who was to Bakunin in Naples and Ischia much what Peter Ivanovitch's "Egeria" was to him in Geneva.

[33] *Aseff the Spy* (New York: Doubleday, Doran, 1934), p. vii.

[34] Typical of the way Conrad used Russian material, seizing the dramatic situation but often reversing roles and compressing many instances into one, may be seen in the scene where Peter Ivanovitch (conglomerate of Bakunin, Kropotkin, and Tolstoy, among others) happens to meet Police Chief Mikulin in a railway carriage and is informed that Nikita, "the arch-slayer of gendarmes," is also a police tool. "Mikulin had wanted to get rid of that particular agent of his own" (*Under Western Eyes*, p. 381). In the story of Azef's exposure, it is the Police Chief Lopuhin who is approached in a railway carriage by the editor Burcev and informed that his agent Azef is acting as a

Another discouraging result was to find that Conrad's desire to seize the very soul of things Russian was so well satisfied by the works of Tolstoy and Dostoevsky that their shadows seem to flit capriciously through the novel. The character of Ziemianitch might have come from any of Tolstoy's peasants or Dostoevsky's laborers. Readers have been aware of this for some time. Jocelyn Baines has documented a number of points at which Conrad employs material from these two authors.[35] Wit Tarnawski (whose recent translation of *Under Western Eyes* [London, 1955] into Polish is greatly admired by Herling-Grudziński) wrote an article in 1948 for a Polish journal in London, discussing the influence of *Crime and Punishment* on the novel, and in it made the following summary:

> Poleska [another Polish critic] quotes the fundamental resemblance, that the heroes of both novels are students psychically shattered by a crime they committed. To this we may add that love is a factor arousing the consciences of both and leading them to the confession of guilt. Resemblances in detail are still more striking: the roles of mother and sister in both novels, the mental derangement of both mothers at the end of the novels, the curious illness of both heroes after committing the crime, the identical roles played by the sledge-driver Ziemianitch and the house-painter, both suspected and at the same time relieving the hero of suspicion. Finally both writers create a similar final situation for their heroes—freeing them of suspicion so that their confessions may arise from their own free will.[36]

Almost simultaneously, in 1928 in France and England, two critics published fine comments on the Conrad v. Dostoevsky debate—a literary feud unique in that it was waged between a living writer and a dead one. In his *Carte d'Europe*, Henri Daniel-Rops

---

terrorist. Burcev merely has his suspicions confirmed that Azef is also a police agent (see *Aseff the Spy*, pp. 1–21). Baines mentions this connection (*Joseph Conrad*, pp. 371–72). Conrad's Father Zosim, the double agent who is also a priest, is another such composite figure. Conrad uses the historical Father Gapon to snipe at Dostoevsky's Father Zosima.

[35] Baines, *Joseph Conrad*, pp. 369–72.
[36] Wit Tarnawski, "O Conradzie," *Myśl Polska* (London, March, 1948), p. 13. This article was translated for me by David Welsh.

tried to distinguish the similarities and differences between the two
Slavic writers and found Conrad, despite his protests, Slavic—

> par cette habitude qu'il possède de faire ce qu'on pourrait appeler
> une psychologie en couches successives; par les singuliers retourne-
> ments moraux dont les pires bandits sont capables dans son oeuvres
> [I question this] et qui témoignent de la richesse psychologique de
> leur tempérament; par son amour pour les dévoyés que le sort hos-
> tile a jetés dans des situations douleureuses, le sort, ou leur nature,
> ou leur tourment; par la sobriété de son récit, où l'analyse (dans ses
> meilleurs livres) est tacite; par cette inquiétude géante qui domine
> toute son oeuvre et pénètre le héros d'une foncière inappétance de
> la vie, si caractéristique de tous les romanciers slaves. C'est le
> slavisme inconscient . . . qui fait que ses héros ne sont jamais
> limités, mais au contraire toujours en mouvement et en augmenta-
> tion, et qu'au lieu d'obéir à la logique, ils obéissent à leur logique
> intérieure, celle qui est vie.

It is in the element of will power that Conrad's characters differ
most from Dostoevsky's:

> Il n'y a pas chez Conrad cet abandon conscient aux forces perverses
> qui caractérise un Stavroguine. Les héros de Conrad résistent; ils se
> battent; ils vont à l'aventure comme à une bataille sans espoir. Tout
> cela . . . est polonais. Et si Dostoevski a exercé sur Conrad une in-
> fluence, c'est celle que M. André Gide a défini l'influence par ré-
> action.[37]

Richard Curle's comment, praised by Morf, merely elaborates
the point made by Gide: that Conrad very likely

> saw in this Russian novelist the most formidable of all antagonists
> to his own theories of a world governed by sanity and method. . . .
> I have an idea that his real hatred was due to an appreciation of his
> power. It is on record that he once told Mr. Galsworthy that Do-
> stoevsky was "as deep as the sea," and for Conrad it was the depth of
> an evil influence. Dostoevsky represented to him the ultimate forces
> of confusion and insanity, arrayed against all that he valued in civili-
> zation. He did not despise him as one might despise a nonentity,
> he hated him as one might hate Lucifer and the forces of darkness.[38]

---

[37] "Joseph Conrad," *Carte d'Europe* (Paris: Perrin, 1928), pp. 60–61.
[38] *The Last Twelve Years of Joseph Conrad* (London: Sampson and Low, 1928),
pp. 28–29.

It is perhaps unnecessary to add that, at whatever distance Conrad held his connection with the Roman Catholic Church, he did not fail to challenge Dostoevsky's attacks on it. He countered with the observation that atheism lay just a little way beneath the Russian's Orthodox ecstasies. In the first pages of *Under Western Eyes*, the argument of Dostoevsky's Grand Inquisitor becomes an even more arrogant manifesto issued not by a Catholic inquisitor but by the Russian Minister of the Interior: "the thought of liberty has never existed in the Act of the Creator."[39] Police officials and revolutionaries alike in *Under Western Eyes* look on Divine Providence as their special guide. The remarks made by the elderly English narrator on "the Russians' extraordinary love of words,"[40] as he describes Razumov's diary at the outset of the story, suggest a criticism of Dostoevsky's style. Conrad's original manuscript shows he at first attached to Razumov's style a "blasphemous quality," which he canceled when trimming Razumov's Russian spirit to a severer pattern. One manuscript passage reads,

> All the fluctuations of his feelings, all the perplexities of his spirit, in short all the profound trouble of his existence, is set down with a terrible minuteness of self-examination interspersed with long speculative passages in a declamatory style. In places he apostrophizes the Deity with considerable violence and bitterness. But this violence and bitterness are robbed of all offensively blasphemous quality by the consideration that Mr. Razumov held no religious faith or belief of any kind.[41]

Another curiosity revealed in the manuscript is the name first given to Sophia Antonovna, Conrad's scourging angel among the revolutionaries. From the page where she is introduced until 232 pages later, she is Sophia Semenovna. Conrad may have realized only then that he was naming her after Sonia, the very different heroine of *Crime and Punishment*.[42]

---

[39] *Under Western Eyes*, p. 8.

[40] *Ibid.*, p. 4.

[41] Razumov, MS pp. 9–10.

[42] *Ibid.*, MS p. 128. Other names changed in the manuscript are Eleanor Maximovna (Madame de S——), originally Alexandrovna; Madcap Kostia, originally Misha; and Louisa Laspara, originally Minnie.

As against Conrad's preoccupation with the ghost of Dostoevsky, his concern with Tolstoy is slight. His treatment of Tolstoy in the person of Peter Ivanovitch (whose beastlike appearance is coupled with a supposedly celestial nature and whose virulent feminism is coupled with the suggestion of impotence—"this big pinkish poll"[43]), reminds one more of Bakunin, who also made a harrowing escape to the West from the prison in Russia that reduced him to a physical wreck. Something of Michael Bakunin was undoubtedly also in the character of Michaelis of *The Secret Agent*.

"At one time all Europe was aware of the story of his life written by himself and translated into seven or more languages."[44] Conrad seems to be thinking somewhat of Kropotkin, too—the most celebrated of the Russian émigrés, who had spent much of his time in Geneva and London and whose *Memoirs of a Revolutionary* (1899) undoubtedly added their bit to the novel on Russia. The English press refers to Peter Ivanovitch as the "heroic fugitive," the teacher-narrator informs us, and one feels a Polish grimace behind his mild English irony.

A slip in the manuscript gives Ivanovitch the patronymic Nikolaievitch,[45] which was Tolstoy's. Tekla's observation in the manuscript—that Peter Ivanovitch wrote "with a cold regard to effect"[46] —shows us how the second Russian "great" was contrasted with Dostoevsky in Conrad's mind. There is doubtless some reflection on Tolstoy's famous conversion in Ivanovitch's perverse reaction to the death of his aristocratic fiancée, which brought about his "conversion" from autocracy to some vague doctrine of revolt based on "the cult of the woman." (One begins to suspect that Conrad's failure to distinguish clearly among the doctrines of anarchism, socialism, and communism is deliberate—a stab at what appeared to him incoherent even after he had grasped their arguments.) At any rate, the parody of Tolstoy's titles in the works of Peter Ivanovitch mentioned in the manuscript emphasizes the morbid

---

[43] *Ibid.*, p. 128.
[44] *Ibid.*, p. 120.
[45] Razumov, MS p. 491.
[46] *Ibid.*, MS p. 645.

character of the premises from which his mystical conversion has sprung. Baines calls attention to two titles from his reading of the typescript, also at Yale.[47] In the manuscript there are four: Peter Ivanovitch's *Resurrection of Yegor* for Tolstoy's *Resurrection*, *The Pride of Darkness* for Tolstoy's play *The Power of Darkness*, *The Pfennig Cantata* for *The Kreutzer Sonata*, and *The Parables of Decay*, which is a slur apparently at Tolstoy's late parables *Work, Death, and Sickness*.[48]

Zabel[49] and Baines have discussed other possible written sources for different characters and events in *Under Western Eyes*, as well as descriptive details. No understanding of the Russian historical background is complete, however, unless one takes into account the source of Conrad's familiarity with the Russian messianic myth, the myth of Holy Russia, which underlies the nationalism of all the Russian characters in the novel. The servants of the autocracy: Prince K——, General T——, Councilor Mikulin, and Razumov himself, no less than the utopian revolutionists, are all possessed by the dream of Russia's sacred mission among the nations of the world—a mission made manifest by Christ Himself and destined to be fulfilled despite every obstacle within Russia or outside.

Haldin is the first to express an aspect of the myth when he gives his interpretation of the immortality of the soul in terms of the Russian national spirit: "My spirit shall go on warring in some Russian body till all falsehood is swept out of the world. The modern civilization is false, but a new revelation shall come out of Russia."[50] The myth is behind Razumov's experience when, after failing to rouse Ziemianitch, he must resort to a justification for delivering Haldin to the authorities: "Like other Russians before him, Razumov, in conflict with himself, felt the touch of grace upon his forehead." Then, the "grace entered into Razumov. He believed now in the man who would come at the appointed time."

---

[47] Baines, *Joseph Conrad*, p. 372.
[48] *Razumov*, MS pp. 458, 591.
[49] Morton Dauwen Zabel, "Introduction," *Under Western Eyes* (New York: New Directions, 1951), pp. xvii–xxiii.
[50] *Under Western Eyes*, p. 22.

Therefore, "absolute power should be preserved—the tool ready for the man—for the great autocrat of the future."[51] Later, Peter Ivanovitch will lecture Natalia Haldin: "Strength is what we want. Spiritual strength, I mean. As to the other kind, what could withstand us Russians if we only put it forth?"[52] Contemptuous as she is of Peter Ivanovitch, Natalia is yet dedicated to the same centuries-old dream of a future miraculously redeemed for the world by Russia:

> The whole world is inconceivable to the strict logic of ideas. And yet the world exists to our senses, and we exist in it. There must be a necessity superior to our conceptions. It is a very miserable and a very false thing to belong to the majority. We Russians shall find some better form of national freedom than an artificial conflict of parties—which is wrong because it is a conflict and contemptible because it is artificial. It is left for us Russians to discover a better way.[53]

It seems almost unnecessary to ask ourselves where Conrad gathered his information on the Russian mania. The national self-justification must have been only too well-known to every Pole. It may even have developed its nineteenth-century traits from Poland's own national messianic myth, though it is more likely that Towiański and Mickiewicz derived their ideas in reaction to the ancient Russian tradition. The major difference between the two myths, as far as I can determine, was that the Poles during their "diaspora" identified their people with the actual body of the crucified Christ. Each person, being a member of the body, was necessary to the "resurrection of the body" which would make possible the resurrection of all mankind. The point of this different emphasis, presumably, would be the greater importance of each

---

[51] *Ibid.*, pp. 34–35.

[52] *Ibid.*, p. 128.

[53] *Ibid.*, p. 106. The foresight Conrad shows into the "better form of national freedom" about to be born in the following decade in Russia was apparent many years earlier to Karl Marx. Having failed to find an English translator for *Das Kapital*, Marx was pleased as well as surprised when a Russian translation appeared as early as 1868. The Russians "always run after the most extreme ideas that the West has to offer," Marx commented to a German friend. Quoted by Edmund Wilson, *To the Finland Station* (London: Secker and Warburg, 1941), p. 350.

individual to the small nation threatened with extinction by a colossal nation (which could afford to waste or ignore lives—a theme pervasive in the Russia of *Under Western Eyes*).

It would be interesting to study in detail Apollo Korzeniowski's attitude toward the Russian myth, since he was one of the Poles who subscribed ardently to the Polish version of it. We know that Conrad rejected his father's mystical nationalism, but we may assume that he read, and was in full agreement with, Korzeniowski's analyses of Russian history and ideology. It is conceivable that his father's pamphlet, *Poland and Russia*, was among the personal books Conrad begged Tadeusz Bobrowski to replace when he lost them during his early years at sea. (But Jean-Aubry does not list this book among the Polish documents he disposed of as Conrad's executor.) At any rate, there seem to be echoes of Korzeniowski's pamphlet not only in Conrad's "Autocracy and War," but in *Under Western Eyes*.[54]

As to his knowledge of the Russian legend, Conrad might have encountered it almost anywhere in the Russian literature of the nineteenth century (in translation), for as Michael Cherniavsky indicates in his splendid article on the history of "Holy Russia,"

> it is virtually impossible to list all the instances of the use of "Holy Russia" in the nineteenth century; it is sufficient to say that, from the middle of the century, it became a commonplace in all kinds of writing.[55]

Pushkin, according to Cherniavsky, discovered a new awareness and a popular national ideal in the epithet "Holy Russia," which had for perhaps three centuries been used in one form or another to signify Muscovite Russia's conviction that she was, "after the Council of Florence and the attempt at the Union of Churches in 1441 . . . the only orthodox land in the world, that is to say . . . the only source of salvation for mankind." In the sixteenth century

---

[54] Compare, for example, pp. 34, 142, and 163 of the novel with Korzeniowski's assessments given above, pp. 265–66.

[55] Michael Cherniavsky, " 'Holy Russia': A Study in the History of an Idea," *American Historical Review* (April, 1958), pp. 626–27.

a monk had written to the Muscovite Prince Basil III: ". . . two Romes have fallen, and the third one stands, and a fourth one there shall not be."[56]

The precise term "Holy Russia" was not, Cherniavsky argues, synonymous with the idea of the "Third Rome," however. It appears to have been used first by a Prince Kurbsky who, in the sixteenth century, wished to curb the power of princes who had only recently assumed the title of Tsar, of "Orthodox and Universal Emperor." The exact epithet "Holy Russia," then, was initiated as a myth needed to oppose the myth of the ruler on behalf of the people. And its long use as "an antitsarist, antistate slogan," if Cherniavsky is right, made it extremely useful in the nineteenth century.[57] At the same time, its continued use must have kept alive the myth of the "Third Rome" which was most useful to Tsar and state. At the turn of the twentieth century, when *Under Western Eyes* takes place, the role of Tsar is in a state of advanced decay, and Conrad's revolutionaries direct their activities principally against the bureaucracy or state. Thus, as Conrad suggests throughout the novel, at the heart of the twofold national myth lies a political contradiction containing no germ of a solution. "Reform is impossible," says Natalia Haldin. "There is nothing to reform. There is no legality, there are no institutions. There are only arbitrary decrees. There is only a handful of cruel—perhaps blind—officials against a nation."[58]

There is nothing—"*C'est le néant*," Bismarck had said of Russia, and Conrad repeats the phrase not only directly but in the imagery that gives us the scene before Razumov's tormented eyes on the night he sends Haldin to death. The style of this novel, as compared with *Heart of Darkness*, *Nostromo*, and *The Secret Agent*, is rather bare of symbolic imagery and allusion. Its few strong images stand out in relief against the scenic and human barrenness of both Russia and Geneva. The snow-covered ground is "a mon-

---

[56] *Ibid.*, p. 619.
[57] Cherniavsky, *Tsar and People: Studies in Russian Myths* (New Haven, Yale University Press, 1961), pp. 101 ff.
[58] *Under Western Eyes*, p. 133.

strous blank page awaiting the record of an inconceivable history."[59] Mickiewicz, in the "Digression" sequence in *Dziady*, Part III, had typified Russia's lack of organic coherence as a nation by comparing its snow-covered plains to "a page prepared for writing."[60] Mickiewicz, Weintraub mentions, is frightened by this blankness because it represents a dreadful question: will Satan cover the page before God has a chance to? The question is posed differently in *Under Western Eyes*, whose author must have known *Dziady*, as his name —Conrad—was taken from it. The future is simply "inconceivable," and the snow-covered ground is also "a sullen and tragic mother hiding her face under a winding sheet."[61]

Again, Conrad might have found these same suggestions in the writings of Russians themselves. Cherniavsky quotes the passage from Gogol's *Dead Souls* expressing this same dreadful riddle as the writer is haunted by reflection on his nation: ". . . an awful cloud . . . looms above my head, and thought is dumb before your immensity. What does this limitless space prophesy? . . . a supernatural power has enlightened my eyes . . ."[62]

Slavophilism, a movement that arose from the degeneration of autocracy and was also a response to the French and German romantic stresses on idealized conceptions of the nation and the source of strength in folk cultures, is imprinted heavily on most of the characters in *Under Western Eyes*, though Conrad correctly indicates that the passionate Christian mysticism pervading the writings of the greatest of the Slavophils, Dostoevsky, was already an empty vessel by the turn of the century as far as the intellectuals were concerned. What is left, of course, is the apotheosis of the Russian laborer (another antithesis to the deification of Tsar and state), expressed most particularly in *Under Western Eyes* by the hallowing of the sledge-driver Ziemianitch and by the servant Tekla's powerful devotion to all broken and downtrodden people.

---

[59] *Ibid.*, p. 33.
[60] Wiktor Weintraub, *The Poetry of Adam Mickiewicz* (The Hague: Mouton, 1954), p. 187. I find Herling-Grudziński has noticed the same echo.
[61] *Under Western Eyes*, p. 33.
[62] Quoted by Cherniavsky (who translates from the Russian), *op. cit.*, p. 168.

To the tavern keeper, Ziemianitch is "a proper Russian man—the pig."[63] Conrad dramatizes a major irony in the extravagances of the Slavophils and *narodniki* (populists), who developed the political potentialities of the "people's will": the irony inherent in the strange mixture of self-exaltation and self-contempt that resulted from the attempt of intellectuals to identify themselves with the religion, customs, and objectives of illiterate peasants. Of course the strength in the simple Christianity of the people gave intellectuals a stick with which to beat a church that had always been a pawn of the state, but it also gave them an argument they needed to explain the "bestiality" and barbarism which Dostoevsky admitted characterized the history of Russia.[64] The idea from Isaiah of "the suffering servant"—"despised and rejected," unattractive and undesirable—made the Russian who identified his people with Christ unashamed to stand in the company of his most degraded countrymen and gave him the convenient as well as exalted conviction that what "Holy Russia" had been wanting all along was the real holiness that could come only through self-abasement and renunciation of all the tyrannous pomp[65] that afflicted intellectuals and their countrymen together. Thus Conrad arrives at Haldin's remarks to Razumov:

> . . . "don't you forget what's divine in the Russian soul—and that's resignation. . . . What do you imagine I am? A being in revolt? No. It's you thinkers who are in everlasting revolt. . . . When the necessity of this heavy work came to me and I understood that it had to be done—what did I do? Did I exult? Did I take pride in my purpose? Did I try to weigh its worth and consequences? No! . . . I thought, 'God's will be done.' "[66]

And the elderly teacher's last view of Haldin's sister Natalia has history to support it:

---

[63] *Under Western Eyes*, p. 28.
[64] Cherniavsky, " 'Holy Russia,' " p. 632.
[65] This renunciation, alas, did not extend to renunciation of Poland, for the Slavophils looked on Russia's empire as the first soil won in the mission of "Holy Russia."
[66] *Under Western Eyes*, p. 23.

> There was no longer any Natalia Haldin, because she had completely ceased to think of herself. It was a great victory, a characteristically Russian exploit in self-suppression.[67]

Cherniavsky concludes his essay with the comment, "All societies seem to need a justification for their reality; the irony of Russian reality was such as to require the most extreme justification of all."[68] And Conrad, in his determination to assess Russia objectively, needed to do little more than present his characters as faithfully as he could according to the Russians' own self-evaluation.

If one imagines that Conrad's image of Russia in this novel is to be found mainly in the revolutionary and counterrevolutionary sets, one misses the main point. For the image of Russia is to be found, above all, in the title character, in Razumov himself. He is not just a sympathetic alter ego to Conrad, thrust into circumstances that are to dramatize the horrors of life in Russia. He is not a Lord Jim (though there are striking similarities between the two characters) caught up in political events and forced to sacrifice his individuality to political pressures alien not merely to romantic egoism but indeed to the fundamental human person. In Razumov's own nature, Conrad figures the central dilemma and tragedy of Russian life, the life of a people who for generations, and particularly in the present century, have naïvely worshipped the state (in the person of Tsar or "soviet") and to further this end, have methodically sought to destroy whatever threatened that holy authority.

Russian youth, as Conrad saw plainly some seven years before the Bolshevik Revolution, was most ideally conceived as an orphan before the state. Thus Razumov, unrecognized natural son of a Russian prince:

> Officially and in fact without a family (for the daughter of the Archpriest had long been dead), no home influences had shaped his opinions or his feelings. He was as lonely in the world as a man swimming in the deep sea. The word Razumov was the mere label

---

[67] *Ibid.*, p. 375.

[68] Cherniavsky, *op. cit.*, p. 637. For fuller discussion of the role of this justification, see *Tsar and People*, pp. 190 ff.

of a solitary individuality. There were no Razumovs belonging to
him anywhere. His closest parentage was defined in the statement
that he was a Russian. Whatever good he expected from life would
be given to or withheld from his hopes by that connexion alone.
This immense parentage suffered from the throes of internal dis-
sensions, and he shrank mentally from . . . taking definite sides in
a violent family quarrel.[69]

Razumov's isolation—so similar in effect to the loneliness of a Jim,
a Tom Lingard, or Nostromo—is thus not self-imposed but is one
of the conditions of his birth. He is "nobody's child."[70]

Among the many Russian intellectuals in the nineteenth century
who might have posed for the portrait of Razumov, one thinks
immediately of Alexander Herzen (1812–70), illegitimate son of a
Russian nobleman, Polish sympathizer and (with Belinsky) one
of the fathers of Russian Westernism, who like Razumov was
accused of being "an Englishman" and who stressed at least two
of Razumov's five principles[71] ("History not Theory" and "Evolution not Revolution"), though he sympathized with revolutionaries a good deal more than did Razumov. Like Razumov, too,
Herzen will be remembered best for his diary (written mainly between 1852 and 1855 and finished in the 'sixties), *My Past and
Thoughts*.

Yet, not to put too fine a point on any one model, Razumov
represents more generally the literate "people" of Russia, caught between autocracy and revolution. His story is an epic of Russia,
written by no sympathizer but by an "artist of the whole matter,"
capable through force of intellect and imagination of a rare degree
of objectivity. The novel is, in fact, the second and only other book
Conrad wrote besides *Lord Jim* which shows him clearly in the
role of epic writer, a role which he fitted through his genius for
seeing the historic destiny of nations in crisis and the fate of individuals so identified with national crisis as to characterize both the

---

[69] *Under Western Eyes*, pp. 10–11.
[70] *Ibid.*, p. ix. One is reminded again of *The Princess Casamassima*, where the
orphaned, illegitimate Hyacinth Robinson, son of an aristocrat and a lower-class
woman, becomes something of a symbol of Europe's political crisis.
[71] *Ibid.*, p. 66.

spirit of the whole people and the struggles of the solitary person within it.

In shaping the character of Razumov, Conrad obviously wanted to reveal a man who, while being no "Westerner," would at once typify the Russian youth of the period and with some degree of awareness be able to reflect upon the Russian character of his fate. He must be inside it, suffering but also seeing—not a Winnie Verloc, who never saw the social and political background of her crisis. In Razumov's case we are to have pure tragedy, not the pathetic tragedy of *The Secret Agent*. But we know, by the nature of Conrad's vision of Russia, that his hero cannot see just as "you or I"— as everyman would see; he can see only the way a Russian could see.

The name "Razumov" suggests that Conrad may have entertained a thought of making the hero the narrator, but the manuscript at Yale has the Professor's voice on the opening page. Razumov's name is a sort of epithet, from the Russian *razumet* (to understand), meaning "the man of reason."[72] He is a student of philosophy, not a "simple character" like Lord Jim. But Conrad is not interested primarily in his intellectual struggle; his tragedy does not grow out of his use of intellect, as does the downfall of that other seeker after truth, Oedipus. Razumov's mind is the universal human faculty that interested Pascal. "I know I am but a reed," Razumov says to Mikulin. "But I beg you to allow me the superiority of the thinking reed over the unthinking forces that are about to crush him out of existence." He pleads for the use of intellect less from any position of eminence than as a man asking simple recognition of his sanity:

"I am reasonable. I am even—permit me to say—a thinker, though to be sure this name nowadays seems to be the monopoly of hawkers of revolutionary wares, the slaves of some French or German thought . . . . But I am not an intellectual mongrel. I think like a Russian. I think faithfully—and I take the liberty to call myself a thinker. It is not a forbidden word, as far as I know."[73]

[72] In *Crime and Punishment* the student who tries to understand Raskolnikov is named Razumihin.
[73] *Under Western Eyes*, pp. 89–90.

Razumov's reasoning powers are complicated by his capacity for sympathetic identification, which makes him appear committed when he is not. "In discussion he was easily swayed by argument and authority."[74] In the manuscript Conrad here adds (and later cancels as possibly conflicting with Razumov's more crucial taciturnity): "Then becoming visibly troubled he would give up his position impulsively. Evidently he could not only see the two sides of every question but he suggested the capability too of embracing either of these with emotional ardor."[75] Thus, Razumov is not the sort of "thinker" who can exclude any part of his whole experience merely for the sake of maintaining a fixed position. The characteristic qualifies him to be trusted by both revolutionaries and police. It also makes him the sensitive instrument needed in the novel to register the psychological and political upheavals of his nation.

Like Jim, then, Razumov is "one of us"—though here we are not to forget that "us" means "Russians." Both Razumov and Jim are men possessed by what Stein would call the essential romantic quality—a "sentiment of existence" (as Jim's is called in the preface to *Lord Jim*), meaning something like "a full sense of life's demands." When Razumov finds Haldin in his room and learns that Haldin is de P——'s assassin, Conrad writes in awkward English, "The sentiment of his life [was] utterly ruined by this contact with such a crime . . ."[76]

As with Jim, again, we are to discover the exceptional quality of human nature in the general. Razumov is exceptional in relation to Haldin (who is also exceptional). They are opposites within a single unity, very much as we have discovered the opposite qualities conflicting in the unity of Conrad's experience. Haldin is not unlike Apollo Korzeniowski, who according to Miłosz was repeatedly expelled from his secondary schools for his "unsound mind."[77] At St. Petersburg University (where Korzeniowski was a student), Haldin is "marked" as "restless" and "unsound," whereas for Razumov (and Conrad) the certificate of achievement in his pro-

---

[74] *Ibid.*, p. 5.
[75] Razumov, MS pp. 12–13.
[76] *Under Western Eyes*, p. 16.
[77] Miłosz, "Apollo Nałęcz Korzeniowski," p. 61.

fession is the "solid beginning."[78] Personal analogy puts Conrad inside his subject: Korzeniowski versus Bobrowski, Conrad versus Conrad. The main purpose of the story is then to show where the analogy fails—between Russia and Poland, Russia and the rest of the world.

Razumov sincerely and honestly identifies himself with the state when the novel opens. He aspires to an administrative appointment. Facing Haldin, he asks himself why he is even hearing him out. His sympathy with autocracy is not as definite at this moment as it will be after he meets Ziemianitch.

The fear and frustration that possess him in his encounter with Ziemianitch show him another aspect of his simple allegiance to authority. There must be authority when the people of Russia— even the "bright souls"—are dead drunk at the time they are most needed. Possessed by "the blind rage of self-preservation,"[79] Razumov beats the unconscious driver and still cannot rouse him. The stupidity of a revolution designed to improve the lot of such people intensifies Razumov's horror at the possibility of losing his security by protecting Haldin, and he turns to the police.

Longing for recognition by a father as well as by his nation drives Razumov to Prince K——. But in General T——'s office an important change comes over him. The goggle eyes of the general, prying into his soul, alienate him instantly. (Later, at secret meetings in an oculist's office, he will be commissioned to use his own eyes to spy for the state.) Cleverly, General T—— reminds him that he, Razumov, alone carries the responsibility for Haldin's death: ". . . if he had not come with his tale to such a staunch and loyal Russian as you, he would have disappeared like a stone in the water."[80] Razumov is alone with his phantom.

In the general's room stood a bronze statue "of an adolescent figure, running." "Spontini's. 'Flight of Youth.' Exquisite,"[81] the prince observes. The statue, which in Haldin's presence might have

---

[78] *Under Western Eyes*, pp. 14–15.
[79] *Ibid.*, p. 30.
[80] *Ibid.*, p. 47.
[81] *Ibid.*, p. 43.

been interpreted as youth soaring to promethean heights, now reaches us only as a youth flying for his life, or as youth—the crucial time of life—running away wasted and lost.[82] Here, perhaps for the first time, Razumov discovers that he and Haldin are bound together by more than accident and hate. The war with Haldin's spirit becomes a war with himself.

In answer to Razumov's suggestion that thinking itself may be forbidden in Russia, Councilor Mikulin answers, "Why should it be forbidden? . . . I too consider myself a thinking man, I assure you. The principal condition is to think correctly,"[83] thus justifying Razumov's imagination of

> his own brain suffering on the rack—a long, pale figure drawn asunder horizontally with terrific force in the darkness of a vault . . . . It was as though he had dreamed for an infinitesimal fraction of time of some dark print of the Inquisition.[84]

The face of the figure is invisible. It might be himself or Haldin.

After the intense concentration and power of dramatic events in Russia in Part I, most critics find the sudden, bewildering change of scene and pace in the Geneva of Part II disappointing. Apparently John Galsworthy (Conrad's closest friend during the composition of the novel) raised this objection and wondered if the novel could not take a different turn. Conrad answered, indicating that what he had written presented the inevitable consequences of Razumov's overt commitment to the autocracy and unacknowledged commit-ment, through self-identification, to the revolutionary Haldin.

> What you see is the residue of very many pages now destroyed, but by no means wasted from an unmaterial point of view. But good

---

[82] Conrad carries this image throughout the novel. Every character touches it in some way. Sophia Antonovna, with her prematurely white hair, "had discovered the secret, not of everlasting youth, but of everlasting endurance" (p. 264). The theme accounts for the curious construction in the opening of Part IV: "Mr. Razumov's youth had no one in the world, as literally no one as it can honestly be affirmed of any human being . . ."
Alexander Herzen, according to E. H. Carr, saw the principal crime of the Russian emperor and his regime to be in the "moral abortion and killing of the souls of the young" (*The Romantic Exiles*, p. 126).

[83] *Under Western Eyes*, p. 90.

[84] *Ibid.*, p. 88.

work takes time: to invent an action, a march for the story, which could have dispensed with Part II as it stands, was a matter of meditation, of trying and retrying for goodness knows how long. This I could not afford to do. I went on the obvious lines and on these lines I developed my narrative to give it some sort of verisimilitude.[85]

What one misses at once in Part II is the earlier absorption of the plot in an overwhelming struggle of conscience, waged in the mind of the "thinker" Razumov. The dull, elderly narrator's voice, recounting in his own words the events and states of mind recorded in Razumov's diary, has little or no effect on the first part. We completely forget his presence. Now, in Geneva, his intervention is necessary: without him there would have been no one to whom Natalia Haldin could have bequeathed the diary, no one sympathetic, colorless, and objective enough to represent the alien West in the Haldins' salon or among the revolutionary "apes of a sinister jungle" in Geneva's *Petite Russie*.[86]

"Unidentified with any one in this narrative":[87] the elderly teacher himself admits the coldness that makes him a poor figure in the group of wonderful narrators Conrad created for most of his full-length novels, who are engaging because they are themselves so deeply engaged in the outcome of the issues raised. The fittingly nameless teacher is something between the Marlow of *Chance* and Alvan Hervey of "The Return," but really not even as interesting as they. Conrad's determination to be objective would not, by itself, excuse the use of such a nonentity to represent the Western perspective. Of course, the marvelously ironic authorial voice of *The Secret Agent* would not do. The irony wanted for this most powerful of all Conrad's tragic situations must be the complex irony maintained by participants in the drama who explain without understanding the full importance of what they are saying. *Lord Jim, Heart of Darkness,* and *Nostromo*—all three so different in respect to their narrators—would seem to indicate Conrad's ability

---

[85] Letter of Nov. 30, 1908, *Life and Letters*, II, 90–91.

[86] *Under Western Eyes*, p. ix.

[87] *Ibid.*, p. 293.

to conceive a wide variety of rich personalities to reveal the necessities of his plots. In *Under Western Eyes* he did not want a rich personality.

The question in *Under Western Eyes* was how to make the observant and knowledgeable Westerner obtuse enough to exaggerate, without realizing it, the loneliness of the man whose diary he is sharing with the reader; yet not so obtuse as to fail in the important task of observing extraordinary passions and circumstances with some degree of understanding. At times the old teacher expresses exact insights: "Nations it may be have fashioned their Governments, but the Governments have paid them back in the same coin."[88] At other times the reader's insight is intensified by the narrator's misconceptions or by the inadequacy of his judgment.

A striking instance of this comes toward the end of the novel, just after Razumov has made his confession to Natalia. The black mourning veil she was wearing falls to the ground (she now "sees" through her delusion), and unthinkingly Razumov snatches it up, covers his face with it momentarily (making one think of a shroud) and stuffs it into his pocket before making his escape. The first words spoken thereafter come from the teacher, who seems interested only in the theft. "That miserable wretch has carried off your veil!" At the same time, Conrad conveys the idea that the Englishman's habit is to interpret less of his own experience than he feels. Beholding Razumov with his face pressed into the veil, the teacher tells the reader, "Something, extreme astonishment perhaps, dimmed my eyes, so that he seemed to vanish before he moved."[89] In this instance, Conrad's evocation of an alien point of view is fully adequate to the power of the situation he has created.

In "Autocracy and War" Conrad seems to give one further clue to why the narrator's voice rings so stupidly in *Under Western Eyes*: "Western thought, when it crosses [Russia's, or perhaps even *la Petite Russie's*] frontier, falls under the spell of her autocracy and becomes a noxious parody of itself."[90] The teacher's Victorian

---

[88] *Ibid.*, p. 25.
[89] *Ibid.*, p. 356.
[90] *Notes on Life and Letters*, p. 98.

prudishness is to some extent Conrad's reflection on Anglo-Saxon self-confidence and complacency as well as a response triggered by the abnormalities of Russian psychology. Douglas Hewitt's comment that there is in *Under Western Eyes* "an implied 'Western' code of behavior which escapes investigation"[91] may be thus partially qualified. And Hewitt's other important objection, that the teacher's "animus against Russia—his belief that it is fundamentally more evil than the rest of Europe—has been introduced into the novel as it stands and not subjected to any process of imaginative re-creation,"[92] is entirely valid only if we fail to be persuaded by the whole imaginative re-creation which is Razumov's story.

The question of what "West" means in the novel raises a point which only Guerard has attempted to answer. He makes clearer than anyone else has that the elderly teacher's protestations concerning the legality, order, and "decency" of Western political institutions tend to become caricatures and to deepen our sympathy for the profounder experiences of trial and suffering in the Russian people. Guerard points to an effect many readers may miss when he notes that the teacher's "astonishment because the revolutionaries visit the deafened Razumov throws an unfavorable light on his own automatic moralism, and a final light on their unexpected compassion."[93]

We have taken it for granted thus far that Conrad was unequivocal in his repeated avowals—throughout his writing life—that Poland was a western nation, unrelated to the eastern Slavs. Yet just as we noted the case of his early attraction to America, later so emphatically reversed, we must acknowledge that in roughly the same period of his unsettled life as a seaman—about 1880–81— he seems to have entertained a notion that Poland might become the leading *Slavic* nation in the Panslavonic movement. Our evidence, as before, is in one of Tadeusz Bobrowski's letters, addressed to Conrad in England but this time sent from Switzerland and

---

[91] *Joseph Conrad: A Reassessment* (Cambridge: Bowes and Bowes, 1952), p. 88.
[92] *Ibid.*, p. 82.
[93] Guerard, *Conrad the Novelist* (Cambridge, Mass.: Harvard University Press, 1958), p. 245.

therefore (as Róża Jabłkowska points out) uninhibited by the Russian censorship. "What you write about our hopes for the future," Bobrowski wrote, "delighted me greatly, for I see that whatever touches our country affects you, though you are so far away. It is right that it should be so, and I count on you never to alter; but there are many who do not trouble about such matters at all, though they remain at home." Apparently Conrad had seen in the decay of the Ottoman Empire at that period a great hope for all Slavic peoples, among whom the Poles considered themselves the most highly civilized. It is evident from Bobrowski's letter that he agreed with his nephew on this point. Bobrowski catches Conrad up short, however, on his unfounded hopes for the Polish future in Panslavism:

> As to what you say about those of our hopes which rest upon the Panslavonic movement, though those hopes are comforting and plausible, they are likely to encounter great difficulties in practice. You do not lend sufficient weight to the prestige which force and mere numbers have in the eyes of the world. A more important nation [Russia] which rests upon Panslavonism and assures the world of its disinterestedness (though it is not disinterested) counts secretly upon its population to secure for it a hegemony. You make the same mistake in attributing qualities to us which are not, accurately speaking, ours. Russia only understands by Panslavism the Russification of all other Slav nations and their conversion to the Orthodox Church. She maintains that she is a country with eighty million of inhabitants (which is false), and that our culture, which is more advanced, and our national history, which is more ancient than hers, are only the culture and history of a single class pretending to be those of a whole people (up to a certain point this is true); and she maintains that it is she, Russia, who can develop the true, popular culture of Poland. She asserts that the Czechs are too small a nation to count; and that we and they represent a bastard culture, a cross between Slavonic and Western influences; while she herself represents the true Oriental Slav culture (which does not exist!). She tells to the other Slav nations that, in the first place, they are too weak to stand alone, and in the second, that being themselves of Eastern origin they ought consequently to submit to Russian sway; she is powerful: without her they will perish . . . . I firmly believe that there will be an end of all this some day; but

when it comes I shall be in my grave, and possibly you will be too. Meanwhile, though we are pariahs, robbed of all political existence and the right to develop as a nation, we ought above all to preserve and defend our individuality to-day till the Nemesis of history long due shall at last become a *fact*, and give us a real national existence.[94]

Although Bobrowski's shrewd diagnosis of the Panslavic movement is worth noticing for itself, what interests us here is that Conrad obviously had embraced for a time certain aspects of the Russian mystique. It may have been during this period that he first read Dostoevsky (in a French translation presumably), who may have transmitted some of his Slavophilism to Conrad. One is interested, too, in the process by which Conrad later not only adopted his uncle's analysis but carried it to the extreme of maintaining that Poland's tradition was in no way Slavic, in no way "Eastern." His position when writing *Under Western Eyes* is perhaps best expressed in his "Note on the Polish Problem" (written some six years later), where he goes as far as to give the name Polonism to the "individuality" cherished by Bobrowski:

> The Poles, whom superficial or ill-informed theorists are trying to force into the social and psychological formula of Slavonism, are in truth not Slavonic at all. In temperament, in feeling, in mind, and even in unreason, they are Western, with an absolute comprehension of all Western modes of thought, even of those which are remote from their historical experience.
>
> That element of racial unity which may be called Polonism, remained compressed between Prussian Germanism on one side and the Russian Slavonism on the other. For Germanism it feels nothing but hatred. But between Polonism and Slavonism there is not so much hatred as a complete and ineradicable incompatibility.[95]

He had known once, nevertheless, what it was to see the "West" with "Eastern eyes." Many readers fail to discover that in *Under*

---

[94] *Life and Letters*, I, pp. 66–67. I have very slightly altered Jean-Aubry's translation in order to come nearer the Polish letter, which Róża Jabłkowska has published in its entirety ("Listy Tadeusz Bobrowskiego do Conrada" [Letters from Tadeusz Bobrowski to Conrad], *Kwartalnik Neofilologiczny* [1956, No. 2, pp. 106–7]). Mitchell Winthrop translated for me from the Polish.

[95] *Notes on Life and Letters*, pp. 135–36.

Western Eyes Conrad to some extent imaginatively revitalizes an
early antagonism to the non-Slavic peoples.

"There runs throughout a counterpoint of East and West," as
Guerard observes, and this "counterpoint becomes necessarily, and
perhaps unluckily for the West, a counterpoint of Russia and
Switzerland."[96] I do not think, however, that Conrad intended the
English narrator's values and convictions to merge entirely in our
minds with what he says of the political atmosphere of Geneva.
Perhaps he took for granted that English readers would spot the
difference through natural identification with their countryman.
At any rate, if one examines the original manuscript of the novel
at Yale, one discovers a decided effort on Conrad's part to distinguish among Western nations those whose ideas are rational,
passionless, detached from organic traditions, and those (by inference among the English, French, and other western nations of
Europe excluding Switzerland) that have "plastic shape" and are
"clothed in flesh," as the teacher-narrator phrases the difference
between Natalia's ideas and his own in the finished book.[97]

Among the many passages in the manuscript which were excised for the finished book, one finds several which, taken together,
reflect an image of "America" sharply contrasted with the narrator's England. In the manuscript this image of "America" coin-
cides exactly with the published book's image of Geneva: "the
respectable and passionless abode of democratic liberty . . .
tendering the same indifferent hospitality to tourists of all nations
and to international conspirators of every shade."[98] Clearly Conrad
himself, without advice from friend, agent, or publisher, canceled all
references to America, which in the original manuscript provide a
continuing contrast in the mind of the teacher of languages. The

---

[96] Guerard, *op. cit.*, p. 244.

[97] *Under Western Eyes*, p. 106.

[98] *Ibid.*, p. 357. In a letter to Galsworthy (*Life and Letters*, II, 136) Conrad acknowl-
edges the extensive surgery he performed on the novel: "You know there are about
30,000 words more than the printed text. Revising while ill in bed, I am afraid I
have struck out whole pages recklessly. The other day I looked at the MS,—1357 pp.
averaging about 120 words per page. There are passages which should have remained.
I wasn't in a fit state to judge them."

contrast is not at all to America's advantage, as one might expect from the Americans in *The Rescue* and in *Nostromo*. The effect of a recurring insistence in the manuscript of *Under Western Eyes* is to suggest at once a similarity and rivalry between the two leviathans, America and Russia, which seriously threaten England and the other nations of Europe.

The excised portions range from trifles to large assertions. Thus for example, in the first draft of section iii, Part II, Conrad originally had Peter Ivanovitch mention an invitation he had had to lecture in New York, whereupon the narrator says, "I kept quiet in my corner, noting in myself the unexpected growth of mystic solidarity with New York."[99] And a bit further in the same section, when the teacher is urging Natalia to return to Russia, he says in the manuscript, "You would be doing good." She answers, "But is that enough?" and he is prompted to recall the character of his widowed sister-in-law in Canada, who also has absurdly altruistic views. Comparing the Russian with the American, he thinks of the "extreme contrast of opulence and misery . . . . One sheltered within her rights like the rich in their warm and lighted houses, the other utterly destitute, wandering in darkness . . . ."[100]

Some hundred pages later in the manuscript appears a lengthier passage, which would have come at the end of the section of the book just cited. While walking alone in Geneva, the English teacher thinks of a letter recently received from his niece in Canada, announcing her forthcoming marriage "with a young but rising journalist [*nota bene*]. It would not interfere with their individual usefulness to the community," the narrator remarks ironically;

> each would preserve an intact personality. She would lecture and he would write. They seemed to have planned their life so as to meet as little as possible—in the day-time, at any rate; but I was comforted to hear that apparently they were to live in the same house. It was to be a boarding house. While writing my congratulations I felt strangely out of it somehow—an outsider in this relation too to the point of asking myself why these two were marrying—how

---

[99] *Razumov*, MS p. 476.
[100] *Ibid.*, MS pp. 523–26.

11 / 1 IS 476.

bread. And all in such confusion, too!
One feels anguish.... The mental
caducity ~~conviction~~! The moral destitution
of that West buried in gold up to
the neck. I ~~refused~~ received lately an
invitation ~~appropriately~~ to New York. They wanted me to ~~talk~~ speak in public over
there. *To deliver some discourses* And do you know what?
~~I was afraid I should never say yes.~~
~~My imagination flinches~~
I could not bring myself to say — yes.
I flinched. That *world* does not think in
the same terms. *with us, there is a barrier. Even* the women
~~themselves~~ *at present*... Ah! You may well
be proud of being a Russian
girl, Natalia..."

noting
I ~~reproach~~ *the* in my corner *pocket*
in myself ~~distaste of~~ *the unexpected* (growth) mystic solidarity with
New York; And ~~that same~~ a ~~faint~~
~~bit~~ *he urged* distaste for that familiar
Natalia on his lips. Eleanor! Na-
talia. This *(easy)* *woman's* use of christian
names must have been a

This passage in the manuscript of *Razumov* (Yale University Library) was canceled before the novel was published. Peter Ivanovitch is speaking to Natalia Haldin,
while the English narrator listens. It is one of several canceled passages, which—
taken together—imply an attraction-revulsion complex existing in the attitudes of
Russians and Americans toward each other.

could they even have allowed such an interference with their precious personalities as falling in love with each other necessarily amounted to.

"We have cheerfully agreed to differ on certain points," my niece announced. Well, of course if their happiness were a matter of formal agreement . . . But all this matrimonial news was dismissed in one page. A lot of strange immigrants[101] from Russia had just been landed on the shores of the Dominion and the press had decided that their fate should be made a matter of interest to the world at large. They were escaping domestic persecution but it seems that on account of their religious tenets they had got into difficulties at once with the authorities of the land of refuge. It seems the Russians' destiny to suffer from lawlessness in servitude and to strive for lawlessness in their freedom. The dear girl . . . thought their religion anti-social and their morality incompatible with the great passionless ideals of mankind. Anyone could see that she was a reasonable person.[102]

Though the tone here is typical of the stodgy professor, one recognizes the fundamental Conrad, who called the gun-toting, Negro-hating boaster from Baltimore a "New Englander" in *The Rescue*, made the San Francisco tycoon Holroyd a prophet of the New World's "purer form of Christianity" in *Nostromo*, and has the "perfect anarchist" of *The Secret Agent* say of the United States: ". . . their character is essentially anarchistic. Fertile ground for us, the States—very good ground. The great Republic has the root of the destructive matter in her. The collective temperament is lawless."[103] "New" Englishmen seeking new freedoms in Canada are clearly one in the author's mind with the rationalist, feminist, tradition-defying, *nouveaux arrivés* of the young and immature United States democracy.[104] The distortion, which would pique

---

[101] Conrad's reference here is to the Dukhobors, a group of whom fled to Canada in the 1890's.

[102] *Razumov*, MS pp. 615–17.

[103] *The Secret Agent*, p. 72.

[104] About this time Conrad wrote to the Galsworthys, "Ford, I guess, is now being entertained in America. No doubt they'll feast him on intellectual roast dog. Perhaps his next book will be written with an eagle's feather" (*Life and Letters*, II, 37). For the particular associations Conrad had with the eating of dog see *A Personal Record*, pp. 32–34. Conrad cut out of the manuscript of *Under Western Eyes* a passage, in the description of Peter Ivanovitch's escape from Russia, where Ivanovitch re-enacts the

most Americans just as much as the remarks in the same passage (and indeed much of the novel as a whole) would annoy most Russians, is interesting chiefly because it reveals Conrad's early intention, in the development of the novel, to suggest a confrontation somewhere in the future between the sort of psychological anomie represented by rationalist, passionless "democracy," on the one hand, and the lawlessness of the morbidly emotional Russian victims of despotism on the other.

We find Conrad returning in *Under Western Eyes* to the kind of problem he set for himself in *The Rescue* (see above, pp. 99–103), and once again withdrawing a part of the argument which complicates and subtilizes the image of the West in the novel. In *The Rescue*, I have suggested, he deleted the important Wyndham episode largely because it involved him in an antithesis between Western civilization and Eastern primitive cultures which placed his refined heroine in a very unbecoming light. In *Under Western Eyes*, on the other hand, his temptation to analyze the West at greater length probably seemed, finally, extraneous and not worth the extra length it imposed on the novel. He was content to confine his animus against Western Hemisphere democracy, we may suppose, within the inferences one might draw from the international city of Geneva.

There is no beauty in the Geneva of *Under Western Eyes*. The lake loved by Jean Jacques Rousseau is only a "lake whose precise, orderly, and well-to-do beauty must have been attractive to the unromantic imagination of a business man."[105] Geneva seems memorable above all, to Conrad, as the birthplace of Rousseau. It is on the little island named after the author of the *Social Con-*

---

wretched episode in *A Personal Record*, but there the dog-eater is more suited to his feast than was Conrad's Uncle Nicholas. "The body of the silent dog carried off by the primeval man afforded sustenance for a couple of days to the dual personality of the convict" (*Razumov*, MS pp. 435–36).

Another view of Conrad's opinion is given by Retinger, who says Conrad "asserted that the Chinese, possessing an ancient culture, are closer to us than the new-rich Americans, to whom he denied all the subtleties of civilization, declaring that their place had been taken by a meddling curiosity" (*Conrad and His Contemporaries*, p. 81).

[105] *Under Western Eyes*, p. 143.

tract that Razumov finally brings himself to write his first pages to the police, to perform his first positive act of betrayal. "There was something of naïve, odious, and inane simplicity about that unfrequented tiny crumb of earth named after Jean Jacques Rousseau. Something pretentious and shabby, too."[106] Conrad seems to be applying to the place words he would like to use for the man commemorated, the father of democracy and revolution.[107]

If the critical objections raised by the character of the narrator and the dreariness of Geneva as a microcosm of the West are put aside, another important obstacle still remains for many readers. G. H. Bantock feels that in the last three-quarters of the novel, "Conrad fails his theme" by allowing it to rely too heavily on the presentation of Natalia Haldin and Razumov's relationship with her. Because both are inadequately fathomed, "the ending is felt to be sentimental" and fails "to resolve the dilemma of the beginning. . . . Razumov's confession is at most a gesture in a void, a purely personal affirmation."[108]

We know from a letter Conrad wrote to Galsworthy that his original conception made even more of the relationship between the lovers.[109] They were to marry and to have a child. And the resemblance of the child to Haldin was, somehow or other, to bring about their death. Even in the cursory sketch, however, we see Conrad reaching past the romantic interest toward some point

---

[106] *Ibid.*, p. 290.

[107] In answer to an invitation by Wielhorski to draft a Polish constitution Rousseau wrote an essay, *Considérations sur le gouvernement de la Pologne*, recommending an elective monarchy for Poland. At the same time Wielhorski applied to the Abbé Mably, who responded with *De La Situation politique de la Pologne*, recommending the introduction of a hereditary constitutional monarchy—a solution considered more appropriate than Rousseau's. Conrad would no doubt have agreed. That he supported the plan of a hereditary constitutional monarchy till the end of his life is clear from his advice to the British Government, written in 1916, on how Poland should be treated after World War I. In this "note" he proposed that "a written constitution" should establish "the Polish Commonwealth *with a hereditary King as its head*. . . ." Apparently deciding later that this advice was premature, Conrad deleted the words I have italicized (which one finds in the Rosenbach manuscript, p. 12) from the paragraph as published in *Notes on Life and Letters:* "A Note on the Polish Problem," p. 140. For further discussion, see below, pp. 326–29.

[108] "Conrad and Politics," *English Literary History* (March, 1958), pp. 134–35.

[109] Letter quoted above, n. 6.

which would bring Razumov face to face with Haldin and force him to terminate the life of deception he had been living.

Haldin had prophesied that his spirit would go on warring in the world after his death. He himself was embodying the spirit of an uncle: "They say I resemble my mother's eldest brother . . . . They shot him in '28."[110] His spirit, too, would pass into a nephew through his sister, and through this nephew, he would have his revenge on Razumov.

As one rereads *Under Western Eyes*, the romantic interest seems to matter less and less to the theme. It is the way with all Conrad's novels—and with the classical tragedies they so closely resemble. Conrad finally decided to compress his original conception and have Natalia Haldin herself bring about the reversal which at first the child was to effect. Her ardor and her presence torment Razumov on two accounts; first, reminding him of the truth he is hiding and, second, confronting him anew with the fatality that came to him in Haldin, now not in the person of an assassin whom he must give up to the police but in a compellingly desirable and innocent woman. Both as Russian and as woman, she plays on his sympathies and antipathies to such a degree that he cannot resist involvement with her. All Geneva considers them fated to be lovers. But surrendering to her will be in part surrendering to and exonerating Haldin, whom he must continue to abhor as a criminal if he is to be true to himself. If he loves her without giving up the convictions that made him betray Haldin, he will be "stealing a soul," Haldin's soul, as it lives on through her.

The intention Razumov described in such words,[111] writing to Natalia in his diary, was not necessarily to be a Mephistophelean snare but something more like a case of loving and living under false pretenses. Conrad employs Dostoevskian language not to convey an image of demonic seduction in the Dostoevskian sense but to suggest (once more rewriting Dostoevsky) that there are depths of evil vile enough for a novelist in the normal human mind

---

[110] *Under Western Eyes*, p. 23.
[111] *Ibid.*, pp. 359–60.

without invading the monstrous. "If [Razumov] is slightly abnormal it is only in his sensitiveness to his position," Conrad explains in the preface. "But I don't think that in his distraction he is ever monstrous."[112] Conrad here seems also to be implicitly attacking Dostoevsky's fantastic invocations of supernatural good and evil. As the saintly Tekla tells Natalia, "belief in a supernatural source of evil is not necessary; men alone are quite capable of every wickedness."[113]

Razumov is finally forced to admit that giving Haldin up "to justice" was yielding his own soul to a "devil" in himself to which he felt himself constitutionally opposed—". . . it was myself, after all, whom I have betrayed most basely."[114] Razumov never felt simple remorse for having sent a fellow mortal to death, for this kind of contrition was always overshadowed by an insistence in his mind on the criminality of Haldin's actions. When he then wrote, "After all it is they and not I who have the right on their side!— theirs is the strength of invisible powers,"[115] he referred to the revolutionary expression of the pure spirit of Russian "justice" to which he discovered himself a traitor. "So be it. Only don't be deceived, Natalia Victorovna, I am not converted. . . . No! I am independent—and therefore perdition is my lot."[116]

If Razumov is not "converted" by the revolutionaries, neither does he mentally banish them from the Russia with which he has identified himself ("I am *it*"). In betraying Haldin, he has be-

---

[112] *Ibid.*, p. ix.

[113] *Ibid.*, p. 151. The enormous difference between Dostoevsky's and Conrad's characterizations—so often said to be similar—might be shown by comparing the two theories of character expressed in *The Idiot* and *Nostromo*. In the former, Dostoevsky himself addresses the reader: "Authors for the most part attempt in their tales and novels to select and represent vividly and artistically types rarely met with in actual life in their entirety, though they are nevertheless almost more real than real life itself." (Translation by Constance Garnett: New York, Bantam Books, 1958, p. 447.) In *Nostromo* (p. 273) Decoud suggests a theory of characterization just opposite to Dostoevsky's, though it appears at first glance the same: "Exceptional individualities always interest me, because they are true to the general formula expressing the moral state of humanity."

[114] *Under Western Eyes*, p. 361.

[115] *Ibid.*

[116] *Ibid.*, pp. 361–62.

trayed himself and also part of the Russian spirit. And for this there can be no Dostoevskian expiation, not even a symbolic Siberia from which one can return cleansed.[117] The effect of his remorse, his punishment, can be only a consequence—the physical embodiment of a mental state already in existence. The exact punishment—deafness—excommunicates him utterly from his world. We see the perfect rightness of deafness as the punishment for Razumov (suggested probably by the Russian exile Stepniak's self-induced deafness,[118] which led to his death in 1895). Blindness (one may think of the blinding of Oedipus) would cut a man off from the *vision* of a horrible set of circumstances, but deafness would separate him from ordinary communication with his fellow men, which is the state that Razumov has already recognized as existing. "I am independent—and therefore perdition is my lot."[119] Of course it is accident or fate which, in Razumov's case, chooses the appropriate

---

[117] Belief in the efficacy of expiation for crimes against one's fellow men was another fallacy, carried over from religious doctrines, that Conrad repudiated in all his novels. He put this important matter very clearly in a letter to Marguerite Poradowska: "I astonish and perhaps scandalize you by my joking about criminals while you think me capable of accepting or even admitting the doctrine (or theory) of expiation through suffering. That doctrine, a product of superior but savage minds, is quite simply an infamous abomination when preached by civilized people. It is a doctrine which, on the one hand, leads straight to the Inquisition and on the other, discloses the possibilities of bargaining with the Eternal. . . . Each act of life is final and inevitably produces its consequences in spite of all the weeping and gnashing of teeth and the sorrow of weak souls who suffer as fright grips them when confronted with the results of their own actions." (Letter of Sept. 15, 1891, *Letters of Joseph Conrad to Marguerite Poradowska*, translated and edited by John A. Gee and Paul J. Sturm [New Haven: Yale University Press, 1940], p. 36).

[118] Edgar Wright, in his thesis on Conrad's techniques and critical principles (see above, p. 170, n. 18), was the first to note the likelihood of this connection between Razumov's fate and the fate of Garnett's friend S. M. Kravchinsky, who called himself Stepniak in exile. See also Baines, *Joseph Conrad*, pp. 370–71.

[119] Gustaw Herling-Grudziński, "W oczach Conrada," p. 31, misinterprets André Gide's remarks in his *Journal*, III (Rio de Janeiro: Gallimard, 1943), 246, 284, on the fatal "inconsistencies" of Lord Jim and Razumov. He believes that Razumov's statement to Natalia ("I am independent—and therefore perdition is my lot"—p. 362) and his statement to the revolutionaries ("Today, of all days since I came among you, I was made safe . . ."—p. 368) are examples of this inconsistency. Far from Gide's meaning, this apparent contradiction reveals Razumov in one of man's aspects as *homo duplex*. The life he might have lived with Natalia Haldin is lost, but a life that matters more—the life of integrity—is saved. There is here, indeed, a comparison with Lord Jim—in his last scene with Jewel, discussed above, p. 68.

punishment, though Razumov goes deliberately to meet it. Tekla, who takes the broken "thinker" into her care, not as Sonia took Raskolnikov but as the daughters of Oedipus received him in his blindness, had much earlier unconsciously described to him her fitness to nurse a noble Russian without recourse to words: "I would know how to keep dumb. . . . I would just as soon bite my tongue out and throw it at [the tyrants] as not. What's the good of speech to me?"[120]

Razumov survives the assertion of his real identity, but as an outcast and a cripple. In this respect he is the spiritual brother of the only Polish hero Conrad ever invited into his fictional world, Prince Roman Sanguszko.[121] The story "Prince Roman," Conrad's one fictional treatment of a Polish subject, was written in 1911, according to Cunninghame Graham, possibly as a sort of afterthought to Razumov's tale. It tells the story of a Polish prince who, like Conrad's namesake in Mickiewicz's *Dziady*, elected to transmute his personal happiness and romance into the devoted service of the Polish nation. After the death of his adored young wife, on the eve of the Polish insurrection of 1831, Prince Roman had thrown up his post as ordnance officer to the Russian emperor. Gradually grief for his wife, in Conrad's words, had opened "his mind to a vaster thought . . . to the existence of another love fraught with pain but as mysteriously imperative as that lost one to which he had entrusted his happiness."[122] Disguising his aristocratic identity, he joined a band of Polish insurgents and thus "brought his offering to his country." After a long campaign, he was taken prisoner by the Russians and was recognized among the captives by an old childhood friend. When the Russian authorities asked for his real name, he "owned up at once." But this was only a preliminary test of his mettle. Later, the investigating authorities

---

[120] *Under Western Eyes*, pp. 236–37.

[121] For a thorough discussion of both the English and Polish sources Conrad may have used in addition to his own memory, see Ludwik Krzyżanowski, "Joseph Conrad's 'Prince Roman': Fact and Fiction" in *Joseph Conrad: Centennial Essays*, ed. by Krzyżanowski (New York: The Polish Institute of Arts and Sciences in America, 1960), pp. 27–72.

[122] *Tales of Hearsay*, p. 41.

showed him every clemency; for, says Conrad, "the hate of Poles was not at that time a cardinal article of patriotic creed as it became some thirty years later"[123]—at the time of Apollo Korzeniowski's imprisonment and exile. They offered Prince Roman a chance to be let off lightly, under the excuse that he had joined the rebels when distracted by grief over his wife, "in a moment of blind recklessness." Foregoing speech, by way of answer Roman writes on a piece of paper, "I joined the national rising from conviction."[124]

Though condemned for life to the Siberian mines, Roman was permitted to return to Poland after twenty-five years—broken in health and stone-deaf. Razumov's history differs from Roman's in being a tale of victimization and degradation at the hands of his own people. The resemblance between the two men appears in that both conceal their identities to serve their nations; both shed their disguises in a self-sacrificing display of personal integrity; both suffer deafness and physical ruin as their reward.[125]

Through Razumov, the hero of his last completed novel on a political theme, Conrad locates Russia in the region of his own deepest personal experience, where like deaf men (and like the dead Homeric heroes), perhaps all who are true to themselves and to their fellow men must exist in "an abode of silent shades."[126] Conrad's father had intended to write "a great Polish novel on the corruption that has come to us from Moscow." Conrad's last political novel was tribute to the father, but tribute also to the common humanity and capacity for suffering of the Russian people. In *Under Western Eyes*, as in *The Secret Agent*, Conrad's last word on politics seems to be that political institutions form the

---

[123] *Ibid.*, p. 51.

[124] *Ibid.*, p. 52.

[125] Another slight similarity between the two stories might be found in the self-sacrificing comfort offered the heroes by a woman of their people. Several accounts of Prince Roman's banishment to Siberia focus on the heroic action of Roża Sobańska, a Polish gentlewoman who stood in the snow waiting for the prisoners to pass so that she might give the prince her own copy of the *Imitation of Christ*. Dostoevsky described another such episode as occurring to him on his way to Siberia seventeen years later. Roża Sobańska was, of course, less like Razumov's Tekla than Tekla is like Raskolnikov's Sonya.

[126] *Tales of Hearsay*, p. 55.

national character of a people. Razumov is human, but subjected as he is to autocratic despotism on one side and to revolutionary despair on the other, his tragedy is, according to Conrad, peculiarly Russian.

"Show me the star Soheil and I will show you the Moon."
Arab proverb

"Ah! the lone tree on the horizon and then bear a little—(a very little) to the right. Haven't we all ridden with such directions to find no house but many curs barking at our heels. Can't miss it? Well perhaps we can't. And we don't ride with a stouter heart for that. Indeed my friend there is a joy in being lost, but a sorrow in being weary . . . .

"Ride on to the tree and to the right—for verily there is a devil at the end of every road. Let us pray to the pot bellied gods, to gods with more legs than a centipede and more arms than a dozen windmills, let us pray to them to guard us from the mischance of arriving somewhere. As long as we don't pray to the gods made in man's image we are sure of a most glorious perdition.

"Don't know tho'. I wouldn't give twopence for all its glory—and I would pray to a god made like a man in the City—and do you know for what? For a little forgetfulness. Say half an hour. Oh bliss. I would give him my soul for it and he would be cheated. To be cheated is godlike. It is your devil who makes good bargains, legends notwithstanding.

"Meantime let us look at Soheil and reflect that it is a speck in the eternal night even as we are. Only we don't shine. At least some of us don't. We are as celestial as the other bodies—only we are obscure. At least some of us are. But we all have our illusion of being wayfarers. No more than Soheil, Amigo! Round to the left or round to the right, what matters if it is a circle. Ask Soheil. And if you get an answer I shall with my own hands give you a piece of the moon."

Letter from Conrad to Cunninghame Graham,
August 26, 1898 (Dartmouth MS)

CHAPTER EIGHT

The Rover and After

In everything Conrad wrote after *Under Western Eyes* and "Prince Roman" there are echoes from the political themes that interested him earlier, but the politics of the later novels and stories do not reward our scrutiny. They present variations on attitudes already struck rather than explorations of new subjects or points of view. Even the subject over which Conrad meditated so long, "the Napoleonic episode," bore fruit of a different kind than was anticipated. What appeared in 1922 with *The Rover*, and with the posthumously published "Warrior's Soul" and fragment of *Suspense*, clearly marked the return of Conrad's creative thought "to old familiar things."[1]

"When *The Rover* appeared," wrote Jean-Aubry (who had helped Conrad collect historical material on Napoleon's career),

> as its setting and epoch were precisely those of Bonaparte's début into public life, we thought that here was the Napoleonic novel we had heard announced: and despite the legitimate success of this novel, many readers were disappointed, especially since instead of

---

[1] R. B. Cunninghame Graham, "Preface" to Conrad's *Tales of Hearsay and Last Essays*, p. xv.

their favorite hero, they could find in it only the great figure of his glorious enemy, Lord Nelson.[2]

Napoleon never makes a personal appearance in any of these last works. He was perhaps to appear at the end of *Suspense*, since it was Conrad's intention to end the novel with Napoleon's escape from Elba. In the 274 published pages of the fragment, Conrad's interest is rather in portraying the state of things Napoleon's career had brought to Europe, what in "Autocracy and War" Conrad called "the body of a Europe which did, indeed, for some dozen of years, very much resemble a corpse."[3] Although it is impossible to tell from the fragment where the real moral pivot of the novel was to come, there is an evident tension in the story between the hostility to Napoleon harbored by the wise old Englishman, Sir Charles Latham (who sympathizes from afar with the anguished and decadent French aristocrats living in Genoa where the plot centers) and the admiration for the fallen emperor expressed by Sir Charles's son Cosmo, the hero of the novel. At the end of the fragment, Cosmo finds himself accidentally joined with a band of revolutionaries, setting out from Genoa at night in a felucca, presumably to play his part in the short-lived liberation of Napoleon. The Italian conspirators trust Cosmo's English "luck," but in the last pages, "the thought flashed through his mind that there was something in him that made of him a predestined victim of remorse."[4] One is left to wonder what there might ever be for him to regret.

There is just enough in the meandering tale to remind us that the period of its setting was a time of intense anxiety, hope and suspense for Poland, whose fate—already sealed by Napoleon's disregard, even before his fall—lay on the table before the Triple Entente at the Congress of Vienna. What it was that made Conrad and other Poles go on brooding over his career is hard to understand, unless it was that he was the last of the great conquerors who

---

[2] Jean-Aubry, Translator's Preface to *Angoisse* (*Suspense*) (Paris, Gallimard, 1956), p. 7. I have translated from the French.

[3] *Notes on Life and Letters*, p. 86.

[4] *Suspense*, pp. 265–66.

might have recut the cloth of Europe to the Polish order. His depredations were to some extent offset, perhaps, by the fact that he was the last statesman of genius who was also a genius in the art of war. He was the last warrior statesman who would ever try to found a dynasty in Europe, and this may have appealed to the Conrad who wanted to re-establish a hereditary monarch in Poland.

So many questions are left hanging by *Suspense* that one would prefer to remember *The Rover* as Conrad's last novel. Jean Peyrol, a far more impressive character than Cosmo Latham, represents an interesting variation from the usual hero of Conrad's political fiction. Unlike Lingard, Marlow, Gould, Winnie Verloc, and Razumov, he is spiritually untouched by—and exempt from—the conflict in which his fellow men are caught up. It is his nature to be aloof. Even Nostromo was more easily beguiled by a political illusion than is Peyrol. As Nostromo was to represent "the people" —presumably of Italy mainly—Peyrol represents the people of France. In 1917 Conrad wrote to Sir Sidney Colvin that "the greatest figure of the times through which we have lived was The People itself, *la Nation*. For 150 years the French people has been always greater (and better) than its leaders, masters and teachers."[5] Peyrol is the embodiment of such liberty, equality, and brotherhood as man is ever likely to possess. The major effect of the novel is to show this incarnate spirit of the French people matched against— not the English, for Capt. Vincent and the other Englishmen are visualized less as the enemy than as the heroic equals of Peyrol— but against two other Frenchmen: Scevola, the pathological image of the French Revolution, and Lieutenant Réal, whom Conrad described as the "child of the Revolution . . . with his austere and pedantic turn of mind and conscience."[6] When describing his characters thus to Garnett after *The Rover's* appearance in 1922, Conrad denies that Scevola (whom Garnett had criticized as merely a "scarecrow") is intended to represent the essence of the Revolution,

---

[5] Letter of April 4, 1917. *Life and Letters*, II, 190.
[6] Letter from Conrad to Garnett, Dec. 24, 1923. Garnett, *Letters from Joseph Conrad*, pp. 298–99.

but in view of what the novel itself conveys, the letter gives us the image of Conrad bowing courteously to his old socialist friend and literary godfather. Scevola is purely, as Conrad says in the letter, "a creature of mob psychology," but this was exactly what the Revolution became. If he was designed as "a weak-minded creature," Scevola extraordinarily resembles—in his monomaniacal suspiciousness—what the man of generous ideals, Robespierre himself, rapidly became after establishing the Terror.

The Rover has been rated generally as the work of the exhausted Conrad. If it is not among his most probing psychological or political novels, it nevertheless deserves a better judgment if only for its portrait of the Provençal peasant-turned-seaman who so curiously represents the France that Poland loved. According to one French critic, Peyrol is the typical Provençal:

> He has the people's total skepticism: the habit of weighing, before accepting them, all the presents thrown by destiny. He has their heavy phlegmaticism, which, when occasion demands, is transformed into instantaneous decision and action. He has their devotion to their own interests: he knows how to keep out of the way, how to calculate and how to demand what is due him, he knows how to find and establish the most suitable place for himself. But he knows too, when destiny calls, how to forget everything, abandon everything—interests and all—and fling his own life, as a last and worthy missile, into the middle of adverse circumstances.[7]

Many readers interpret *The Rover* as Conrad's expression of a wish to return to Poland. If it was, the wish included the necessity of returning as such a man.

"He is the only one who provokes an inquietude not spoiled by some neurosis, an inquietude of the normal man."[8] The estimate of Conrad's place among novelists made by Crémieux in 1922 could be defended still in the 1960's when the anxieties Conrad expressed

---

[7] Denis Saurat, "Conrad et la Provence." *Perspectives* (Paris, Stock, 1938), p. 230. I have translated from the French.

[8] Benjamin Crémieux, review of *Within the Tides*, *Nouvelle Revue Française*, July 1, 1922, pp. 108–9. I have translated from the French.

for man's future in *Under Western Eyes* have proved all too well founded. We are more conscious today than men were during Conrad's lifetime that human perversity—the normal condition of man's nature—may deviate into monstrosities, may degenerate into a savagery worse than any known by the unscientific, primitive jungle peoples of Conrad's early works.

There has always been a current of criticism that calls in question Conrad's basic humanity as well as his politics, and this criticism must be weighed against Crémieux's evaluation. Two of the most formidable of these criticisms in our language are those of David Daiches, in *The Novel and the Modern World*, and Irving Howe, in *Politics and the Novel*. Howe asserts that in all the political themes Conrad handles, apart from *Nostromo*, one is likely to find unbalance and injustice. In *The Secret Agent*, says Howe, Conrad denies his characters "the mildest claims to dignity and redemption. . . . So peevish an irony must have its source less in zeal or anger than in some deep distemper."[9] Daiches decides *The Nigger of the "Narcissus"* "reveals that society as such is inevitably corrupt, that the ties of affection and hatred that link men in community are really disguises for emotional self-indulgence and self-love."[10] He reads *The Secret Agent* as a travesty of essential human motives and affections, and sees that the "great society . . . is reduced at the end of the novel to the little society which is both terrible and crazy and incomprehensible."[11] *Heart of Darkness* suggests to Daiches "that outside individual experience there is perhaps no reality, that society can never be wholly real."[12]

What astonishes one about these comments is their similarity to the official opinion of the Soviet Union, with which undoubtedly neither Daiches nor Howe would intend to agree in critical estimates. The *Great Soviet Encyclopedia* of 1937 blamed Conrad for his preoccupation with "weak, broken people" and for his lack of

---

[9] Irving Howe, *Politics and the Novel* (New York: Horizon Press, 1957), p. 96.
[10] David Daiches, *The Novel and the Modern World* (Chicago: University of Chicago Press, 1960), p. 29.
[11] *Ibid.*, p. 57.
[12] *Ibid.*, p. 40.

interest "in real situations and actions."[13] A later edition (1953) of the same encyclopedia (which omits both *The Secret Agent* and *Under Western Eyes* from the list of Conrad's works) sums up more succinctly: "The departure of Conrad from real social problems into exoticism and subjectivism brings him close to the bourgeois decadents."[14]

Polish critics (whether living in Communist Poland or outside), who should be among Conrad's most discerning readers, are often (like Daiches and Howe) so fretful over particular political issues raised in a novel that they fail to appreciate the full implications of the work taken as a whole. Ever since Eliza Orzeszkowa's attack on Conrad in 1899, he has served as a political symbol in Poland, and his value has risen or fallen, depending on the changing fortunes of the country. After World War I, when Poland regained her independence, a group of young Polish poets, publishing a magazine called *Skamander*, reaffirmed Conrad's innocence of the charges Orzeszkowa had brought against him. One of the most moving tributes offered by this group was a long poem called "Dialogue on the Love of Country Between Joseph and Stefan," by Antoni Słonimski.[15] In it Conrad returns to Poland in order to visit his father's grave and, meeting the Polish novelist Stefan Żeromski, explains why he had to leave Poland. His words are to the effect that the earth in Poland was too much like a prison. The country was a rock on which his father's ship was wrecked, and he— Conrad—had to put out to sea, to breathe the free air, see the larger earth, and find love unconstrained by oppression. The novelist who remained in Poland argues with him that only in one's native land can one really breathe and love and find a refuge. Conrad has

---

[13] *Bol'shaia Sovetskaia Entsiklopediia* (Moscow), 1937 edition, XXXIV, Col. 30. This biographical note on Conrad was translated for me by Stephen Hay.

[14] *Ibid.*, 1953 edition, XXXII, 399.

[15] Antoni Słonimski, "Dialog o miłości ojczyzny między Josephem a Stefanem" *Skamander* (Warsaw), April, 1923, pp. 17–21. In 1927 Słonimski changed the speakers in the poem from Conrad and Żeromski to an unnamed "Host" and "New Arrival." The poem appears thus in his collected poems, *Rozmowa z gwiazdą, 1916– 1961* (Warsaw: Państwowy Instytut Wydawniczy, 1961), pp. 74–81. I am indebted to Maria Kuncewiczowa and Wiktor Weintraub for this information. Kuncewiczowa translated the poem for me.

the last word in this poem celebrating the rebirth of Poland. He ends by clasping the hand of his compatriot, but his last words once more hail the experience of feeling one's ship revive, urged forward by the wind after a calm.

Even in this lovely dialogue the pure response of the poet to the two speakers is distorted by an extraneous political message. Słonimski devotes a long speech of "Joseph" to an argument for his own pacifist sentiments, and the illusion of truth drops away when he makes Conrad say he would never defend Poland against an enemy: everyone who is armed is a murderer; one does not defend truth with a sword. Słonimski overlooked Conrad's repeated insistence that he was "not a peace man." It was in answer to a protest from the Polish critic Borowy, who saw the misrepresentation in Conrad's portrait, that Słonimski made the two speakers anonymous in his dialogue when it was republished in 1927. Żeromski (who admired Conrad and fostered the first complete Polish translation of Conrad's works) may have voiced his objection, too.

In recent commentaries, Herling-Grudziński and Miłosz, both émigrés, make Conrad too much a partisan against the current expression of communism. Still, one turns to them naturally as to men who reflect a common history (in so many ways unique and influential on all their works) with Conrad. Wit Tarnawski, who chose England as his land of exile as Conrad did before him, has a wonderfully broad and deep understanding of Conrad and helped to give me courage in many of the opinions I have expressed. Maria Dąbrowska,[16] unlike these last three, lives in Poland and yet criticizes Conrad from a point of view so similar to my own that I have found no point on which to disagree with her. One obviously cannot divide Conrad's Polish critics neatly according to the countries where they have chosen to live.

Conrad was perhaps fortunate in that circumstances gave a shape to his life which made it vividly represent—as a myth represents—history in the centuries he spanned. This coincidence may have

---

[16] Ujejski quotes frequently from Maria Dąbrowska. Recently, her essays on Conrad have been collected and published as *Szkice o Conradzie* (Warsaw: Państwowy Instytut Wydawniczy, 1959).

rendered it unnecessary for him to seek a separation, as T. S. Eliot claims the artist must do, between his private personality and his public or creative mask. Indeed Conrad's whole effort seems to have been to do just the reverse, to integrate as fully as possible the man who suffered and the mind that created. His worst novel, *The Arrow of Gold*, may have failed as it did because what he told about Monsieur Georges amounted to telling a lie about himself. His remarks about the technical devices he used to achieve impersonality will mislead us if we do not read in them a simple lesson of self-discipline, necessary to the right performance of any craft. If Shakespeare, as Hazlitt held, was the least egotistical of artists, Conrad was surely one of the most egoistical, and this may be why the novel was the only genre he found congenial. Other writers anxiously seek "objective correlatives" to private experience. Conrad found them in his own life, as others seem to verify who (like Eliot) have used Conrad's imagery as a correlative for their own experience. Conrad presents the almost isolated example of a modern artist able to produce the generative archetypes on which other artists depend.

Conrad alone among the English novelists of our time qualifies as a "political novelist" in the sense in which we have understood the phrase in this study. For others, man is a political animal more by accident or by choice than by nature. If Conrad was "infected" by man's personal isolation as much if not more than the rest, it was in part because he suffered from the loneliness of a man separated from his nation ("Woe to the stragglers!"), in part because he saw more precisely than the others why a man *has* to alienate himself at times from political circumstances that threaten his very life. When D. H. Lawrence complained cryptically that Conrad bothered him by always "giving in," Lawrence seems to have been disappointed that defiance was not the *final* gesture of Lord Jim, Kurtz, Monygham, Winnie Verloc, or Razumov. Conrad was burdened with, rather than inspired by, modern man's acute sense of individual identity. He cared more than Lawrence about the integrity of the nation or society in which false illusions, sham politicians, and tyrannous traditions make betrayal, either of one's own convictions or one's fellow men, a condition of citizenship.

The political realism that Conrad inherited from his uncle's legal mind included a proscription against his father's exalted vision of political conspiracy. Conrad's decision to take up life at sea reminds one of Goethe, who said that it was the terrible developments in German politics that turned him to a serious study of what was most remote—the Chinese Empire. Only in this light can one interpret Retinger's statement concerning Conrad that, when it comes to "principles of governing mankind he was not a very moral person, I am afraid, and with Montesquieu he shrugged his shoulders at the thought of a Chinese Mandarin killed thousands of miles away."[17]

Retinger's reminiscences of Conrad are highly unreliable, partly because he made little effort to verify them but largely because his point of view was so different in political matters that Conrad often froze into an extreme position during their conversations. As a fellow Pole and a born political agitator, Retinger was irritated with a man he could not stir into political action. His complaint was not that Conrad had become too anglicized. Conrad was as detached from British politics, when it came to direct action, as from Polish intrigues. And if he never voted in an English election, it was probably because no British party represented his political opinions— the Labour Party being consistently pro-Russian and pacifist and the Conservatives consistently imperialistic. Much that Retinger has to say is interesting, nevertheless, if we think that apart from the Kliszczewski family in Cardiff, Conrad had no other close Polish associate in England.

Thus Retinger's remark that Conrad "thought himself completely incapable, mentally and physically, of meddling in politics or attempting to guide public opinion,"[18] is probably true up to a point. That Conrad "had no faith in politics as a factor which might bring any substantial relief to suffering humanity, because, he reasoned, politics cannot change human nature, which alone is

---

[17] Joseph Retinger, *Conrad and His Contemporaries* (London: Minerva, 1941), p. 41.
[18] *Ibid.*, p. 43.

the origin of good and evil,"[19] is true as to Poland but not, I think, as to England. Poland never comes into his political novels except as an unmentionable, suspended ideal (as we saw in *Heart of Darkness*). But all his political novels indicate that politics is capable of affecting human nature deeply, and all reflect in some measure the power of law to express the higher impulses in mankind.

Comparing the happiness of his own family life in Poland with the tragic story of Conrad's youth, Retinger does not conclude that Conrad had any reason for taking a different course from the one he himself pursued as an international agitator in Europe and America, but he does say that Conrad "resolutely decided against the past . . . He chose a road totally new, different and alien to the one followed by the people to whom he belonged, but in no way opposed to them."[20]

The passage from *Nostromo* referred to above (pp. 183–84) is especially poignant when read next to Retinger's comment. There was no command to which Conrad was disobedient. But the possibility of Korzeniowski's disapproval of Conrad's English life must have hung over him. In *Nostromo*, Charles Gould resolves to use disobedience as a means of conquering the evil fate that had killed his father:

> That irreparable change a death makes in the course of our daily thoughts can be felt in a vague and poignant discomfort of mind. It hurt Charles Gould to feel that never more, by no effort of will, would he be able to think of his father in the same way he used to think of him when the poor man was alive. His breathing image was no longer in his power. This consideration, closely affecting his own identity, filled his breast with a mournful and angry desire for action. . . . Only in the conduct of our action can we find the sense of mastery over the Fates.

In all the years before World War I, Conrad's relation to Poland was somewhat like the dilemma of Aeneas, driven from the burning Troy. For Conrad, the commands of an oracular uncle, urging him to find a new land, supported his own impulse. Like Aeneas,

---

[19] *Ibid.*
[20] *Ibid.*, p. 18.

he carried in silence and piety the memory of a family and nation that he considered dead except in spirit:

> . . . whatever may be the changes in the fortunes of living nations, for the dead there is no hope and no salvation. We have passed through the gates where *"lasciate ogni speranza"* is written in letters of blood and fire, and nothing remains for us but the darkness of oblivion.[21]

Similarly, the French novelist Cherbuliez had used an image of Poland that Conrad often echoed, the image of a man buried alive but continually raising the lid of his coffin.[22] To Cherbuliez, this was proof of Poland's remarkable vitality. To Conrad, it was macabre and horrible.

In 1914, when Conrad was fifty-seven, an opportunity presented itself in which he saw the first real occasion for direct action in Poland's behalf. If he had not been visiting in Poland when the war broke out, or if the war had not broken out when he was in Poland, he might not have taken the step he did. Seeing Poland again, for the first time in over twenty years, gave him a clear picture of how life was surviving in the tomb. The war—setting Austria and Germany against Russia—inspired all Poland with the hope that major changes in the map of Europe would result and the boundaries of Poland be drawn again.

Our first evidence that Conrad recognized the situation as designating in some sense his "watch on deck" is in the Polish memorandum Conrad wrote and left in the hands of Dr. Teodor Kosch, a Cracow lawyer, in 1914. Recently translated into English and published by Ludwik Krzyżanowski, the document expresses Conrad's intention to use what influence he commands to "bring up and accustom the English public to the idea that the Poles should have legal recognition of their *nationality* in the defeated as well

---

[21] Letter to Spiridion Kliszczewski, Oct. 13, 1885, *Life and Letters*, I, 81. See also the opening of "Prince Roman" (*Tales of Hearsay*, p. 29), where "the speaker was of Polish nationality, that nationality not so much alive as surviving, which persists in thinking, breathing, hoping, and suffering in its grave."

[22] Quoted in George Brandes, *Poland: A Study of the Land, People and Literature* (New York: Macmillan Co., 1904), p. 47.

as in the victorious states "(i.e., in Germany and Austria-Hungary, as well as England, France, and Russia). The memorandum focuses on the need for England to detach Austria from her alliance with Germany, and ends with Conrad's pledge to show that "it will be in the interest of England (even in conditions unfavorable to herself) to support Austria's Polish policy, the development of a Polish spirit hostile to the Germans in this Monarchy . . . in which the parliamentary institutions so liked by the English people are developed best of all European states."[23]

During the next two years Conrad apparently confined himself to personal contacts, writing nothing of a public nature until 1916 when he wrote the draft (now in Philadelphia at the Rosenbach Foundation) of "A Note on the Polish Problem." From another letter in Krzyżanowski's collection, it becomes apparent that Conrad and Retinger presented this note—proposing that Poland be made an Anglo-French Protectorate—to a Mr. Clark at the British Foreign Office and later talked their proposal over with him in his office. Retinger was dissatisfied with Mr. Clark's response, but Conrad found it quite appropriate and even encouraging. He wrote to Retinger soon afterward in an effort to show him the reasonableness of Clark's attitude. (Conrad's letter is in French, but I have translated it, observing his capitalization.)

> In view of Clark's position at the Foreign Office and the fact that the interview took place in his office in the Ministry itself, he could not say more than he did say. My memory is that You were the first to remark that it would be difficult for England to talk of Polish affairs anywhere other than in Petrograd; even though English Taste would rather seek its inspiration in the wishes of the Poles. To Your precise question:—if the British Gov. (of course with France) approved the general idea of a (triple) Protectorate, he answered: Let the Poles express their clearly formulated ideas first. Not a burst of enthusiasm, but a reasonable demand supported by serious personalities representing as completely as possible all the political and social opinions of Poland. . . .
> It seems to me that with an answer like that (coming from a man

---

[23] Ludwik Krzyżanowski, "Joseph Conrad: Some Polish Documents," in Krzyżanowski's Joseph Conrad: Centennial Essays, pp. 123–25.

If her existence as a State is admitted as just expedient and necessary Poland has the moral right to receive her constitution not from an enemy, but from the Western Powers with the fullest participation and concurrence of Russia.

This constitution elaborated by ^a committee of Poles nominated by the three governments ~~with be theirs~~ will be (after 'due' discussion and amendement by the High Commissioners of the Protecting Powers) presented ~~to~~ Poland as the initial document, the charter of her new life freely offered and unreservedly accepted.

It should be as simple and short as ~~such~~ a written constitution can be — establishing the Polish Commonwealth with a hereditary King on its head, settling the lines of representative ~~government~~ institutions, the form ~~of the~~ Judicature and leaving the greatest measure ~~of~~ self govern-ment ~~to the~~ provinces forming part of the re-created Poland.

This constitution will be promulgated immediately after the three powers had settled the frontiers of the new state including the town of Dantzic (free port) and a proportion of seaboard.

Conrad's nostalgic loyalty to the hereditary monarchy of the old Polish Republic is suggested by the phrasing, later canceled, in this original manuscript of his "A Note on the Polish Problem." (The Philip H. and A. S. W. Rosenbach Foundation)

obliged by his high official position to an extreme reserve) one can, one must, march. The task before You is to gain the agreement of all Polish parties on this project. For it is better to receive the gift of national existence from the hand of friends than of enemies. And agreement on that subject would in no way curb the freedom of action of all parties in the future.

The problem is to begin to live, to breathe again, to gain a body, first. Afterwards the battle of ideas will develop in the framework of fundamental institutions as in all free countries.[24]

More documents will undoubtedly appear, revealing to us the Conrad who stood ready if there should be a clear call to revive Poland's national existence. Encountering the two documents just quoted, in addition to the political essays in *Notes on Life and Letters*, one wonders how Retinger can insist so repetitiously that throughout his life Conrad held aloof from whatever was of interest to Poland.

He fled from a nation in flames in order to save himself for the life that must go on. Self-preservation, however, meant preservation of the national image too. It is egoism that saves everything, he wrote Cunninghame Graham—everything that we hate as well as everything that we love. Having been born to the idealized political imperative of an Aeneas, Conrad carried it as part of the ego's burden. He could not help but reassert in one form or another the existence of his nation's spirit. The life of a ship at sea was for him a surrogate for a free society, existing perilously against the tyranny of the sea; existing perilously, too (the paradox is recurrent in *The Mirror of the Sea*), because of the very freedom of the sea. Everything we know of Conrad's life at sea convinces us that he found there the natural fulfilment of inclinations both toward heroic engagement and master craftsmanship on the one hand, and on the other toward escape and inertia.

From the sea to life in England was a difficult transition, made possible because by then *Almayer's Folly* was an accomplished fact, a living proof that the unaltered identity of Konrad Korzeniowski, asserted according to its own definition at sea, could now be re-

---

[24] *Ibid.*, pp. 132–33.

asserted in writing fiction and on British soil. "It was imperative sometimes to know how to disobey the solemn wishes of the dead. He resolved firmly to make his disobedience as thorough (by way of atonement) as it well could be." Apollo Korzeniowski's gesture of defeat in burning his papers before he died (an image firmly stamped on Conrad's mind though its accuracy has been questioned) could have been a sign to Conrad that the mission of writer-rebel devoted to Polish irredentism was a closed imperative —like Charles Gould's father's command to get rid of the mine. Again, however, in his late thirties, Conrad found himself—as on board ship—personalizing and renewing under conditions peculiarly his own his profound engagement in questions of the lonely man's fidelity to his society and to his fellow men. His father's activity, like the elder Gould's, "had been the cause of an absurd moral disaster; its working [as a many-faceted theme in Conrad's fiction] must be made a serious and moral success." Being above all an artist, Conrad could write his personal tragedy into the very different tragedy of Costaguana's republican "king."

According to Retinger, whenever he tried to press Conrad into action in support of Poland, Conrad would reply, "*Il ne faut pas aller contre le courant des choses.*"[25] Fatalism, or "triumphant passive resistance to life," this was the response to his Polish political imperative that first turned his action inward to his novels. It is in this somber light that we must read Ford Madox Ford's remark that for Conrad "the writing of novels was the one thing of importance that remained to the world . . ."[26] It was, at least, the one means he found of remaining faithful to a special tradition within the dictates of the highly imperious "egoism" or "temperament" which was for him not the least mysterious part of "*le courant des choses.*" When he refused the academic degrees offered him by both of Britain's leading universities in the last years of his life (he refused a knighthood, too), he did so, he said, out of regard for the inner consistency of a life lived with a passionate desire to be

---

[25] Retinger, op. cit., p. 65.
[26] *Joseph Conrad: A Personal Remembrance* (London: Duckworth, 1924), p. 35.

true to all the commands he felt to have a hold on him.[27] In being true to his own "special tradition," he had to exclude ruthlessly whatever was incongruous. He had charted for himself perhaps the most difficult course known to man: fidelity to traditions stamped forcefully upon his character, without recourse to any institution whether of school, party, or church in support of them.

Because he allowed his faith nothing visible to lean upon, it appears in his novels often to falter shamelessly, and leaves the reader who attempts to follow it floundering when he discovers Conrad to be triumphantly passive in the face of apparent contradictions: for instance, his paralyzing attacks on the two best alternatives open to modern politics, capitalistic democracy and nationalistic socialism; or his equal impatience with both the theocentric and the materialist conceptions of the universe. One of Conrad's best Polish critics concluded wistfully that "a revelation of a decisive nature, either from without or within, never illuminated his spiritual horizon."[28]

In *The Destructive Element*, a title taken from *Lord Jim*, Stephen Spender describes a state of mind similar to Conrad's:

> In times of rest, of slow evolution and peace, society is an image of the individual living his life and obeying the laws. In violent times the moral acts of the individual seem quite unrelated to the immense social changes going on all around him. He looks at civilization and does not see his own quiet image reflected there at all, but the face of something fierce and threatening, that may destroy him. It may seem foreign and yet reasonable to his own face. He knows that if he is not to be destroyed, he must somehow connect his life again with this political life and influence it.[29]

The detached individual, shunning yet seeking engagement, is Lingard, Dr. Monygham, Razumov, and the "heroes" of all Conrad's best novels; and often the mirror that reflects him, the narrator, is

---

[27] "Three Autograph Letters," *Saturday Review of Literature* (May 21, 1927), p. 845. The letter refusing a proffered knighthood was written to Ramsay MacDonald in 1924.

[28] Joseph Ujejski, *Joseph Conrad*, translated from Polish into French by Pierre Duméril (Paris: Éditions Edgar Malfère, 1939), p. 112.

[29] *The Destructive Element* (Boston: Houghton Mifflin Co., 1936), pp. 18–19.

his double. Utterly disengaged, the narrator himself turns action inward to thought and feeling, although his concern is right action.

Nathaniel Hawthorne, looking at the political experiment of Brook Farm, must have had something in common with Conrad. Miles Coverdale's description of his role exactly typifies Marlow's position in *Lord Jim*:

> It resembled that of the Chorus in a classic play, which seems to be set aloof from the possibility of personal concernment, and bestows the whole measure of its hope or fear, its exultation or sorrow, on the fortunes of others, between whom and itself this sympathy is the only bond. . . . It is his office to give applause when due, and sometimes an inevitable tear, to detect the final fitness of incident to character and distil in his long-brooding thought the whole morality of the performance.[30]

What this narrator is to the modern novel, Conrad was to the "whole morality" of modern politics.

---

[30] *The Blithedale Romance*, in *The Complete Novels of Nathaniel Hawthorne* (New York: Modern Library, 1937), p. 496.

Bibliography

Only those works are listed that have been quoted or extensively used in preparing this study.

I. MANUSCRIPT MATERIALS

NOVELS AND NOTES

CONRAD, JOSEPH. "A Note on the Polish Problem." Holograph; complete. Philip H. and A. S. W. Rosenbach Foundation, Philadelphia.
———. *Congo Diary.* Two holograph notebooks; complete. Harvard University Library.
———. *Heart of Darkness.* Holograph; complete with exception of first 11 pages and some 17 others. Yale University Library. Some few pages, in typescript, are in the Henry W. and Albert A. Berg Collection, New York Public Library.
———. *Nostromo.* Holograph; many pages are missing. Rosenbach Foundation.
———. *Razumov,* holograph of *Under Western Eyes;* complete. Yale University Library.
———. *The Rescue.* Holograph; complete, although the work is unfinished. British Museum (Ashley 4787).
———. *The Secret Agent.* Holograph; complete. Rosenbach Foundation.
———. "Tuan Jim." Holograph notebook; complete, although the work is unfinished. Harvard University Library.
WALPOLE, HUGH. Note, dated Jan. 26, 1927, in a volume of *The Secret Agent.* Yale University Library.

LETTERS

CONRAD, JESSIE. Holograph letter of Aug. 2, 1925, to Edgar H. Wells. Harvard University Library.

333

CONRAD, JOSEPH. Holograph letter of Aug. 22, 1896, to T. Fisher Unwin. Berg Collection.

———. Holograph letters of Jan. 7, July 30, and Aug. 26, 1898, Oct. 14, 1899, to R. B. Cunninghame Graham. Dartmouth College Library.

———. Holograph letter of Feb. 8, 1899, to Cunninghame Graham. Yale University Library.

———. Holograph letter of Feb. 22, 1917, to Reginald Leon. Berg Collection.

———. Typescript letter of Apr. 2, 1917, to Sir Sidney Colvin. Yale University Library.

———. Typescript letter of Oct. 8, 1923, to Gordon Gardiner. Harvard University Library.

II. PUBLISHED WRITINGS OF JOSEPH CONRAD

WORKS

CONRAD, JOSEPH. *Nostromo*. New York: Modern Library, 1951.

———. *Works*. Collected Edition. 22 vols. London: J. M. Dent, 1946–55.

CONRAD, JOSEPH, and HUEFFER, F. M. *The Inheritors*. New York: Doubleday, Page, 1923.

LETTERS AND NOTES

BLACKBURN, WILLIAM (ed.). *Joseph Conrad: Letters to William Blackwood and David S. Meldrum*. Durham, N. C.: Duke University Press, 1958.

CONRAD, JOSEPH. "Three Autograph Letters" (to the vice chancellor of Oxford University, the vice chancellor of Cambridge University, and the Rt. Honorable Ramsay MacDonald), *Saturday Review of Literature* (May 21, 1927), p. 845.

CURLE, RICHARD (ed.). *Conrad to a Friend, 150 Selected Letters from Joseph Conrad to Richard Curle*. New York: Crosby Gaige, 1928.

———. *Notes by Joseph Conrad Written in a Set of His First Editions in the Possession of Richard Curle*. London: privately published, 1925.

GARNETT, EDWARD (ed.). *Letters from Joseph Conrad, 1895–1924*. Indianapolis: Bobbs-Merrill Co., Inc., 1928.

GEE, JOHN A., and STURM, PAUL J. (trans. and eds.). *Letters of Joseph Conrad to Marguerite Poradowska*. New Haven: Yale University Press, 1940.

JEAN-AUBRY, G. (ed.). *Lettres françaises*. Paris: Gallimard [1930].

———. *Joseph Conrad: Life and Letters.* 2 vols. New York: Doubleday, Page, 1927.

III. BIBLIOGRAPHY, BIOGRAPHY, AND
CRITICISM OF CONRAD

ALLEN, JERRY. *The Thunder and the Sunshine.* New York: Putnam's Sons, 1958.
BAINES, JOCELYN. "The Affair in Marseilles," *The London Magazine* (November, 1957), pp. 41–46.
———. *Joseph Conrad.* London: Weidenfeld & Nicolson, 1959.
———. "The Young Conrad in Marseilles," *Times Literary Supplement* (London; Dec. 6, 1957), p. 748.
BANTOCK, G. H. "Conrad and Politics," *English Literary History* (June, 1958), pp. 122–36.
———. "The Two 'Moralities' of Joseph Conrad," *Essays in Criticism* (April, 1953), pp. 125–42.
Bol'shaia Sovetskaia Entsiklopediia (Moscow). 1937 Edition, XXXIV, Column 30; 1953 Edition, XXXII, p. 399.
BRADBROOK, MURIEL CLARA. *Joseph Conrad: Poland's English Genius.* New York: Macmillan Co., 1941.
A Catalogue of Books, Manuscripts, and Corrected Typescripts from the Library of the Late Joseph Conrad. London: Hodgson and Co. (March 13, 1925).
COMMAGER, HENRY STEELE, JR. "The Problem of Evil in *Heart of Darkness*." Bowdoin Prize Essay, Harvard University, 1952.
CONRAD, JESSIE. *Joseph Conrad and His Circle.* New York: E. P. Dutton & Co., Inc., 1935.
CRÉMIEUX, BENJAMIN. "En Marge des Marées," *Nouvelle Revue Française* (July, 1922), pp. 108–9.
CURLE, RICHARD. *The Last Twelve Years of Joseph Conrad.* London: Sampson and Low, 1928.
DĄBROWSKA, MARIA. *Szkice o Conradzie.* Warsaw: Państwowy Instytut Wydawniczy, 1959.
DAICHES, DAVID. *The Novel and the Modern World.* Chicago: University of Chicago Press, 1960.
DANIEL-ROPS, HENRI. "Joseph Conrad," *Carte d'Europe.* Paris: Perrin, 1928.
DAVIS, H. E. "Conrad's Revisions of *The Secret Agent*," *Modern Language Quarterly* (September, 1958), pp. 244–54.
EDEL, LEON (ed.). *Selected Letters of Henry James.* New York: Farrar, Straus and Cudahy, 1955.

EPSTEIN, JACOB. *Autobiography*. London: Hulton Press, 1955.

FEDER, LILLIAN. "Marlow's Descent into Hell," *Nineteenth-Century Fiction* (March, 1955), pp. 280–92.

FERNANDEZ, RAMON. "L'art de Conrad," *Nouvelle Revue Française* (December, 1924), pp. 730–37.

FORD, FORD MADOX. *Joseph Conrad: A Personal Remembrance*. London: Duckworth, 1924.

————. *Portraits from Life*. Boston: Houghton Mifflin Co., 1937.

————. *Return to Yesterday*. New York: Liveright, 1932.

————. *Thus to Revisit*. New York: E. P. Dutton & Co., 1921.

————. "Tiger, Tiger" in *The Bookman* (New York; January, 1928), pp. 495–98.

FORSTER, E. M. *Abinger Harvest*. New York: Harcourt Brace & Co., 1936.

FRYE, NORTHROP. *Anatomy of Criticism*. Princeton: Princeton University Press, 1957.

GIDE, ANDRÉ. *Journal*. 4 vols. Rio de Janeiro: Gallimard, 1943.

GRAHAM, R. B. CUNNINGHAME. "Inveni portam; Joseph Conrad," *Saturday Review* (Aug. 16, 1924), pp. 162–63.

GORDAN, JOHN D. *Joseph Conrad: The Making of a Novelist*. Cambridge, Mass.: Harvard University Press, 1940.

————. "The Rajah Brooke and Joseph Conrad," *Studies in Philology* (October, 1938), pp. 613–34.

GREEN-ARMYTAGE, ADRIAN. "The Religion of Joseph Conrad," *The Tablet* (London; Dec. 7, 1957), pp. 501–2.

GUERARD, ALBERT J. *Conrad the Novelist*. Cambridge, Mass.: Harvard University Press, 1958.

HALLE, LOUIS. "Joseph Conrad: An Enigma Decoded," *Saturday Review of Literature* (May 22, 1948), pp. 7–8.

HALVERSON, JOHN, and WATT, IAN. "The Original Nostromo: Conrad's Source," *Review of English Studies* (February, 1959), pp. 45–52.

HARKNESS, BRUCE (ed.). *Conrad's "Heart of Darkness" and the Critics*. Belmont, Calif.: Wadsworth, 1960.

HART-DAVIS, RUPERT. *Hugh Walpole*. London: Rupert Hart-Davis, 1952.

HAY, ELOISE K., "Lord Jim: From Sketch to Novel," *Comparative Literature* (Fall, 1960), pp. 289–309.

HERLING-GRUDIŃSKI, GUSTAW. "W oczach Conrada," *Kultura* (Paris; October, 1957), pp. 16–32.

HEWITT, DOUGLAS. *Joseph Conrad: A Reassessment*. Cambridge: Bowes and Bowes [1952].

HOWE, IRVING. *Politics and the Novel*. New York: Horizon Press, 1957.

JABŁKOWSKA, RÓŻA. *Joseph Conrad (1857–1924)*. Wrocław: Ossolineum, 1961.

———. "*Listy T. Bobrowskiego do Conrada*," *Kwartalnik Neofilologiczny* (1956, nr. 2), pp. 82–120.

———. "*Polska Conradystyka za granicą*," *Ibid.* (1958, nr. 1–2), pp. 101–14.

JANTA, ALEKSANDER. "*Skąd 'fatalne dziedzictwo' Conrada?*" *Losy i ludzie*. New York: Polski Instytut Naukowy w Ameryce, 1961.

JEAN-AUBRY, G. *Joseph Conrad in the Congo*. Boston: Little, Brown & Co., 1926.

———. "*Préface du Traducteur*," Joseph Conrad's *Angoisse* [*Suspense*]. Paris: Gallimard, 1956, pp. 7–22.

———. *Vie de Conrad*. Paris: Gallimard [1947]. Translated by HELEN SEBBA as *The Sea Dreamer*. New York: Doubleday & Co., Inc., 1957.

KRZYŻANOWSKI, LUDWIK (ed.). *Joseph Conrad: Centennial Essays*. New York: Polish Institute of Arts and Sciences in America, 1960.

LAWRENCE, D. H. *The Letters of D. H. Lawrence*. New York: Viking Press, 1932.

LEAVIS, F. R. *The Great Tradition*. London: Chatto and Windus, 1948.

LENORMAND, H.-R. "*Note sur un séjour de Conrad en Corse*," *Nouvelle Revue Française* (December, 1924), pp. 666–71.

LOHF, KENNETH A., and SHEEHY, EUGENE, P. (eds.). *Joseph Conrad at Mid-Century: Editions and Studies, 1895–1955*. Minneapolis: University of Minnesota Press, 1957.

MÉGROZ, R. L. *A Talk with Joseph Conrad*. London: Elkin Mathews, 1926.

———. *Joseph Conrad's Mind and Method*. London: Faber and Faber [1931].

MIŁOSZ, CZESŁAW. "*Apollo Nałęcz Korzeniowski*," *Kultura* (Paris; February, 1956), pp. 60–80.

———. *The Captive Mind*. Translated from Polish by JANE ZIELONKO. New York: Knopf, 1953.

MORF, GUSTAV. *The Polish Heritage of Joseph Conrad*. London: Sampson Low, Marston [1930].

MOSER, THOMAS C. *Joseph Conrad: Achievement and Decline*. Cambridge, Mass.: Harvard University Press, 1957.

———. "*The 'Rescuer' Manuscript: A Key to Conrad's Development and Decline*," *Harvard Library Bulletin* (Winter, 1956), pp. 325–55.

MUDRICK, MARVIN. "The Originality of Conrad," *Hudson Review* (Winter, 1958–59), pp. 545–53.

PIETRKIEWICZ, JERZY. "Patriotic Irritability," *Twentieth Century* (December, 1957), pp. 545–57.

PRITCHETT, V. S. "The Exile," *New Statesman* (Aug. 24, 1957), p. 229.

———— "The Moralist of Exile," *New Statesman* (Jan. 30, 1960), pp. 157–58.

RETINGER, JOSEPH. *Conrad and His Contemporaries.* London: Minerva [1941].

ROTHENSTEIN, SIR WILLIAM. *Men and Memories: 1900–1922.* 3 vols. London: Faber and Faber, 1932.

RUSSELL, BERTRAND. *Portraits from Memory.* New York: Simon and Schuster, 1956.

SAURAT, DENIS. "Conrad et la Provence." *Perspectives.* Paris: Stock, 1938, pp. 229–33.

STEINER, GEORGE. *Tolstoy or Dostoevsky.* New York: Alfred A. Knopf, Inc., 1959.

TARNAWSKI, WIT. "Introduction," *Lord Jim, opowieść.* Translated by ANIELA ZAGÓRSKA. 2 vols. Jerusalem: Interim Treasury Committee for the Polish Question, 1946.

————. "O Conradzie," *Myśl Polska* (London; March, 1948), pp. 13–14.

TARNAWSKI, WIT (ed.). *Conrad żywy.* London: Świderski, 1957.

TERLECKI, TYMON. "Conrad w kulturze polskiej," *Conrad żywy.* London: Świderski, 1957.

THALE, JEROME. "Marlow's Quest," *University of Toronto Quarterly* (July, 1955), pp. 351–58.

UJEJSKI, JÓZEF. *O Konradzie Korzeniowskim.* Warszawa: Dom Książki Polskiej. 1936. Translated into French by PIERRE DUMÉRIL as *Joseph Conrad.* Paris: Éditions Edgar Malfère, 1939.

WARREN, ROBERT PENN. "Introduction," *Nostromo.* New York: Modern Library, 1951.

WHITING, GEORGE WESLEY. "Conrad's Revision of 'The Lighthouse' in Nostromo," *Publication of the Modern Language Association* (December, 1937), pp. 1183–90.

Wiadomości (London; Apr. 10 and July 10, 1949): "Conrad's Place and Rank in English Letters."

[WOOLF, VIRGINIA.] "Joseph Conrad," *Times Literary Supplement*, Aug. 14, 1924), pp. 493–94.

WRIGHT, EDGAR. *Joseph Conrad: His expressed views about technique and the principles underlying them with a study of their relevance to certain novels.* Thesis presented for the Degree of Master of Arts in the University of London (March, 1955).

WRIGHT, W. F. *Romance and Tragedy in Conrad*. Lincoln: University of Nebraska Press, 1949.

ZABEL, MORTON DAUWEN (ed.). "Introduction," *Joseph Conrad: Tales of the East and West*. Garden City, N.Y.: Hanover House, 1958.

——. "Introduction," *The Portable Conrad*. New York: Viking Press, 1947.

——. "Introduction," *Under Western Eyes*. New York: New Directions, 1951.

——. "Introduction," *Youth*. New York: Doubleday Anchor Books, 1959.

——. "Joseph Conrad: Chance and Recognition," *Sewanee Review* (Winter, 1945), pp. 1–22.

IV. HISTORY, POLITICS, AND LITERARY BACKGROUND

ALDANOV, MARC (pseud. for MARC ALEKSANDROVICH LANDAU). "Asef," *Les oeuvres libres* (November, 1930), pp. 343–79.

ANDERSON, SIR ROBERT. *Criminals and Crime*. London: Nisbet, 1907.

——. *The Lighter Side of My Official Life*. London: Hodder and Stoughton, 1910.

——. *Sidelights on the Home Rule Movement*. London: Murray, 1906.

ARISTOTLE. *Politica*. Translated by BENJAMIN JOWETT, *Introduction to Aristotle*, edited by RICHARD McKEON. New York: Random House, 1947.

Blackwood's Magazine (Edinburgh). Vol. CLXIII (January–June, 1898).

BRANDES, GEORGE. *Poland: A Study of the Land, People and Literature*. New York: Macmillan Co., 1904.

BROGAN, D. W. "Re-thinking Imperialism," *Encounter* (May, 1960), pp. 75–77.

The Cambridge History of Poland. 2 vols. Cambridge: Cambridge University Press, 1941–1950.

CAMUS, ALBERT. *The Rebel*. New York: Alfred A. Knopf, Inc., 1957.

CARR, E. H. *Dostoevsky*. Boston: Houghton Mifflin Co., 1931.

——. *Michael Bakunin*. London: Macmillan Co., 1937.

——. *The Romantic Exiles*. London: Gollancz, 1933.

The Castle Review, Journal of the Royal Greenwich Observatory Social and Sports Club (March, 1955).

CHERNIAVSKY, MICHAEL. " 'Holy Russia': A Study in the History of an Idea," *American Historical Review* (April, 1958), pp. 617–37.

————. *Tsar and People: Studies in Russian Myths.* New Haven: Yale University Press, 1961.

COLERIDGE, SAMUEL TAYLOR. "Hamlet," *The Complete Works,* IV. Edited by W. G. I. SHEDD. New York: Harper & Bros., 1884.

The Commonweal, A Revolutionary Journal of Anarchist-Communism (London; Feb. 17, 1894).

"Conrad's Place and Rank in English Letters," *Wiadomosci* (London;

DOSTOEVSKY, FYODOR. *Crime and Punishment.* Translated by CONSTANCE GARNETT. London: William Heinemann, 1922.

————. *The Idiot.* Translated by CONSTANCE GARNETT. New York: Bantam Books, 1958.

————. *The Possessed.* Translated by CONSTANCE GARNETT. London: Dent, 1931.

EASTWICK, EDWARD B. *Venezuela.* London: Chapman and Hall, 1868.

FLAUBERT, GUSTAVE. *The Selected Letters of Gustave Flaubert.* Translated and edited by FRANCIS STEEGMULLER. New York: Farrar, Straus & Young, Inc., 1953.

HAHN, EMILY. *James Brooke of Sarawak.* London: Barker [1953].

HALL, CAPTAIN BASIL. *Extracts from a Journal written on the coasts of Chile, Peru, and Mexico in the years 1820, 1821, 1822.* 2 vols. Edinburgh: Constable, 1824.

HAWTHORNE, NATHANIEL. *The Blithedale Romance* in *The Complete Novels of Nathaniel Hawthorne.* New York: Modern Library, 1937.

HERZEN, ALEXANDER. *My Past and Thoughts.* Translated by Constance Garnett. New York. Alfred A. Knopf, Inc., 1924–28.

JACOB, GERTRUDE. *The Raja of Sarawak.* 2 vols. London: Macmillan Co., 1876.

JAMES, HENRY. *The Princess Casamassima.* 2 vols. New York: Macmillan Co., 1948.

KEATS, JOHN. Letter of Oct. 27, 1818, to Richard Woodhouse. *Complete Poems and Selected Letters,* ed. C. D. THORPE. New York: Odyssey Press, Inc., 1935, pp. 575–77.

LANGER, WILLIAM L. *The Diplomacy of Imperialism, 1890–1902.* New York: Alfred A. Knopf, Inc., 1951.

MASTERMAN, G. F. *Seven Eventful Years in Paraguay.* London: Sampson Low, Son, & Marston, 1870.

MOSSE, W. E. "England and the Polish Insurrection of 1863," *English Historical Review* (January, 1956), pp. 28–55.

MICKIEWICZ, ADAM. *Forefather's Eve.* Translated by D. P. RADIN. London: King's College, n.d.

NIKOLAJEWSKY, BORIS. *Aseff the Spy.* New York: Doubleday, Doran, 1934.

Perez, Triana S. *Down the Orinoco*. London: William Heinemann, 1902.

Piltz, Erasmus (ed.). *Poland, An authorized version of Petite Encyclopédie polonaise*. London: Jenkins, 1909.

Plato. *Phaedrus*. Translated by R. Hackforth. Cambridge: Cambridge University Press, 1952.

———. *The Republic*. Translated by F. M. Cornford. Oxford: Clarendon Press, 1941.

Polanyi, Michael. *The Logic of Liberty*. London: Routledge and Kegan Paul, 1951.

Saleeby, Najeeb M. *History of Sulu*. Manila: Bureau of Printing, 1908.

Ségur, Paul Philippe, comte de. *An Aide-de-Camp of Napoleon*. Translated by H. A. Patchett-Martin. London: Hutchinson, 1895.

Shils, Edward. "Ideology and Civility," *Sewanee Review* (Summer, 1958), pp. 450–80.

Słonimski, Antoni. "Dialog o miłości ojczyzny," *Rozmowa z gwiazda, 1916–1961*. Warsaw: Państwowy Instytut Wydawniczy, 1961, pp. 74–81.

Speare, Morris Edmund. *The Political Novel, Its Development in England and America*. New York: Oxford University Press, 1924.

Spender, Stephen. *The Destructive Element*. Boston: Houghton Mifflin Co., 1936.

St. John, Sir Spenser. *Rajah Brooke*. London: Fisher Unwin, 1899.

Strauss, Leo. *Persecution and the Art of Writing*. Glencoe, Ill.: Free Press, 1952.

The Times (London; Feb. 16–20, 1894).

Tolstoy, Count Leo. *War and Peace*. Translated by Constance Garnett. New York: Modern Library [1931].

Tschiffely, A. F. *Don Roberto*. London: William Heinemann, 1937.

Weintraub, Wiktor. *Literature as Prophecy: Scholarship and Martinist Poetics in Mickiewicz's Parisian Lectures*. The Hague: Mouton, 1959.

———. *The Poetry of Adam Mickiewicz*. The Hague: Mouton, 1954.

Wilson, Edmund. *To the Finland Station*. London: Secker and Warburg, 1941.

Index

Index